The Hidden Folk:

Are Fairies and Poltergeists Just the Same Thing?

By SD Tucker

Typeset by Jonathan Downes,
Cover and Layout by SPiderKaT for CFZ Communications
Using Microsoft Word 2000, Microsoft Publisher 2000, Adobe Photoshop CS.

First published in Great Britain by CFZ Press

**Fortean Words
Myrtle Cottage
Woolsery
Bideford
North Devon
EX39 5QR**

ISBN: 978-1-909488-40-3

"Something there is that does not love a wall,
That wants it down." I could say "Elves" to him,
But it's not elves exactly, and I'd rather
He said it for himself.

From Robert Frost, 'Mending Wall'

Morgan le Fay, King Arthur's female arch-nemesis. Such romantic figures seem to have grown up out of ancient beliefs about 'fairy-women', but was Morgan 'fay' because she *was* a fairy, or because she had fairy-*like* powers of enchantment? Scholars cannot agree.

Contents

This is the elaborate frontispiece to a 1568 edition of the famous *Tischreden* (or *Table-Talk*) of Martin Luther. The book contains the first ever account of poltergeist phenomena in which the specific phrase '*polter geyst*' is actually used.

Introduction:

What is a Poltergeist, Anyway?

Ask the average person nowadays what they think a poltergeist is, and they will, if they believe in such things, most probably tell you straight out that it is a spirit of the dead. We can recognise such creatures easily, they may go on to add, because of the commonly-accepted *modus operandi* of their actions; they rap, they tap, they scratch, they throw things around, they start up fires, they play tricks on people, they smash windows and vases. Therefore, even though they are generally thought of as being invisible, it is quite easy to tell when a person has encountered one. The following tale, for example, is obviously about a poltergeist ... isn't it?

On 9th January 1907, John M'Laughlin, an elderly farmer from the coastal area of Magilligan in County Londonderry, Northern Ireland, decided to sweep out the soot from his kitchen chimney, after which various strange phenomena immediately began occurring around his household. He buried the soot he had dislodged in his garden, but found it sitting back in the kitchen again a few minutes later. Bemused, the puzzled farmer reburied the soot; once more, it reappeared inside the house. Soon, soot was smearing the walls and being dumped inside kitchen utensils, with piles of it moving around from room to room. In addition to this plague of black stuff, crockery broke by itself and volleys of stones assailed the house, appearing from nowhere. As many as 30 panes of glass were smashed, and many of the missiles seemed able to pass through matter itself. A piece of bathbrick kept inside a closed cupboard was seen by several people to hurl itself across the kitchen and then smash violently into seven or eight pieces against the window-sash. Furthermore, a stone weighing two pounds was also observed to run about the place, turning around corners before passing, *through the closed door*, into the parlour. Here, it shattered the window-pane and ripped the curtain. In addition, the milk vessels in the pantry were found filled with pebbles, the threshing machine in the barn allegedly began to work of its own accord, and rocks made loud crashing sounds on the roof and landed on the kitchen floor without making any holes in the ceiling.

That, then, seems like as clear a case of poltergeist-haunting as could ever be; except that it was explained by locals at the time as being down not to a ghost, but to a troop of browned-off brownies. A modern reader may be tempted to laugh at this assertion. It would be only too easy to presume that the witnesses were all merely uneducated peasants who simply attributed these events to the fairy-folk due to them probably being entirely ignorant of what a poltergeist actually was. In a way, this is a fair enough assumption. After all, it is indeed exceedingly unlikely that the average County Londonderry farm-worker would have even heard of the word 'poltergeist' back in 1907. There is actually rather more to this story than first meets the eye, though ...

The whole haunting seems undeniably to have had something to do with Mr M'Laughlin's sweeping out of his chimney. After all, the ghostly events only began just after he had cleaned it, and the initial phenomena centred entirely around soot. To M'Laughlin's neighbours, however, these facts will have come as no great surprise; in making himself a proverbial new broom to sweep his flue out with, the foolish farmer had chosen to chop down a nearby holly bush. The locals had warned M'Laughlin that the particular shrub he was interfering with was a so-called 'fairy-bush' – one of any number of such plants to be found dotted around Ireland and thought to be sacred to the fairies in some way, perhaps even their homes – but he had chosen not to listen. As such, the fairies' revenge was surely only to be expected [1]. This may sound initially absurd but, as this book progresses, we shall come across more and more cases of ostensible poltergeist manifestations wherein the entity apparently responsible turns out, upon closer inspection, to have had a whiff less of the graveyard and rather more of the fairy-fort about it.

Are fairies just poltergeists, then? It is a difficult question to answer. The whole issue of creating a definition for what the poltergeist is, and is not, is an incredibly complex one. As the writer Janet Bord notes in her commentary upon M'Laughlin's case in her excellent 1997 book *Fairies*, for example:

> "Students of psychic research will quickly have noted that the happenings in the farmhouse would nowadays be attributed to a poltergeist; though using that term no more explains the mechanism behind the events than would attributing them to the fairies." [2]

Bord is quite correct here; that term, 'poltergeist', actually means surprisingly little. Linguistically-speaking, it is almost what is termed a 'symbol without a referent'; much like the term 'fairy', in fact. What this means is simply that both words refer to things which cannot very easily be defined; both classes of entity have been imagined to be very different things by very different people. They blur into one another around the edges. In fact, one man's fairy could very easily be said to be another man's poltergeist. As will become increasingly clear, it is very hard indeed to draw a definite boundary-line between what is a poltergeist or a fairy, and what is not, something which can perhaps best be illustrated by examining the linguistic history of both terms.

The Devil's Dictionary
It seems obligatory to note in any book about this subject that the word 'poltergeist' is derived from the German phrase *'polter geyst'*, meaning 'noisy/rapping ghost'. Actually, however, the very familiarity of this oft-cited fact is hiding an interesting truth about the term – that it is actually a loan-word. Loan-words are phrases taken from other languages and then used in lieu of any newly-coined native term for an item or concept. English has thousands; 'alligator' is originally a Spanish word, for example, and 'karaoke' Japanese. Just like with these examples, there is, it seems, no

direct English equivalent for the term 'poltergeist' – the investigator Guy Lyon Playfair did propose 'rattleghost' back in the 1970s [3], but it didn't catch on.

This is an important point, as the usual reason for the adoption of loan words into a language is to allow its speakers to be able to describe new inventions or concepts. The English during the Renaissance, for example, had no idea what an 'alligator' was until they heard the term from the Spanish explorers who had discovered the creature, so they simply adopted the Spanish phrase as their own word for it, seeing as there was no native equivalent, either of the animal or of the name [4]. It was a new discovery, a new concept, for which no native term existed. No indigenous term originally existed in English – or in most other non-German tongues – for the poltergeist, either. Does this not likewise imply that the whole idea of the poltergeist is also a human invention?

I do not mean by this that poltergeists do not exist, as such, simply that the term may be to a certain extent a false category. Its written roots can be traced back to a German dictionary named *Novum Dictionarii Genus*, published by the German humanist, poet and religious reformer Erasmus Alberus in 1540, where it was written as two words, namely '*polter geyst*'. Obviously, though, the phrase must have been in spoken usage for some time previously, otherwise it would not have been able to pop up inside a dictionary. The word's most famous early written appearance, however, was in the 1566 publication *Table Talk*, a compilation of the sayings and anecdotes of the eminent Protestant reformer – and, indeed, apparent *polter geyst* victim – Martin Luther. This book has a whole chapter, 'The Polter Geysts', about such beings, apparently the first ever written [5]. However, the fact that the term was originally written in German as two different words, only being joined to form the single word '*poltergeyst*' later on, once the concept's meaning had become more well-established, is key. This allows us to see quite clearly that the word '*polter*' in Alberus' dictionary entry is just being used as an adjective, meaning 'noisy', that is in fact separate from the noun meaning 'ghost', '*geyst*'. It would be better treated as being a *behavioural description* of a ghost rather than as a *distinct classification* of spirit, surely?* Imagine, for a moment, that someone had seen a glowing ghost – and many people have. Some ghosts glow. But we don't yet have a category where we can speak of 'glow-ghosts' (or '*glitzerngeists*') do we?

According to the excellent French scholar Claude Lecouteux, who has also written at length about the similarities between poltergeists and fairies, the use of the word '*geist/geyst*' by German speakers of the time was a further complicating factor when considering the early meaning of the term. '*Geist*', after all, means simply 'spirit' – a generic label which can be used to describe any number of different supernatural entities, from demons to devils to ghosts and fairies. Whilst Luther himself was certain that these *geysts* were essentially Satanic in their nature, to many others this was not necessarily the case. The term may primarily have indicated a spirit that made a racket, but what precisely the underlying nature of this spirit was thought to be was down largely to a combination of personal preference and the influence of prevailing local tradition.[6]

---

* That the phrase is essentially a description of the spirit's actions rather than of its specific underlying nature can also be seen in the fact that there was initially a very similar competing German term available, namely '*rumpelgeist*'. This is derived from the verb *rumpeln*, meaning 'to make a racket', with the added implication of knocking things over and creating a mess. 'Rumpus' might be its closest English equivalent.

A Trick of the Language

We can see from all this, then, that the modern English word 'poltergeist' is only a partially accurate term and is, to a great degree, simply a trick of the language. It is a useful word, in a broad sense, but the designation of invisible supernatural entities as being such in English is really a phenomenon less than two centuries old. When William Hazlitt made a translation of *Table Talk* into English in 1848, for instance, he renamed the chapter about poltergeists 'Of the Devil and His Works', having no convenient English equivalent to work with [7]. If only he had waited to read the popular writer Catherine Crowe's bestseller of that same year, *The Night-Side of Nature*, which, by common consent, contains the first usage of the term in English. This landmark came in a chapter-heading reading, significantly enough, 'The Poltergeist **of the Germans**, and Possession' [8]. Clearly, Crowe felt that the word had to be introduced as being an unfamiliar foreign term, and erroneously conflated it with another (albeit related) phenomenon altogether.

According to the folklorist Michael Goss, the word was then popularised amongst parapsychologists and the initial members of the then-infant SPR (Society for Psychical Research) by the investigator Frank Podmore as a result of his own personal researches in the 1880s – a rather ironic fact given that he didn't actually believe in them [9]. The famous ghost-hunter Harry Price, meanwhile, tells us that the word only began to get genuinely widespread currency in the English tongue as a result of excited Press reports of his experiments with Eleonore Zugun, the famous so-called 'poltergeist girl' (whom we shall meet briefly later) in 1926 [10]. Price's own 1945 book *Poltergeist Over England* also seems to have had an impact upon the popular acceptance of the word, as did the immense success of Tobe Hooper/Steven Spielberg's 1982 blockbuster film *Poltergeist*. Perhaps we should consider the poltergeist as being to some extent a media creation too, then?

Before this point had been reached, a bewildering variety of entities would have been blamed for such disturbances, in any number of different nations. According to the ancient Syrian Neoplatonist philosopher Iamblichus, it was the spirits of Greek heroes who made a racket like the poltergeist, these being the type of ghosts around whom "sounds echo around" when they wish to make their presence known [11]. The Swiss Protestant Louis Lavater, writing in 1572, defined entities known as *lemures* and *spectra* as being those kind of ghosts that "haunted some houses, by appearing in divers and horrible forms, and making great dinne." [12] King James I, however, used these two terms in his 1597 *Daemonologie* to refer more generally to spirits of the dead, without any poltergeist-like qualities necessarily being appended to them [13]. An old Catholic formula once used at the benediction of churches, meanwhile, contained injunctions against the *spiritus percutiens*, or spirit who makes 'percussive sounds' – clearly, a rapping poltergeist [14]. Even the German folklorist Jacob Grimm, in his 1882 book *Teutonic Mythology*, called such beings 'house-sprites', equating them with a breed of fairy [15]. Had he never read his Martin Luther?

Even after the best efforts of Catherine Crowe and the SPR, though, non-German confusion about what to call invisible ghosts was rife, well into the twentieth century, at least outside specialist circles. Around the turn of the century, the word 'poltergeist' was still commonly being translated quaintly into English as 'hobgoblin' [16]. A schoolteacher witness during the

Scottish Sauchie case, which occurred as late as 1960-61, meanwhile, professed to have never even heard of the word. When told that a pupil might have a poltergeist by her Headmaster, she presumed that it was some kind of "obscure but mild" medical complaint [17]. Nowadays, however, after numerous Hollywood movies and TV shows, some basic comprehension of the term seems almost universal. The average person knows that a poltergeist is just an 'invisible ghost' and is quite happy to leave it there. Clearly, though, as even this brief study of the word has shown, the situation is in fact much more complex than that. The jumbled and confusing history of the word 'fairy', however, is even more so!

Meet the Fairy-Folk

The folklorist Noel Williams wrote what is perhaps the best introduction to the convoluted history of the word; he called it, appropriately, *Making Meaning Out of Thin Air* [18]. Obviously, in this post-Disney age when images of Tinkerbell are used to sell everything from lunchboxes to glittery pink-spangled t-shirts for toddlers, we are introduced towards a very concrete and easily-graspable conception of what a fairy supposedly is from a very young age. It is so sweetly saccharine in its nature that it provokes instant reactions amongst small children, who can read its imaginary implications immediately; girls gravitate towards such characters, whilst little boys instinctively act towards them with revulsion and label them as 'soppy' (I know I did). It has proved convenient for marketing-purposes for the media, entertainment and toy industries to package fairies for a modern childhood audience in this way.

Originally, however, fairies were a matter of concern not just to small infants, but to the adults who surrounded them, too. Whilst the meaning of the word 'fairy' might, nowadays, seem to be more-or-less fixed in a modern world where even tiny tots are treated as being potential consumers, this was not always the case. In 1907 in County Londonderry, for instance, the word 'fairy' apparently meant something potentially nasty, that lurked in haunted holly-bushes and hurled stones around when riled. Nowadays, however, such unpleasant characteristics have been labelled instead with the word 'poltergeist'. Did the word 'fairy' originally just mean 'poltergeist', then? Or have the malicious qualities of the fairy-folk merely been quarantined off safely in a corner with that new, German-derived name placed upon them like an albatross around their neck? The issue is undeniably complex.

Historical sources show that there have been at least 50 different possible ways of writing down the word 'fairy' in English at various times and in various different places throughout the British Isles (the area upon which I shall most concentrate within this book). Some of these – 'faerie' and 'faery', for example – are still used today, in certain New Age contexts. Some more unusual ways of writing the word 'fairy' can be found when looking through old texts too, though; 'fae' and 'ffey', for instance [19]. These particular spellings are significant, because they seem to back up the generally-accepted idea about where the word 'fairy' originally came from, namely that it is a derivation from the Old French word *fae*, which was itself derived from the Latin word *fata*, meaning one of 'the Fates', those old Greek goddesses (Clotho, Atropos and Lachesis) who were responsible for spinning out the path of a man's life. There appears a general presumption that this word *fata* was adopted by the Celts living in France to refer to their own tripartite goddesses, but that, somewhere along the line, the 't' was dropped in pronunciation, leaving us with the word *fae*. However, it must be admitted that there is no actual written evidence for certain of these changes taking place; it is instead mere assumption [20]. Such uncertainty amongst scholars about where the word ultimately comes from seems to speak of a wider truth, of direct relevance to this book, though – that, when it comes down to it, *nobody actually really knows what fairies are*!

Quibbling Over Words

The first known written examples of use of variants of the word *fae* (such as *fee* and *fay*) can be found in some of the Old French and Anglo-Norman romance-cycles of the twelfth century. Confusingly, though, the word seems here to have been used not just to refer to Celtic goddess-figures, but also certain more ambiguous females with supernatural powers – enchantresses, perhaps (think of Morgan le Fay in the Arthurian romances, for example). Whether these female figures were called *fae* because they simply *had* magic powers, or because they actually *were* inherently magical in and of themselves, being not really human but instead some form of supernatural beings which just *looked* like women, is another source of confusion. Either way, it is then presumed that the word *faerie* came from *fae* as a kind of extension of it; if a *fae* was an 'enchantress', then *faerie* meant 'enchantment'. Then, from this already muddied soup, further complications arose. Whether due to misunderstandings, deliberate extensions of the word or whatever, *faerie* came also to mean 'fairy-land' and also to be used as the plural 'enchantress*es*'. [21]

The specifics of the next part of the word's history are disputed, but let us simplify and look at the state of affairs when the Middle English words *fay* and *fairy* enter the English tongue, in whatever form. Here, no longer does either word just refer to female sorceresses; instead, they are more commonly being used as adjectives, in order to describe things which seem somehow 'enchanted' in their nature [22]. Sometimes the words are used to refer to 'enchanted creatures' (of whatever kind), for sure, but more often the word 'fairy' seems, in essence, to be a medieval equivalent of our modern word 'paranormal', which can encompass any number of different phenomena or entities, from UFOs to hauntings to crop-circles to demons ... or, indeed, to fairies and poltergeists.

For as long as fairies have been discussed by folklorists and antiquarians, different explanations have been recorded in order to account for what they really are. Some traditions said that they were fallen angels, too bad for heaven but too good for hell, and doomed to walk the earth forever in a kind of eternal limbo. Others have averred that they are forms of demons, or elementals. Others still have said that they were nothing more than diminished folk-memories of the old Pagan gods. They can't all be right. Or can they? If the word 'fairy' was largely used when it entered Middle English as a kind of catch-all adjective meaning 'supernatural in nature', then there is a sense in which they probably could. 'Fairy' is the ultimate umbrella-term for the supernatural in old tradition; 'poltergeist' may well be its direct modern equivalent in more contemporary, living experience. Both words, it might be said, can cover a multitude of ghosts.

Who Are You Calling a Fairy?

Who originally used the word 'fairy', though? Seeing as scholars have to rely entirely upon written records to try and work out this kind of thing, the only answer we can give with any real degree of confidence would be 'the literate'. This, certainly, is the opinion of Noel Williams, whose fascinating researches I am still largely following here. Williams expresses the view that, despite its original origins in speech-terms over in France, by the time it came over to England, the word 'fairy' should be "best regarded as primarily a literary word" being used by the relatively small proportion of the population of Britain at that time who could actually write. After the successful Norman invasion of 1066, these people would, disproportionately, have been likely to have been influenced by Old French literary models. The ordinary, illiterate English peasant, meanwhile, would still have used his old traditional vocabulary in order to describe the denizens of the hidden supernatural world he conceived of as being present all around him.

Seeing as communities tended to be more isolated from one another back then, the names given to the ghostly creatures which were meant to haunt woods, fields, barns, homes and hearths would have varied vastly from region to region. A *scin* may have been blamed for a haunting or strange event in one place, a *drymann* in another, and an *orc* yet somewhere else [23]. We can't really know what precisely these terms actually referred to at this distance of time; for all we know they may have been largely the same thing. As such, the word 'fairy', to a more literate, fashionable and Norman-influenced person, would have been valued as being a useful general term which could be used when writing in order to unify an otherwise very varied and ambiguous vocabulary under one simple and convenient heading. Or, as Williams puts it succinctly:

> "There was not, as folklorists tend to express it, a 'confusion' of fairies and elves in medieval belief, but a tendency of the more generic and more fashionable word to attract and take over the associative meanings of its rivals." [24]

And yet ... were *bugges*, *schuckes*, *thurses* and *gobelyns* all exactly the same thing, precisely? Whilst we can reasonably deduce that many of these words were little more than competing regional synonyms, we cannot necessarily presume that they *all* were. Ever since the celebrated folklorist Katharine Briggs published her *Dictionary of Fairies* in 1976, numerous other writers have fallen over themselves to get their own field-guides to *The Personnel of Fairy-Land* (Briggs' initial working-title) [25] into print. Thousands of words have been expended laying out exactly the difference between a boggart and a bull-begger, a kelpie and a knocker and a spriggan and a sprite, an entertaining exercise if nothing else. Whilst looking through these taxonomies, however, it might strike the attentive reader that many of the different species of fairy listed are different only in name; Jack-o'-Lanterns and Will-o'-the-Wisps are obviously identical, as are Kit-with-the-Candlestick and perhaps even corpse-candles, too. Jack-o'-Lanterns are not boggarts, however. One is a kind of flitting supernatural light, generally rationalised away today as being spontaneously-ignited marsh-gas; the other is a big hairy man who lives up a chimney.

Or, at least, the boggart is this *sometimes*. When annoyed, and smashing dishes in the kitchen, he is invisible and indistinguishable from a poltergeist. At other times, he merges away into the brownie, that breed of helpful little domestic fairy which will perform small tasks around the household at night in return for offerings of food. This is the brownie who gives the Girl

Guides their nickname; he does good turns to help those who need him. It is highly unlikely, however, that Brown Owls tell their young charges of the brownie's occasional alternative depiction as being a big, hairy, naked man, much like the boggart. In Scotland, meanwhile, the brownie (or 'broonie') is sometimes said to be the ghost of an old tramp, with white beard and piercing blue eyes, who rewards those who are generous to him and punishes those who are not. And which of these competing versions is the 'real' version of the brownie? As the folklorist Jeremy Harte puts it most concisely in his own discussion of this entity, "There is no answer to that." [26] This, once again, sounds very similar to the poltergeist; which is the 'real' form of that entity? Demon, spirit of the dead, angel, elemental ... or fairy? I am afraid that I can only echo Harte's conclusion about it all.

Name-Games

The fairies, in my view, are probably the most interesting of all alternative poltergeist identities we can examine. They are just so damned ambiguous in and of themselves! Sometimes, they are invisible, like polts; sometimes, on the contrary, they are perfectly visible – and yet, when they are seen, upon one occasion they are tall, upon another small. Sometimes, they manifest as balls of light, like UFOs; sometimes as shadowy spectral figures, like ghosts; sometimes as supernatural animals, like Black Dogs. They, just like the poltergeist, are more a kind of imaginative nexus in their nature than they are anything specific. Explaining a fairy as being a poltergeist, or a poltergeist as being a fairy, is just trying to account for one unknown in terms of another.

Personally, it is my opinion that what we now term 'poltergeist activity' does genuinely exist, but that in the end we have very little idea of what it is that is ultimately behind it all. Words like 'poltergeist' and 'fairy' are just masks which we use to hide this ignorance. I think that this truth has often been alluded to – presumably unconsciously – in one of the great tenets of traditional fairy-lore; namely, that *'they should not be referred to directly by their name'*. A name, of course, is just another form of mask. Look too closely behind it, and what it apparently means begins to fall away.

As is well-known, the fairies have traditionally been alluded to indirectly instead of being named outright, by virtue of people making use of various colourful and often flattering descriptive epithets for them instead, such as 'the Little People', 'the Good Folk', 'the Gentry', 'the Hidden People' and 'the Hill Folk' (the literal meaning of *sidhe*, the native word for the celebrated Irish fairies). In Wales, they can be called *y tylwyth teg*, meaning 'the fair family' or *bendith y mamau*, 'their mother's blessing'. But why? According to the writer Janet Bord, it was thought to be unlucky to use the fairies' real names as "to know the name gave one power over the individual", like in the tale of Rumpelstiltskin, something which the fairies would not be happy about [27]. A similar process can perhaps be seen going on in all those well-known folktales of helpful brownies who flee from the farms and houses they once helped maintain as soon as their 'masters' leave out nice new liveried clothes for them, or stay awake at night to catch a glimpse of what they actually look like. Immediately as they are pinned down with servant's livery or made comprehensible by sight, they vanish into the ether; there is a moral in there somewhere [28].

The well-known psychical researcher Harry Price's 1945 work *Poltergeist Over England* was the first English-language book to feature the word 'poltergeist' in its title, and played a key role in popularising the term in the UK and elsewhere. Earlier, reports of Price's 1920s experiments with Eleonore Zugun, who was dubbed 'the poltergeist girl' by hacks, had also helped to spread the word about polts.

Four typically twee Victorian illustrations of fairies as rather camp child-like flower-beings with wings, and clothing made from petals. Whilst such images do draw upon some genuine fairy-lore – the association with toadstools and nature – they are also sentimentalised and airbrushed to the nth degree. The true nature of the fairy-folk in genuine tradition was much more ambiguous than this admittedly cute rubbish – and they *didn't* have wings!

The famous Irish poet, playwright, statesman, folklorist and fairy-scholar William Butler Yeats, who travelled the Irish countryside with his friend and patroness Lady Augusta Gregory collecting tales and lore about the *sidhe*. The kind of towering cultural figure the modern age just cannot seem to produce any more.

Dermot MacManus, busily performing one of the healthy, outdoor activities he felt were good for a person's soul – just like he thought the Irish fairies were.

A Blueshirts brigade in action; many people nowadays dispute that the organisation to which Dermot MacManus belonged was truly fascist in nature, but such images appear to suggest that Mussolini had certainly influenced the aesthetics of the group, at any rate ... It seems strange to think that fairies could have been co-opted as yet another symbol of Irish nationalism by some such persons, especially given the effeminate modern connotations of the word.

To me, this tale-type sounds almost like a kind of folk-recognition of the fairies' constantly-shifting nature. Hobs, silkies, cluricauns, korrigans, brownies, elves, knockers, *kobolds*, brags, boggarts, *lares* and poltergeists; we *can't* properly name these things and, thereby, get a form of 'power' over them – namely, that of their coherent conceptual comprehension by us – because they are, essentially, unknowable as any one thing in and of themselves. They all merge away into one another at the margins. As such, we can't finally name and classify them, in any comprehensive taxonomic sense, because that would be reductive; as soon as we try, contradictions begin to proliferate. Brownies are brownies, for instance – except when they get annoyed and start acting like boggarts and poltergeists.

In the view of the great Irish poet and mystic WB Yeats – whom we shall encounter often in this book – the fairies had no inherent form to them at all. According to him:

> "Many poets, and all mystic and occult writers, in all ages and countries, have declared that behind the visible are chains on chains of conscious beings, who are not of heaven but of the earth, who have no inherent form but change according to their whim, or the mind that sees them ... The visible world is merely their skin." [29]

Perhaps fairies and poltergeists, then, are very much what the individual observer wishes to make of them – personalised or culturally-influenced thought-forms, maybe. Even the view of Yeats that they are, inherently, shape-shifters, is ultimately an attempt to conceptualise them by him, really, when you think about it.

A Fairy-Romance

How have people tried to conceptualise poltergeists and fairies in different ways, then? In terms of poltergeists, there are two main competing modern interpretations. Firstly, there is the idea that they are the invisible dead. The dead are supposed to have returned in all ages, of course, and in this view the poltergeist is merely their modern vehicle. Alternatively, we have the opinion which currently predominates in parapsychology, that poltergeists are not really any kind of entity at all, but, rather, merely the result of unintentional psychic emissions upon the behalf of (most commonly) disturbed teenagers. The theory goes that youths accidentally release these psychic powers, cause dishes to fly around and smash, and furniture to rumble, and then blame a 'ghost' for it all. The precise form that this 'ghost' takes is then attributed largely to a combination of the personal psychology of the person involved (usually termed the 'focus') and the prevailing cultural outlook of the times. Such a theory is generally known as the 'RSPK hypothesis'. It stands for 'Recurrent Spontaneous Psycho-Kinesis' – this latter word referring to the paranormal movement of objects by use of no known force – and is an attempt by contemporary ghost-hunters to reclassify spooks as a kind of 'rational' phenomenon which can be studied by science rather than something mysterious and occult. It is not, perhaps, a terribly romantic idea.

Fairies, however, are the very essence of romance. As such, some persons of a poetic bent have occasionally attempted to reclaim poltergeists as being fairies for their own aesthetic purposes. This process took place most often with the fairies of Ireland. Here, during the late nineteenth and early twentieth centuries, the *sidhe* came in literature and art to symbolise a kind of 'native genius', a sort of ancient imaginative Celtic bulwark against the increasingly-resisted rule of the commercially-minded and thus materialistic British Empire. The English may have owned Ireland *physically*, the profusion of native folklore collectors and commentators of the time appeared to say, but not *mentally*. Englishmen, after all, didn't believe in fairies any more.

Because of this kind of thinking, reactions against the modern figure of the poltergeist amongst certain Irish persons could sometimes be quite violent. For example, the writer Dermot MacManus, in his excellent compendium of modern Irish fairy-lore *The Middle Kingdom*, discusses a haunting in a Dublin cemetery during 1935 in which the lodge-keeper, a Mrs Dean, was bothered by ghosts making loud crashes upon her door. In his account, MacManus seems almost indignant that the woman chose to blame the unquiet dead for these incidents rather than the more traditional native agent of the fairies (or 'earth spirits' as he here has it), writing slightly inaccurately that:

> "I feel quite sure that she was mistaken, and that all these goings-on were coming from ill-natured earth spirits ... this crash on the door is a performance typical of poltergeists, though I have not yet been able to find out what exactly a poltergeist is meant to be. The word is entirely artificial and was coined in Germany about a century ago to cover this sort of manifestation." [30]

There is clear distaste in that word 'artificial', a sense that the concept of a 'poltergeist' is really little more than an unpleasant and unnecessary foreign import, yet another pollutant sent forth from the disagreeable morass of predominantly Anglo-Saxon modernity to help undo the old Celtic beliefs and put more materialistic and weakly internationalist ones in their place instead. MacManus, indeed, was a fairly extreme right-wing Irish nationalist, but of a now virtually-extinct romantic order; half-Brownshirt, half-folklorist, equal parts William Butler Yeats and Sir Roderick Spode. A member of an old Catholic gentry family from the west of Ireland, he was trained at Sandhurst but ended up joining the IRA in 1920 and the newly-formed Free State forces a few years later, was a general organiser for the Blueshirts movement (a body of ex-IRA pseudo-fascists, to simplify immensely) and claimed numerous mystical experiences for both himself, his family and his acquaintances [31]. The following extract, taken from his introduction to *The Middle Kingdom*, gives us a brief yet illuminating flavour of his basic philosophy:

> "In olden days the strength and vitality of a race lay in its healthy and virile country communities, living their self-sufficient lives according to nature's plan ... Their lives were interwoven with the wonders of the eternal seasons, of birth and of death, of fertility and growth. They knew and loved ... the beauty which God has evolved by His divine law of nature, and the spiritual outlook was never absent from them. Today the country is merely the adjunct of the cities, and in these the balance of power lies; the dwindling rural districts have been degraded into a mere food factory to supply the teeming millions of the towns. The more universally rule and factory regulations are brought into the country, the more materialistic the country must become and the more divorced from beauty and from the spirits of nature ... And as materialism comes in, in many lands, so the old contacts with the spirit world of nature go out. Even in Ireland the materialists in the towns, with their newly-acquired superficial education without wisdom, are attacking vigorously. But

contacts with the spirit world have not yet vanished from Ireland and please God they never will, and this book shows that they are still here." [32]

Who would ever have thought that fairies could function as *völkisch* propaganda?

Getting Back to Nature

MacManus, of course, was a good friend – and political confidant – of WB Yeats, and the two men clearly shared some of the same views upon the subject. Indeed, MacManus' opinions were in many ways little more than a continuation of Yeats' own early writings about the imaginative and racial significance of the *sidhe*. For example, in his short essay *Irish Fairies*, written in 1890, Yeats could pen the following paragraph about the matter:

> "The world is, I believe, more full of significance to the Irish peasant than to the English. The fairy populace of hill and lake and woodland have helped to keep it so. It gives a fanciful life to the dead hillsides, and surrounds the peasant as he ploughs and digs with tender shadows of poetry. No wonder that he ... can ... make up proverbs like this from the old Gaelic – 'The lake is not burdened by its swan, the steed by its bridle, or a man by the soul that is in him'." [33]

Yeats' folklore writings are full of this kind of stuff – "Do you think the Irish peasant would be so full of poetry if he had not his fairies?" [34] he asked in 1892 – and it is all part of a conscious and deliberate attempt by him to facilitate the birth of some kind of new and vital national consciousness in his countrymen by marking out for them a set of perceived racial characteristics which made the Irish essentially different from their English overlords. If the English were a nation of shopkeepers, then (to Yeats at least) the Irish were a nation of poets – and the fairies their dancing, melancholy, hill-dwelling Muse.

As we have just seen, however, as the twentieth century dawned, the infant science of parapsychology was attempting to take all the poetry out of poltergeistry; and thus, by implication, from the fairies, too. If you agreed with Yeats' views upon the significance of the *sidhe* – and Dermot MacManus evidently did – then this process had to be resisted. Presuming that it was the fairies, and not the poltergeists, who ennobled the country-folk of Ireland, who connected them back to the purity and beauty of the indigenous landscape, and thus up through some kind of 'invisible chain of being' right back to God Himself, it had to be maintained by MacManus either that they were different things entirely, or that the German term was merely an inferior, spuriously 'scientific' label for what had always existed and been known about in the Irish countryside. True Celts, it seemed, should not really believe in poltergeists. Fairies were just so much better for the soul.

As the industrial age progressed, however, belief in fairies did inevitably begin to be replaced in Ireland either with belief in poltergeists, or else in nothing. This, for example, is the plaintive response of a farmer from the Northern Irish hamlet of Derrygonnelly, near Enniskillen, whose haunted house was, in 1877, the scene of one of the first 'scientific' investigations of poltergeistry ever conducted, when questioned by Professor Sir William Barrett, FRS, as to what exactly he thought was responsible for producing the phenomena in question:

"I would have thought, sir, it do be fairies, but them late readers and knowledgeable men will not allow such a thing, so I cannot tell what it is. I only wish, sir, you would take it away." [35]

Pretty soon, of course, science would indeed take the fairies away from the Irish farmers – if MacManus had read this reply, no doubt he would have been both despairing and furious. To him, poltergeists really *were* fairies.

Was he right? For myself, I doubt that fairies exist, *absolutely*, as fairies, any more than poltergeists exist, *absolutely*, as poltergeists. Both terms are somehow meaningless, in essence, though certainly evocative. But aren't the two classes of entities really little more than aspects of one another, at root? Whenever we encounter the invisible world, we seem to need to 'clothe' it, somehow, to give it some kind of an identity in order thereby better to understand it. If this view is correct, though, and the 'fairy' and the 'poltergeist' are but two different culturally-conditioned terms for what is, in essence, the same basic thing – namely, the invisible creation of ostensibly supernatural mischief – then we would expect to be able to find numerous overlaps between the kinds of things that are said to occur during fairy-hauntings, and the kinds of things which are said to occur during poltergeist-hauntings. Well, we can indeed find many such overlaps – and it is the purpose of this book now to point them all out at length.

AUTHOR'S NOTE: HOW TRUE ARE THESE STORIES?

I have already said at the outset that I think there really are poltergeists (or that there really is such a thing as poltergeist *phenomena*, at any rate). Not all readers will agree with me, of course; but I'm not entirely sure that this matters. My basic thesis is simply that fairies and poltergeists have much in common – and, as such, whether you view the stories detailed throughout as being factual or merely invented is actually not of too much real import. If both poltergeists and fairies alike are *said* to have caused people to levitate, say, or to have materialised coins out of thin air, then this is still enough to suggest very strongly that the poltergeist is little more than the modern version of the fairy, even if the actual accounts of them doing so should turn out to be nothing more than made-up nonsense. Such narratives, ancient and modern, still show that fairies and poltergeists were *conceived of* as being able to do the same kinds of things, after all, which is surely enough to support my main idea. You can, therefore, approach this book as either sceptic or believer, and still get something out of it.

However, just because I think that poltergeist phenomena are real does not mean to say that I accept *all* of the stories detailed herein. Far from it! I will frequently bring in obvious folk-tales and then discuss them alongside other possibly more genuine instances of supernatural activity. Rather than attempting to discuss the truthfulness of each specific case detailed, though, I generally assume that the reader is able to make up his or her own mind as to which tales in this book might have been real, and which entirely literary or fictional in their nature (many would appear to be a bit of both). Some readers might object to this method, but I would point out that even untrue stories could have been based, at some point, upon actual, observed fact – so, just because some elaborate yarn about a brownie ploughing a farmer's field for him is manifestly not a true one, that does not necessarily mean that the original tale-tellers in question might not have picked up upon certain elements of authentic supernatural reality when concocting their appealing fictions.

This book is, then, entirely what you choose to make of it. You might want to say that it provides some proof suggestive of the notion that fairies actually still exist in some sense, here and now, in the present day; or, alternatively, you might seize upon the data provided to say that the obvious similarities between polts and fairies merely act to prove that people for some reason feel the need to populate the world around them with imaginary beings of an essentially similar type, whatever the age or culture they should happen to be living in. It really is up to you. My only aim is to point out the correspondences; what you then do with them is your own business.

The ſtrange

VV I T C H

AT

G R E E N VV I C H,

(Ghoſt, Spirit, or Hobgoblin) haunting
a Wench, late ſervant to a Miſer, ſuſpected
a Murtherer of his late VVife :

With curious Diſcuſſions of walking ſpirits and ſpectars of
dead Men departed, for rare and myſticall knowledge and diſcourſe,
By HIERONYMUS MAGOMASTIX.

Eme Lyſippe, novus, tota ſonat Urbs, Libellos.

April 24. 1650. *Imprimatur.* JOHN DOVVNAME.

An English pamphlet about an invisible spirit from 1650 reveals typical contemporary confusion over what to call the thing – a witch, ghost or hobgoblin? Certainly not a poltergeist, as only Germans knew the word back then!

Two photographic portraits of Sir William Barrett, FRS, in one of which he appears to think he is Napoleon. One of the first of a new breed of Victorian scientific investigators of psychical phenomena, his examination of a haunting in the Irish hamlet of Derrygonnelly in 1877 marked a turning-point in educated investigators' opinions about such matters; unlike the farmer at the centre of the case, Barrett thought that the entity involved was a poltergeist rather than a fairy.

PART ONE: Behaviour

Mrs. X was absolutely terrorised by ghostly manifestations. As the Institute investigators stared, glasses, lamps and chairs flew into the air by themselves and doors slammed shut mysteriously.

A psychonalyst bravely confronts polteregists in his consulting-room in this uni-dentified old magazine illustration. In centuries past, however, exactly similar phenomena would have been blamed upon fairies, not invisible ghosts.

1.

High Spirits: Stone-Showers, Object-Movements, Apports and Rappings

During an interview with an old Shetlander named Andrew Hunter, born in 1888, the late folklorist Alan Bruford heard an interesting story. Whilst still a boy during the 1890s, it seemed, this inhabitant of the northern isles had been walking with his dog, his mother and an elderly female friend of hers towards this latter woman's home. As they went along, the dog began to make "queer noises" and act up. Looking to one side momentarily, the boy began to see why; there were "a multitude" of little men and women, the men dressed in dark clothes and their wives wearing white aprons, capering about in the fields. Neither adult saw them, however, the boy's parent dismissing his vision as being simply "a lot of foolishness". And yet ...

After this apparent sighting of the 'trows' (as the fairy-folk were known locally), the old woman who was being escorted home began to be troubled by what Bruford terms "something that sounded to me like a poltergeist". It did indeed sound like a poltergeist. The old woman and her sister, who lived together, continually found cups, saucers and other small utensils having been moved around inside their kitchen by unknown means whilst they were out. Furthermore, they were both kept awake at night by certain "dreadful noises", which would only cease when one sister read out loud from the Bible. Hunter's opinion upon these curious facts was clear. He always felt that the little people he saw "had something to do with that lady" and her poltergeist-haunting [1]. It seems highly unlikely – we might almost say impossible – that he had even heard of the word 'poltergeist' back in the 1890s when the incidents actually occurred, though. He would have had to have been familiar with Catherine Crowe and the *Proceedings* of the SPR, which small boys living on remote Scottish islands tend generally not to be. Poltergeist *phenomena*, however, do appear to have been known to him; and he put it all down to the doings of the fairies. It seems as if he was not alone.

Everybody Must Get Stoned

This is because fairies and poltergeists tend often to perform the same basic tricks; throwing stones or causing them to materialise from out of thin air, for instance. This is thought of as being one of the main stereotypes of poltergeist behaviour today, but it was not always so. For example, the Episcopalian Minister Robert Kirk, one of the most notable early writers upon fairy-beliefs, recorded in his important book *The Secret Commonwealth of Elves, Fauns and Fairies* the opinion of his seventeenth-century Scottish parishioners that "those creatures that move invisibly in a house, and cast huge great stones but do not much hurt" are "souls that have not attained their rest".[2] His flock thought that they were the unquiet dead, then, who had perhaps been murdered or else had buried treasure to reveal. Kirk himself, however, was very firmly of the opinion that:

> "... these invisible wights [beings] which haunt houses seem rather to be some of our subterranean inhabitants [i.e. fairies] ... than evil spirits or devils, because though they throw great stones, pieces of earth, and wood at the inhabitants, they hurt them not at all, as if they acted not maliciously like devils but in sport like buffoons and drolls." [3]

A haunting from mid-sixteenth-century Spain also featured a fairy being blamed for stones and pebbles being tossed about. The account has been cited in several modern books, but it is not generally mentioned that many locals at the time blamed the events not upon a ghost, but upon what they called a *trazgo* – a kind of Spanish brownie. The haunting probably occurred during the 1560s, and was detailed by the Spanish Renaissance writer Antonio de Torquemada in his picaresque 1573 book of wonders and travellers' tales, *The Flower Garden*. In this tome, Torquemada relates how, back when he was attending the University of Salamanca, then one of Europe's chief seats of learning, a rumour spread around that a *trazgo* was haunting the home of an elderly but rich local widow and her several maids. This being reputedly liked to manifest itself invisibly on top of the woman's roof and throw large numbers of stones at passers-by, causing annoyance but no actual physical harm. Eventually, a local magistrate (or the Mayor of Salamanca, in some translations) decided to get to the bottom of the matter and took 20 men and a constable around to investigate. They examined every corner by torchlight and even ripped up floorboards, but could find no explanation. Nonetheless, the magistrate was still sceptical and told the old widow that her maids were probably responsible; gossip was abroad that some of the prettier servants were simply pretending to be spooks in order to provide a distraction so they could sneak their lovers inside.

As the magistrate and his men went downstairs to check the cellar, however, they were surprised to hear a loud noise, followed by "such a mass of stones that it seemed someone had thrown three or four baskets full" rolling down the stairs after them and, in some versions, sweeping them off their feet. Thinking some prank was afoot, the magistrate sent his men back upstairs to perform another search. Whilst they were doing so, though, a second shower of stones began falling down from the sky at the entrance to the property, bouncing onto the floor. A constable picked one of the largest up and set the spook a challenge. "Whether this is a devil or a *trazgo*, send this stone back to me!" he said arrogantly, and hurled it away over the rooftops. Immediately, in full view of everyone, the stone shot back over the roof and hit the constable on the head, just above his eyes. Whilst it now had to be admitted that this was no hoax, there was nonetheless a difference of opinion amongst those present about what exact kind of being the noisy spirit was, as the constable's slightly equivocal terms of address here indicate. Some saw it as being a fairy; others said it was a demon, whilst yet others felt it was all the result of witchcraft.[4] It is only more modern Spaniards who would be likely to blame a poltergeist for such entertaining escapades, it seems.

The same phenomenon, then, accounted for in different ways by different people; it has ever been thus. Perhaps we could say quite truthfully in light of such tales that the poltergeist is the fairy of actual *experience*, not of legend; there are no crystal castles lying deep within the enchanted forest, nor magnificent banquet-halls filled with golden candle-light hidden magically beneath the forbidden hill, but there really are cases of flying stones and other objects being hurled around by forces unseen. People have always encountered those – but they did not always have the word 'poltergeist' available to conveniently describe them with. Instead, they had to conceptualise such events as being down to mischievous gnomes and fairies.

A Familiar Description
Descriptions of polts both looking and acting like fairies and gnomes are legion in texts dealing with such subjects published before and during the Renaissance, when belief in them could still be very strong. Writing in 1666, for instance, the Bohemian-German mathematician and astronomer Johannes Praetorius said that, during Classical times:

> "The ancients could only believe that poltergeists had to be veritable human beings, who looked like small children and wore little robes of multicoloured garb." [5]

I do not know Praetorius' ultimate source for this assertion but, if what he says is true, then the fact surely makes my whole case for me in microcosm. Even implausible descriptions of dwarfs living and working in underground mines were sometimes related to poltergeist-like phenomena in the past. In 1561, for example, the Swiss theologian and preacher Pierre Viret wrote of how what he termed "mountain dwarves" habitually bothered human miners by throwing gravel and stones at them underground, although, characteristically, these missiles would never genuinely hurt anybody. Despite them sounding just like subterranean poltergeists here, though, Viret describes the dwarfs' alleged visible form as being that of "little" and "elderly" persons of a height of a mere "three palm spans" and dressed up like human miners, with smocks and leather aprons.[6] Mere legends, naturally – but legends in which fairies act very much like modern pebble-throwing spooks.

Such quaintly gnome-like visual descriptions of apparent poltergeists can even be found in some old pieces of fiction – a prime example being the thirteenth-century German fable of *The Little Crier and the Polar Bear*. This traditional fairy-tale tells the story of a Norwegian traveller who passes through Germany with his pet, a tame polar bear, until he arrives at the home of a poor peasant and asks if he can stay the night. The peasant agrees, but warns him that the house is haunted by a malicious spirit named 'Crier'. Crier, apparently, was "the minion of the Devil", although the peasant also refers to him as a *kobold* (a German brownie). If he had lived a few centuries later, however, he would undoubtedly have called him a *polter geyst*; Crier delighted in "juggling" furniture and tools, making a racket, hurling stones, disturbing the stove and upsetting crockery. The brave Norwegian says he will stay there anyway. That night, when Crier arrives, he sees the polar bear asleep in front of the hearth and is displeased, so much so that he goes and punches it, which is never a wise thing to do with a polar bear. A fierce fight ensues and, that next morning, Crier approaches the peasant and asks him nervously if the giant white cat is still there. Seeing his opportunity to exorcise the spook, the peasant lies that the 'cat' is indeed still present, and that it has given birth to several huge kittens overnight! Disturbed by this news, the cowardly Crier leaves the peasant's house for good.

Significantly, the spirit in this tale is described visually in terms very similar to those used by Praetorius in his description of the tangible form of a poltergeist; Crier is a human-like being "hardly three hand-spans in size" and wearing a red cap. In other words, then, this particular poltergeist, when seen, turned out to be nothing less than a stereotypical picture-book fairy! Evidently, the fable is not a true one – but, nonetheless, it would seem obvious that it picks up on some genuine old folk-beliefs. As Claude Lecouteux says about it, "Is this literature or the transcription of a belief? Undoubtedly it is a blend of both."[7] Indeed it is.

Follets and Fairies

Here, meanwhile, is another highly relevant old description, this time of what the French used to term *follets* and *lutins* – fairies – but what we ourselves might now reasonably be expected to call poltergeists. Apparently, these French fairies of old:

> "... make their presence first known in a house by various silly pranks and idle japeries. Trinkets and knickknacks belonging to the house and more especially to the person whose attention the lutin wishes to attract vanish from the place where they had been laid down, only to reappear shortly afterwards in another spot. These tricksters next annoy people by hiding in dark corners and laughing suddenly, or calling aloud as one passes; they will even pluck the sheets off the bed from sleepers, or tweak one's nightcap ... Very often they beset tender girls, to whom they manifest themselves as handsome gallants, hot young amorosos, who pursue them with obscene suggestions, whispering in their ears the most indecent words at unguarded moments."[8]

Other sources say that these *lutins* enjoy playing childish tricks such as filling shoes with pebbles, or shaving people's beards off while they sleep, and that they can appear in animal form, for instance as entirely white cats. Indeed, the verb *lutiner* – meaning 'to behave like a *lutin'* by playing harmless little poltergeist-like pranks on people – has survived in the modern French tongue even today.[9]

In Italy, meanwhile, *follets* were often known as *foliots*. According to the consummate sixteenth-century Italian Renaissance man Gerolamo Cardano, these *foliots* would "frequent forlorn houses" where they would then:

> " ... make strange noises in the night, howl sometimes pitifully, and then laugh again, cause great flame and sudden lights, fling stones, rattle chains, shave men [in their sleep], open doors and shut them, fling down platters, stools, chests, [and] sometimes appear in the likeness of hares, crows, black dogs, etc."[10]

Apparently, then, polts have always been with us, under a variety of different local names. Two modern European scholars, Erika Lindig and Claude Lecouteux, have even imitated the writings of Renaissance authors like Cardano, and created their own 'typologies' of the sort of things that household fairies were spoken of as doing in the past. Their respective lists include the following activities: rapping and knocking, throwing objects, moaning and groaning, creating the noise of invisible footsteps, laughing and singing from thin air, slamming and opening doors, pressing down upon sleepers at night, knocking things over, pulling away bedclothes, hitting children, scaring animals, appearing in a variety of apparitional forms, playing tricks, creating fear, throwing people out of bed, knocking people over, spoiling or stealing food and just generally creating an almighty racket. [11] We need not labour our point with such lists any further. A few specific examples of directly witnessed poltergeist-like fairy-behaviour might not go entirely amiss here, however.

A Load of Cobblers
The alleged ability of fairies to move objects around invisibly, for example, is commonly reported. Take, for instance, Dermot MacManus' account of some invisible fairies living in a field in County Longford, north-west Ireland, a few years before WWII, who took exception to farm-workers placing a hay-cock, six feet or so tall, upon a large flat rock which the *sidhe* had evidently already claimed as their own. An hour or two after it had been placed there, one of the child-labourers present screamed out and directed everyone's attention to the hay-cock; it was floating in the air! It rose up from the rock, moved a few yards to one side, and then landed upright on the grass with "not even a wisp" of hay left on the stone. The workers left the hay where it now stood, fearing that the boulder must have been the home of the Little People. [12]

Another of the most frequent signs of a poltergeist's presence is the production of strange rapping and scratching sounds. Fairies, too, can pull this kind of trick, though. For instance, in August 2000 a curious letter appeared in *Fortean Times*, the marvellous 'Journal of Strange Phenomena', from a Mr J Keen of Leighton Buzzard in Bedfordshire, concerning weird hammering noises which he had heard emanating from a tree in an unnamed 'gentleman's park' near his childhood home one night in the 1930s. They seemed, he said to be coming from high up in a pine tree with "three hits, hammer laid down, three more hits, and so on." Keen's father mended shoes, and he thought the din sounded just like that. All the local residents, including those from the nearby 'big house' and their servants, were out peering up the tree, such was the loudness of the rapping. A torch was shone into its branches and commands made for the noise to stop, but to no avail. The racket continued for over an hour, then stopped forever. [13]

What could have caused these sounds, though, presuming that it was not simply some animal? Apparently, it was not a poltergeist. Many years later, Mr Keen says, he met a woman professing to be "something of an expert on folklore" who told him it was a brownie, which she defined, slightly eccentrically, as being a fairy shoe-maker (a role reserved in Ireland for leprechauns) hard at work in the tree. How can we know this, though, without appealing blindly to tradition? Had he had not met this woman who said that a brownie had caused the bangings, then would Mr Keen ever have come to this conclusion independently? I think not.

A brownie's noisy shoe-mending, it seems to me, would be essentially indistinguishable from a poltergeist's characteristic knocking and rapping – unless, perhaps, the brownie was actually *seen* mending shoes, which, needless to say, they never are. The phenomena, I think, are real and constant throughout time; the explanations we invent for them are not. Nobody today still believes in 'Knocky Boh' – a Yorkshire goblin who was supposed to spend his whole life tapping and rapping behind a house's wainscots [14] – but plenty are still prepared to lend credence to the idea of a poltergeist doing exactly the same thing.

Hello Sailor

Sometimes, though, we are privileged to come across an intermediate case, a haunting which occurs in a time and place where conceptions and definitions of the paranormal seem to be in the process of shifting around from a belief in one kind of spirit and over to another kind. In such instances, it seems, fairies and poltergeists can happily coexist. One remarkable such case occurred in Massachusetts in 1844-49, and centred around a physician, a certain Dr Larkin, and his maidservant, named Mary Jane. I doubt that this Dr Larkin believed in fairies, really; but, given what soon started going on in his home, it seems that young Mary Jane, presumably being less educated and polished than her master, did.

Events began when Larkin, who had been interested in what was still then termed 'animal magnetism' for about five years, decided to send Mary Jane under hypnosis in order to try and cure some fits from which she was suffering. Once he had done so, however, he found that the girl, in her fugue state, was able to accurately diagnose the conditions from which some of her employer's patients were suffering, and to prescribe appropriate cures. By way of 'explanation', Mary Jane said that, whilst under hypnosis, she was visited by a fairy called Katy, who had come all the way from Germany to help Larkin out. Katy, who was described by Mary Jane as being of "rare beauty and exceeding goodness", was often surrounded by other similar beings and was apparently a highly-qualified physician, as it was in fact she who was diagnosing and prescribing for Larkin's patients.

However, as time progressed, poltergeist phenomena started to occur during Mary Jane's sessions of fairy-trance. Initially, loud knockings were heard emanating from within articles of furniture. Then, the young girl began being 'possessed' by another spirit, who caused her to utter "the most blasphemous and rude speeches"; and, whilst Mary Jane gave vent to these foul oaths, heavy furniture and other items would move about from place to place, and various objects suddenly materialise around her. This new spirit claimed to be a sailor-boy and, whenever he came to the house instead of Katy, havoc ensued. Most disturbingly, Mary Jane's limbs were twisted and dislocated, then tied up around her torso and each other in bizarre and seemingly impossible 'knots', all whilst the disembodied voice of the sailor-boy laughed, mocked and made obscene jokes from thin air. Once the ghost had eventually left the scene, Dr Larkin would then be obliged to use his professional expertise to reset the poor girl's limbs back into their joints again.

Once, the sailor-boy stole a handkerchief and professed to have carried it off to Germany; it later reappeared inside a man's open palm, apparently from nowhere. The spook even began trailing after Dr Larkin on his rounds, producing loud poundings on doors and following him

A cute (but possibly *slightly* politically-incorrect) knitted trow-doll on sale at Scalloway Museum gift shop in the Shetlands. The days when such fairy-beings could be blamed for causing poltergeist phenomena are evidently long gone, but the account of islander Andrew Hunter certainly proves that there once was such a time. [muckle-shetland.blogspot.com]

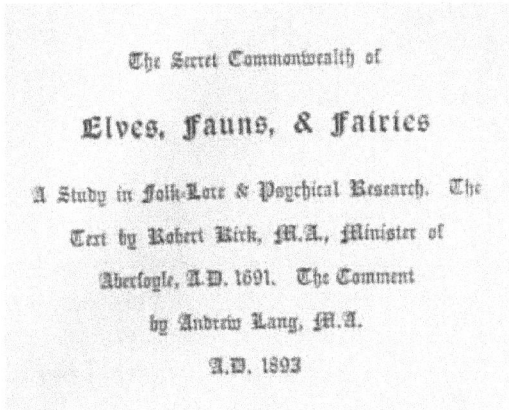

The Secret Commonwealth of

Elves, Fauns, & Fairies

A Study in Folk-Lore & Psychical Research. The Text by Robert Kirk, M.A., Minister of Aberfoyle, A.D. 1691. The Comment by Andrew Lang, M.A.

A.D. 1893

The title-page of an 1893 edition of *The Secret Commonwealth*, prepared for publication by the noted Victorian folklorist Andrew Lang. It was not until after the beliefs of Kirk's parishioners were long-dead that they actually received any meaningful public attention, sadly. Note how the book is by now being marketed as 'A Study in Folk-Lore and Psychical Research', two terms which did not even exist when Kirk actually wrote the thing!

JARDIN (58.
DE FLORES
CVRIOSAS, EN QVE SE TRA-
TAN ALGVNAS MATERIAS DE HV-
manidad, Philofophia, Theologia y Geo-
graphia: con otras cofas curiofas, y
apazibles: compuefto por
Antonio de Tor-
quemada.
***

DIRIGIDO AL MVY ILLV-
ftre y Reuerendiſsimo ſeñor don Diego
Sarmiento de Soto mayor, Obiſpo
de Aſtorga. &c.

Va hecho en feys tratados, como parecera en la
tercera hoja de efta obra.

Impreſſo con licencia.

En Leyda, por Pedro de Robles, y Ioan de
Villanueua, Año de. M. D. LXXIII.

CON PRIVILEGIO.

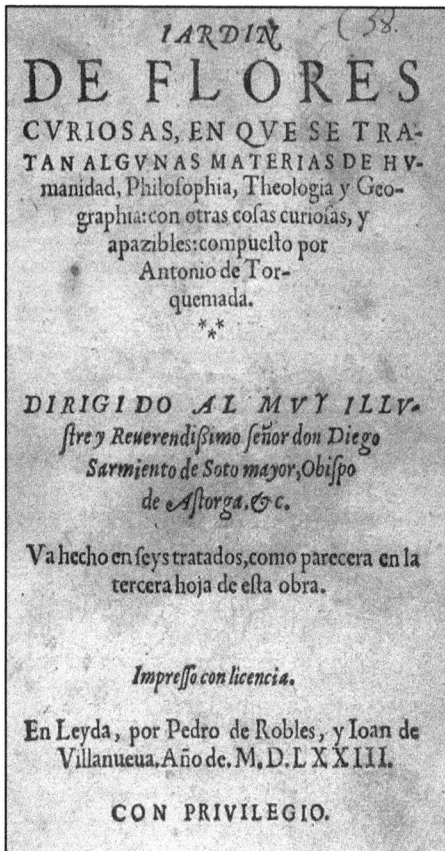

On the left is the title-page of the Spanish Renaissance writer Antonio de Torque-mada's book of anecdotes and travellers' tales *Jardin de Flores* (*The Flower Garden*), in which he tells the strange tale of the stone-throwing *trazgo* of Salamanca. On the right is a 19th-century French illustration of a pesky stone-throwing poltergeist which bothered a house in Paris during 1846. Were the behaviour of the 'fairy' and the 'ghost' really any different in either case, however?

'The Mad Merry Pranks of Robin Goodfellow'

From Oberon in fairyland,
the king of ghosts and shadows there,
Mad Robin I, at his command,
am sent to view the night sports here:
  What revel rout
  Is kept about,
In every corner where I go,
  I will o'er see,
  And merry be,
And make good sport with ho, ho, ho!

More swift than lightning can I fly,
and round about this airy welkin soon,
And, in a minute's space, descry
each thing that's done beneath the moon,
  There's not a hag
  Nor ghost shall wag,
Nor cry "goblin!" where I do go,
  But Robin I
  Their feats will spy,
And fear them home with ho, ho, ho!

If any wanderers I meet
that from their night-sports do trudge home,
With counterfeiting voice I greet
and cause them on with me to roam,
  Through woods, through lakes,
  Through bogs, through brakes, –
Over bush and brier with them I go;
  I call upon
  Them to come on,
And wend me, laughing ho, ho, ho!

Sometimes I meet them like a man,
sometimes an ox, sometimes a hound;
And to a horse I turn me can,
to trip and trot about them round.
  But if to ride
  My back they stride,
More swift than wind away I go;
  Over hedge and lands ,
  Through pools and ponds,
I whirry, laughing, ho, ho, ho!

When lads and lasses merry be
With possets and with junkets fine,
Unseen of all the company,
I eat their cakes and sip their wine;
  And to make sport,
  I fart and snort,
And out the candles I do blow;
  The maids I kiss,
  They shriek, "Who's this?"
I answer nought, but ho, ho, ho!

Yet now and then, the maids to please,
I card at midnight up their wool:
And while they sleep, snort, fart and fease,
with wheel to threads their flax I pull:
  I grind at mill
  Their malt do still,
I dress their hemp, I spin their tow;
  If any wake,
  And would me take,
I wend me, laughing, ho, ho, ho!

When house or hearth doth sluttish lie,
I pinch the maids there black and blue;
And from the bed the bed-clothes I
pull off, and lay them naked to view:
  twixt sleep and wake
  I do them take,
And on the key-cold floor them throw;
  If out they cry,
  Then for they I,
And loudly laugh I, ho, ho, ho!

When any need to borrow ought,
we lend them what they do require:
And for the use demand we nought,
our own is all we do desire:
  If to repay
  They do delay,
Abroad amongst them then I go,
  And night by night
  I them affright,
With pinching, dreams, and ho, ho, ho!

When lazy queens have nought to do
but study how to cog and lie,
To make debate, and mischief too,
twixt one another secretly:
  I mark their gloss,
  And do disclose
To them that they had wronged so;
  When I have done,
  I get me gone,
And leave them scolding, ho, ho, ho!

When men do traps and engines set
in loop-holes, where the vermin creep,
That from their folds and houses get
their ducks and geese, their lambs and sheep:
  I spy the gin,
  And enter in,
And seem a vermin taken so,
  But when they there
  Approach me near,
I leap out, laughing, ho, ho, ho!

By wells and gils in meadows green,
we nightly dance our hey-degies,
And to our fairy King and Queen
we chant our moonlight harmonies.
  When larks 'gin sing,
  Away we fling,
And babes new-born steal as we go;
  And if in bed
  We leave instead,
And wend us, laughing, ho, ho, ho!

From hag-bred Merlin's time have I
thus nightly revelled to and fro:
And, for my pranks, men call me by
the name of Robin Goodfellow:
  Fiends, ghosts, and sprites
  That haunt the nights,
The hags and goblins do me know,
  And beldames old,
  My feats have told,
So Vale, Vale, ho, ho, ho!

The 1628 poem *The Mad Merry Pranks of Robin Goodfellow*, probably by Ben Jonson (pictured above), clearly describes the arch-fairy Robin acting like a contemporary poltergeist in any number of prank-pulling ways.

An old illustration to the classic fairy-story of 'The Elves and the Shoemaker'. Did *Fortean Times* reader Mr J Keen really encounter such a being repairing some foot-wear up a tree sometime in the 1930s? He thinks so. [gutenberg.org]

On the left, a leprechaun mends a shoe with a tiny hammer; their traditional role in Irish folklore. On the right, an enlarged detail from Hogarth's print *Credulity, Superstition and Fanaticism: A Medley* illustrates the famous 17th-century English ghost story of the 'Drummer of Tedworth'. Are both images merely false mental representations of the invisible entities which actually create such mysterious rapping sounds, however?

A levitating table. But should we blame a poltergeist or a fairy for such an uncanny occurrence?

The British SPR have set up an 'Operation JOTT' in recent years, in order to try and gather evidence for the inexplicable movement and dematerialisation of everyday household objects. But are such things really supernatural, or mere tricks of the memory?

A sign erected in 1977 to celebrate the well-loved fairy-tale of the 'Green Children of Woolpit'. Another 'little green man' was seen during a poltergeist-haunting by a Mrs Lynn Connolly of Hull, however. Was he a fairy, or a mere hallucination?

Alleged apports – or inexplicably-materialising objects – can come in many shapes and sizes.

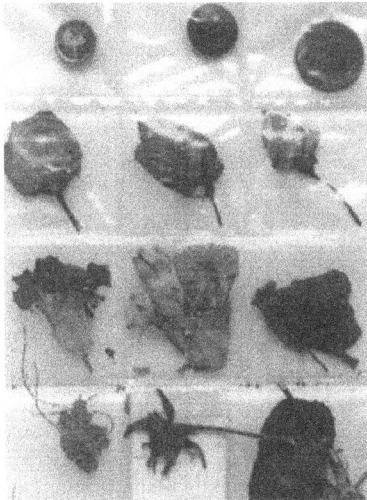

A collection of apports reputedly materialised by the English medium Minnie Harrison.

unseen to dinner parties, then reporting back to all and sundry about various minor embarrassing incidents which had happened to him there. Amazingly, even at this relatively late date, the incidents caused such a stir locally that Mary Jane was arrested, tried on charges of necromancy – or 'raising the dead' – and sentenced to 60 days' solitary confinement in Dedham jail, just outside Boston. [15]

Was this all down to a fairy, the dead, a poltergeist, fakery, hitherto-latent psychic powers being released by the power of hypnosis, or good old-fashioned witchcraft, then? Your answer to that question, I suspect, will depend largely upon your cultural background and own personal prejudices. Evidently, 1840s Massachusetts was a place and time in history when at least three or four of these explanations were able to compete plausibly within the minds of those involved. I doubt that, if the same thing had happened to Mary Jane today, she would have gone around claiming to have spoken to a German fairy, though ...

Having a Laugh
The 'sailor-boy' in this weird tale, it will be noted, was heard to laugh; it appears obvious that he found the pranks he was playing on Mary Jane to be amusing. Why else would he have played them? Fairies, too, are meant to have laughed at their innocent dupes, however. This, for example, is an account gathered from the island of Reachrai, off the coast of Northern Ireland, about the fairy-folk making an islander's grandfather 'pixie-led' – or inexplicably lost within an entirely familiar environment – at some unspecified time in the past:

> "They [the fairies] played a trick on my grandfather one time. He came out to fodder the horses, and he went round the stable a dozen times, couldn't get the door. He was an hour out, and they went out to look for him, and they asked him what kept him. He said, "Them wee buggers!" Made a fool of him! And he could hear them laughing up on the hill. He couldn't see them." [16]

Whether this was true or merely a socially-acceptable way in which the man could cover up the true reasons for his prolonged absence may be a moot point, but the idea of invisible laughter is a trope still commonly encountered within poltergeist cases. The famous Lamb Inn poltergeist, for example, whom we shall examine later, was sometimes heard to laugh from out of thin air, a "ha! ha! ha! like a hollow shrill voice" being observed during the haunting. [17] A more recent, but evidentially-weak, case comes from a woman named only as 'Claire' who, in 2000, moved into a flat near to the allegedly haunted Greyfriar's Cemetery in Edinburgh. Here, she was bothered by minor poltergeist events and, in bed one night, realised that she could hear some unseen person in the room with her, breathing. On closer listening, she realised that something was, in fact, blowing raspberries into her ear. Her lover, meanwhile, identified the sound not as raspberry-blowing, but as "the sound of giggling". [18] All this does suggest that polts, just like fairies, might have a certain puckish sense of humour to them at times.

One of the best examples of this idea involved a being identified specifically as a "brownie" which, in 1615, haunted a castle in the old province of Dauphiné in south-east France. This brownie, though essentially benign – he never really hurt anyone, and lay low completely on Sundays and Holy Days – performed many infantile poltergeist pranks. If we can believe the story, he broke vases and caused the water to float over people's heads before drenching them with it, filled other vases with cabbage-leaves instead of flowers, put bits of metal into visitors' food after begging their forgiveness for the quality of the meals being served, and hid various objects inside sealed rooms. He certainly seems to have been a merry old soul, and could sometimes be heard invisibly singing, drumming, playing music and laughing at all the jokes he had played. Sadly, he was eventually expelled by a ceremony of exorcism, in spite of his apparent respect for Church holidays. [19]

Dermot MacManus has a whole chapter – entitled 'Pranks and Mischief' – devoted to cataloguing things like this, wherein we can read, for example, of a female artist, a 'Mrs EM', who in summer 1947 was staying in the western Irish district of Connemara, painting landscapes. Getting off the bus one June afternoon at an isolated spot, the artistic visitor placed her canvas on the slope of a small hill, then returned to her bicycle to fetch some other tools of her trade. Turning around, however, she found to her shock that the canvas was no longer there! A thorough search of the area turned up nothing but bewilderment and, giving up, she sat down to eat her lunch and smoke a leisurely cigarette. After half an hour, though, she turned back to face the hill – only to find the canvas sitting back there in the exact same spot she had left it in the first place. Returning to the bus-stop, and talking to the (apparently near-ubiquitous in these tales) old woman who dwelled nearby about her experience, Mrs EM was met with no surprise, merely a little laughter and the suspiciously stereotypical comment "What else would you expect now? Sure, isn't that a fairy hill!" [20]

Hide and Seek

This whole issue of mysteriously appearing/disappearing objects is yet another one which pops up frequently in tales of both poltergeists and fairies alike. In a 2005 *New York Times* article about continuing modern Icelandic belief in fairies, for example, Elly Erlingsdóttir, a woman from the port-town (and alleged elf hot-spot) of Hafnarfjördur, told a reporter how she still believed in the reality of the Hidden People. She had to, she said; some of them had recently borrowed her kitchen scissors, taking them from their usual place and then returning them a week later to a spot which she was sure she had repeatedly checked. [21] We may laugh, but the idea of elves taking people's tools and then giving them back some time later is actually a standard motif of fairy-lore, so Ms Erlingsdóttir is actually standing within a long and old tradition when making such unlikely claims.

However, rather than elves, most of us would surely prefer to blame our short-term memories for such incidents. We all occasionally misplace our wallets and our glasses, and no doubt most of these minor mishaps are down to nothing more sinister than mere absent-mindedness. Losing our keys is, in all likelihood, 'just one of those things'. But are *all* such incidents explicable in similarly banal terms? Not according to some researchers.

An SPR member named Julian Isaacs, for example, once asked for volunteers to take part in some 'metal-bending' experiments with him, in which the participants were tasked with trying to twist spoons using only the power of their minds, like Uri Geller. One couple involved found that there were annoying side-effects to their involvement, though; their spanner, which they kept hanging on a hook inside their locked garden shed, simply vanished, poltergeist-like, from its place sometime after October 1982. No sign was then seen of this item until March

1983, when it was found sitting on top of a wardrobe in their five-year-old daughter's room, rusty and not at all in the mint condition in which it had been left. [22] Hearing similar tales repeatedly, the SPR has now set up something called 'Operation JOTT' ('Just One of Those Things'), in order to gather more information about the topic. Log onto the SPR website, and one of the first things you come across is an appeal for accounts of:

> "... incidents often dismissed as Just One of Those Things – typically your computer glasses, which live on the desk, vanish; you find them, eventually, in the kitchen drawer, though you are sure you did not put them there. Or perhaps after diligent search you find them sitting where they ought to have been all the time. Or, if you are really unlucky, you never see them again. You may even find another pair of spectacles nearby, very similar to yours but not quite the same. Incidents of this sort are known as jottles." [23]

But why should the SPR care about such tales, really? In a world supposedly full of much more sensational paranormal phenomena, why bother collecting stories about such apparently trifling material as this? The answer the SPR provide is in fact rather a good one. Jottles, they say:

> "... may look trivial, but a small hole in a large balloon can cause a total collapse, and a discontinuity in the fabric of the environment may lead us to radical ideas about the nature of reality." [24]

Very true. These "slips in spatial continuity", as the SPR calls them, whether down to poltergeists, fairies or something else, would be just as significant indicators that our current view of reality may be incorrect as are levitating hay-cocks and flying pebbles; it is just that they happen to be somewhat less spectacular in appearance. They are also, however, by their very nature profoundly anecdotal and as such quite difficult to accept as being definite evidence of anything much at all, really.

Little Green Men

Fortunately, however, there are many weirder cases of objects inexplicably appearing and disappearing on record than the ones cited immediately above. What are we to make of the truly strange case of Mrs Lynn Connolly of Hull, for instance, who was hanging out her washing on 21st October 1975, when she felt a tap on her head? Reaching up to see what had caused it, she found that a small silver-cased notepad had somehow appeared from nowhere and become lodged in her hair-do. Removing it, she found a six-pointed star carved on the front together with some initials and the stamped word 'Klaipeda', which later turned out to be the name of a Lithuanian port. Inside, only 13 pages remained. Perhaps you could say a bird dropped it, if you were sceptical. Other readers, however, may wish to term it an 'apport' – the technical name given by specialists to such objects which seemingly materialise from nowhere.

Intrigued by news of this bizarre occurrence, a rather eccentric enthusiast named AJ Bell went to investigate, and reported back on his findings in an early issue of *Fortean Times*. He discovered that Mrs Connolly had been experiencing poltergeist phenomena in both her current and previous homes for some time, with electrical items malfunctioning, breathing sounds being heard, doors opening by themselves, and animals acting oddly. Once, when Mrs Connolly's husband was seriously ill in hospital during 1964, both she and her sister saw the sick man's profile appear suddenly and clearly on the living-room wall. Even more remarkable, what is described as "a Little Green Man" was occasionally sighted by Mrs Connolly, "seated cross-legged on a wall, repeatedly turning pages in a book and doffing his Trilby". [25] Even if this was just a hallucination, then its fairy-like nature, occurring as it did to somebody who would nowadays surely be characterised as being a poltergeist-focus, is surely still of great interest. Maybe the notepad belonged to him?

Perhaps more credibly, in *The Night Side of Nature* Catherine Crowe gives an account of the haunting of the castle of a certain Prince Hohenlohe in Silesia during 1806. Here, numerous bizarre occurrences were experienced by both guests and residents – phantom noises were heard, objects thrown around, lights and apparitions seen, and a jug of water tilted up and then 'drank itself' in mid-air. Most relevantly for our current purposes, though, was the following puckish event which allegedly occurred to a book-keeper named Dorfel who was staying at the castle:

> "He once laid his cap on the table by the stove; when, being about to depart, he sought for it, it had vanished. Four or five times he examined the table in vain; presently afterwards he saw it lying exactly where he had placed it when he came in." [26]

Taken in and of itself, this could very easily be dismissed ... but in conjunction with so many other remarkable phenomena having taken place within Castle Hohenlohe, it seems at least possible to have been down to what the German poet and mystic Justinius Kerner, from whom Crowe ultimately got the story, called "goblins" – but what we would surely term 'poltergeists'.

Pixilation Problems

How should we best approach such matters, though? Are they worth seriously considering, or not? Patrick Harpur, an excellent writer upon the unknown, calls the phenomenon of mysteriously appearing/disappearing objects pixilation (after the pixies), and views it in a very interesting way. In a 2006 article of his, *The Problem of Pixilation*, Harpur gives several odd examples involving his mother. Her engagement-ring disappeared on her once, for instance, whilst she was on holiday in Brittany. She had removed it, in front of her two sisters, before bathing in the sea. When she returned to shore, however, it was gone – only to turn up, ten days later, safely ensconced inside her jewellery box back home in England.

The most remarkable such occurrence cited, however, is actually quite scary. Harpur's mother's pot of face-cream, it seems, had long had the annoying habit of disappearing from her dressing table whilst she was sat there chatting to her sister. One day, in order to try and get to the bottom of this mystery, the siblings performed an experiment; both put their fingers upon every item on the table, whilst calling out its name, in order to make sure of what was there and what was not. There was definitely no pot of face-cream present – until Harpur's aunt let out a sudden scream. The pot had abruptly materialised from out of thin air and now rested inexplicably within her sister's curled fingers right there on the dressing table!

Are such things really important, then, or not? Yes and no, says Harpur. Compared to a full-on poltergeist or fairy-haunting, perhaps, isolated incidents of skin-cream and engagement-rings going missing are indeed small-fry. Yet, he hints, maybe the true significance of such occurrences lies buried within their very insignificance, saying that perhaps the real purpose of pixilation is:

> "… to introduce us to the in-between world. It opens a nagging crack in the fabric of our comfortable reality, a crack small enough to ignore or overlook if we wish … [It] is a tiny fault-line symbolising the moment … when we are suddenly opened up like wounds to … the beginning of the deeper, imaginative life of the soul." [27]

Through such little things as missing rings and misplaced credit-cards, then, seeps through fairy-land, and by a mere shift of perspective a pair of mislaid keys is transformed into an act of communion with another world. The word 'fairy', as we saw earlier, originally seems in English to have meant something like 'enchanted' or 'supernatural', as well as referring to the land of faery itself. Given this fact, it is surely highly appropriate to describe much reported poltergeist activity in such terms. Falling stones, flying furniture, apports and jottles; all *are* 'fairy', in its adjectival form, because they give a brief glimpse into something magical, wonderful and somehow 'other' in its very nature. With every rap, scratch and howl, the poltergeist gives each of us who contemplates it from a certain perspective a free pass away into the magic of fairy-land. We just have to look at it in the right way in order to be able to enter fully through its gates – or does that just sound too much like Dermot MacManus for comfort?

2.

The Ley of the Land: Poltergeists and Fairies in the Landscape

Mostly poltergeists are conceived of as being internal, domestic creatures. There are numerous types of domestic fairies, too, but the Good Folk are also frequently said to live outside, in various sacred spots throughout the countryside. This seems like an obvious difference between the two classes of entity, then, but in fact the situation is not quite so clear-cut. There is, for example, an occasional – if often dubious – association in existence between both fairies and poltergeists and what are now popularly termed 'ley-lines'.

I think we have to be careful with these particular slippery landscape-features, however. There is a woolly perception amongst some that these things were some kind of ancient 'cosmic energy paths' used by druids/pagans/UFOs (delete as applicable) at some undefined point in the distant, prehistoric past. However, they were only really noticed – and named 'leys' – in 1925 by the inventive antiquarian Alfred Watkins, in his classic book *The Old Straight Track*. Noticing that various ancient sites, from churches to stone circles, within the English landscape seemed to be aligned with one another and linked via half-vanished straight tracks, he theorised that these old, forgotten paths were simply antique trading-routes. Notions of them being associated with mystical 'earth-energies' and suchlike are essentially a 1960s invention, stemming largely from the work of esoteric writers like John Michell. Far from being ancient, the notion of a ley-line is in fact a very recent one.

However, this is not to say that there is necessarily *nothing* to such ideas. Ley-lines may not really be plotted-out UFO flight-paths, as some once naively thought, but the association of fairies with some of them is real enough. For instance, in Ireland what an Englishman might now term leys were known as 'fairy-paths'. The Irish *sidhe*, as is well-known, were meant to live in places called 'raths' 'lisses' or 'fairy-forts', circular areas characteristically surrounded by a bank and ditch, and often located on a hill, knoll or other small raised area. Originally, most were Iron Age 'ring-forts', defensive encampments in which the ancient Irish lived, but which were now supposedly occupied by the fairies. However, a widespread tradition lingered on in Ireland well into the twentieth century that the *sidhe* frequently marched between these raths and other fairy-places in the landscape – such as fairy-bushes and supposedly enchanted hills, mountains and lakes – in something known as the 'fairy-troop'. In order to do this, they made use of fairy-paths, imagined as being straight routes running between and thereby linking up all of these special sites.

There is some possible evidence of similar-sounding beliefs surviving in England – where Neolithic forts were also sometimes said to be haunted by fairies – into the twentieth century, too. The folklorist Katharine Briggs, for instance, in her book *The Fairies in Tradition and Literature*, quotes from a speech given by the vice-president of the Edington branch of the Women's Institute in 1962, in which she spoke of "all sorts of odd things" happening in her rural Wiltshire cottage. Specifically, she talked of one of her bedroom doors which would shut itself for no reason and then refuse to open no matter how hard you pushed or pulled on it, "just as if it was bolted". However, it would open instantly on such occasions if asked politely to do so, something which the woman accounted for by saying that her house lay on the old Pilgrim's Way to Glastonbury and that, as such, the fairies probably just popped in to visit the place at times. [1]

Get Off My Land!
The researcher Paul Devereux, probably the leading light in this field, has, in his splendid book *Spirit Roads*, linked these fairy-paths – and, by implication, ley-lines themselves – to various ancient traditions of so-called 'paths of the dead', like those found in the traditional Chinese system of landscape divination known as *offeng shui*. Readers may be familiar with a bastardised version of this current in the West today, wherein highly-paid *'feng shui* consultants' will offer to rearrange your household furnishings in order to bring good luck, but the original concept was related partially to the idea of keeping houses and buildings away from certain parts of the landscape over which the dead were said to pass; the 'spirit-paths'. Building in the way of these procession-routes was said to be dangerous, and any house which blocked the way would be highly likely to end up being noisily haunted by irate ghosts. Other legends about processions of the dead – everything from phantom-funerals to the Wild Hunt of Germany – seem likely to be related to these very old beliefs. [2]

So does the idea of the fairy-troop; in many Irish traditions, the wandering fairies are linked pretty closely to the dead. Time and again, we can read stories of departed persons being seen amongst their number; some have even held that *all* trooping fairies were nothing more than the dead in disguise. If you happened to come across the fairy-troop, then the chances were that you would see the soul of someone deceased you had known in life walking there amongst them, it seems. Whatever the Irish fairies ultimately were, though, the warnings concerning what would happen to you if you built your house in their path were much the same as the warnings the Chinese once gave about disturbing their own troops of the dead – namely, that there would be bad luck, sickness and death for all concerned, with the house inevitably ending up being haunted, generally by noisy and destructive poltergeist-type beings.

You would think that talk of the fairy-troop, spirit-processions and the Wild Hunt is just folklore. However, be this as it may, in *Spirit Roads* Paul Devereux gives some interesting examples of fairy-hauntings taking place in apparent revenge for stupid humans inconsiderately obstructing the route of fairy-paths with their buildings. A house built less than a mile from Caherhurly Crossroad in eastern County Clare, for instance, was once inhabited by a lady interviewed by Devereux. Whilst living there, the woman said, she had become sick and depressed, and one night had seen a number of small, shadow-like figures passing through the wall at one end of her living room and out through the opposite one, apparently in a procession. The end of the building through which the figures passed, said Devereux, stood on a direct line running from a nearby fairy-fort to the crossroads – something which she, as a non-native to the area, had not known. [3]

A more spectacular instance cited by Devereux, meanwhile, came from Cloonagh, County Clare, where a man named Billy Brennan allegedly found that his cattle were sick and dying, the situation growing steadily worse until a disembodied voice – a surprisingly common facet of poltergeistry – told him to shift the position of his gable from out of the way of the fairies' wanderings [4]. A public house in the County Kerry village of Knocknagashel, likewise, was also once supposedly plagued by invisible forces pulling sheets from beds and odd, shadowy forms wandering around the place at night due to its being built in the way of what some said must surely have been a fairy-path [5]. Dermot MacManus tells us of another such case; that of a certain Paddy Baine, one corner of whose home jutted out over a fairy-route. Not long after it had been built, phantom noises, "as if the whole house was about to tumble down" were heard coming from the end of the building which was in contravention of the unwritten local planning-laws. Baine had to employ a stonemason to cut across the offending corner before peace finally prevailed [6]. The tale from Knocknagashel is particularly interesting, as what locals called a 'fairy-path' was in fact a 'Mass-path' – a straight route used to link communities with churches, and along which coffins were once carried on their way to burial [7]. This detail clearly demonstrates the confusion which has long-existed in Ireland (and elsewhere) between the fairies and the marching dead.

Paranormal Planning Permission
Ireland is not the only place in which beliefs about fairies living within the landscape can still sometimes be found, though. Iceland is another modern stronghold of such ideas, a 1998 public opinion poll allegedly finding that 54% of all Icelanders believe in a kind of 'hidden world' of elves which surrounds them [8]. In 1992, for instance, Reykjavik, the capital, became the first city in the world to employ the services of an 'Elf-Finder General', an apparent clairvoyant (and part-time piano teacher) named Erla Stefánsdóttir. Together with the city's planning department, she drew up a map displaying the main dwelling-places of elves across the city and its environs. Whilst it was implied at the time that the map was supposed to be taken into account when making future planning decisions, however, its main purpose actually appeared to be for tourism. Nonetheless, the map itself was quite detailed, with fairy zones delineated as belonging to Elves, Light-Elves, Gnomes, Dwarfs and Huldufólk (or 'Hidden People') littering the landscape [9].

Perhaps most famously, though, there have been numerous reported instances of Vegagerdin, Iceland's national road-building company, allegedly altering its construction plans in order to accommodate fairy-habitats. If you try and contact the Icelandic Roads Administration (ICERA) about this issue, though, then you will simply receive a standard response written by a rather frustrated-sounding official named Victor Arnar Ingólfsson to the effect that:

> "The environmental impact is assessed for many construction projects ... It cannot be

denied that belief in the supernatural is occasionally the reason for local concerns, and these opinions are taken into account just as anyone else's would be. This is simply a case of good public relations." [10]

However, rather contradicting this viewpoint was the furore which surrounded a large boulder called the Klofasteinar ('Cloven Rock') that stood in the way of a new stretch of the Westfjords highway in 1995, and which was slated to be moved. Naturally, given the way of such things, machines involved in construction broke down, and minor accidents occurred. Locals blamed the elves who supposedly inhabited the rock. The contractor in charge, hearing this, immediately announced that he did not wish to be responsible for the boulder's removal. An elf-medium named Regina was therefore called in who laid her hands on the rock in order to commune with its spirits. There were not, she said, any elves in it – but there were some living in two other nearby boulders. She asked the elves, who she said were old friends, for their permission to move the cursed rock out of the way and closer to their present homes, thus presumably giving them more living-space. The elves, seeing that their precious boulder was not simply about to be destroyed, agreed, and the medium stayed around to supervise matters – together with what were termed some "rather worried elves" who stood there by her side throughout [11].

Erla Stefánsdóttir has more such stories. In a recent interview, for instance, she spoke out about a troubled building-site located near a waterfall in the Borgarfjördur region, just north of Reykjavik, a place slated to be transformed into a holiday resort and golf course but which was also, in her view, "densely populated by gnomes, nymphs, fairies and trolls". Because of this fact, she said, progress on-site was unnaturally slow, with a 50-ton excavator having twice tipped over by itself for no apparent reason. The site-manager, mystified, asked Erla to attend, and she spoke to the resident elves who agreed not to hurt any workers, but still pledged to defend their homes by interfering with the project invisibly [12]. Cynics, however, might speculate that Erla was only invited to the site and fed the whole yarn in order to gain some free publicity for the new resort from her visit...

Rock Legends

It seems that, if encountering poltergeist-like phenomena in the home is the otherworldly punishment for building in the *path* of the fairy-troop, then encountering 'curses' involving things like mysteriously breaking-down equipment and construction-machines falling over is the equivalent penalty for interfering with the sacred sites which are actually *linked* by those paths. There was even one Icelandic case, from the fishing village of Bolungarvík on the north-west coast, in which elves angered by builders were blamed for a massive shower of stones and clods of earth raining down over the place during June 2011. It later turned out that the deluge was not down to poltergeists, however, but a freak explosion in a mine being dug through the nearby mountain of Tradarhyrna by contractors Ósafl in order, ironically, to provide the place with large rocks for a new avalanche-defence barrier. However, seeing as tunnel-builders had dug through another nearby mountain supposedly inhabited by Hidden Folk the previous year, locals saw fit to blame elves for the catastrophe, especially seeing as Ósafl's machines had recently begun malfunctioning too. After the local council refused to offer an official apology to the elves, various Bolungarvík residents took matters into their own hands and held a ceremony intended to bring about peace between the two realms by singing and offering up prayers to the slighted trolls [13].

It is thought that humans having consideration for the elves in this way can actually lead to positive outcomes; in the late 1970s, a road being built over a place called Tröllaskard ('Trolls' Pass') in the Skagafjördur district of northern Iceland was disrupted by various misfortunes after a number of supposedly fairy-filled rocks were pencilled in for demolition. Concerned road-engineers allegedly communicated with the trolls at a series of séances held by a well-known Icelandic medium named Hafsteinn Björnsson, and the site's foreman claimed that these beings began appearing to him in his dreams, warning him not to dynamite the rocks. Eventually the boulders were spared, the path of the road being altered somewhat unnaturally to accommodate them, and all was well. The fact that there have been no serious or fatal accidents on the road in question since it was laid is interpreted by some locals as being a reward from the trolls for this sensible compromise [14].

Another recent news story, meanwhile, told of the efforts of an Icelandic MP named Árni Johnsen to relocate a 30-ton boulder from a place called Sandskeid, where it was threatened by roadworks, to his home of Höfdaból in the Westman Islands, an archipelago off the south coast of the country. He wanted to do this because, in his view, the boulder was the home of three generations of elves – a young couple with children living on the ground floor, and the kids' grandparents on the upper one – who had helped to save his life when he had been involved in a serious car accident near to the rock in 2010. Seeing as his SUV was a write-off, but he had survived unharmed, Johnsen could only conclude that the boulder-elves had saved him, something which a psychic he consulted confirmed. She also told the MP that the elves would be delighted to move back home with the grateful politician, on the proviso that the rock's 'window-side' be turned to face the sea-view, and that it be placed on grass so that the fairy-family would be able to keep and feed a flock of tiny elfin sheep, conditions to which he gladly agreed [15].

Secrets of the Stones

So far, these tales of fairy-haunted stones seem just cases of dubious superstition which could easily be attributed to mere coincidence or wishful thinking. However, there are a few cases on record of ancient stones – once thought of as being fairy-stones, perhaps? – being moved around which appear to have led to the outbreak of what would be classified by most people nowadays as being poltergeist phenomena. Some are purely legendary, such as a curious tale from the Lancashire village of Dilworth. Here, on a lane leading towards a place called Written Stone Farm, lies a ... well, a 'written-stone'. It is about nine feet long, two feet wide and one foot thick, and is inscribed with the following message: 'RAUFFE RADCLIFFE LAID THIS STONE TO LYE FOR EVER : AD 1655'.

And *why* did Rauffe Radcliffe lay this stone? In truth, nobody can remember, so a lie had to be invented instead. The tale, as first recorded in the 1870s, goes that there was a "cruel and barbarous murder" (what other type is there?) on the spot many centuries beforehand, which led to the victim returning and haunting the lane in the form of a malicious boggart. In order to put a stop to this, the stone in question was lain down in order to appease the spirit somehow, perhaps by giving it an appropriate memorial-marker. However, some time later, an unwise owner of Written Stone Farm is said to have decided that the stone would make a good worktable for making butter on, and so removed it into his farmhouse. However, the boggart soon expressed its disapproval of his actions by turning poltergeist; any pots, pans or other items of crockery placed upon the stone were knocked over, spilling their contents, the angry ghost causing these items to keep up an unceasing noisy dance all through the night. Eventually, so it is said, the chastened farmer had no choice but to replace the stone, before taking the extra precaution of planting magical holly-bushes all along the lane to bind the boggart back into its prison, a particularly fairy-like touch [16].

However, other tales about polt-haunted stones purport to have their basis in fact, not quaint rural legend. For instance, in 1944 a number of weird events were said to have occurred in the Essex village of Great Leighs after US troops stationed there moved a rock, known locally as the 'Witches' Stone', from a crossroads where it was obstructing their trucks. Within hours of this having happened (or so it is said ...) the bell in the local church tower began tolling for midnight at 2.30 in the morning, with nobody there to ring it. Meanwhile, hens stopped laying or were found drowned in water-butts, whilst a local farmer, Ernest Withen, discovered that his haystacks had been knocked down and scattered all across his yard, despite it having been a windless night.

More sinisterly, 30 sheep and two horses were then discovered lying dead in a field one morning, and chickens in a run and rabbits in a hutch were found to have changed places overnight without the fasteners having been in any way disturbed. One farmer's flock of sheep were even found in another field from their usual one, despite the hedges and fences in-between being unbroken. One farmer reported that the hay wagons had been turned the wrong way around in his sheds at night, too – all of which sounds not unlike the typical activities of a *stallspuk*, a specific breed of farmyard fairy/poltergeist we shall meet again later. Furthermore, traditional poltergeist phenomena started to break out in an already reputedly haunted bedroom at the local St Anne's Castle Inn, where a heavy wardrobe moved about, chests of drawers tipped onto their sides, and bedclothes were found strewn across the floor. All of this, according to the standard version of the story, occurred within the first week of the Witches' Stone being moved; but events were soon put a stop to when a group of villagers recovered the rock from where the GIs had dumped it, and replaced it back in its rightful place at the centre of the crossroads [17].

It must be said that many of these events could easily have been faked, though, as has been suggested in a recent article by the researcher Robert Halliday, which plausibly implies that a combination of pranksters and publicity-seeking pub landlords were to blame [18]. Even Harry Price, who went to Great Leighs to investigate, concluded that the phenomena were only "partly genuine, partly the work of a practical joker, and partly due to mass hysteria." [19] According to Halliday, the stone involved had, suspiciously, gathered no apparent folklore around it at all prior to the alleged events of 1944, and had in fact been moved several times before by road-workers without any ill effects. Even so, it is still interesting that the jokers involved – if jokers there were – chose to play pranks of exactly the kind that were reputedly performed by various breeds of rural fairies in the past. Whilst locals and the Press chose to play up some kind of spurious witchcraft element, claiming that a notorious hag had been buried beneath the stone with a stake through her heart during the 1600s, any fakers involved

A rare photograph of the Icelandic elf-medium Erla Stefánsdóttir in her youth; if you think there are any fairies living inside a rock near you, then she's the one to call! (She can also help if you need piano lessons).

In the town of Kópavogur, not far outside Reykjavik, lies a street named Álf-hólfsvegur, where the road suddenly narrows. This is not a method to deter speeding motorists, but a concession to the Icelandic elves (or Huldufólk – 'hidden folk') which allegedly inhabit the rock formation on the right of the picture and who were supposedly responsible for a series of misfortunes and equipment break-downs whenever road-builders tried to plough their way through the sacred rock. The street's name means 'Elf's Hill Way', and according to local bureaucrats the Álfhóll is actually preserved purely for heritage reasons as a culturally-important ice-age rock formation rather than as a nature-reserve for fairies; or, at least, that is the official line ...

Fairies dance and sing around a cromlech (dolmen/standing stone) in an illustration to the old Welsh fairy-tale of 'The Shepherd of Frennifawr'.

You never knew when you were going to come across a fairy-palace hidden secretly within the landscape.

As these two images clearly show, whilst hardly in the middle of nowhere, the Humber Stone does not lie directly next to any houses – so how much did it *really* have to do with the 1980 haunting of the Billingham family home?

The Humber Stone, as viewed during the 19th century when it was rather larger than it is now. Did this local yokel survive messing about with it?

'RAUFFE RADCLIFFE LAID THIS STONE TO LYE FOR EVER: AD 1655'. Indeed so; but was this really done to trap an annoying boggart who kept on playing poltergeist on a nearby farm? The unlikely legend of Lancashire's 'Written Stone' certainly suggests so.

The picturesque Essex village of Great Leighs, where Harry Price investigated an alleged outbreak of poltergeist phenomena related to the movement of a so-called 'Witches' Stone' in 1944.

At a haunted house on Russian Hill overlooking San Francisco Bay in 1856, a "frightfully lean" 'goblin' with a hideous face was seen emerging from a shaking bush. The description given makes him sound not unlike Count Orlock here, from the seminal silent movie *Nosferatu*.

The Latoon fairy-tree, the subject of an act of senseless vandalism with a chainsaw one night in 2002, but since thankfully recovered. There are not too many trees that can say they have caused the alteration of a stretch of highway.

A Green Lady hangs down ominously from the limb of a dogwood tree; did Betsy Bell's innocent attempts to pick some flowers trigger off America's most infamous poltergeist haunting?

The Bell Witch story in potted form as shown on Historical Marker 3C-38 in Tennessee.

A so-called 'fairy-fort' (also known as 'raths' and 'lisses'). Often the remains of iron-age hill-forts or other such raised areas in the landscape, the Irish imagination has populated them with fairies for countless generations now. The Irish name for the fairies – *sidhe* – actually means 'hill folk'.

An illustration of the famous 'Wild Hunt', a legendary phenomenon known from all across Europe in the past; the Irish fairy-troops were probably its Celtic equivalent.

An illustration of a fairy-funeral taken from James Bowker's 1878 book *Goblin Tales of Lancashire*. The researcher Paul Devereux collected testimony from a woman living near Caherhurly Crossroad in Ireland that she, too, had witnessed a procession of small, black shadow-figures marching in line through her house one night.

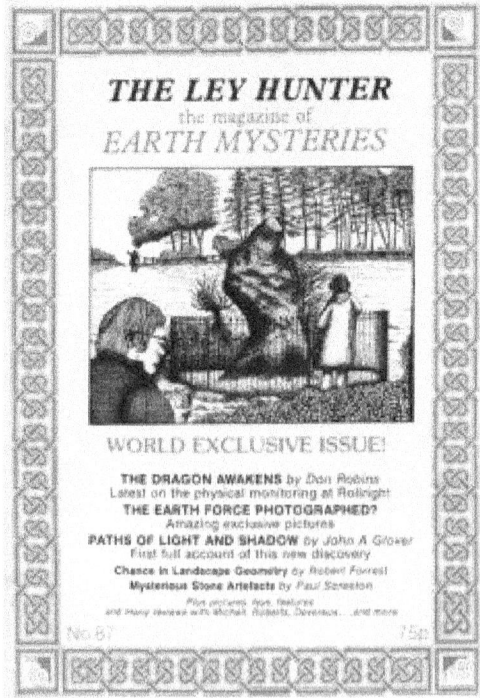

Alfred Watkins, the 'discoverer' of ley-lines. He had no idea that his theories about straight lines in the countryside marking out old trading-routes would later be picked up on by those of a more esoteric bent and then transformed to fit their own notions about 'earth-energies' and 'UFO flight-paths' in influential magazines like *The Ley Hunter*.

were in actual fact imitating fairies rather more than they were witches!

One Hell of a Stone

Another ancient stone often associated with ghostly phenomena is the Humber Stone (also known as the Hell Stone, Holy Stone or Host Stone) near Leicester, a large glacial deposit which is alleged to have once been used for certain ill-defined ritual purposes. This item is located in a village which is actually called Humberstone, and the rock itself, a large granite block, was originally called the 'Hoston Stone', or simply 'Hoston', the name probably deriving from the Old English *har stān*, meaning 'hoary (or grey) stone'. It used to loom much larger than it does now, some upper parts of the rock having been broken off and the place where it stands levelled out for agricultural purposes. According to local lore, the farmer responsible for this outrage was cursed, his land never prospering afterwards, something which supposedly led to him dying penniless in the workhouse. Perhaps this was only to be expected as, in times gone by, it was rumoured that fairies frequented the stone; one popular fable has it that some unnamed local foolish enough to pay a visit to the boulder alone one day heard it utter a deep groan, causing him to flee the scene for fear of meeting the Little Folk. [20]

This is all just legend, but in 1980 it was reported as fact in the local Press that a house sitting close to the Humber Stone was haunted. A ten-year-old boy living there drew a Pan-like creature with a goat's head, long horns, cloven hoofs and a man's body whilst at school. His teacher commented upon it, and the boy volunteered the information that the entity was something that he had frequently witnessed standing at the bottom of his bed at night. The Press seized hold of the story, and soon got more out of the boy's parents, a Mr and Mrs Billingham. They said that they had also experienced numerous disturbing poltergeist-related incidents inside the house, hearing the crying of phantom children and seeing a ghostly cat there, which had jumped up onto the couple's bed. When Mrs Billingham's parents stayed over to babysit one evening, meanwhile, her mother woke up in the middle of the night after being strangled by invisible hands which, she told reporters, were "exerting a vice-like grip" around her throat. Eventually, the Billinghams felt compelled to move away; and their successors in the property left themselves within two months, too. Supposedly, neighbours also complained of phantom monks haunting their own houses and two exorcisms were reportedly carried out in the area. [21]

Apparently, then, the Humber Stone was haunted – or, perhaps less sensationally, you could choose instead to say that some houses which just happened to sit quite near to it were. How close were these residences, though? Not as close as you might be led to think. In fact, there *are* no houses standing right next to the damned stone, as accounts of these events tend not to mention! As such, whilst the polt may well have been real, the conflation of it with the Humber Stone appears to have been largely invented to sell newspapers.

Indeed, it seems that legends of curses and paranormal activity surrounding the Humber Stone, whilst not originally *invented* by the media, are nowadays largely promulgated through such channels. For example when, in 1981, Leicester Council was considering removing the rock and building a housing estate around it (proof positive that no houses surrounded the thing in 1980!), they thoughtfully consulted the Old Humberstone Historical Society for advice. A Mrs J Bailey, of the Society, advised the authorities publicly through the *Leicester Mercury* not to excavate it, citing various anecdotal misfortunes which she said had occurred to those who had attempted to interfere with it in the past. Should the builders choose to go ahead with their plans, however, then Mrs Bailey had some odd advice for them:

> "Talk to it. I believe that if you told it that it would be removed to a safe place where no damage would come to it, there would be no trouble. I believe there would be disastrous results otherwise." [22]

And, with that, it sounds almost as if we are back in Iceland with Erla Stefánsdóttir again.

Save the Trees!

In Iceland, then, people are punished for messing about with elf-stones; in Ireland, however, as we saw earlier with the case of John M'Laughlin, they are cursed for chopping down fairy-thorns. This lingering belief has sometimes led to stories very similar to the ones from Iceland being told in the Emerald Isle. In 1968, for example, it appears that the planned route of a new road passing through Donegal had to be altered after large numbers of workmen refused point-blank to chop down a nearby lone tree, believed locally to have been a haunt of the *sidhe*. "I have heard so much about these fairy trees that I would not risk it," said the foreman in charge, Roy Green [23]. In County Carlow in November 1959, meanwhile, it is said that a farmer named John Byrne was bulldozing a bush from his land when a three-foot-tall "wee red man" suddenly ran out from beneath it and across the field before jumping over the fence – something which was, supposedly, witnessed by three other people. Beneath this bush, the men allegedly discovered a large flagstone covering a hole. This stone proved impossible to shift, with gelignite placed on it failing to explode, and eventually, so the story goes, Byrne stopped all landscaping work on the field and left the fairies to it [24]. This was actually reported on in the *Belfast Telegraph* for 9th November 1959, apparently with a straight face.

Credence was still being given to such beliefs in the 1980s; when the American businessman John DeLorean famously set up a plant to build his futuristic-looking but wildly impractical cars in Belfast only for the entire venture to fail massively, for instance, an urban legend that he had been cursed because a fairy-bush had been uprooted when he built the factory soon began to spread [25]. Sadly, though, Irish belief in the power of fairy-trees is now diminishing; at least if the depressing fate of the Latoon fairy-tree in County Clare is taken to be indicative. This particular sacred old whitethorn was threatened by a new motorway being built between Limerick and Galway in 1999 but, thankfully, the authorities were sympathetic to its plight and made slight alterations allowing it to stand next to the road surrounded by a protective wooden fence. One night in August 2002, however, some cretin armed with a chainsaw came along and hacked off all its leaves and branches, leaving it half-dead (although, cheeringly, by 2003 its leaves were sprouting once more) [26]. Given this wanton act of vandalism, however, it would be very interesting to know if any urban legends have since sprung up in which the chainsaw-wielding criminal is said to have been cursed to suffer either misfortune or poltergeist phenomena by the wrath of the wronged fairies...

A Bird in the Bush

WB Yeats, meanwhile, also collected a few instances of fairy-haunted bushes, including one set in "a house in a village that I know well" where lived a man who found £300 on the quay at Sligo one day and kept it. The sea-captain who had lost this money committed suicide in mid-ocean, fearing the consequences of his loss. After this, the man who found the cash died, and his soul could not rest; "strange sounds" and voices were heard around his house, and the dead man's wife took to praying to a bush in the garden at all hours, where the dead man's ghost would appear. This lone bush, said Yeats, was still standing there in his day; still nobody dared to cut it down. As for the poltergeist in the house, it did not depart until, allegedly, a snipe flew out of the solid plaster of one of the walls when repair-work was being done there. This bird, said the neighbours, was the "troubled ghost" of the dishonest owner, freed from the earthly prison of his own guilt at last [27].

Yeats' other story about a fairy-bush is just as strange. He said that a man had told him of how, when a child, he had once gone with another boy to "a certain field full of boulders and bushes of hazel and rock roses and creeping juniper" that lay by Coole Lake in County Galway. Seeing one particular bush, the boy bet to his companion that he could hit it with a pebble. Doing so, he was shocked to then hear "the most beautiful music that ever was heard" emanating from the plant. The boys fled and, looking back, saw a woman dressed in white walking round and round the bush: "First it had the form of a woman and then of a man", Yeats was told. [28]

But what was it that lived inside these haunted bushes, exactly? Ghosts or fairies? Probably it was a confused fusion of both at once; as the Elizabethan poet Michael Drayton put it in his *Nimphidia*, Robin Goodfellow "Oft out of a bush doth bolt/Of purpose to deceive us." Disembodied voices and noises around the house were certainly attributed to the actions of the dead in the first of Yeats' tales, but the idea of the dead man's apparition living inside a bush, and his soul being sighted in the form of a bird, speak very clearly of both the old Celtic fairy-faith, and of a now long-forgotten Irish folk-belief in metempsychosis – the idea that the souls of the dead could transmigrate into the bodies of animals like birds after death, or else reappear in the form of spectral animals. In the second tale, meanwhile, the woman who walked out of the bush sounds like a stereotypical ghost of the so-called 'White Lady' sort; yet her shape-shifting nature, the beautiful music and the fact that she lived in a shrub are all much more suggestive of her being some kind of *fay* rather than a spirit of the dead. How can we make sense of stories like these, whether genuine or mere fantasy?

Local Boy Chops Wood

One way to try and understand such narratives would be to examine an intriguing French story quite reminiscent of the tale of John M'Laughlin with which this book began. It so happened, according to this undated account, that an unnamed man from Lourourer-Saint-Laurent decided one day to cut down a box-tree in his garden because it was annoying him. Once he had done so, however, the tree began annoying him even more; the spirit which had formerly inhabited it awoke him every midnight by violently knocking upon his door thrice. Then, the tree-spirit would make the sound of an axe appear from thin air together with strange grunts and muffled sighs, all of which kept the man from his sleep until cock-crow, whereupon the poltergeist-like din stopped. This racket continued for the next six weeks until the man paid for a Mass to be said, which quietened the ghost for good. [29]

As Claude Lecouteux says in his discussion of the case, this particular tale features "a melding and superimposition" of various traditional ideas. For instance, it plays upon the old Classical belief that all trees had their *numen*, or guardian-spirit, in the form of dryads, nymphs and so forth (an idea which lingers on still in some fairy-lore), the notion that the souls of people buried near trees could sometimes pass up into them, presumably through their roots, and the later Christian alteration of these ancient beliefs into the new idea that condemned souls could sometimes be sentenced by God to live out the rest of their damned existence inside trees instead of in Hell. This weird notion eventually found its expression in the obscure medieval Christian practice of *obligationes ad arbores*, in which, before certain trees were chopped down, placatory offerings were made to the ghosts who were supposed to be living inside them. If this practice sounds to the reader rather more pagan than it does Christian, however, then you would be right; as was commonly done in centuries past, the Catholic Church merely co-opted an old pagan rite, gave it a new narrative and then passed the idea off as its own until eventually its original, non-Christian origins became almost totally forgotten with the passage of time. [30]

The status of the tree-dwelling poltergeist in this instance is actually quite ambiguous, then; was it some nature-fairy, or the condemned soul of a sinner? The fact that it was ultimately dispelled by having a Mass said can also be taken in two ways. Was the Mass intended as an official Church exorcism of an evil fairy, or as a request for God to take pity upon the suffering soul of a poor sinner? In such cases all of these old but competing traditions have become so mixed up that they can no longer really be untangled. Yeats' initially incomprehensible stories of haunted bushes, then, can only properly be understood as being imaginative composites of various different beliefs.

Polt-Plants

This is all legend, though. Have any haunted trees and bushes been encountered within any specific real-life poltergeist cases? They have, but very rarely. One good example comes from the famous Bell Witch case, an incredibly elaborate haunting from nineteenth-century Tennessee which we shall examine in much more detail later. Here, one of the many apparitions supposedly seen upon the haunted Bell farmstead by the daughter of the family, Betsy Bell, was particularly fairy-like. Gathering spring blossoms to decorate the house one day, so the story goes, Betsy heard a voice calling out to her as she went to pick some dogwood flowers from a tree. "Betsy Bell, don't break a flower; if you do, you will pay well for it," it said, ominously. Looking up, Betsy reputedly then witnessed "a ghostly-looking woman, dressed in pale green" hanging from a branch on a nearby red-oak tree with her "frail figure" swaying in mid-air. The children who had accompanied Betsy to the woods could not see the apparition, it seems, but she herself stopped what she was doing, made some feeble excuse for not picking any flowers after all, and took her young charges back home [31]. One version of the story – which calls the ghost "a pretty little girl dressed in green", not a fully-grown woman – implies that this sighting of the Green Lady was made immediately before the initial poltergeist phenomena itself broke out upon the farm, which could prove significant. [32]

This particular green-clad apparition, quite clearly, sounds more like some kind of nature-spirit or fairy-maiden than it does a typical poltergeist. It has implicit within it apparent echoes of such obscure old British plant-guardian fairies as Lazy Lawrence, who was said to protect orchards, Melch Dick, who guarded unripe nut thickets, and Awd Goggie, who made it his business to scare away children from unripened gooseberries [33]. There is even a tale from 1950s Ireland which seems like a direct parallel to this supposed event, the only real difference being that the *numen* involved was male rather than female. The narrative originates with a farmer living near the Mournes mountains in County Down, who told how, one Sunday afternoon in 1951, he and his childhood friends were vandalising a thorn tree. Seeing as the farmer was then only "a little tot", he stayed at the bottom whilst his pals broke off branches and threw them down. The boys' fun was interrupted, however, when a "wee man" in a "big broad hat" suddenly appeared at the base of the tree and began angrily shouting "Come down out o' that! Come down out o' that!" before disappearing [34]. The implication of such stories, surely, is that interfering with certain sacred trees or bushes can bring down the curse either of the fairies or the invisible dead upon a person, as happened to both John M'Laughlin and the Frenchman who chopped down the box-tree at Lourourer-Saint-Laurent.

The House on Haunted Hill

The often-overlooked haunting at a house on Russian Hill overlooking San Francisco Bay in 1856, meanwhile, is another notable example of poltergeist activity involving an apparently *numen*-haunted plant. This particular case, it must be said, was very weird, and involved a multitude of polt phenomena, with a black servant being repeatedly assaulted and hurled around by invisible hands, objects being smashed and rappings being heard. Two female residents of the place had recently spent a long time living in the Sandwich Islands, it seems, and felt that the spooks bothering them might have been some of the native *kanaka* spirits which had followed them home. Maybe; but are *kanaka* spirits meant to appear in the following apparitional guises? First of all, a so-called "goblin" was seen there, which, according to one witness:

> "... certainly bore the human form, though in distorted and frightful disproportion. It was of gigantic height and frightfully lean. Its face was hideously long, thin and distorted; blacker than any idea of blackness I ever had before; but its expression I never can portray. I can only say it was an appalling mixture of rage, hate and despair ... He wore a large white robe thrown fully around him and partly covering his immensely long lean head; and there he sat, reclining on the bench, full in the moonlight, silent, still and ghastly, in all his appalling ugliness." [35]

What is of specific interest to us here, though, is that this 'goblin' – like all the other apparitions which subsequently appeared around the house – arose from a bush in the garden which had begun "shaking so violently" a few moments beforehand that everyone present thought it would be "torn up by the roots". The next night, for instance, the *kanaka* spirits appeared from this same bush in the guise of a girl aged about 10 or 12 who bore a "slightly stooping attitude" and "flitted several times back and forth before the window." As she did so, someone screamed and the ghost floated off towards the kitchen where she disappeared "as if she had melted out". In her place immediately appeared another figure, seemingly male, but "gigantic in height, very thin and extremely shadowy". This seemed to pass right through the wall of the house before then reappearing, half-in and half-out of the wall, "melting" in and out of it repeatedly before finally vanishing. [36]

The third night, the assembled company asked, via séance, to see the apparitions again. They were granted their wish; the bush outside shook once more, and the young girl stepped out of it again. This time she faded away almost immediately, leaving behind a glowing light which was "at first a mere glimmer", but in a few seconds grew to be "the form and size of a large globe lantern". Soon, the light began changing shape rapidly into "a great many singular forms" before finally assuming "the exact shape of a long grave, about six feet in length, and close to the ground" which stretched into a "thin long line of light" and disappeared [37]. This is all a quite remarkable echo of the old folk-motif of haunted fairy-bushes from out of which, as we have seen, shape-shifting apparitions could sometimes apparently emerge; but were the witnesses at Russian Hill consciously aware of this trope? It seems unlikely – and yet the events, we are told, really happened. How to account for this fact is, I think, down to the individual reader.

3.

Ask and Ye Shall Receive: Fairy-Money and Coin-Apports

I am sure that many readers of this book will be familiar with the name of the so-called 'Demon Drummer of Tedworth', perhaps the most famous of all English poltergeists. Events began in March 1661 at the home of a local magistrate, John Mompesson, in the Wiltshire village of Tedworth (now Tidworth), not long after Mompesson had tried an itinerant drummer and conjuror named William Drury for begging and vagrancy. Finding him guilty, Mompesson banished Drury from the area and confiscated his drum, which allegedly led Drury to curse him. Apparently, his curse worked, as weird events soon broke out in the Mompesson household; rapping and drumming noises continued for days on end, giving the ghost its name, objects moved around, ashes and ewers were emptied into beds, animals assaulted, and a disembodied voice cried out the words "a witch, a witch", over a hundred times. One visitor to the house even found that the coins in his pocket all suddenly turned themselves black for no apparent reason. But then, all this is well known, thanks to its being detailed in the theologically-motivated investigator Joseph Glanvil's influential 1681 book upon such topics, *Saducismus Triumphatus*, and the case is now celebrated as being one of the earliest poltergeist manifestations ever to have been subjected to reasonable investigative scrutiny.

Most relevant to us here, however, is what the 'Demon Drummer' reputedly did one night in relation to the twin topics of fairies and of money. According to a letter written by Mompesson:

> "A neighbour coming and discoursing with my Mother, told my Mother that she had heard storyes of Fayries, that did use to leave money behind them in Maydens shooes [as a reward for cleanliness and moral behaviour], and the like; My Mother replied, I should like that well if it [the Drummer] would leave us some money to make us satisfaction for the trouble and charge it putts us to. And that night there was such a chinking of Money all about the house, that we thought we should have found all the house strewed with halfe Crownes in the Morning." [1]

They didn't, though; it was all just an auditory trick. The poltergeist, apparently, had deliberately imitated a fairy; or, perhaps, had simply regressed back to being one.

The aspect of fairy-belief being referred to by Mompesson's mother here is an old and venerable one, though. For example, in an interview conducted with an elderly Welsh blacksmith named William Jones in 1969, one folklorist recorded a modern survival of such ideas. Jones, according to his own words, had been told by his grandfather that the local Welsh fairies:

> "... had given many treasures to some people, especially if they had done good deeds in this world. Then they would be given a prize for those deeds. A widow having lost her husband, she gets up the next day and finds a purse of money on the table." [2]

How convenient. Such a narrative sounds not unlike an alternative version of that old folk-motif of the poor peasant praying to God for something they desperately needed and then waking up the next morning and finding that they had been miraculously provided with it as a reward for their unshakable faith and general Christian way of living.

Pennies from Heaven
It seems appropriate, then, that the lives of the Christian saints have also featured the miraculous provision of money – presumably from God rather than fairies – as one of their recurring themes. Some of the most remarkable such instances are alleged to have occurred during the life of St Jean Baptiste Vianney, the famous Curé d'Ars, nowadays often portrayed as being a notable poltergeist victim himself, due to the fact that he was plagued throughout much of his life by an invisible prank-playing 'devil' he called *grappin* [*]. Vianney lived a life of the most abject poverty in nineteenth-century rural France, though he still managed to set up an institution for the poor and hungry children of his parish, the village of Ars-sur-Formans in the east of the country. In order to provide this charity, of course, he needed cash; fortunately for him, it repeatedly kept on appearing, apparently from out of nowhere. He would put his hand in his pocket and pull out coins, or find money from Heaven lying inside his drawers, sitting on his table, or even heaped up amongst the ashes of his hearth (a highly appropriate location to find such gifts, it might be thought ...).

According to the Curé, this was all nothing less than "celestial money" and it would sometimes appear in response to specific requests; after deciding to set up a foundation in honour of the Heart of Mary, for instance, he addressed a prayer to the Virgin, telling her that "if this work is pleasing to thee, send me the means to establish it." He then opened a drawer and found 200 francs inside which, he claimed, had not been there before. At other times, he would observe his empty purse visibly growing and bulging; opening it, he would find it filled

---

[*] The word means something like 'grappling hook'. Interestingly, there was a type of French fairy with a similar name – the '*gripet*'. This being was said to live up a chimney, make rapping noises at night, scare animals and take the cover off the stew-pot before interfering with the food inside. Intriguingly, this latter trick had its own direct parallel in the case of the Curé; one day, *grappin* was said to have got inside Vianney's stew-pot and dropped meat in to try and trick him into eating some on an abstinence-day. Did the Curé perhaps know of the legends surrounding this *gripet*, and so name his own invisible tormentor accordingly?

with gold. Sometimes, so much money materialised inside his pockets that Vianney found it difficult to walk. Apparently, he gave most of it away. At other times, mysterious strangers would appear to him during his moments of direst need and hand him large sums for no good reason. This, at least, is the implausible story as it is told in his *Life* [3]. If he hadn't been acclaimed as a saint, then the country-folk around him might well have said that Vianney was blessed by the fairies instead; more modern readers, however, now seem equally keen to ascribe his fortune to the work of an occasionally benevolent poltergeist.

An account written by the Freudian parapsychologist Nandor Fodor of his experiences with a poltergeist-focus named Mrs Forbes during the well-known Thornton Heath case of 1938, meanwhile, actively plays up such resemblances between poltergeistry and the lives of the saints. Mrs Forbes, it appears, collected 'bread-checks' – small plastic tokens which, older readers may recall, could once be purchased and then used to pay bakers with instead of real coins. These money-substitutes, says Fodor:

> "... multiplied like loaves and fishes. Their number grew to twelve. When the baker's boy came, Mrs Forbes handed him one out of the twelve and put back eleven. Miss C, a friend of hers, saw movement on the shelf. Mrs Forbes counted them. There were twelve again. After this she marked the bread-checks which she gave to the baker's boy with a cross. They did not come back but two more, unmarked, were found in the pile." [4]

Mrs Forbes, as Fodor's book makes clear, was really no saint at all – but this aspect of her life, apparently, was not a million miles away from certain aspects of St Jean Baptiste Vianney's.

Beware of Ghosts Bearing Gifts

All that has changed between the beliefs of William Jones and those surrounding the Curé d'Ars and Mrs Forbes are the specific agencies which have been blamed for making the money appear. If you believe in ghosts, then they were ghosts; if in fairies, then they were fairies. Devout Catholics may prefer to credit God. The phenomena stay the same; only the interpretations differ. As far as I know, this particular aspect of poltergeistry has rarely been discussed at length before, so I wish to examine it here at some length. We shall begin with probably the strangest (and scariest) case of monetary apports that I know of. The tale is set near to a haunted bridge in 1930s Sicily, a place which was rumoured to be the home of a drowned man's shade, and was detailed in a letter to *Fortean Times* by an occasional correspondent of theirs named Jack Romano.

It seems that a friend of Romano's father, then aged around nine or ten, underwent some very extraordinary experiences by the bridge in question. According to his own account, he was "regularly accosted" there by a "beautiful young woman" who was "bathed in golden light" and "radiant". She was wearing what was described as being a "semi-bridal dress" with an "electric sheen" to it, which "sparkled and crackled". Apparently, she was beckoning towards the boy in a sensual manner, as if offering herself up for sex, whilst mouthing silent words to him. Scared, the boy would have simply fled; except that he heard the characteristic jangling sound of coins falling to the ground nearby. Looking down he saw two *lire*, brand new and shiny, which he promptly pocketed. Looking up again, he found that the lady had gone.

The promise of money, though, drew the boy back. Every day he went to the bridge and saw the woman, and every day more coins would materialise from nowhere, almost as if they were being used as bait. The lad had soon amassed quite a tidy sum from this game (so much so that his father wanted to know where it was all coming from), but the woman was coming closer and closer and beckoning to him with greater sexual intensity each time, so he began to get nervous. But he still wanted the cash, so asked his sister to tag along with him to provide moral support. She agreed, but could not see the spirit when it was pointed out to her. She did, however, witness two brand-new *lire* falling out of thin air, just as she had been told would happen. [5]

This was presented in Romano's letter as being a true story, and not a mere folk-tale. But, if so, then what was the boy actually seeing? Might it have been a female fairy? A beautiful, sexually-entrancing yet obviously supernatural lady does sound very fairy-like, although not perhaps in the more familiar modern sense of the term. She sounds not unlike one of the old fairy-maidens, the *fees* and *fays* of French-influenced Romance cycles, or the *fates* of Italian tradition, whom we met in this book's introduction; even, perhaps, one of the ancient Greek nymphs. These specific classes of female fairy were described by the writer and scholar CS Lewis, in an overview of such figures as they appeared in Renaissance and medieval literature, thus:

> "The encounter is not accidental. They have come to find us and their intentions are usually ... amorous ... whenever they are described we are struck by their hard, bright, and vividly material splendour ... Where a modern might expect the mysterious and the shadowy he meets a blaze of wealth and luxury." [6]

Such duplicitous supernatural temptresses aim to entice people into the faery otherworld, then, with explicit shows and promises of sex and wealth; much, it might be said, like the shining sexy lady living under the bridge in Sicily supposedly did ...

Throwing Money Around

In no way, obviously, am I attempting to claim that this young Italian boy actually encountered Morgan le Fay, the Queen of Elfame or Keats' *La Belle Dame Sans Merci*. His sister, when she went to the bridge with him, did not even see the spectre. But she did, apparently, see or hear the money falling down onto the path before her. We can speak of hallucinations quite easily – but hallucinatory money which can be spent in shops seems most unlikely. The boy's father, remember, wanted to know where he had got it from, so it must have been solidly material in its nature. In folkloric fairy-stories, gifts of money often transform themselves magically into mere piles of worthless leaves when their human recipient gets them home; but not here.

This disturbing account is, though, (as far as I know) unique in terms of its strange and sexualised apparitional elements. However, mysteriously-appearing coins are heard of all the time during more standard poltergeist hauntings, without any fairy-ladies being seen to account for it all. Usually, the invisible dead are blamed instead. For example, a haunted garage in South Yorkshire was featured in the Press in 2010. Here, alongside stones being tossed around and tyres being moved mysteriously, the spook's signature trick was to

The well-known frontispiece to Joseph Glanvil's 1681 book *Saducismus Triumphatus*, detailing various different kinds of supernatural phenomena which are discussed rather gleefully within, from witchcraft to levitation.

The infamous 'Drummer of Tedworth' caught in action over John Mompesson's house; an enlarged detail from Glanvil's frontispiece. Whilst clearly depicted as being demonic in nature here, it seems that at times the poltergeist also deliberately pretended to be a money-dispensing fairy.

A portrait of Joseph Glanvil, now often described as being an 'early psychical researcher', though in fact his motives for collecting tales of ghosts and witchcraft were purely theological.

Henry Meynell Rheam's interpretation of John Keats' *La Belle Dame Sans Merci*, a dangerous fairy-succubus figure, one of whose close relatives was apparently encountered by a young boy living in 1930s Sicily.

Lady Augusta Gregory, who accompanied WB Yeats in his forays out into the Irish countryside to collect local folklore, recorded one interesting tall tale about a lucky find of fairy-money.

St Elisabeth's Church in Reddish, Stockport, where in May 1981 a series of inexplicable coin-showers apparently took place, puzzling the incumbent vicar, the Reverend Graham Marshall (pictured here using an umbrella to avoid such strange rain).

materialise money from out of the very ether. Frequently, upon opening up of a morning, the garage-owner, Nick White, would find old pre-war copper pennies placed on the floor; at other times, items of small change would suddenly go whizzing about the place from nowhere. The building, we are told, served as a mortuary during WWII; and, perhaps appropriately, a figure dressed in 1940s garb would sometimes be sighted walking around the building. It was presumed that this must have been the ghost responsible. [7]

A poltergeist haunting a house in Cardiff during the late 1980s was just as numismatically inclined; it often left coins and notes, sometimes to the value of £70, lying around the place, and occasionally pinned banknotes up on the ceiling [8]. Presumably its 'victims' (the wrong word?) will have blamed a dead person for the fact.

Even some of the most famous polts in history, such as that which infested a home in the Indian city of Poona (now Pune) during 1927-30, have caused repeated coin-apports, as shown in this entry from the journal of a Miss H Kohn, who witnessed the events concerned:

> "On several occasions in broad daylight we saw coins fall among us from above ...
> At first we could not always see the coins in mid-air, but merely saw them fall,
> being startled by the contact of the coin with the floor. Soon, however, we were
> able to observe more closely, and actually saw the money appear in the air ... In
> some cases these seemed to be coins which were missing from our purses; in
> other cases we could not account for the coins." [9]

Miss Kohn did not, however, think to mention the word 'fairy' anywhere in her account. Neither did the famous American anomalist Charles Fort use the word during his account of the "flows" of copper coins and coal which apparently plagued the Robinson family, of Battersea, London, in 1928, within several closed rooms [10]. This is despite the fact that the apports were of both coal – surely an appropriate symbol for a hearthside fairy – and coins. Maybe the Robinsons were just being rewarded for their household cleanliness by an approving brownie or boggart?

Easy Money
Meanwhile, it seems that some people just can't help attracting money to themselves. For example in 1989 Albert Williamson, then 71, of Ramsgate, Kent, proclaimed proudly to the British Press that "Coins have been falling on me from the skies for the past six years." Apparently, this remarkable tendency was catching somehow – his neighbour, Kim Moody, claimed also to have been hit by a shower of coins whilst waiting for a bus one day [11]. Once, people might have tried to explain such incidents by saying that Mr Williamson and his friends were simply being 'favoured by the fairies'. After all, there are plenty of folk-tales about people who were.

For example, there exist a number of stories purportedly told by one 'Robert the Tailor' (a real person, despite the soubriquet) about donations of fairy-money which he himself had supposedly been fortunate enough to receive at some point during the 1800s. A Welshman, Robert went to the village of Cerrigydrudion in Conwy to get his clock repaired one day. It cost him half a crown, which was all the money he had in the world – so he must have *really* loved that clock. The next day, however, he put his hand inside his pocket and pulled out a new half-crown. His wife then opened a drawer and found another half-crown sitting inside that, too. Robert then began discovering more half-crowns hidden about the place and declared that it must be the work of the fairies, something which his wife confided to their neighbours. As soon as she had done so, however, the fairy-bank apparently decided that they could no longer responsibly lend out such sums in the current financial climate, and the couple received no more otherworldly cash to aid them [12].

Likewise, a man living near the town of Corwen in Denbighshire, North Wales, another old yarn tells us, used continually to find silver coins lying about in his garden. When his wife asked about the source of this wealth, he told her that he believed the fairies were responsible. Shortly after giving away his secret, though, the man supposedly died, and the coin-supply immediately dried up [13]. Compare that (presumably) invented story now to a real one, though, as detailed by Mike Bending of the East Sussex village of Robertsbridge, where he owned an old cottage:

> "Every time I ventured into the garden, I'd find coins – lots of coins. I'd weed a bed (no digging involved), find a coin or two, come back a few weeks later, weed again and find more coins – even though they definitely weren't there when I last looked." [14]

Some of the coins were extremely old and, you would imagine, relatively rare – such as a Napoleon III three-centime piece from 1853. I wonder if he still kept on finding them once he had revealed his secret on the letter-pages of *Fortean Times*, though? Somehow, I doubt it.

Lucky Finds

People of a certain romantic bent may still choose to invoke fairies in order to 'explain' such matters. For example, when he was eight, the writer Patrick Harpur – whose ideas concerning 'pixilation' we examined earlier – wished and wished "as only small boys can" for a fishing rod, but, wish as he might, he was still half a crown short of the price of one. One long, hot summer's afternoon, he lay on the grass outside his home, idly pulling up weeds, longing and longing for that elusive money – until, of course, he lifted up one particular weed and found a half-crown, green with age, tangled up in its roots. As Harpur puts it:

> "The boy marvelled at the coincidence ... He half-believed that the money had materialised there especially for him." [15]

A gift from the fairies? Harpur seems to half-suggest so when he links his account to the story of a man named John Phelan given in the aristocratic folklorist Lady Gregory's 1920 book *Visions and Beliefs in the West of Ireland*, a collection of orally-gathered folk-narratives which she collected and wrote up in collaboration with her friend WB Yeats. According to Phelan:

> "I met a woman coming out one day from [the County Leitrim village of] Cloon and she told me that when she was a young girl, she went out one day with another girl to pick up sticks near a wood. And she chanced to lay hold of a tuft of grass, and it came up in her hand and the sod with it. And there was a hole underneath full of half crowns, and she began to fill her apron. She called to the other girl, and the minute

she came there wasn't one to be seen. But what she had in her apron she kept." [16]

Obviously, Harpur doesn't *literally* believe that the fairies allowed him to buy his fishing-rod; but perhaps the Irish girl, coming from a society in which it was the done thing to believe in the reality of the *sidhe*, genuinely did think that her gift came from fairy-land rather than from someone just burying a small treasure-trove in the place where she happened to dig. Or, then again, maybe Phelan just made the whole thing up to please his famous inquisitors.

Finders Keepers

It is surely tempting, though, to rationalise such narratives as being merely naive attempts by lucky persons who come across free money to account for their finds. Stumble across a stash of coins lurking beneath a grass-tuft and, hey-presto, it automatically becomes a 'leprechaun's treasure' in the minds of some. One other speculation about the ultimate origin of the term 'fairy' which we did not discuss earlier, however, is that it may have stood originally (in the form of *fata*) for the concept of 'fated*ness*', as opposed to the Fates themselves. 'Fatedness' (or 'luck', basically) is defined by Noel Williams, in the essay of his about this topic which we examined earlier, as follows:

> "... a quality in the world which can control and direct the actions of humanity, and hence is more powerful than humanity." [17]

Certainly, any force which can direct a person to find money in unlikely places, or from thin air, does indeed seem to be 'more powerful than humanity'. The word 'luck' itself also later came to refer in English to certain helpful household deities or fairies of a brownie-like nature which helped to ensure that the families to whom they were attached prospered in terms of wealth and the harvest. Again, this concept can easily be explained away as being merely an attempt by jealous onlookers to account for some families' success in agriculture; but, if the word 'fairy' is to a certain extent a synonym for luck itself, then it is perhaps no surprise that such creatures have become associated in some way with the fortunate uncovering of coins and treasure.

A formerly-common and clearly-related motif from ghost-lore, meanwhile, was that of ghosts acting as either guardians or revealers of treasure-troves. Fairies could also sometimes fulfil this role, however, as in an account given by that well-known Scottish chronicler of fairy-matters, Robert Kirk, of an event which supposedly occurred in a neighbouring county to his parish in about 1676. Apparently, during a regional shortage of grain, a "marvellous illapse and vision" was experienced by two women who lived "a good distance from one another", revealing that some treasure was hidden in a place called *sith-bhruaich*, or 'fairy-hill'. This vision was then followed by a disembodied voice naming the place in question, to which both women purportedly hastened. Meeting one another there, they dug into the hill and found a hoard of ancient coins which they took back home and exchanged for grain with their neighbours. As Kirk puts it, though:

> "... whether it was a good or bad angel, one of the subterranean people, or the restless soul of him who hid it that discovered it, and to what end, I leave to the examination of others." [18]

Nowadays, of course, Kirk could very easily add the word 'poltergeist' to that list.

A Very Friendly Ghost

Probably the very best case on record of a man who apparently attracted coin-apports (and was therefore 'lucky') is that of a Hungarian lawyer investigated by Everard Feilding in 1913-14. Feilding, a fellow-barrister and one-time Honorary Secretary of the SPR, referred to the entity that was supposed to be responsible, rather jocularly, as being "a Jinn ... a friendly, sportive hobgoblin ... the most desirable imp anyone could ever wish for." Why so desirable? Feilding explains:

> "This creature first started operations at a time when, for lack of pence, the lawyer wanted to commit suicide. He suddenly found money in his pocket which he knew wasn't there before. He thought he must have stolen it in a fit of aberration. Then money began to drop on to the table, and he thought he was mad. Then stones fell beside him as he walked out, and ... all sorts of things were chucked into his room at all hours of the day and night. Bromide tablets fell on his bed when he couldn't sleep; bottles of Schnapps in his carriage of a cold night; cigarettes out of the air when he had run out of them, and cigars bearing the Emperor's monogram!"

This amazing, fairy-tale fortune wasn't to last forever, however. According to Feilding, as the lawyer's financial plight eased:

> "... the character of the phenomena changed, and now the things are mostly ancient and useless tagrags and bobtails, ranging from bottle-tops to an elderly pump ... slabs of marble, 5-foot poles, pieces of wood, heavy iron screws, pincers, knives, wire lampshades, toy animals – all hurtle into the room at unexpected moments .... And they do: I have seen lots of them." [19]

To make up for this unfortunate degeneration in the nature of his gifts, the 'Jinn' later made use of a Ouija board to reveal that he was, in fact, none other than the spirit of a certain Baron von Schindtreffer, who had sent his son to Brittany in 1713 with nine cases of money and jewels which were to be buried in a secret spot to protect them from robbers. A thorough verbal map of the hoard's whereabouts was then gifted by the ghost to the sitters and, upon their examining a real map, the details given of the area in question were deemed to be accurate. Upon travelling to the supposed burial-site, however, Feilding and the lawyer found no treasure there at all. [20]

Its seems very much as if the ghost was playing a joke here; which is why Feilding put it all down whimsically to the actions of a "friendly, sportive hobgoblin". The idea seems appropriate, as it does all sound very much like a kind of modern-day fairy-tale. There is a definite sense of puckish humour involved, and a kind of moral, as with so many fairy-tales, is reinforced. The message seems to be 'don't be greedy and wish for more than you really need'; otherwise coins and cigars will soon start changing themselves into rusty pumps and useless toy animals, and you will be sent out on wild-goose chases halfway across Europe in pursuit of buried treasure which doesn't even exist.

Funny Money

Just to be awkward, though, some showers of fairy-money seem to be entirely random and show no demonstrable sense of humour or intelligence behind them whatsoever. In such cases, 'teleportation' (a term often used to avoid implying that any sentient agency is involved) is often blamed instead. On 28th May 1981, for instance, a young girl walking through the churchyard of St Elisabeth's Church in Reddish, Stockport, saw a 50-pence piece fall "from nowhere" in front of her. Word spread, and soon youngsters were busily gathering more such coins to buy sweets. They would hear a tinkle behind them and then find coins on the path where there had been no coins before. Some were found embedded in the ground by their edges. The vicar, Graham Marshall, made a spectacle of himself, getting fistfuls of coins and hurling them as hard as he could at the ground to see if he could reproduce this peculiar aspect of the phenomenon – all to no avail. No plausible explanation for the events was ever provided; it seemed as if the universe had simply chosen to rain 50ps down upon the area for no reason at all one day. [21]

There are several reports of such recurring but apparently random coin-showers on record. According to the noted French atmospheric scientist and psychical investigator Camille Flammarion, for example, a "rain of small coins" fell every evening over some unspecified amount of time in the Rue Montesquieu in Paris, probably during the 1840s, attracting crowds of what he contemptuously termed "boobies" [22]. The famous American anomalist Charles Fort says that the same thing once happened in Trafalgar Square, too, over a period of several days, disrupting traffic and causing annoyance to police [23]. He claims to have had more such tales, but to have misplaced the references!

Some coin-apports do seem to show a demonstrable sense of both timing and humour in their occurrence, however; so it seems likely that there is some sentience behind them, at least some of the time. In 1917 or 1918, for example, a Finnish woman named Ester Hallio was living with a student friend of hers called Inni Siegberg in the Finnish capital, Helsinki. Alone in the house with another friend, Hallio and the girl began to tell each other ghost stories ... and *something* sensed that this would be the perfect moment to play a prank on them. According to Ester's own account:

> "Suddenly a faint click was heard, and then another one. We looked around and found two large overcoat buttons on the floor. We suspected each other, protesting that this was not a proper time for jokes. The next click sounded clear, metallic. A coin had fallen on the parquet floor, rolling and revolving before coming to rest. More coins fell at intervals of five, ten or fifteen minutes. Pale with fear we went next door to ask an Estonian lady to come and witness the miracle ... [She] suggested that her brother-in-law, a deeply religious man, should be asked to stop the phenomenon. He came with his Bible, read some incantations and commanded the phenomenon to cease, but after his "Amen", a coin fell on his Bible, and he panicked and escaped." [24]

Bizarrely, that same night, Inni's sister, a nurse, had been plagued at her hospital by odd tinkling sounds resembling falling coins – although there were no coins actually to be found on the floor when she looked down for them. Speaking to Inni's sister about these weird events over the phone, another coin dropped onto the table next to Hallio and her friend. By the next morning, around ten Finnish marks had appeared in the students' house, so they decided to make the best of matters, went out to a local restaurant and spent it all on apple-pie and coffee!

Taken as a whole, these cases do seem to suggest that there is some kind of invisible force – or entity – in existence which enjoys playing puckish little tricks on people with money. Whether you decide to call it a 'fairy' or a 'poltergeist' is, however, likely to be entirely immaterial. Certainly, though, there are far worse varieties of spook which you could encounter than ones which deign to compensate you financially for any trouble they might cause – as the next chapter will demonstrate.

4.

Pins and Needles: Attacks and Assaults

Fairies nowadays are generally thought of as being nice, pleasant, friendly creatures. This is not, however, always the picture painted for us by folklore and old tradition; in fact, these supposedly benign creatures were frequently said to be quite violent. Often, the specific patterns of their violence appear to mirror certain aspects of modern poltergeist-lore. For example, both classes of being are said to have had a penchant for persecuting people with pins. Famously, for instance, the celebrated nineteenth-century Canadian victim of poltergeist activity Esther Cox, of the town of Amherst in Nova Scotia, was repeatedly assaulted by an invisible entity calling itself 'Bob', who allegedly enjoyed jabbing large numbers of pins into her body. These pins, apparently, appeared from nowhere. According to the case's original investigator, a travelling actor named Walter Hubbell, both Esther and her sister Jennie were repeatedly scratched with pins by the ghost, being marked "from head to foot" with crosses etched into their flesh. Whilst staying with the Cox family, Hubbell tells us that he was occupied with constantly pulling out pins from Esther's pierced body:

> "... they came out of the air from all quarters, and were stuck into all the exposed portions of her person, even her head, and inside of her ears." [1]

There are many other such cases. Margaret Rule, a 17-year-old girl, was carried out from the church of the famous New England preacher Cotton Mather on September 10th, 1693. She was fitting, and producing pins from inside her body as well as suffering from invisible pinches which marked her skin blue, and is even said to have levitated, whilst objects moved around in her presence [2]. Witchcraft was blamed for her sufferings at the time. The Freudian parapsychologist Nandor Fodor, meanwhile, investigated a particularly abhorrent 1936 Hungarian haunting during which a two-year-old girl was subjected to torture by having pins, needles, matchsticks and thumbtacks suddenly materialise inside her mouth, under her armpits, and even in her vagina [3]. A 1718 haunting at the home of Reverend Robert McGill in the Perthshire town of Kinross, Scotland, was even weirder. Here, the polt delighted in packing all food found on the premises full of pins. Even boiled eggs were, impossibly, found crammed with needles when they were cracked open, and any bread baked in the house was simply inedible. One maid who swallowed some meat soon vomited it back up, together with five sharp tacks. McGill's wife, Isabel, determined to beat the spirit, carefully prepared her husband a meal, obsessively checking at every stage of proceedings that each ingredient was unpolluted. Thinking that she had outwitted the spook, she placed the pin-clean meal down upon the table – whereupon, quite suddenly, it became riddled with needles anyway. Just like Cotton Mather, the McGills blamed witchcraft. It was thing to do, at the time [4].

A more recent such case occurred in 1965 in Brazil, when an 11-year-old girl named Maria José Ferreira attracted the attentions of an initially-friendly poltergeist who would apport objects such as candy and flowers to her feet when she wished for them, not unlike the Hungarian 'jinn' whom we met earlier. However, Maria's spook soon turned nasty. Invisible hands started to slap and bruise her, she was bitten by unseen jaws, and cups and glasses were forced over her nose and mouth whilst she was asleep so that she could not breathe. Allegedly, an attempt was even made at rape. Eventually, attacks with needles began. They would "simply appear thrust deep into the girl's tender flesh", apparently, always in her left heel, and even when she had shoes and socks on. Once, 55 had to be removed at the same time. Even when her bleeding heel was bandaged up it did no good – the ghost just pulled the bandages off again. Then, as if things were not bad enough, her clothes suddenly began bursting into flames for no reason! Whether because of the strain caused by these events or otherwise, Maria eventually killed herself by swallowing a soft drink laced with formicide (an insecticide) in 1970 and the spirit simply disappeared [5].

However, surely the best-attested pin-pricking polt was the famous Lamb Inn entity, which haunted said hostelry in Bristol between 1761 and 1762, and which was notoriously violent. The infants at the centre of events, Molly and Dobby Giles, were very severely treated by the ghost, as this account from a local man called Henry Durbin who went out to the Inn to investigate shows:

> "I was determined to try an experiment … I made Molly sit down in a chair in the middle of the parlour: I took a large pin and marked it at the top with a pair of scissors; I put her hands across, and bid her not move … I then put the marked pin in her pincushion … As I moved my hand … she cried out … and directly was pricked in the neck (her hands being still across). The identical pin I had marked was run through the neck of her shift, and stuck in her skin, crooked very curiously …We then marked four other pins, and I put them in her pincushion singly, as before; and all of them were crooked and stuck in her neck. I examined the pincushion (after we took every pin out of her neck) and found the pins gone … Some of them were crooked in half a minute, in such a manner as no human hand could do in the time." [6]

Durbin collected these pins – which were all bent into weird shapes – and sent a large number off to the editor of the pamphlet in which he laid out his experiments, who wrote in his preface to this rare work that "it would have tortured the ingenuity of man" to have invented the "vast variety of fantastic figures" which the pins exhibited [7].

It's a Blast!

Folklore insists, however, that fairies too can insert needles inside people supernaturally. This particular form of elf-attack was known as 'the blast', and involved the fairy-folk gaining revenge upon one who had wronged them by shooting some magical projectile (perhaps a form of so-called 'elf-shot'[*]?) at them. Wherever on their body these missiles struck a person, it is said, they would soon begin to experience pain and debilitation which could only be eased by opening up the flesh and pulling out the cursed substances that had been placed within – which might be such common items as grass, bones, cloth or, very often, pins and needles. Some oral fairy-narratives collected by folklorists like Barbara Rieti (whose researches I am following here) in Newfoundland, Canada, for example, speak of a man losing the use of his arm after the fairies had filled it with needles, and of another man whose abdominal pains were only cured when his side was opened up and a big darning needle fell out[8]. The standard interpretation of such stories is that the alleged appearance of the fairy-needles inside the body is a kind of folk-rationalisation of strokes, rheumatism and suchlike; losing the use of an arm being, of course, a typical symptom of such real-life maladies.

Whilst pins and needles were some of the most common blast-weapons, however, it would be only fair to point out that other sharp (or sometimes simply disgusting) substances were said to have been shot inside people too, from rabbit bones, dead moths, hare's teeth, pieces of rags and felt[9], to straw[10], to pieces of broken comb[11], to unfeasibly long pieces of string[12]. Because of this, you could probably justifiably claim that the blast may also have been a kind of folk-explanation for the occasional but actually entirely natural presence of foreign objects within the human body. A few tales, though, appear more difficult to account for in such terms.

For example, there is an intriguing narrative of a young girl in Newfoundland walking around minding her own business before feeling "something like a hand" smack her in the face. She went away with a pain in her cheek and then, a few days later, it is said, piles of rusty nails and needles fell out of her face, together with some old cloth and bits of rock and clay. This was blamed by locals upon the girl "walking across the path of ghosts", which again only goes to show how the fairies merge away imperceptibly into the dead in many traditions[13]. Another female informant, from the town of Clarke's Beach in Newfoundland, told one folklorist that such things were also known locally as being "flicked by the dead", although the older members of the community still called it being "flicked by the Good People". This woman recalled a case known to her in which a young boy had been 'flicked', causing his foot to become painful. After it had been poulticed, two "old weatherbeaten bones" had been removed by the boy's mother, who kept them preserved in a jar of alcohol as proof of what had happened.[14]

The fact that the older generation here attributed such attacks to fairies whilst the younger people preferred to blame ghosts seems symptomatic of a general shift which has taken place across wider society over the past 150 years or so in which poltergeists (or the 'invisible dead' as the average person would no doubt conceive them) are now blamed for performing exactly the same kinds of

---

[*] 'Elf-shot' was meant to be a kind of supernatural weapon dropped down upon people and cattle from above by fairies, killing or maiming them; they were supposed to be made from sharpened stone, and to be shaped like darts. General opinion has it that these projectiles were actually those prehistoric stone arrow-heads which are sometimes found in fields, however. (See, though, Alaric Hall's book *Elves in Anglo-Saxon England* for a far more involved and nuanced discussion of this topic)

actions for which fairies would once have been held responsible. Whilst these Irish-Canadian tales of the blast are obviously just legends, they do nonetheless demonstrate clearly how the concepts of 'fairy' and 'ghost' have now become quite thoroughly mixed.

Enough to Make You Sick
However, the motif of supernatural attack by needles is not associated only with fairies and poltergeists. Bewitched people, for instance, were supposed frequently to vomit up blast-like materials – bones, nails, needles, pins, faeces, balls of wool and hair – during the famous 'witch-scares' of the medieval and early Renaissance periods. Joseph Glanvil, as well as chronicling the tale of the Drummer of Tedworth, also describes in his writings the case of a girl from the Somerset town of Taunton who was forced to swallow pins by a witch which then later passed unnaturally out from her body in various large swellings. A supposed Elizabethan hag, meanwhile, is spoken of by one writer as having the rather unlikely ability to fill a letter full of needles, "in such a Mathematicall order", that, when its recipient opened it, they would all magically "flye into his body as forceably as if they had beene blowne up with gunpowder." Witches were even conceived of during this period as being able to make pins and needles be magically 'wished into' people's livers [15].

A curious echo of such beliefs can be seen in the fact that Molly and Dobby Giles claimed to have seen the apparition of "a woman dressed in a dirty chip hat with a torn ragged gown" during the course of the Lamb Inn haunting – which sounds a clear enough description of a stereotypical witch. The noted poltergeist-scholar Father Herbert Thurston, commenting upon this fact, says that the Giles sisters were just "responding no doubt to the folk beliefs still widely prevalent in 1762" when saying this, implying that they were simply "inclined to romance" [16]. Maybe so; back then, fairies, poltergeists and witches were evidently much-confused in the public mind.

It is not just witches, though. Nowadays, extraterrestrial invaders are also alleged to insert needles into supposed 'abductees' aboard their spaceships for nefarious medical purposes, and to place mysterious 'implants' – the modern version of the old blast materials? – beneath their victims' flesh. This is particularly curious because numerous contemporary commentators, most notably Jacques Vallee in his classic book *Passport to Magonia*, have made a plausible case for ufonauts being simply more modern manifestations of demons and fairy-folk, reimagined anew for the space-age. Famously, he compared the alleged experience of Betty Hill – the most famous UFO abductee of all – reputedly having a long needle inserted into her navel by aliens to a depiction of demons similarly torturing sinners in Hell by inserting long needles into their abdomens on a fifteenth-century French calendar, the *Kalendrier des Bergiers* [17]. Here, the picture is muddied even further, showing again how all these things seem to merge into one another endlessly around the margins.

The specific issue of people vomiting up pins, needles and other typical blast materials is, however, a particularly confusing one to examine, as many such instances exist on a very indefinite borderline between poltergeistry and witchcraft. In 1696/97 at a Scottish laird's house named Bargarran in the county of East Renfrewshire, for instance, the laird's daughter, an 11-year-old girl called Christian Shaw, notoriously began to suffer fits

A propaganda poster from WWII accidentally taps into a distinctly violent vein of fairy-lore.

A photograph allegedly showing the home of Esther Cox in Amherst, Nova Scotia, where the defenceless young Canadian girl famously found herself being assualted by a pin-wielding polt going by the unlikely name of 'Bob' during 1878/79.

The New England Puritan preacher Cotton Mather, from whose church a 17-year-old girl named Margaret Rule was carried out after she began vomiting up pins from her belly during September 1693. In the era of Salem, witchcraft and the Devil were blamed for the uncanny occurrences, and not poltergeists *per se*.

Two undated photographs purporting to show the building in Bristol which was once a hostelry known as 'The Lamb Inn', where in 1761/62 two little girls named Molly and Dobby Giles were said to have been violently tormented by an evil, pin-jabbing spirit.

An archaeological illustration of some 'elf-shot' – actually prehistoric flint arrow-heads and not the weapons of the wee folk at all – published in 1868.

Unpleasant demons torment sinners by inserting giant needles into them, in an illustration from the medieval *Kalendrier des Bergiers*. The French ufologist Jacques Vallee has pointed out the similarities between this image and certain modern accounts of alien abduction.

Another inadvertantly amusing propaganda poster about violent imps from WWII.

An alarmed-looking Betsy Bell awaits yet another attack from the Bell Witch. The poor girl was supposedly forced to vomit up an entire hardware store's worth of pins by the invisible entity.

An enlarged detail from Hogarth's engraving *Credulity, Superstition and Fanaticism: A Medley*, showing William Perry, the so-called 'Boy of Bilson', vomiting pins. Allegedly a victim of demonic possession, he was in fact exposed as a fraud who had been taught the trick of pin-swallowing by an old man in 1620. Were Betsy Bell's episodes of pin-swallowing similarly exaggerated, a case of allotriophagy, or the genuine results of poltergeist-possession?

MISCELLANIES,

UPON THE

Following SUBJECTS.

I. DAY-FATALITY. II. LOCAL-FATALITY.
III. OSTENTA. IV. OMENS. V. DREAMS.
VI. APPARITIONS. VII. VOICES. VIII. IM-
PULSES. IX. KNOCKINGS. X. BLOWS
Invisible. XI. PROPHESIES. XII. MARVELS.
XIII. MAGICK. XIV. TRANSPORTATION
in the Air. XV. VISIONS in a Beril, or Glass.
XVI. CONVERSE with ANGELS and SPIRITS.
XVII CORPS-CANDLES in *Wales*. XVIII. ORA-
CLES. XIX. EXSTASIE. XX. GLANCES of
Love and Envy. XXI. SECOND-SIGHTED-
Persons. XXII. The Discovery of Two MUR-
DERS by an APPARITION.

Collected by JOHN AUBREY, Esq; F.R.S.

The SECOND EDITION, with large Additions.

To which is Prefixed,

Some ACCOUNT of his LIFE.

LONDON:

Printed for A. BETTESWORTH, and J. BATTLEY in *Pater-Noster-Row*, J. PEMBERTON in *Fleetstreet*, and E. CURLL in the *Strand*.
M.DCC.XXI. Price 4 s.

The esteemed 17th-century English antiquarian John Aubrey, whose book *Miscellanies* includes an account of a certain Mr Brograve being slapped about by invisible hands near a place suggestively called Puckridge.

A

NARRATIVE

OF

SOME EXTRAORDINARY THINGS

THAT HAPPENED TO

Mr. Richard Giles's CHILDREN,

AT THE LAMB, WITHOUT LAWFORD's-GATE, BRISTOL;

SUPPOSED TO BE THE EFFECT OF

Witchcraft.

BY THE LATE MR. HENRY DURBIN, CHYMIST,

Who was an Eye and Ear Witness of the principal Facts herein related.

(NEVER BEFORE PUBLISHED.)

To which is added,

A LETTER

From the Rev. Mr. BEDFORD, late Vicar of *Temple*, to the
BISHOP OF GLOCESTER,

Relative to one THOMAS PERKS, of Mangotsfield,
Who had Dealings with Familiar Spirits.

Bristol :

PRINTED AND SOLD BY R. EDWARDS, BROAD-STREET;
SOLD ALSO BY T. HURST, AND W. BAYNEL, PATERNOSTER-ROW,
LONDON; AND BY BULGAR, AND BROWNE, BATH.

1800.

[Entered at Stationer's Hall.]

A rare copy of Henry Durbin's pamphlet about the Lamb Inn affair, printed in 1800.

during which she is said to have vomited up bent pins – as well as straw, hair, animal bones, hot wax, stones, feathers, glowing coals and even human turds. Shaw supposedly soon also began floating around the household, being audibly beaten by invisible hands, and on one occasion had her glove picked up and returned to her by something unseen. Whilst witnesses at the time blamed witchcraft, however, leading to several executions taking place, the case is nowadays generally spoken of as being a case of poltergeist activity – or, more realistically, as being an exaggerated piece of religiously-motivated propaganda. [18]

Why Did You Have to Bring That Up?
The notorious Bell Witch affair, which took place in Tennessee, largely between 1817 and 1821, featured some particularly remarkable instances of alleged pin-vomiting. The 'Witch' in this instance, of course, was actually no witch at all; it was a disembodied voice, often harsh and metallic in nature though at times sweet and musical, which spoke from thin air and played all kinds of remarkable tricks upon the remote farmstead of a certain John Bell and his family. Modern commentators are united in looking at this haunting and classing it as being a poltergeist manifestation rather than witchcraft – either that or dismissing it all as pure folklore. Either way, John Bell had a daughter, Betsy, and it was around her that much of the phenomena centred.

The specific occurrence which concerns us here, though, came after Betsy had been offered some vile concoction by a local self-styled 'witch-doctor' which, he claimed, would cure her immediately of all her problems. It seems to have been an emetic; the idea, rather naively, was that it would enable Betsy somehow to 'vomit out' the ghost, the poor girl evidently being conceived of by the quack as being a victim of possession. However, when she did spew up, her sick was found to be full of brass pins and needles. The Witch "fairly roared with laughter" at this, delightedly sneering that, if Betsy would just throw up again, she would have enough pins to set up a hardware store. [19]

We should be careful here, though, because vomiting things like pins is a textbook symptom of 'possession' in the pathological sense – that is to say, as an expression of mental illness. There is even a specific psychiatric term, 'allotriophagy', which can be used to describe the practice of disturbed people deliberately swallowing small, sharp objects, only to then vomit them up later. Many modern commentators have speculated that this is what actually happened during the case of Christian Shaw of Bargarran; a 1996 article in the *Scottish Medical Journal* specifically diagnosed her, retrospectively, as having some kind of dissociative personality disorder [20]. However, in Betsy Bell's case this is not presented as being plausible. According to the testimony of Lucinda Rawls, the daughter of Betsy's best friend, there were so many pins in her sick that "As a matter of course Betsy could not have lived with such a conglomeration in her stomach" which led Lucinda to speculate that the Witch must have "dropped the pins and needles in the excrement [vomit] unobserved." [21]

This particular ghost, then, did act rather like a witch would once have been expected to do, although the main reason it became known to posterity as the 'Bell Witch' was due to the fact that the ghost's voice claimed falsely to be coming from the soul of a local eccentric called Kate Batts, whom it slandered as being a witch, an identity which stuck. This is what it once supposedly said:

> "I will not tell you a lie. I am Kate Batts' Witch [i.e. her 'projected soul'?]. You just watch her pretty close, and you will see and hear her do many things that will convince you that she is a witch. She begs every woman she meets to give her a brass pin and when she gets as many as she wants, she puts them on a stump in John Bell's woods, and tells me to use them. Haven't you seen that old long-legged devil writhe and twist, and say that something was sticking pins all over him?" [22]

Apparently, John Bell was indeed tortured in this way by the ghost. Indeed, it seems that pins were frequently found sticking up out of pillows and chair-seats around the Bell household, as though the place was in fact haunted by Dennis the Menace, and not by a 'witch'. Because of these events, a rumour soon sprang up that Kate Batts was always going around begging pins from people, and that anybody who was foolish enough to hand one over would instantly be placed under the power of her and her pet polt. [23]

Getting Handy
One other common way (though more common of polts than of fairies, admittedly) in which invisible entities have been said to harm people, meanwhile, is simply to slap, hit or punch them, as in this verbatim account taken from the seventeenth-century English antiquarian John Aubrey's curious 1696 book *Miscellanies*, a collection of odd bite-sized folkloric titbits:

> "BLOWS INVISIBLE: Mr Brograve, of Hamel, near Puckridge [now Puckeridge] in Hertfordshire, when he was a young man, had a blow given him on the cheek: (or head) he looked back and saw that nobody was near behind him; anon he had such another blow, I have forgot if a third. He turned back, and fell to the study of the law; and was afterwards a Judge." [24]

Nowhere does Aubrey attempt to account for what it was that struck Mr Brograve so rudely in the face, however – though he could hardly have answered 'poltergeist' in the 1600s. As for myself, I am intrigued to know just how close the future judge was to the village of Puckridge when the blows rained down on him; maybe it was Puck himself who punched him?

Similar accounts of acknowledged poltergeists doing the same kind of thing are numerous, and only a few need be detailed here. A good case involved a certain Professor Schuppart, a theologian from the German town of Giessen, who was bothered by a spook which appeared to genuinely hate him. Not only did it slap his wife with blows which resounded throughout the whole household (though they caused her little pain), it also punched and tormented him with pins upon any portion of his flesh which was exposed to thin air. This was how Herr Schuppart put it himself:

> "Often I have been for four weeks together without taking off my clothes. It has struck me in the face, it has pricked me with pins, it has even bitten me so that both rows of teeth could be distinguished. The two big fangs stood out plainly and they were as sharp as pins." [25]

The young Romanian 'poltergeist-girl' Eleonore Zugun – who was famously bitten by her own notorious vampire-like spook during the 1920s – was also sometimes slapped as if by an invisible hand. She also had objects thrown at her, was scratched by pins and needles, thrown over, pushed out of bed, and had her hair pulled. She said that this was all being done by something she called 'Dracu' – the Romanian word for the Devil. [26]

Pinching is another common activity of both polts and fairies; one well-known tradition was that fairies would pinch the bodies of slatternly housemaids who didn't clean up around the place properly. This idea was widespread, and is mentioned by several of the giants of English letters; in John Milton's poem *L'Allegro*, for instance, a maiden speaks of how "She was pinched and pulled she said" by fairies, and Ben Jonson, in his *Entertainment at Althorp*, speaks of Mab, by the 1600s securely crowned as being the legendary 'Queen of the Fairies', who, he says, "pinches country wenches". Poltergeists also pinch, though. Professor Schuppart was pinched as well as punched, for instance, and so were the Giles sisters at the Lamb Inn, "the impressions of nails" apparently being left upon their skin by the ghost's hand [27]. Maybe they should have just got their dusters out...

Getting it in the Neck

Strangulation is another occasional theme. A Scottish correspondent of John Aubrey once wrote to tell him about the famous Highland faculty of 'second-sight'; the ability some Scots allegedly had to see events happening at some distance away from them in both space and time. According to this correspondent, the most common explanations for this ability were that the men who possessed it either gained it "by compact with the Devil" or "by converse with those daemons we call fairies." In any case, it was not permitted of these Highland wise-men to let on too much about their mysterious powers; if they did, then "they are sure of their strokes from an invisible hand." The letter-writer illustrates this by giving the tale of "one Alien Miller", a man with the second-sight who, getting drunk one night, let on too much about his abilities to his companions. This, apparently, was a big mistake; unseen powers (presumably either Satan or the fairies) "suddenly removed him" to the far end of the house, where he was then "almost strangled" by invisible hands [28].

Such a motif of strangulation by angry fairies is a rare one; but it does exist. Yeats, for example, in his guise of folk-tale collector, spoke to one informant who told him of how her husband had been 'taken' by the *sidhe*. Lying in bed with him one night, the woman woke and heard him move, it sounding to her as if there was somebody else there in the room with them. Putting out her hand, she got a brief feel of one of the fairies; apparently, it had "an iron hand, like knitting needles it felt." After this, the woman:

> "... heard the bones of his neck crack, and he gave a sort of choked laugh; and I got out of bed and struck a light, and saw nothing, but I thought I heard someone go through the door." [29]

That just sounds like the woman was romanticising her husband's death to me; although possibly I should not be quite so cynical, given that there are numerous stories of poltergeists strangling people on record, perhaps the best-attested such case being the Lamb Inn entity. Here, whilst everyone present could clearly see the necks of Molly and Dobby Giles being squeezed in by the ghost, the two little girls themselves claimed to be able to see a disembodied hand actually performing such acts. According to Henry Durbin's disturbing account:

> "We ... saw the children pinched with the impressions of nails, and the children said they saw the hand that did it ... Dobby cried the hand was about her sister's throat, and I saw the flesh at the side of her throat pushed in, whitish as if done with fingers, though I saw none. Her face grew red and blackish, as if she was strangled, but without any convulsion or contraction of the muscles. We went to her, and I touched her head. It went off in a moment and she was well ... Soon after Molly was struck twice on the head and we all heard it ... After that, seven of us being there in the room, Molly said she was bit in the arm, and presently Dobby cried out the same. We saw their arms bitten about twenty times that evening ... We examined the bites and found on them the impression of eighteen or twenty teeth, with saliva or spittle all over them, in the shape of a mouth, almost all of them very wet, and the spittle smoaking [sic] as if just spit out of the mouth. I took up some of it on my finger to try the consistence of it ... we found it clammy like spittle, and it smelt rank." [30]

An interesting point about this case is that the children's wounds do seem genuinely to have been inflicted externally, by an outside force. We can note in Durbin's description of the strangulation, for example, that Molly's throat appeared to be being pushed in, as though with invisible fingers. Another witness, meanwhile, took a lit candle under the bed, intending to search out any deceit, but instead felt "three or four fingers" catch hold of his wrist and pinch him "so hard that the prints were visible and grew black the next day." [31] Bites, scratches and cuts still appeared on the children even when their flesh had been covered up with petticoats and sheets, apparently without any damage occurring to these items, however – so evidently the 'hands' and 'teeth' that attacked the Giles children were not corporeal in any ordinary sense of the word.

They're Coming to Take You Away

Are poltergeists responsible for such things, then, or fairies? Even WB Yeats could get confused about the matter. For instance, writing in 1898, he tells us of how:

> "I was told at Sligo about four years ago of a man who was being constantly beaten by a dead person. Sometimes it was said you could hear the blows as he came along the road, and sometimes he would be dragged out of bed at night and his wife would hear the blows, but you could never see anything." [32]

Apparently, the man is said to have moved away from his home-village in order to escape the spirit, but it merely followed him to his new lodgings. For some reason, it was concluded by all and sundry that it was the man's dead uncle who was haunting him like this. But in what sense? Yeats cited this story in a longer essay about the old Irish belief that people could be 'taken' (as the term has it) by the fairies and forced to live in fairyland or march in the fairy-troop as their slaves, should they take a fancy to them. These people's 'dead bodies' left behind to be buried would actually be no such thing, according to this tradition; rather, they would be things like inanimate logs which had merely been enchanted in order to look human. This is how Yeats explained the matter:

"The most of the Irish country people believe that only people who die of old age go straight to some distant Hell or Heaven or Purgatory. All who are young enough for any use, for begetting or mothering children, for dancing or hurling, or even for driving cattle, are taken ... by 'the others', as the country people call the fairies; and live, until they die a second time, in the green 'forts' ... or under the roots of hills, or in the woods, or in the deep of lakes." [33]

Therefore, the 'dead man' who was assaulting the poor country-lad with invisible blows in the tale from Sligo might not literally have been believed to be *dead*, as such; he could just have been thought of by the locals as awaiting his true final death within the land of faery. Was he a poltergeist, then, or a full-blown member of the fairy-troop? You may as well ask whether victims of the Newfoundland blast were injured by ghosts or by gnomes, or whether Betsy Bell was forced to swallow pins by an invisible witch or by an invisible spirit which merely *belonged* to that same witch. There are no answers to questions like these; there are only the phenomena themselves. The names we use to 'explain' them with are merely culturally-plausible lies.

The Victorian medium DD Home levitates in front of a group of astonished onlookers. Opinions differ as to precisely how genuine/fraudulent Home was, but one thing's for sure – he never credited fairies with giving him his alleged powers!

5.

Walking Through the Air: Levitations and Teleportations

The fairies of old tradition, whilst they did *not* have wings (such an image being pure Walt Disney), were often thought to be able to fly. They were also sometimes thought of as being able to make *people* fly, too, and legends about the topic of fairy-levitation are legion. The most famous such account concerned a series of bizarre events which supposedly affected a butler at the Earl of Orrery's house near Cork in the south-west of Ireland sometime between 1660 and 1665 [*]. This man, who was prone to fits, was sent by the neighbour who employed him over to Orrery's property to borrow some cards. On his return, he fell down into a typical spasm. Coming round, he explained that he had encountered a gathering of strange people – the fairies – dining at a table in the middle of a field. They invited him to eat and dance with them, but one of their company whispered to him not to do so. Realising the danger, he refused their offer and they vanished, "table and all". This is a typical fairy-lore motif and need not be considered as being real in anything other than a visionary sense. No doubt the man saw, during one of his fits, exactly what he had expected to see lurking out there in the Irish countryside. What allegedly happened next, however, was not quite so typical.

The following night, one of the people who had been feasting in the field – later identified as being a dead man who was seemingly now one of the fairy-troop – appeared at the butler's bedside and warned him that, if he dared set foot outside the next day, the *sidhe* would steal him away. Unable to resist tempting fate, however, the foolish man set one foot over the threshold that next evening anyway. Immediately, a rope was lassoed around his midriff and he was carried away running at great speed, like a man tied to a bolting horse. The entire household ran after him, but were unable to keep up. Eventually a horseman, coming in the opposite direction, saw the man coming towards him, drawn along by a rope pulled by invisible hands. He grabbed hold of one end of the rope, managed to hold on, and stopped the butler's unwilling progress away to fairyland.

---

[*] According to the writer ARG Owen, this particular Earl was probably Roger Boyle, Lord Broghill, brother of the famous scientist Robert Boyle. Boyle held the Earldom between 1660 and 1679, thus dating the incident.

When the Earl of Orrery heard of this unlikely miracle, he asked for the butler to be sent around to his house for examination. Whilst there, he told the Earl that the dead man had visited him once more and warned him that the fairies would return for him again that day. Accordingly, he was locked up inside a large room, with many people – including the then-famous Irish 'faith-healer' Valentine Greatrakes – to guard him. All was well until late afternoon when the butler, so it is said, started to rise up from the ground, leading Greatrakes and another "lusty man" present to clap their hands over his shoulders and try to hold him down. The levitationary force proved too strong for them, however, and the butler went flying around "in the air to and fro over their heads" for "a considerable time" with the assembled company running around madly beneath him with their arms stretched out wide to catch him should he fall – which, at length, he did, right into their embrace. He was later visited once more by the dead man, who gave him some medicine to cure both his fits and his levitations – a remedy which, apparently, worked [1].

Of course, it is very hard to accept the whole story, as told by Greatrakes to a gathering of early psychical researchers at Ragley Hall in Warwickshire in 1665, as being entirely true. The vision of the fairy-folk at their feast was a natural one for an Irish country-butler to have had during one of his fits, as we said earlier, and the dead man's appearances could also have been hallucinatory. The story of the rope, meanwhile, was merely reported upon hearsay by Greatrakes, who did not actually witness it himself. The levitation itself, however, appears to have had several witnesses of high standing. Whilst it has been suggested that Greatrakes' account was merely a naive description of the difficulties to be encountered when trying to restrain someone who is fitting [2], this is rather hard to square with the specific description of him flying "to and fro" above the witnesses' heads.

You'll Believe a Man Can Fly
We can also find stories of fairy-teleportation. A Mr T Leece, for instance, of the Isle of Man, told such a tale to the American folklorist and mystic WY Evans-Wentz when the latter was travelling around the island in search of modern-day fairy-tales. Apparently, the man's uncle was a tailor by trade and had an 18-year-old apprentice, by the name of Humphrey Keggan. I have no idea of how good a tailor Humphrey was, but as a worker of wonders he was first-rate. By all accounts, whilst walking home with his boss after work, he would frequently simply disappear from view, often in the very middle of a conversation, perhaps a particularly dull one. Once this had happened, there was no point in looking for him – he would not turn up until the next morning, exhausted and bedraggled. The cause of his woes, the boy claimed, was a "crowd" of "little men" who made him get down on all fours so they could use him as a horse upon which to gallop across fields and fly over hedges [3].

Such supposedly truthful accounts seem to have their legendary equivalent in the old folk-belief of the 'fairy-host'. This was perhaps the aerial equivalent of the fairy-troop; a kind of supernatural wind in which the invisible *sidhe* travelled and which was once popularly believed by many on the Celtic Fringe to pick up men against their will before then depositing them back down again far, far away. On the Western Hebridean island of Barra, for instance, Evans-Wentz interviewed a woman called Marian MacLean, who told him of how the fairy-hosts used to travel past "particularly about midnight" making a sound "like a covey of birds", looking out for men to kidnap and then force to shoot fairy-javelins at milk-maids. Obviously, this is mere fancy, but once again in Ms MacLean's account mere fancy merges away weirdly into alleged first-hand experience, the woman telling Evans-Wentz that her father and grandfather knew a man who claimed to have physically flown to Barra from the island of South Uist himself whilst caught up in the fairy-host [4]. Likewise, we have on record the testimony of a man called Edward Jones, of the Welsh town of Llanidloes in Powys, who claimed to have encountered a troop of fairies one night who, annoyed by his intrusion upon their revels, offered him the chance of being carried off by a "high wind, middle wind or low wind". He chose the first, and was "whisked high up into the air" until he suddenly found himself being dropped down into the middle of a garden near Ty Gough, several miles away. [5]

Are these tales actually true, though? We may have reasonable cause to doubt it, but specific people and places are actually named in them, and the teleported people themselves could once have been produced to vouch for the truth of such yarns to sceptics. It would be easy to accuse them of lying; but, evidently, all lived in societies in which they expected that any such lies would be believed. This fact causes the modern reader obvious problems. For instance, how different from the above narratives, really, once all of the fairy-tale elements have been stripped away from them, is the oft-cited case of Francis Fry, a 21-year-old domestic servant from the Devon village of Spreyton who, John Aubrey tells us, was in 1682 caught up by what we would now term a poltergeist:

> "... by the skirts of his doublet, and carried into the air; he was quickly missed by his master ... and a great enquiry was made for Francis Fry, but no hearing of him; but about half-an-hour after Fry was found whistling and singing in a sort of quagmire ... coming to himself an hour after, he solemnly protested that the daemon carried him so high that he saw his master's house underneath him no bigger than a haycock ... The workmen found one shoe on one side of the house, and the other shoe on the other side; his periwig was espied next morning hanging on the top of a tall tree." [6]

This final detail has its direct equivalent in many old yarns about the passing fairy-host abducting passers-by, the now oft-neglected novelist and antiquarian Sir Walter Scott telling us that it was not an uncommon feature of such stories in Scotland for the kidnapped man being whisked away to "leave his hat or bonnet on some steeple between, to mark the direct line of his course." [7] An extremely dubious account of a supposed male witch named 'Old Stranguidge' who is said to have been carried through the air on a black hog to a witches' Sabbat in Cambridge, only to tear his breeches on a weathercock on the steeple of Shelford Church, also sounds suspiciously similar [8]. Should this all make us more suspicious of the truth of the tale of Francis Fry, then, or does it lend it further credence? We may well suspect the former. After all, the main source for Fry's tale was a letter copied out second-hand for Aubrey from a local clergyman, the then-Rector of Barnstable – a man who fully admits that he never actually went out to Spreyton to investigate himself.

Going Underground
On the other hand, that there were poltergeist disturbances of *some kind* going on in Spreyton during 1682 seems to be an acknowledged fact. Furthermore, there are numerous other instances of teleportations and levitations having been directly witnessed taking place during

seemingly genuine poltergeist cases on record. A particularly interesting example occurred at the village of Sandfeldt in eastern Germany in 1722, when, during an especially weird haunting, a number of children were apparently seen by adults to disappear into thin air "in the twinkling of an eye." When they eventually returned to our world, they said that they had been transported underground where they met a race of "little crooked people" who had offered them coins to stay in elf-land. Upon refusing this offer, they were returned to the surface. Despite this bizarre element, the case is generally nowadays classified as being a poltergeist one. [9]

Probably the most well-known instances of poltergeist-teleportations, though, were those which took place during the Poona case, referred to earlier. The two young adopted boys at the centre of events, Damodar and Ramkrishna Ketkar, were transported around by the ghost several times. On more than one occasion, Damodar found himself being teleported into a car sitting safely within a locked shed. One witness actually claims to have seen the re-materialisation of Damodar's elder brother, Ramkrishna, taking place before her very eyes on April 23rd 1928. It seems that he suddenly appeared in front of the startled woman in a doorway – but "He didn't come through any door." The posture adopted by the child during this incident was most remarkable. He was:

> "... bending forward; both his arms were hanging away from his sides, and the hands hanging limp – his feet were not touching the floor ... [there was] a distinct space between his feet and the threshold. It was precisely the posture of a person who has been gripped round the waist and carried, and therefore makes no effort but is gently dropped at his destination." [10]

Upon another occasion, Damodar was witnessed by a doctor, JD Jenkins, to rise into the air after he had been put to bed. According to him:

> "I saw the bedclothes pulled off the bed on which the lad was lying, the bed was pulled into the middle of the room, and the lad actually lifted off the bed and deposited gently on the floor. The lad could feel the arm of an unseen person at work." [11]

Similar things happened during the now-notorious Enfield poltergeist case from North London in 1977-78, the teenage girl at the centre of events, Janet, seemingly being teleported through her bedroom wall and into the house next door [12]. As proof of this incident really having occurred, Janet's neighbour went into the room and found a book belonging to the child lying on the bed. A few minutes beforehand, it had been sitting innocuously upon Janet's mantelpiece in her own room next door. Another time, the girl was actually seen to levitate by a passing lollipop lady named Hazel Short. In her words, she looked up through Janet's bedroom window and saw the girl:

> "... going up and down as though someone was just tossing her up and down bodily, in a horizontal position, like someone had got hold of her legs and was throwing her up and down." [13]

The fairy-folk, too, have occasionally been said to have the power to make people pass

The 17ᵗʰ-century Irish faith-healer Valentine Greatrakes pictured laying hands upon a sick youth, a method of treatment which led to him being given the soubriquet of 'The Stroker'. Even he, big burly man that he was, could not prevent a butler at the Earl of Orrery's house from levitating after an encounter with feasting fairies and a mysterious member of the troop of the dead, however.

An old illustration shows the Devil carrying a woman off through the air (and apparently looking up her dress whilst he does so). A similar thing was said to have occurred to a poltergeist-victim named Francis Fry in the Devon village of Spreyton in 1682.

The 1722 pamphlet in which the haunting at Sandfeldt was first detailed.

The levitating Icelandic medium Indridi Indridason; proof positive both that men can fly and that stupid footballer-type hairstyles are by no means a modern invention.

St Joseph of Cupertino, at it again; with more than 70 instances of alleged levitation on record, it is perhaps no wonder that he has since been made the patron saint of air-travellers and astronauts!

Two images of Spanish witches engaging in acts of magical flight, taken from Goya's grotesque 'Los Caprichos' sequence of engravings.

Laughing goblins levitate some unfortunate lad in this old drawing.

through solid walls, however. In 1960, for example, a Malaysian man, Mohamed Akhir, claimed to have been carried away from his home by 'forest elves', who left him in a debilitated condition for all of five years. Then, however, on 5th May 1977, he returned home to find his wife missing – but the strange thing was that he was initially unable to gain access to the house because all of the doors and windows had been locked from the *inside*. His neighbours blamed the 'invisible people' who lived in the forest for the crime, theorising that they had come to reclaim Mohamed but had settled instead for carrying off his wife, seeing as he was not there. Clearly, then, these forest elves were conceived of by the villagers as having the power to teleport human beings through solid matter [14].

Hold On Tight!

Some cases of alleged poltergeist-levitation, meanwhile, sound rather comic and could be characterised almost as being some kind of 'supernatural tug-of-war', as can be seen in this account of events which supposedly took place at a séance in Boston in December 1855:

> "The medium was lifted bodily from the floor at various distances, whilst we held him by either hand. He was lifted from the floor and placed, standing, on the centre of the table ... Being seated in his chair, himself, chair and all, was elevated several inches, and hopped about the room like a frog. Suddenly it was lifted, medium and all, into the centre of the table ... it was drawn up so high that the medium's head knocked against the ceiling; and finally the medium was thrown out of it upon the bed, while the chair was hurled upon the floor." [15]

Easily the most entertaining instance of this kind of caper, however, involved the remarkable Indridi Indridason, a young Icelandic medium, and the actions of his friend Mr Oddgeirsson, together with a Mr Kvoran, the president and archivist of the Icelandic SPR, and a Mr Thorlaksson, a senior clerk in that nation's Ministry of Industry and Commerce, who tried to prevent the boy from being levitated off into the ether one night in 1907. The events were recorded by the Reverend Haraldur Nielsson, and are so astonishing that they deserve to be repeated here at length:

> "During the night the medium shouts that he is being dragged out of bed and is very terror-stricken ... Mr Odgeirsson takes his hand, pulling with all his might, but cannot hold him. The medium is lifted above that end of the bed against which his head has been lying and he is pulled down on to the floor, sustaining injuries to his back ... The medium is now dragged head foremost through the door and along the floor in the outer room, in spite of his clutching with all his might at everything he could catch hold of, besides Mr Kvaran and Mr Oddgeirsson pulling at his legs ... Two nights later a similar scene occurred. Indridi on this occasion has Mr Thorlaksson and Mr Odgeirsson sleeping in the room with him. Ewers and other crockery were hurled about and smashed. The two watchers, while throwing themselves upon the medium and exerting all their strength, could hardly prevent him from again being dragged out of bed, and while this was happening, the table which was standing between the beds was lifted and came down on Mr Odgeirsson's back ... the medium, after partially dressing, once more asked for help. Mr Thorlaksson had been standing in the outer room, but now rushes in to his medium, and then sees that he is balancing in the air with his feet towards the

window. Mr Thorlaksson takes hold of him, pulls him down into bed and keeps him there. Then he feels that the medium and himself are being lifted up, and he shouts to Mr Oddgeirsson to help him. Mr Oddgeirsson goes into the bedroom, but a chair is then hurled against him ... Mr Oddgeirsson swerved aside to avoid the chair, and went on into the bedroom. Mr Thorlaksson was then lying on the medium's chest. Mr Oddgeirsson threw his weight on to the medium's knees, who was at the moment all on the move in the bed. Then a bolster which was under the medium's pillow was thrown up in the air ... Simultaneously the candlesticks which were in the outer room came through the air and were flung down in the bedroom." [16]

At this point, it seems, the medium was saved. Indridason put the blame for these assaults upon the ghost of a recent suicide who was known to him – but when similar things happened to Lord Orrery's butler back in seventeenth-century Ireland, it was not the dead, but the fairy-folk who were accused of perpetrating such assaults. The clear similarities which exist between this account and that of Valentine Greatrakes, however, would appear to be obvious.

The Unbearable Lightness of Being
This whole issue is further complicated for us, however, by the fact that, on numerous other occasions, neither poltergeists nor fairies have been so much as mentioned in relation to apparently identical accounts of persons supposedly seen whizzing around through thin air. For example, several Christian saints are said to have been levitators, and their alleged ability put down to God's grace, or whatever. St Joseph of Cupertino, an Italian saint who lived from 1603-1633, is the most famous such 'holy flier'. Whatever you think of such unlikely tales, there are more than 70 separate occasions upon which he is recorded as having allegedly levitated; all it took to set him off was a pious observation or two, whereupon he would go into ecstasies and float away. One time, he rose up into a tree and perched on a branch, which quivered as gently as if he had been a bird. Another time he was seen to remain kneeling in mid-air, having begun to levitate whilst engaged in prayer. Once, so overjoyed was he by the sound of holy music at a Christmas service, that he floated above the altar in the church for 15 minutes. Yet another time, upon seeing some men struggling to erect a weighty cross, he uttered a shriek, flew over to them and then – seemingly making the cross as light as air too – put it up with ease. [17]

Sometimes, though, levitations which occur within a religious context can be said by their observers to be demonic rather than holy in origin. For example, sometime during the 1970s (details about this case are vague, making me suspicious) an Italian nun, Sister Rosa, is said to have been tormented in her convent in Rome by violent and invisible powers. In her vicinity, objects apparently levitated – and so did she. Once, she is said to have been witnessed slowly floating up to a ceiling and then simply passing through it, rather like Janet with her bedroom wall at Enfield. Exorcists who were called in blamed demons rather than God for such occurrences [18]. At a convent in the French city of Louviers between 1642 and 1647, strange things also started happening to nuns. They began acting bizarrely, blaspheming, running around in impossibly contorted positions, fainting, having visions, and shouting obscenities. The most logical conclusion that could be drawn at the time was that they were all 'possessed by demons'. If so, then these demons were also able to make people as light as air. Apparently one nun, known only as 'Sister of the Saint-Sacrament', jumped up into a tree where she was seen to be seemingly "in imminent peril of her life", leaping around from tiny branch to tiny branch, each of which nonetheless supported her entire weight. Such was her apparent lightness of being here that one bystander cried out "She is flying like a bird." [19]

Interestingly, there had been a previous instance of alleged levitation in Louviers, when a 16-year-old servant-girl called Françoise Fontaine was seen by a Provost Morel and his men to rise up into the air in a horizontal, prone position, and come flying right towards them. Nervous, the officials went out of the room in the court building where she was being held, and locked the door on her; whereupon she tried to fly through another exit, heading for a door leading out onto the street. This, too, had to be locked, in order to keep her from floating away like a loose balloon. When efforts were made to purify Françoise by giving her holy communion or shaving her head, she would immediately shoot up into the air, and it would take the combined efforts of several men to bring her back down to earth again. Strangely, when she was hovering like this it is said that her skirts would sometimes, quite naturally, fall out of place so that you could (if you were so inclined) stare right up them; but at other times, they would remain impossibly and miraculously in place, preserving both her modesty and her virtue [20]. It seems likely that the possessed nuns at Louviers had heard of this girl, and so perhaps she provided a kind of unconscious 'model' for them to follow during their own, later states of 'possession'?

Or, then again, maybe the Louviers nuns were familiar instead with the life-story of a rather neglected thirteenth-century German saint, now known as Blessed Christina of Stommeln, who was also supposedly hurled around through thin air by demons. Being an ecstatic and visionary, she took the time to count how many of them were tormenting her; apparently, there were 40,050 of the little blighters. Not only did they make her levitate, they also played various poltergeist-like tricks upon her, such as snatching away her bedclothes, beating and biting her, replacing her pillows with hard stones, throwing shit at her and her visitors, making a skull fly around her room, setting her clothes on fire, sticking red-hot stones to her flesh, and more. Most interestingly, upon several occasions she claimed to have been dragged out of bed and taken through the air by demons, being found in the morning insensible and left up on rooftops, tied to trees and even buried up to her neck in a pit of mud – this latter event sounding rather similar to Francis Fry being found in his quagmire [21]. It is curious indeed how such obscure details appear to persist across time and space.

Unexpected Flying Objects

Amongst other cultures, meanwhile, mystical flight and teleportation were supposed to be the preserve not of Christian saints, but of native holy-men called shamans. Amongst the Niassan people of Sumatra, for instance, it was said that those chosen to become shamans suddenly disappeared from their villages into the skies, before returning again three or four days later. If they did not return, however, then search-parties were sent to look for them; usually, the newly-revealed holy-man would be found sitting at the top of a tree to which he had supposedly been transported, sometimes seemingly out of his mind and claiming to converse with spirits [22]. This seems likely to have simply been a kind of ritually-enacted folk-drama used by the Niassans in order to help make a holy-man's sense of 'calling' seem comprehensible to them. And yet, at the same time, there are some definite similarities between some of these accounts and those of the Christian saints. Ancient Hungarian shamans, for example – called *táltos* – could reputedly "jump up in a willow tree and sit on a branch that would have been too weak for a bird." [23] And so, we have just seen, could Joseph of Cupertino and one of the nuns at Louviers ...

Several supposed UFO abduction cases have also featured people being lifted around by beams of light or other such mysterious rays – for instance, one account of the so-called 1976 'Allagash Abductions' case features the following description of how two American abductees were supposedly returned from a spacecraft and to their home:

> "Both were literally floated across the lawn from the craft to their house, through the unopened front door and to their bedroom." [24]

When witchcraft was seriously believed in, meanwhile, this kind of thing happening was simply put down to the effects of evil spells. In 1661, for example, there was a trial at Cork Assizes wherein a supposed Irish witch, Florence Newton, was accused of bewitching a servant girl named Mary Longdon. During this 'bewitchment' Mary had fits, vomited strange objects and was followed by showers of small stones. She was also allegedly teleported and levitated about, in a fairly comic fashion. Apparently:

> "... sometimes she should be removed out of her bed into another room, sometimes she should be carried to the top of the house and laid on a board betwixt two Sollar Beams [rafters?], sometimes put into a Chest, sometimes under a parcel of wool, sometimes between two feather-beds, and sometimes between the Bed and the Mat in her Master's chamber in the daytime." [25]

Fly-By-Nights

Witches, of course, were meant to be able to fly through the air themselves, rather than just causing their unfortunate victims to do so. Most commonly, they would put a hurdle or stick between their legs and ride off on it, perhaps having initially covered themselves with some kind of 'witches' ointment', on their way to their famous Sabbats (a kind of midnight orgy with Satan and his imps). According to Isobel Gowdie, for instance – the most famous Scottish witch of all, tried at Lochlay in 1662 – she and her fellow witches:

> "... will fly like straws when we please; wild straws and corn straws will be horses to us, and we put them betwixt our feet and say horse and hillock in the devil's name. And when any see these straws in a whirlwind and do not sanctify themselves, we may shoot them dead at our pleasure." [26]

These particular delusional beliefs also have their echo in certain aspects of fairy-lore, though, particularly from Ireland. According to Yeats, the word *sidhe*, as well as referring to the 'hill-folk', was also the Gaelic word for wind. The fairies journeyed around in the "whirling winds", he says, and when country people saw leaves whirling around, they believed the *sidhe* were passing [27]. He even mentions one Irishwoman who saw a pile of wood-shavings blowing around and instantly knew that they were fairies and not really shavings at all, she said, "because there was no place for shavings to come from." [28] Because of these beliefs, whenever what Yeats terms "the peasantry" saw straw and leaves blowing in the wind, they would remove their hats and say 'God bless them' in order to protect themselves [29]. The country-folk did well to do so, it appears; for the *sidhe* travelling in the wind were in fact nothing less than the fairy-host, who would give unwary travellers the blast, carry them away, or shoot them with their elf-shot. According to Isobel Gowdie, however, so would she – but then, she did claim to have met the Queen of Elf-Land during her nocturnal flights of fancy. This, perhaps, is where she sourced her fairy-weaponry from.

Gowdie's accounts of transforming straws into flying horses during her forays into the air also have their parallels in fairy-lore. In Ireland, for example, it was once believed that *bucalauns* – ragweed plants – were special fairy-plants. At night, according to Yeats, the fairy-troop would "come out of their green hills and change the *bucalauns* into horses, and ride furiously all night long." [30] If they didn't have any such plants available to them, however, then they might choose to use human victims as horses instead – and we will remember that the alleged teleportations of poor Humphrey Keggan on the Isle of Man were explained away in just such a fashion. The *sidhe* could also pick up bits of straw and fly using them, just like Isobel Gowdie could. This all seems most confusing. Why are there all these strange and unexpected parallels present between accounts of levitation in fairy, poltergeist, witchcraft, UFO and demon-possession cases? I think that one potential answer to this conundrum could well lie contained within the works of that great American anomalist, Charles Fort.

Spirited Away

Fort, as many readers of this book will no doubt be aware, was one of the most significant writers in our field. He scoured through literally thousands of obscure newspapers and journals for many years, searching out accounts of the weird and the fantastic – a rain of blood here, a spontaneous combustion there – and then recorded them for posterity in four excellent and amusing books. He also kept a look-out for cases of levitation and teleportation; indeed, the latter word was actually of his own invention. One such account he gives is of the Pansini brothers, Paolo and Alfredo, both of junior-school age, of the Italian city of Bari, and the subjects of numerous alleged teleportations. Their first in 1901 took them to within the walls of the Capucine convent at Malfatti, some 30 miles away from the town of Ruvo where they had begun their day that morning; perhaps the monks should have acclaimed them as living saints, like Joseph of Cupertino was. In 1904, meanwhile, they were transported to a relative's house in another town, Trani, arriving in what Fort terms "a state of profound hypnosis." Best of all, however, was the time that they are supposed to have flopped down from out of the sky into the Mediterranean – right into a fishing-boat! [31]

You can believe this or not, of course; and, I suspect, you probably won't. What interests me here, though, is the agency which Fort habitually used to blame such occurrences on. Was it fairies? Angels? Poltergeists? Devils? None of these, in fact. He simply blamed the force of 'teleportation' itself. Even though the first phenomena reported around the Pansini brothers were actually of the poltergeistic variety, with objects moving about and crockery being broken [32], Fort's view was that such instances might simply be the result simply of some inanimate force inherent within the universe, rather than down to the actions of specific supernatural entities as such.

For Fort, the universe was all one big organism; and, just as antibodies and suchlike are naturally distributed throughout other living organisms according to specific biological needs, so matter is naturally and unthinkingly distributed throughout the universe, he says. Or, at least, so it was once; nowadays, this teleportive force has become senile and unreliable, he proposes. Famously, Fort gave an account of two farmers, George and Albert Sanford, hoeing in a field near the city of Trenton, New Jersey in June 1884, when stones began falling on them from the sky. Going public, the farmers returned with a crowd of 40 or 50 persons – and stones continued to fall, just where they weren't wanted; in a field that was being hoed [33]. These events led Fort to pen one of his most well-known passages:

> "It could be that, in reading what most persons think are foolish little yarns of falling stones, we are, visionarily, in the presence of cosmic constructiveness – or that once upon a time this whole earth was built up by streams of rocks, teleported from other parts of an existence. The crash of falling islands – the humps of piling continents – and then the cosmic humour of it all – or utmost spectacularity functioning, then declining, and surviving only as a vestige – or that the force that once heaped the peaks of the Rocky Mountains now slings pebbles at a couple of farmers, near Trenton, NJ." [34]

Fort, as always, means all this half in jest, of course; and yet, his distaste for the idea that sentient agencies of the type we have been calling poltergeists and fairies are responsible for such things does seem to have been a genuine one. If we can trust at least some of the testimony provided in this chapter, then teleportation and levitation of the human frame are, it would seem, genuine – if exceedingly rare – occurrences. When people witness such things in action, however, they need to account for them somehow. Once, they would have been blamed upon fairies. Now, we blame poltergeists. For myself, not unlike Fort, I simply accept the apparent reality of the phenomenon itself, not its masks. Sometimes, it would seem, people appear to float in the air, or teleport instantly from one place to another. Nobody, as of yet, really knows why. Saying that it is all down to demons, aliens, fairies or ghosts merely allows us temporarily to pretend that we do. That, I think, is one of the main points being made by Fort in his writings – and, in my opinion, he deserves to be listened to.

6.

The Stolen Child: Baby-Theft and Associations with Children

In his *Chronicon*, Ralph of Coggeshall, the medieval English chronicler and monk, tells an interesting ghost-story from East Anglia, about a spooky little girl called 'Malekin'. The tale, in Father Herbert Thurston's translation from the Latin, goes thus:

> "In the reign of King Richard [i.e. Richard I – reigned 1189-1199] at Dagworth in Suffolk, in the house of Sir Osberne de Brandewelle, a certain whimsical ... ghost appeared on many occasions and for a long time together [was] talking with the family of the aforesaid knight, and imitating in its tones the voice of a baby girl. She called herself Malekin and said that her mother and her brother made their home in a house nearby. Moreover she declared that she was frequently scolded by them because she left their company and made bold to talk with human beings. She both did and said things which were extravagant and amusing, and sometimes she revealed the secret doings of other people. When she first was heard to speak, the knight's good lady and the whole household were very frightened, but afterwards, when they had become accustomed to her diverting tricks and speeches, they talked with her familiarly and confidently, asking her all sorts of questions. She spoke in English, using the local dialect, but sometimes also in Latin, and she would debate about the Scriptures in all seriousness with the chaplain of the aforesaid knight as he himself informed me. She could make herself heard and felt, but was never seen; though on one occasion a little waiting maid beheld her in the form of a tiny babe clothed in a white frock ... She confessed that she had been born at "Lanaham" [probably the Suffolk village of Lavenham] and that while her mother took her with her into the fields when she was reaping with a number of others, the little one, who had been left by herself in a corner, was seized and carried off by another woman. She had now been seven years in this woman's company, but she

said that after another seven years she would return to live with mortals again as before. She also made known that she and others wore a sort of cap which rendered them invisible. She frequently demanded food and drink, which, being left on top of a certain chest, disappeared and were seen no more." [1]

The fairy-tale elements here are obvious; snatched from a field by a strange woman, Malekin (a name very much like one of those traditionally attributed to witches' familiars) seems, though somewhat incoherently, to be claiming to be a human child trapped in fairy-land; someone who has been 'taken', as it were. Frequently, tales of human children kidnapped by the fairies feature the detail that the Good Folk could only get at them in the first place because their imprudent human mothers had left them unattended in a field whilst they got on with doing farm-work; there is a version of this tale-type set in the Staffordshire village of Ipstones, for example, in which a woman left her baby out on a pile of hay beneath an umbrella whilst she went off to labour amongst the crops, enabling malicious goblins to replace her healthy baby with a sickly one of their own [2]. Perhaps such stories were originally meant as being coded warnings for mothers against the very real dangers of leaving young babies unattended outdoors; the modern equivalent, perhaps, would be 'watch out a gypsy doesn't steal them!'

And yet, despite these similarities, Malekin also seems to a modern reader like a classic poltergeist: "She could make herself heard and felt but was never seen." As Father Thurston astutely points out in his own discussion of the case, however, her story "obviously does not quite hold together." [3] Perhaps what we have here, then, is a poltergeist making use of several then-current folkloric elements in order to make up a semi-plausible identity to try and account for itself? The 'seven years' motif in fairy-stories, for instance, is well-known, as is the 'cap of invisibility' *. The fact that Malekin demanded offerings of food also links her with various types of friendly but hungry household fairy-familiars for whom small tributes of bread, milk and honey were often left out by appreciative country-folk during the past. But then, of course, the word 'poltergeist' did not exist, even in German, during the days of King Richard I. If it had, then perhaps Sir Osberne would have called it one, and the spirit would have dropped those outlandish claims about being trapped in fairy-land altogether. Even Ralph of Coggeshall seems to be in two minds about whether or not Malekin really was who she said she was – his original Latin account calls the spirit, literally, one that is *'fantasticus'*. This word has its origins in the Greek word *'phantasia'*, meaning something whose appearance or image is potentially illusory [4]. The implication of this wording would seem to be that Malekin was merely *pretending* to be a child trapped in another world, then ...

* Other translations say 'hood' – which could perhaps be said to link Malekin with the so-called *genii cucullati*, ambiguous spirit-beings depicted on a number of stone carvings found across both Britain and Europe. The name means something like 'hooded spirits of place', and is derived from the Latin word 'cucullus', a kind of full-length hooded robe. The exact focus and purpose of their cult is as-yet unknown, but it would appear that they were considered to be some kind of guardian-like fairies or elementals in nature – some say that they were originally representations of the three Fates, from whom we derive the word *'fae/fay'*. Others say that they may have been early versions of brownies. Yet others speculate that the spirits' hoods were meant to indicate their owners' invisibility. The now-familiar idea of a fairy wearing a hood or pointed cap apparently has a long history to it, then, one into which 'Malekin' seems to have purposely tapped.

Changing the Baby
The main folklore motif being played upon here, however, is that well-known old idea that the fairies liked to go around snatching people's children. Fairies, so it was said, were prone to kidnapping healthy infants and then replacing them with so-called 'changelings' – sickly, old and unhealthy members of their own community disguised as human babies – in their cots. The easiest way to look at Malekin, I suppose, was as yet another stolen child, trapped for twice seven years within the realm of faery.

But surely it is the case that stories of changelings are just folklore? In a literal sense, yes. The generally-accepted modern explanation for such tales is that they were told in order to account for once-high rates of infant mortality or the birth of disabled children in societies of the past. Here, for instance, is a description of a typical changeling from the Isle of Man in the 1720s:

> "... tho' between five and six years old, and seemingly healthy, he was so far from being able to walk, or stand, that he could not so much as move any one joint: his limbs were vastly long for his age, but smaller than an infant's of six months ... he never spoke, nor cryed, eat scarce anything, and very seldom [was] seen to smile, but if anyone called him a fairy-elf, he would frown and fix his eyes so earnestly on those who said it, as if he would look them through." [5]

Examining such accounts, some modern commentators have made the obvious conclusion that such infants were simply ill, and as such have grouped various childhood medical disorders under the general heading of 'changeling syndrome'. Thus, by calling any baby born with one of these disorders a 'changeling', parents were making use of a widely-available supernatural method of explaining certain babies' failure to thrive for whatever reason.[6] Then, any blame for a baby's subsequent demise could be placed not upon neglectful parents or an uncaring universe, but upon the dastardly child-snatching fairy-folk; and the parents of disabled infants, attitudes being what they once were, were also provided with a psychologically useful means of denying that the disabled baby was even theirs in the first place.

If they should then choose to 'test' whether the baby was really human or not by subjecting it to some kind of horrific trial of such a nature that, realistically, was bound to kill it – throwing it into a fireplace, for instance, burning it alive on a red-hot shovel, exposing it to the elements on a dung-heap or leaving it on a beach to see if the tide would sweep it away – then, in actual fact, these were probably no more than what one writer has termed "socially countenanced forms of infanticide" for 'useless' mouths that would otherwise need feeding[7]. The word 'oaf' is derived from the word 'elf' – and if the 'oaf' you were killing was actually thought by you to be an elf, well then, there was no need to feel any guilt about it all [8]. By killing your baby, you were simply doing what was natural – because, of course, the infant was not *actually* your baby at all, it was an evil imposter.

Invasion of the Baby-Snatchers
There is, then, no good reason for us to presume that tales of changelings are in any sense literally true. Fairies do not steal babies and take them away with them under the fairy-hill ... or, at least, not permanently. Curiously, however, there are a number of allegedly first-hand

stories in existence in which invisible fairies have been blamed for either temporarily stealing people's children, or for attempting to do so. In Wirt Sikes' 1880 book *British Goblins*, for example, there is recorded the purported experience of one Jennet Francis of Ebwy Fawr Valley in Gwent, Wales, who claimed to have awoken one night to find some unseen force pulling her baby out of her arms. She screamed and began praying, eventually succeeding in pulling the infant back, or so she says [9]. Another story, from the Isle of Man, tells of a woman whose babies kept on mysteriously disappearing shortly after their birth, accompanied by strange noises around the family home. Eventually, each of her babies was found having been dropped on the floor by the fairies, their attempts at kidnap having failed. The woman's third child, however, was meant to have been seen by her being levitated away by some invisible force. Crying out, her husband entered her room and pointed out that the baby was safe and sound and lying by her side. Looking at it, though, the mother knew instantly that it was not her baby; it was a sallow, wrinkled thing, not at all like her real, healthy child, and it only lived on for a few years more, during which time it learned to neither walk nor talk. [10]

Of course, these tales are dubious; the second one in particular was obviously just a fictional narrative invented by distressed parents trying to account for the fact that one of their children had been born disabled. Another such story, however, possibly with rather more of a ring of truth to it, was reported to the folklorist WY Evans-Wentz by one of his fairy-tale informants on the Isle of Man, a fellow named Samuel Leece:

> "... this did happen to my own mother in the parish of Kirk Patrick about eighty years since. She was in bed with her baby, but wide awake, when she felt the baby pulled off her arm and heard the rush of *them*. Then she mentioned the Almighty's name, and, as *they* were hurrying away, a little table alongside the bed went round about the floor twenty times. Nobody was in the room with my mother, and she always allowed it was the *little fellows*." [11]

A dancing table, then – and a snatched baby, to boot – but tables danced at Victorian séances, and invisible poltergeists have been known to snatch babies, too. To give but one example initially, a haunting from Paraguay in 1973 featured the disturbing detail that a sleeping ten-month-old baby vanished – pram and all – from inside its parents' house. After a desperate search, the infant was found, still asleep, under a tree; and, supposedly, as dry as a bone, even though it was raining at the time! [12] In Mexico, however, this exact same kind of child-snatching behaviour is well-known – and attributed not to polts, but to a form of local fairy known as the *chaneques*. These *chaneques*, described as looking like small children with the heads of old men, are noted for supposedly taking babies in the night and then hiding them beneath their beds. [13]

An Indian tribe from the Pacific North-West of the USA, meanwhile, the Nez Perces, believed in a type of fairy called the 'Stick Indians', so called because they lived deep within the forests, amongst the twigs and branches. They were often invisible, but when spotted were spoken of as being quite wizened, with small eyes, wrinkles and long, uncombed hair. They were supposed to wear deerskins, be very strong, and kidnap both humans and livestock – including, it seems, small babies. One Indian informant, for example, told the following tale:

> "One time when some people were huckleberrying near Mount Adams [in Washington State] they locked their baby in the car, for safety. No one else was in the car. While they were picking berries, they heard the baby cry. They went to the car and found that the baby was gone. Then they heard it cry from another direction. They went over there, and they found it. The Little People had taken the baby out of a locked car. This did happen." [14]

The same thing happened in reverse to young Damodar Ketkar at Poona in 1927-30, readers will recall, the boy there somehow being teleported into a car kept inside a locked garage from outside. My point here is not necessarily that the tale about the Stick Indians was definitely a real one, merely that such motifs are common to both poltergeist and fairy-lore.

Child Abuse

There are actually a surprising number of cases of babies and infants being bothered by poltergeists on record. One of the most notable comes from a haunted Portuguese villa in the city of Coïmbra belonging to a Mr Homem Christo, which in 1919 became the scene of much disruptive poltergeist activity. Screams and laughter were heard from thin air, rappings and knockings broke out, and invisible assaults were perpetrated upon the house's inhabitants. The police were called in, but could do nothing; the ghost just beat one of them up! One evening, the spook even decided to have a go at Mr Christo's baby. In the middle of the night, Christo heard his wife screaming that she was being dragged down the stairs. Being Latin in temperament, he immediately discharged his revolver in the direction where he thought the unseen spirit must have been lurking. His wife then fainted in his arms, and Christo got a blow on the cheek which, he said, felt like he had been hit by "five small sticks". Dragging his bride upstairs to their bedroom, he banged the door shut and she seemed to recover. Christo takes up the story from here:

> "My wife, feeling herself saved ... rushed to the cradle of her child: *the cradle was empty*. Then she fainted away. Savagely watching the circle of feeble light which the lamp shed around me and the woman on the floor for a sign of the something which would no doubt appear there, I waited. It was useless to think of defence. Knife, revolver, all this became powerless against an enemy who could not be seized. From afar the servants, having heard the firing, howled like dogs at the moon. I know of nothing more demoralising than the cries of women in the night. But the soft wailing of a baby which seemed to come from under the floor awoke me from my moral feebleness. It had to be found, the little mite, for I knew from my wife's fainting fit that it was not she who had put it away. So I had the courage ... to search the whole ground floor, holding the lamp on high. I found the infant, quite naked, all its swaddling-clothes taken off, placed on its back in the middle of a marble table, like an object of no value abandoned by the redoubtable robber in his haste to escape in the night." [15]

This is certainly a dramatic story – especially given the hyperbolic way that Christo writes it all up – and you can easily understand the man's panic. When poltergeists move around children, it seems only natural for their parents to presume that the ghosts are trying to harm them, whether this is actually the case or not. Sometimes, their malicious intent appears undeniable, though. One Brazilian case reported for us by the noted poltergeist-expert Guy Lyon Playfair in his classic book *The Flying Cow*, for example, is described by him as being "nothing less than attempted murder." It concerns a house in a town outside the city of São Paulo where several attempts were apparently made by a polt to burn a baby to death. On one occasion, the spirit tried another tactic and the baby simply disappeared; after a desperate search, the father of the household heard stifled cries coming from a basket full of dirty clothing. Ripping the clothes off, he found his child lying at the bottom, half-suffocated to death. The family concerned eventually abandoned the home – they had to, as the angry spirit smashed its roof in and burnt all of their furniture. [16]

A very early report of another attempt at condemning a baby to a fiery death, meanwhile, comes from an eighth-century account of the life of the Northumbrian missionary St Willibrord written by the learned English scholar and ecclesiastic at the Carolingian Court, Alcuin:

> "A certain father of a family and his household suffered grievous trials from a mocking demon, the presence of the spirit of evil in the home being made manifest by the fright he occasioned and by his malicious tricks. On a sudden he used to carry off food, clothing and other necessary things and throw them into the fire. He even took a little child while it was lying in bed between the father and the mother, they being fast asleep, and threw it likewise into the fire. But the parents, being aroused by the infant's wailing, were able to rescue it, though only just in time." [17]

According to some translations of this passage, the baby was not just thrown onto the fire, but actually buried deep beneath the burning coals, a position from which it could only be extracted with difficulty. [18]

Baby-Love
However, surely the weirdest account of a poltergeist – or incubus (demon-rapist) as it was termed at the time – getting involved with babies was chronicled for us by the noted seventeenth-century Franciscan scholar Father Ludovico Sinistrari. Sinistrari's tale concerns a native woman of the Italian city of Pavia, where Sinistrari taught theology, a "married woman of excellent morality" named Hieronyma. Despite Hieronyma's "excellent morality", this tale in fact begins with something of a moral; don't take what doesn't belong to you. One day, we are told, Hieronyma took some bread to a tradesman to be baked. When he brought it back he also gave her a large pancake "of very peculiar shape" which, she protested, had not been made with any of the ingredients she had given the man. The baker disagreed, insisting that he had had no other customers that day, so where else would he have got them from? Making the best of an awkward situation, Hieronyma shrugged and accepted the delicious food, sharing it that night as a meal with her husband and tiny daughter.

This, however, proved to be a serious error; accepting a gift of food from fairy-land always is. The following night, Hieronyma was awoken by an "extremely fine" voice, "somewhat like a high-pitched whistling sound", whispering in her ear. It asked her if she had enjoyed the pancake. Terrified, Hieronyma made the sign of the cross and invoked the names of Jesus and Mary. "Fear naught," replied the voice, however. "I mean no harm to you. On the contrary,

Fairies snatch a baby from its distraught mother in this evocative illustration to Wirt Sikes' 1880 book *British Goblins*.

The mysterious hooded fairy-like figures of the *genii cucullati*, as carved on the Roman fort of Housesteads at Hadrian's Wall. Was 'Malekin' actually just such a being?

A demon steals a baby and leaves behind an evil horned replica in its place; detail from a 15th-century painting by Martino di Bartolomeo.

THE
CHANGELING:

As it was Acted (with great Applause)
at the Privat house in DRURY LANE,
and *Salisbury Court.*

Written by {THOMAS MIDLETON,
and
WILLIAM ROWLEY.} Gent*.

Never Printed before.

LONDON,
Printed for HUMPHREY MOSELEY, and are to
be sold at his shop at the sign of the *Princes-Arms*
in St *Pauls* Church-yard, 1653.

The existence of a famous Jacobean play about the subject demonstrates quite
clearly how widely-known the idea of fairy-changelings once was.

A baby is bothered in its cot by typical poltergeist phenomena in this 19th-century engraving. The maid in the background is Adolphine Benoît, around whom the ghostly events in this case centred.

DEMONIALITY

OR

INCUBI AND SUCCUBI

A Treatise

wherein is shown that there are in existence on earth rational creatures besides man, endowed like him with a body and a soul, that are born and die like him, redeemed by our Lord Jesus–Christ, and capable of receiving salvation or damnation,

By the Rev. Father

SINISTRARI of Ameno

(17th century)

Published from the original Latin manuscript discovered in London in the year 1872,
and translated into French by Isidore Liseux

Now first translated into English
With the Latin Text.

SCIENTIA DUCE

IL

A 19th-century translation of Father Ludovico Sinistrari's classic text about the perils of sexual intercourse between humans and demons – a 'specialist subject' if ever there was one.

there is nothing I would not do in order to please you. I am in love with your beauty, and my greatest desire is to enjoy your embraces." Whilst the invisible ghost said this, Hieronyma felt that someone was kissing her cheeks, "but so softly and gently that she might have thought it was only the finest cotton down that was touching her." This persecution lasted for around 30 minutes before the incubus went away. That next day Hieronyma went to see her priest and had her house exorcised – but all to no avail. The amorous demon just kept on coming back for more.

Soon, the incubus was trying a different approach; he appeared to her "in the figure of a young boy or small man with golden, curling hair, with a blonde beard gleaming like gold and sea-green eyes ... elegantly dressed in Spanish vestments." Fashionably-dressed though the spirit may have been, however, still Hieronyma did not yield. In annoyance, therefore, the incubus began acting more like a typical polt, as Sinistrari explains:

> "First, he took from her a silver cross full of holy relics and a blessed wax or papal lamb of Pope Pius V, which she always had on her. Then, rings and other jewels of gold and silver followed. He stole them without touching the locks on the casket in which they were enclosed. Then he began to strike her cruelly, and after each series of blows one could see on her face, arm, or other areas of her body bruises and marks, which lasted one or two days, then vanished suddenly, quite unlike natural bruises, which go away by degrees. Sometimes, as she suckled her daughter, he took the child from her knees and carried her to the roof, placing her at the edge of the gutter. Or else he would hide her, but without ever causing her harm. He would also upset the household, sometimes breaking to pieces the plates and earthenware. But in the blink of an eye he also restored them to their original state." [19]

Both the fairy-tale and poltergeist elements to this case are obvious, even if there will always be those who suspect that Sinistrari either embellished or invented the whole narrative in order to suit either his pedagogy or the propagandistic purposes of his Mother Church. However, as we have just seen, there are other similar cases of spooks transporting babies about on record, so perhaps we should not be quite so sceptical. Whilst the standard explanation for the changeling myth we explored earlier, centring around the supernatural rationalisation of infant disability, is clearly the true one, it may just be that alleged experiences like those of Hieronyma had their part to play in the dissemination of such ideas, too. After all, if babies should occasionally find themselves being transported around from place to place by invisible beings, then witnesses in the past would, most likely, have tried to assimilate such events into their own pre-existing world-view. If you'd heard tales about babies being 'taken' by the Good Folk and then saw a floating baby, then that would probably act simply to reinforce your acceptance of these same beliefs, would it not? Whilst such narratives may not have been the ultimate origin of belief in the changeling myth, then, it is at least possible that they may have acted occasionally to *strengthen* it.

Will You Be My Friend?
One other issue which deserves to be discussed here, meanwhile, is that of invisible childhood friends. Are these just fiction? Mostly. There are a few tales on record, though, which might

make us think twice. Around Easter-time 1970, for example, something strange began happening to a 17-year-old servant girl called Aida in the house where she worked in the Philippines. Smooth, black stones started rolling across the floor towards her, stopping just a few inches from her feet. All the doors and windows in the house were closed; yet still the stones appeared, rolling towards her from all directions, following her around wherever she walked. Even though it was raining outside, these stones were warm and dry to the touch. A local 'wise-man' who was consulted said that it was nothing to worry about, though. Aida had just attracted the attention of what he called a "playful gnome" who wanted to be her friend. The gnome, he assured Aida's mistress, was harmless; but if she wanted to expel it, all she had to do was sprinkle salt around the house at sunset. The woman did as she was told, and the phenomena came to an instant halt. [20]

Whatever the entity behind these events truly was, it seems to have encompassed elements of fairy, poltergeist and invisible childhood friend. But perhaps this is just a matter of exotic cultural interpretation? Surely there are no accounts in existence from Western sources of invisible friends having any kind of objective reality to them, are there? Remarkably, there are. *Invizikids*, an interesting and unique book by the well-regarded English paranormal investigator Michael J Hallowell, details a number of such cases. For example, there was the bizarre story of John Tatters from Birmingham who, in the 1940s, was aware that his son had an invisible friend called Stephen. Mr Tatters thought nothing of this; until, one day, he saw his son playing catch with Stephen in the garden. As he shouted out "Here Stephen ... catch!" the ball "seemed to stop in mid-air" and then began to "sail" back across the lawn to the little boy, "as if thrown by an invisible pair of hands." Shocked, Mr Tatters dragged his son in and made him promise never to play with Stephen ever again. Apparently, he didn't. [21]

Perhaps the most poltergeist-like imaginary friend detailed in Hallowell's book, however, was Douglas, a seven-year-old boy clad in grey shorts, white shirt and flat cap, who befriended a five-year-old lad named Lewis in his rural home. Lewis would speak to Douglas, who told him that he was a ghost; he had lived on a farm, he said, and one day had fallen asleep nestled inside a haystack. However, his father had then thrust his pitchfork into the hay, not knowing that he was asleep there, accidentally impaling and killing him. This is a somewhat unlikely story, of course; but, whatever the truth of Douglas' sad demise, the poltergeist phenomena which broke out around the household seemed real enough. Objects would vanish and then reappear several days later, rapping noises were heard, drawers and cupboards would open by themselves and, in a most fairy-like touch, pennies would appear from nowhere or fall down from the ceiling. When he got angry, meanwhile, the ghost would growl, pull people's hair and dim the lights. [22]

In 1984, meanwhile, a 'child genius', Anthony McQuone, then aged two, of Weybridge in Surrey, was widely reported upon in the British Press. Amongst other things, Anthony could speak Latin, and had definitely-formed right-wing political views. He sensibly detested Arthur Scargill, for instance, the then-leader of the National Union of Miners, but described Margaret Thatcher as being "bonum" – Latin for 'good'. But how did he learn such things? Not from his father, he said. Instead, Anthony claimed to have an invisible tutor named Adam who followed him around at all times. This Adam was tall, had black hair and brown eyes, and wore a white toga and sandals – which Anthony referred to, quite correctly, as being *caligae*. He also said that Adam had a Van Dyke beard; he used this specific phrase to describe it, thereby illustrating the mysterious depths of his pognophilic knowledge, apparently being imparted to him by a dead Roman. [23]

Billy Gnome-Mates

The interesting thing about imaginary childhood friends for our present purposes, however, is that they often seem to appear in the guise of elves, pixies, gnomes or other elementals. According to Michael J Hallowell, these particular kinds of invisible friends "almost always live out-of-doors, often by the coast and in remote areas where, presumably, they are unlikely to be seen" – not unlike the fairy-folk. They also, he says, were described to him by the people he interviewed when writing his book as having bizarre names, like Mol-Mol, Koddy-Koddy, Ball Eagle and Wumpy [24]. Fairies also tend to have weird non-human names in folklore, like Rumpelstiltskin. There are very few elves I know of with names like Gertrude Shufflebottom or Derek Jarvis!

A typical description of an elf-like childhood friend is provided for us by a certain Jack Holloway, who knew just such a being going by the name of Pete-Pete who appeared at the bottom of his aunt's garden in Ashburton, Devon, during the 1950s:

> "He was always smartly dressed, and I don't recall ever seeing him wear any other colours than brown and green ... in a multitude of shades." [25]

Pete-Pete, it seemed, was obsessed with the peas which used to grow in this garden; if given permission to eat some, he would be "off like a shot", stuffing his mouth and filling his pockets. Other such descriptions contained within Hallowell's book sound somewhat fairy-like, too: "My friend Gron used to appear in the woods. He was small, and had strange skin. It was shiny." [26] "I think Venton Clay was a bit like an elf, or possibly a gnome." [27] "She was small, elfin-faced – almost urchin-like." [28] "Gumby was only two feet in height, thin and usually turned up in a green suit." [29] An odd little being called Mr He who lived in one garden, meanwhile, "had the knack of changing the colour of his garments to match his surroundings" and "existed solely on lupin seeds". [30] Finally, as a child, a woman named Karen Miller said that she became aware of a number of small beings, looking like "sprites or elves", who were living in a magical kingdom inside her walls. They would speak to her, and had "a hermaphroditic quality" together with "windswept, spiky hair" which stuck impossibly upright, and wore "gossamer-like" clothing which was both "translucent and insubstantial". [31] Imagination? Of course – but, curiously, there are parallels with such tales from all around the globe.

In South America, for example, dwarf-like fairies known as the *duende* are said to enjoy watching children playing with balls and then later appear to them, either to make their friendship or to steal their toys (although some people say that they prefer to eat infants than simply make their acquaintance). These *duende*, suggestively, are supposed to live inside the bedroom walls of small children; which sounds not a million miles away from Karen Miller's story, quoted above. [32] Interestingly, the *duende* are basically just an alternative name for the Spanish *trazgos*, one of whom we encountered in a previous chapter invisibly throwing stones around a house in 1560s Salamanca. Whilst most imaginary friends are just that, then – entirely imaginary – it does seem that a select few overlap in a most confusing way with both poltergeists and with fairies. If you should ever happen to overhear your own child alone in their room and talking to someone unseen called Malekin, therefore, it might just be time for you to panic ...

7.

From Out of Thin Air: Music and Voices

O ne thing which fairies like to do most, it seems, is dance – there are dozens of first-hand accounts in existence of people who claim to have seen them doing just that – and, in order to dance, you first need some music. It is perhaps unsurprising, then, that we also have numerous testimonies on record of fairy-melodies being picked up and listened to by human ears. This, for example, is the statement of John Graham, an old man who had lived by the famous Irish fairy-hill of Tara for most of his life, as given to WY Evans-Wentz during his travels across the Emerald Isle:

> "As sure as you are sitting down I heard the pipes there in that wood ... I heard the music another time on a hot summer evening at the Rath of Ringlestown [in County Meath], in a field where all the grass had been burned off; and I often heard it in the wood of Tara. Whenever the Good People play, you hear their music all through the field as plain as can be; and it is the grandest kind of music. It may last half the night, but once day comes, it ends." [1]

This testimony contains detailed within it many of the most commonly-reported traits of fairy-music; it is beautiful, played invisibly, occurs within known fairy-haunts and disappears in a trice. Such typical traits can also be found in the account of a servant-boy employed on Dermot MacManus' family estate in County Cork who was scything down nettles one afternoon when he heard music and dancing coming from an old, derelict garden-house at the other end of the grounds. Nobody, surely, should have been carousing in there, thought the boy – the doors and window-panes were gone, it was empty and unfurnished, and most of the staircase had collapsed. Going over to check on affairs, though, he could hear the party getting louder; laughter, stamping feet and merry conversation could all be discerned quite clearly. But then, as he got within a short distance of the place, these sounds all stopped in an instant and the area fell down into a dead silence. Puzzled, the boy ran inside the wreck, heaved himself up onto the top floor, and found that there was no-one anywhere to be seen. Looking out through the empty door-frame, however, he realised that the fairy-fort of Lis Ard lay directly in the path of the old house, less than a quarter of a mile away. He knew then that it must have been the fairies having one of their dances and decided to retreat, the unearthly music springing up again behind him as he did so, as if to mock him. [2]

This is an extremely picturesque and evocative story, and sounds almost like a classic folk-tale in its beauty and otherworldliness – and yet it is presented, at least, as having been a genuine occurrence. Given Dermot MacManus' already-explored beliefs about fairies and the Irish soul, however, is it reasonable of us to suspect that it might perhaps have been somewhat embroidered? Not necessarily. There are, after all, several other accounts on record of named persons, not of a notably Celtic-nationalist bent themselves, who have also heard such performances. For instance, Thomas Wood, the well-known English composer and author, once heard a disembodied voice calling his name whilst out camping in the wilds of Dartmoor in 1922. The next day, he returned to the same spot in which the voice had sounded, and heard music emanating from the ether instead:

> "It was overhead, faint as a breath. It died away, came back louder, over me, swaying like a censer that dips. It lasted 20 minutes. Portable wireless sets were unknown in 1922. My field glasses assured me no picnickers were in sight. It was not a gramophone nor was it an illusory noise in my ears. This music was essentially harmonic, not a melody nor an air. It sounded like the weaving together of tenuous fairy sounds. I listened with every faculty drawn out to an intensity ... The music drifted into silence. No more came, then or since. I was reasonably certain that I had been deliberately encouraged to listen to the supernatural." [3]

Hearing Things

This all sounds pleasant enough so far, but sometimes the fairy-music which is heard is said to be ominously hypnotic, if not dangerous, in its nature. For example, some fairy-music which is meant to have been heard by a Welsh servant from the Gwynedd area named David Williams sometime in the 1800s seems to have led to a classic 'missing-time' experience, of the kind so beloved of contemporary ufologists. Walking home behind his mistress one night, Williams thought she was merely a few minutes ahead of him. When he arrived home, however, he professed himself to be amazed that she had in fact got there three hours before him. Why was this? Apparently, it was because Williams had undergone some kind of a vision. First of all he had seen a "brilliant meteor" in the sky, followed by a "ring or hoop of fire" inside which two small people, one male and one female, and both "handsomely dressed", were stood. This hoop descended down to earth, the two fairies jumped out of it, and drew a circle on the ground inside which dozens of tiny men and women then appeared, dancing round and round to the sound of "the sweetest music that ear ever heard". Entranced, Williams stopped for a few minutes – or so he thought – and listened. Eventually, the hoop of fire returned and the original two fairy-folk jumped up inside it and flew off into the night sky, their companions disappearing into nothing. [4] Of course, this could have always just have been an imaginative excuse by Williams for his getting home late; but if not, then the story certainly speaks eloquently of the entrancing power of the music of the fairies.

And 'entrancing' is surely the right word to use here; such experiences do sound very much as if they have taken place in some kind of trance-state, perhaps implying that fairy-music has its origins very much within the head (or ears) of the beholder. This explanation for the phenomenon seemed to be suggested by the maverick American psychologist Julian Jaynes, in an account of his own experiences with such things. In his youth, Jaynes tells us, and right through into his twenties, whilst "walking in woods or along a beach, or climbing hills or almost anything lonely", he would:

> "... quite often suddenly become conscious that I was hearing in my head improvised symphonies of unambiguous beauty. But at the very moment of my becoming conscious of the fact, not loitering even for a measure, the music vanished. I would strain to call it back. But there was nothing there. Nothing but deepening silence." [5]

For Jaynes the psychologist, of course, this was not truly fairy-music at all but was, rather, "undoubtedly being composed in my right hemisphere and heard somehow as a semi-hallucination." Phantom music in this view is thus merely an unusual auditory hallucination being caused by the unconscious functioning of the right-hand side of the brain.

The Choir Invisible

Phantom music is also associated with poltergeists and not just fairies, however, although both types of tune seem in many ways to be extremely similar. Often, for example, poltergeist-music is said to sound every bit as beautiful and ethereal as fairy-music does, sometimes being so lovely that it is deemed to be somehow spiritual or holy in nature. Sounds of "ineffably sweet" and "most exquisite" music were heard during the haunting of a young girl named Mary Jobson at her house near Sunderland in 1839/40, for instance, a case during which numerous bizarre religious phenomena were said to have occurred alongside the more typical poltergeist incidents, with the apparition of a lamb (the symbol of Christ) being sighted, and voices claiming to be those of the Virgin Mary and Jesus being heard. The heavenly music itself reappeared here continually over the course of some 16 weeks, sometimes sounding "something like ... an organ, but more pleasing", and often featuring audible angelic voices singing the words to holy songs. Upon one occasion, Mary's father heard what he called "the sweetest music" for a period of nearly two hours, and another visitor to the home professed to have heard up to three disembodied voices singing hymns "very distinctly". Another witness, meanwhile, said that this "most beautiful music" sounded as if it was being produced by "musical glasses, when skilfully played upon". [6]

Sometimes such pleasant music is heard at the culmination of a poltergeist haunting, as with the case of a spirit calling itself 'Ann Merrick' in 1850s Ohio. This ghost, after throwing a tantrum with the furniture, suddenly decided to leave its victims in peace, the haunted house becoming quiet for a period only for "strains of the most exquisite harmony" to then burst out, even though there were no musical instruments present inside the building. The ghost played some "familiar airs" to all and sundry, but the best and most touching seemed to be of its own composition. Presumably this was intended to indicate that 'Ann' was flying up towards the gates of Heaven at last. [7]

Such accounts pale into insignificance when compared with the ghostly musical activities reported from séances during the nineteenth-century heyday of Spiritualism, however. The historian of the religion EW Capron, for example, gives the following remarkable account of musical phenomena he allegedly experienced in the presence of an American medium named Mrs Tamlin:

> "After sitting for a few minutes, we heard a low sound like a distant locomotive whistle. Soon, however, the sound grew louder, and softened into the most exquisite music. One of the company was requested to sing and she did so; the most beautiful music accompanied. It was like the notes of an exquisite Aeolian harp, but any attempt to describe its beauty would fail ... At times it would resemble the finest conceivable tones of the human voice and almost seem to be dissolved into words." [8]

To Spiritualists, such music came from the friendly dead, eager to demonstrate the beauty and refined sensibilities which lay on 'the Other Side'. To others, such sweet airs were an incontrovertible sign of a fairy-haunting. That such assumptions were merely cultural constructs, however, can easily be demonstrated by the fact that descriptions of phantom music also exist free of any association whatsoever with either poltergeists or with fairies. An account of a vicar from the county of Cardiganshire collected during the well-known 'Welsh Revival' of 1904-05 (when there was a widespread upsurge in faith amongst the Protestants of that country), for example, shows this fact very clearly. At Christmas 1904, this man was riding up a hill to see some parishioners, when all of a sudden he heard voices singing from above. At first, he thought he was imagining things, but then:

> "... the voices seemed to increase in volume, until at last they became quite overpowering ... the wonderful harmony seemed to be borne on me entirely from the outside, and was as real to my senses as anything I have ever heard. The moment the refrain would come to an end it would be restarted, the volume becoming greater and greater. To me it was an exquisite sensation." [9]

To the vicar, however, these were angels singing, not fairies or poltergeists.

Come Dancing

In several of these instances, the airs were heard not by some lone passer-by, as in most of the fairy-narratives we have so far cited, but by a number of people at once. If these were also hallucinatory in their nature, as someone like Jaynes might suggest, then they seem to have been collective hallucinations which also, in some cases, reoccurred again and again in the same place over a period of some time. These are not normal hallucinations in any usual sense of the word. There is also the problem that collective visual hallucinations have sometimes taken place in association with fairy-music being heard. A Welshman named Evan Roberts, for instance, interviewed in 1973, described the following tale as having been passed down to him by his grandmother:

> "... the women and all the family would go up to the peat bog on a fine day to help with the peat – to dry it and carry it into ricks. And there on some warm misty day they would hear the fairies – so they said. They heard some sound – some music, sweet music. Then the mist would open and suddenly they would see a circle of tiny

Fairies dance in a ring around an understandably entranced country-maiden in this picture by the prominent Pre-Raphaelite painter John William Waterhouse.

A famous and oft-reproduced old woodcut of a ring of fairies dancing around to music. Note the door leading into the fairy-hill on the left, and the apparent 'nature-spirit' in the leaves of the tree to the right. Was this the kind of sight that David Williams of Gwynedd saw whilst walking home behind his mistress one fateful night during the 1800s?

Fairies are often said to have been seen dancing to the music they supposedly create, as in these two paintings by William Blake and William Holmes Sullivan.

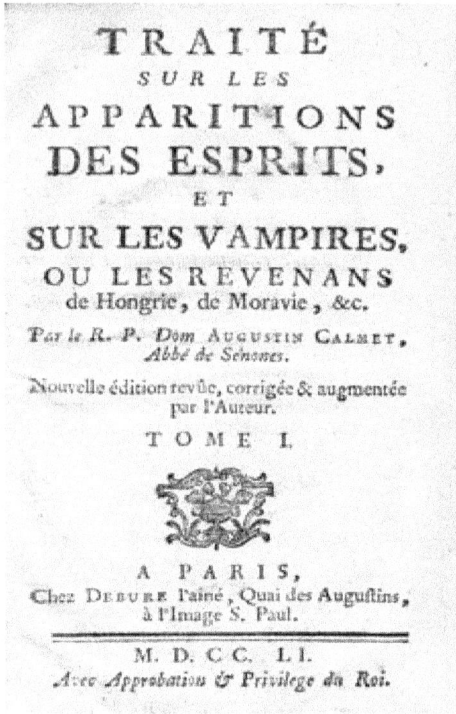

Dom Augustine Calmet's 1751 *Traité sur les Apparitions des Esprits ...* in which the strange tale of Garnier the Ghost was told, and Martin del Rio's 1599 *Disquisitionum Magicarum ...* in which the story of the Drepano spook first appeared. Both were very talkative, and both were probably incorrigible liars.

Hark! The herald brownies sing.

beings dancing and disappearing immediately. That was the story of the fairies and my grandmother conscientiously believed that she had seen such a thing." [10]

The appearance of the dancing fairies here, however, was perhaps simply a case of people seeing what they expected to see. It is conceivable that if you live in an environment where you have been told that phantom music is produced exclusively by fairies, you will have been culturally predisposed towards having some kind of confirmatory vision in order to account for any such experience. It is significant that, in many such tales, the fairy-sighting occurs *after* the music itself has already been heard. In such cases the visual apparition, it might be said, simply backs up the preceding auditory one.

For instance, in Dorset there is a well-known tradition of 'Music Barrows' – hills (actually burial tumuli) upon which, it was said, if you sat down at certain magical points of the day, you would hear fairy-music. Perhaps it was familiarity with such legends which supposedly allowed a Reverend ART Bruce to rest upon a Dorset barrow named Bottlebrush Down one evening during the 1920s and then see "a crowd of little people in leather jerkins" appear from nowhere and begin to dance around him. [11] If you live in a culture in which fairies are not supposed to exist, though, then when you hear phantom music it seems less likely that your brain will conjure up accompanying sights in order to account for the fact; and, if the source remains unseen, then it seems not entirely unreasonable for someone to attribute the event to a ghost or poltergeist.

The Witch Who Sang

Probably the most incredible musical spirit of all, though, was the Bell Witch, whom we met earlier on making a young girl vomit up pins. The Witch enjoyed singing a great deal, it seems, and even composed her own songs. The lyrics of her favourite self-penned ditty were recorded for posterity by Richard Williams Bell, one of the sons of the affected household, and go like this:

> Come my heart and let us try
> For a little season
> Every burden to lay by
> Come and let us reason.
>
> What is this that casts you down?
> Who are those that grieve you?
> Speak and let the worst be known,
> Speaking may relieve you.
>
> Christ by faith I sometimes see
> And He doth relieve me,
> But my fears return again,
> These are they that grieve me.
>
> Troubled like the restless Sea,
> Feeble, faint and fearful,
> Plagued with every sore disease,
> How can I be cheerful?

The Witch sang this song to the sick mother of the Bell household every day in an attempt to aid her recovery, apparently. According to witnesses, it was delivered with great skill and beauty: "No rhythmical sound or melody ever fell upon the ear with greater pathos, coming as it did like a volume of sympathy from a bursting heart." [12] No doubt the delivery was better than the rather saccharine and evangelical lyrics reproduced above, then. RW Bell does claim to have heard this song being performed by the Witch several times himself, incidentally; whilst many readers will no doubt find his claims hard to believe, unlike with many of the supposed events in this haunting the ghost's song does not appear to have been a later folkloric addition to the narrative.

Strangely, however, the land surrounding the Bell farmstead in Tennessee was also noted for manifestations of what might, if the Witch had never been heard of there, simply been called fairy-music. For instance, in 1866 two men, John A Gunn and AL Bartlett, had occasion to be in the vicinity of the Red River, which runs for 100 miles throughout Kentucky and Tennessee, on the side where the Bells owned land. After drinking from the river they started up a nearby hill, when suddenly "a sweet strain of music pierced their ears like a volume of symphony vibrating the air." Both men, entranced, stopped and sat down, listening to the "ravishing melody" for half an hour. Apparently:

> "It was unlike any music they had ever heard. The modulating sound was indescribable and unsurpassingly sweet. It was utterly impossible to discover from whence it came. The whole atmosphere seemed thrilled with vibrating euphony and the gentlemen were caught up, as it were, on wings of ecstasy." [13]

The source of this music was later said to have been the Witch – despite the fact that this music was heard in 1866, and the Witch had disappeared from the area almost 50 years earlier. But then, as the tale's recorder says, the spirit "was a musical witch, and the circumstance is characteristic of the acts performed years before."

Heard But Not Seen
If poltergeists and fairies could sing, though, then it does follow, quite naturally, that both must have been conceived of as having voices. Apparently this is indeed so. According to an analysis performed upon 500 historical hauntings by the researchers Alan Gauld and Tony Cornell during the 1970s, for instance, 26% of cases in their sample involved what they termed 'voices, groans, whistles, etc' (a slightly portmanteaux categorisation, sadly[14]). Medieval and Renaissance authorities upon such topics are equally clear upon the matter; the fairy-folk were thought to be able to talk in human tongues. When discussing the topic of brownies, for instance, the medieval English writer Gervaise of Tilbury, in his *Otia Imperialia*, a notable thirteenth-century compendium of wonders, says that you can recognise when a home has a brownie living there quite easily – as, first of all, the unseen spirit would pass amongst stones, wood and household objects making a noise and, secondly, because they would talk to their victims just as easily as if they were human beings themselves. [15]

Sometimes, such spooks could be quite chatty, and a few made use of their ethereal voices in order to spin their human victims implausible yarns about their ultimate places of origin, just like we saw 'Malekin' doing earlier. Another such instance is supposed to have occurred in the

German town of Cyrenbergh in 1349, when a disembodied hand of the type seen surprisingly often during poltergeist hauntings suddenly appeared in a certain house and allowed itself to be both seen and touched. This hand – which was "small and gracious", apparently – used to create an almighty din whenever visitors who it deemed to be 'shameless' were allowed into the house by the place's owners. We know that this was the reason why the spook created a noise, as it developed a disembodied voice and told everyone so! It also said that its name was Reyneke, that it was a living man not a ghost, and that, despite this fact, it lived with several of its fellow-beings inside some unspecified nearby "hollow mountain", as if it was a dwarf or *kobold*. [16]

Telling Tales
Another such spook which made use of a disembodied voice to tell tall tales is said to have appeared in 1135 in the French city of Le Mans, in the house of a certain magistrate called Nicolas. At first, the invisible spirit played the usual pranks; it made loud crashes, making the building shake, threw stones, drummed, moved plates, cushions and other items around, lit candles placed far away from any fire, put soot and seed pellets in food, and twisted and knotted up thread which the magistrate's wife was intending to spin into fantastical and elaborate patterns which could not be unravelled. At night, a disembodied young female voice could be heard, sighing and repeating mournfully that her name was Garnier. When asked where she had come from, this 'Garnier' spun a tale every bit as elaborate as the patterns she had made in the thread:

> "Oh dear, where have I come from? From what far away country, through how many storms, dangers, snows, cold, fire and bad weather have I arrived at this spot?"

Garnier didn't specifically say where exactly this "far away country" was, but the implication seems to have been that it was actually purgatory. After all, the poltergeist explicitly asked for Masses to be said for its soul, and asked Nicolas' wife Amica – whom it referred to as "sister-in-law" – to donate some clothes to the poor in its name. The ghost also implied that, though it had been given no power by God to do evil over them, it had been followed to the house by a troop of unclean demons, or "wicked troops", against whom it recommended Nicolas and his family seek protection in the sign of the cross. It also took advantage of its privileged position to inform several people in the household whether they were destined for damnation or salvation after death, and to answer questions about past and future events.

The tale exists in a few slightly different versions, however, and is full of potential confusions. One version has it that Nicolas did indeed have a dead sibling named Garnier, and that the spirit's reference towards Amica being its "sister-in-law" was meant literally. Another account, though, says that Nicolas had no such relative, and that the reference to Amica was intended only affectionately or metaphorically. This is because, in the translation of the narrative into French by the Benedictine monk Dom Augustin Calmet, who included the tale in his 1751 *Traité sur les Apparitions des Esprits*, he uses the word *génie* to describe the ghost. This is the French version of the Latin *genius*, which refers not to a spirit of the dead as such, but to the tutelary or ancestral spirit of a particular family; a brownie or *lar* (a type of Roman household god we shall examine later), essentially. However, in the original 1180

Latin account by the ecclesiastical historian Hugues du Mans, the poltergeist is described as "a fantastic being, usually called a faun in pagan books".

Whilst there is much uncertainty about what type of spirit precisely this entity was, then, there is at least some suggestion that it was more a kind of invisible tutelary fairy than it was a returning dead person. This too raises questions, though – for fauns and brownies were not meant to inhabit purgatory, where it appears that Garnier was claiming to have come from. Only the sinful dead lived there. We can presume from all this, perhaps, that whichever version should turn out to have been the most accurate, the spook was simply lying. Maybe this is why, when the Bishop of Le Mans eventually sent out several learned exorcists to speak with and then banish it, Garnier simply refused to talk to them and seems to have just disappeared. To engage in argument with such erudite persons would only have exposed its own ignorance, maybe. [17]

Liar, Liar

Martin del Rio, a Spanish Jesuit theologian and chronicler of sorcery, ghosts and other allied topics, provides another especially interesting example of a fairy-poltergeist that could both talk and sing in his influential book *Disquisitionum Magicarum*, or 'Investigations into Magic', first published in 1599. In this book, he talks of what he terms a "familiar spirit" – that is, a ghost attached to members of a certain specific family, like a tutelary brownie – which haunted a house in Drepano, Greece, during 1585. Here, it did the usual things, like throwing around stones and other objects. Somewhat less expectedly, however, when the unseen fairy heard a young man playing a musical instrument, it decided to accompany him verbally by singing what del Rio termed "scandalous songs". Another time, meanwhile, the family familiar is supposed to have accompanied the man and wife of the house on a trip to another town, going ahead of them on the way back and issuing "loud shouts" to the household staff, warning them that their master and mistress had got soaked in the rain and instructing them to light the fire so that they could dry themselves off.

Far from being touched by this considerate and distinctly brownie-like behaviour, however, the entity's master was annoyed at all the fuss being made and threatened the ghost with being exorcised by a Jesuit. Indignant, the brownie turned boggart and began making a great noise and using its voice to make threats, saying that it would simply hide when the exorcist arrived. The priest never did arrive, though; when the distressed householders went to see him, he simply gave the daughter of the household (who, typically, was most affected by the spirit) a holy amulet and recommended that the family stop talking to the ghost and asking it to reveal "hidden things" as they had been doing. In his opinion, the fairy was of the Devil's party, and its words all lies in any case, so there was no point in talking to it. The family did as advised and, ultimately, the spook disappeared, no doubt bored of the one-sided conversations in which it was now fated to engage. [18]

The stories of Reyneke, Garnier and the Drepano brownie are all very old, of course, and it is anyone's guess as to whether or not they refer in some way to real events or are simply quaint literary inventions; what is interesting, however, is that all seem to feature genuine motifs of both fairy-lore and poltergeistry, thereby illustrating once more the nexus that exists between these creatures. If these stories teach us one thing, though, it is that both ghosts and fairies alike have long been deemed to be incorrigible liars – and bizarrely, it is not just through our ears that their untruths can enter. As our next chapter shall show, they can apparently enchant our eyes to receive their absurd fictions as well.

8.

Seeing Things: Glamour, Pishogue and Apparitions

Two particularly interesting old types of fairy trick were labelled by the Irish under the names of *glamour* and *pishogue*. *Glamour* is where the fairies cast a kind of spell on something intending to alter its appearance somehow; *pishogue* is where they cast a spell on *us*, making us see things that aren't really there. The classic example is of the mischievous *sidhe* making a hungry traveller see a pile of horse manure as a lovely, sweet cake lying by the roadside – with predictable results. In some versions of the joke, the manure is full of pins. I sometimes wonder if analogous processes might not have an absolutely central role to play in some poltergeist phenomena.

Take, for example, the actual appearance of the fairies themselves, whenever they deign to make themselves visible to human eyes. Are they really there in the first place or just some kind of visual representation being created – whether by the mind of the percipient, or by the 'fairies' themselves – in order to account in some way for the presence and actions of invisible entities, to make them seem more comprehensible to us somehow? The writer Janet Bord certainly suggests so, when she tells of the "race of little red men" who, the native Embu people used to say, inhabited the hills of a place called Kwa Ngombe in Kenya. An elderly man called 'Old Salim' described his own encounter with these entities to some Western visitors in the 1920s, telling them how, when he had climbed to the top of the hills one time, an "icy cold wind" blew, before he and his native companions were "pelted with showers of small stones by some unseen adversaries." Looking back up as he retreated, Old Salim described how he saw "scores of little red men hurling pebbles and waving defiance from the craggy heights." [1] As far as I can tell, no Westerners have ever seen these particular African fairies, however. But why is this? Bord's proposed explanation is a good one:

> "Did Salim really see the little red men? Or did the stones have some other origin? They might have been hailstones, or they might have been a poltergeist manifestation, with in both instances the frightened natives seeing the little red men because they expected to see them. When an area becomes populated

with dwarfs, real or imaginary, they tend to be blamed for all negative events; this is human nature, all over the world." [2]

Maybe so. After all, it is eminently possible for people to hallucinate fairy-like beings and then blame hauntings upon them, even in the modern West. The paranormal researcher John Keel, for example, unearthed a very strange 1970 case from the New York neighbourhood of Forest Hills, in which a 12-year-old girl with a medical history of blackouts, seizures and hallucinations began seeing a series of 'red men' of a different kind around her home – namely, apparitions of Native American Indians! These entities seemed so real to the girl that she actually engaged in full-blown conversations with them. Strangely, however, the beings were also quite real to the girl's mother – albeit whenever she saw them they were not adult-sized, as they were to her daughter, but appeared "diminutive". This is particularly interesting in light of the fact that, traditionally, the Good Folk were often said to be able to alter their size in a similar manner, making these particular apparitions seem quite fairy-like in nature. Either way, after seeing them, both females decided that their house was haunted, and moved away[3]. Whilst we must suspect, given the medical history of the main witness involved, that these particular spectres were merely hallucinatory, we can well imagine, if doors had begun slamming around the household in question, or pebbles being flung, who would have found themselves getting the blame for it all ...

Going Postal

Look now at another fairy-sighting, this time from the Isle of Man, in light of what has just been said above. The postman involved was interviewed personally by the folklorist William Martin, around three years after the strange events concerned. According to Martin:

> "One evening during the summer months of 1884, the driver of the mail-cart from one of the towns in the island started on his round to collect the mail-bags from the surrounding district in the usual manner. He was due at his destination about half-past one o'clock in the morning, but did not arrive until nearly half-past five, when he appeared dreadfully scared and agitated. Being asked to account for his delay, he solemnly related that when six miles from home he was beset by a troop of fairies, all of whom were particularly well-dressed in red suits and provided with lanterns. They stopped his horse, threw the mail-bags into the road, and danced around them in the well-known manner usual with fairies. The poor postman struggled with them in vain. No sooner did he succeed in replacing a bag than it was again immediately thrown out. This continued until the appearance of daylight, when the fairies apparently thought it was time for them to take their departure, which they eventually did, leaving the postman in a highly nervous and exhausted state. After resting a short time to collect his scattered wits, he succeeded in replacing the mails in his cart, and reached the end of the journey without further adventures." [4]

If it was possible for Old Salim to see little red men in order to account for objects invisibly flying around him, then why should a Manx postman not also see little men *dressed* in red when something similar happened to him? Perhaps the subconscious minds of both men just drew upon well-known (to them) cultural tropes, and then used corresponding visual representations of them somehow in order thereby to 'explain' the fact that various objects around them were quite flagrantly disobeying the laws of physics. After all, we moderns, if confronted by such an event nowadays, would 'see' something there in order to account for it all, too; namely, the actions of an invisible agency of the type we now term 'poltergeists'. No actual visual representation is even necessary when such a *mental* representation takes place, it will be noted. Hallucination – or *glamour*, or *pishogue* – is no longer even needed.

Kids See the Funniest Things

Apparitions do appear necessary to certain witnesses of poltergeist phenomena, however, perhaps because they make such things seem more comprehensible. For example, there is a very odd Irish case from County Cork in 1928, wherein the children of a polt-infested farmhouse saw some self-evidently ridiculous but clearly fairy-related sights such as "a great many" people milling about in the fields, some of whom were old men with "flowing grey beards" and wearing "high hats", but most of whom appeared to be women and small boys without any shoes on, and wearing leather belts around their waists. Most peculiar of all, one of them was walking on his head; the children who saw him thought he had no feet! An elderly female fairy came up to the little girl who was watching this scene amazed with her brother, and demanded that she remove her overalls. She then added that, if she saw her again, she would make her take off her dress and hand it over too, as she rather liked it. The next morning, these same overalls were found draped over the garden gate.

Prior to these sights being seen, however, more typical phenomena had been experienced upon the haunted farm; knives, clothes and bars of soap were thrown about the house, people's caps were pulled off, and inept threats written on pieces of paper dropped down from the ceiling (one of which read, perhaps significantly, "I will come *down the chimney* and steal Nana's glasses"). Perhaps the children saw their visions in order to help them comprehend these strange events, then? Maybe so, for after the Little People had been sighted in the fields, the poltergeist phenomena actually began to become more fairy-like in nature; the children were pinched by unseen hands, money went missing (eventually the father of the children was forced to take all his cash to the bank, as scrawled notes from the ghost threatened to rob them of every penny), and a bizarre black cat appeared inside the house. It would get into beds during the day, and had a very odd appearance, seeming "very small at times, and very big at other times with very long hind legs." At night, it could be seen exiting the house through a window, even though it was shut; from there it would get inside the hen coop and steal the eggs. This all makes it sound less like a real feline, of course, and more like the *cait sidhe/sith*, the well-known supernatural fairy-cats of Irish and Scottish tradition. Furthermore, tools were even taken away and 'borrowed', just like the fairies were supposed to do with human tools in folklore. Upon one occasion a pick-axe disappeared and then was returned, broken, together with an apologetic note from the spirits saying how they had taken it to use for themselves, but sadly could not avoid having broken it into little pieces.

Other apparitions were seen around the farm too, however. Having speculated in a letter about how the curse of a dismissed servant-girl may have been to blame for events, the farmer who owned the affected property then seemed to gain ostensible confirmation of this suspicion in a very silly vision experienced by his daughter who, as the man put it:

> "... said she saw the servant maid I had employed ride up the yard on a horse, her mother following after on a motor bicycle, and then followed by a long train of red-coated figures on horseback." [5]

Overall, then, we can see how the child's visions during this haunting seem to have been a garbled mixture of traditional Irish fairy-lore (red-coated figures, high-hatted people dancing) and half-digested suppositions about the presumed guilt of the sacked servant-girl. The people on horseback could even be viewed as being a version of the *Tuatha dé Danann*, the half-god, half-ancestor figures from Irish mythology who were supposed still to ride across the countryside on their magic steeds, or to appear in diminished form as the *sidhe*. It is tempting to suggest with this case that, at first, the girl saw fairies around the farm because she was culturally-primed to account for poltergeist phenomena in such a way; but that, when the idea about the maidservant's curse took root in her head later on, she began to adapt her visions accordingly. Whatever happened, it is surely worth mentioning that the girl's father said that he could not account for the whole haunting himself, "unless it is what people call a 'Pishogue', or a demon sent to annoy us." [6] Even he seems to have thought that his children were being made to see things which were not really there, then ..

Gnome Gym

However, it does seem to be a curious fact that certain persons who we would *not* expect to be culturally-primed to see fairies in order to account for poltergeist activity sometimes claim to have witnessed odd, gnome-like beings during hauntings too. For instance, a strange tale is told about some alleged events which supposedly took place in an Edinburgh flat in that city's Rothesay Place, probably between 1958 and 1961, after the flat's owner, a certain 'Mrs van Hoorne' (a pseudonym), bought a second-hand dressing-table. This dressing-table had apparently previously belonged to a sailor who had since died, and the poltergeist events centred around the item of furniture accordingly. Its drawers are said to have repeatedly opened and closed by themselves, and various objects placed on top of it would inexplicably throw themselves down to the ground. In addition, a "shimmering circle of light" was claimed to have been seen moving across the flat's walls, a phenomenon seemingly in possession of a certain amount of responsive intelligence. Most interestingly, though, Mrs van Hoorne is reported to have witnessed a full-blown apparition flitting around the haunted flat as well. It was about one foot tall, and dressed nattily in a brown jacket and red trousers. Obviously, it was a fairy! [7]

Another such unexpected sighting of a ghostly gnome allegedly occurred during the 1950s at Wildenstein Castle in the southern German state of Baden-Württemberg. The castle had been said to be haunted for at least a century, with various apparitions being sighted and poltergeist phenomena such as floating wine glasses being experienced there [8]. It was only at the surprisingly late date of 1955, however, that the place's resident 'goblin', as it became known, was first seen. According to the fortress' owner, a Baron Hofer von Lobenstein, he was letting the castle dogs out one night when he saw a little man with a beard, who was lit from behind by a small blue flame – blue flames being a traditional indication of the approach of a ghost, it might be noted. Weirdly, this gnome-like being came up to the Baron and hopped around him before then suddenly disappearing. The Baron's wife saw the little bearded man one day too; she said that he was two-foot tall, dressed in a peaked cap and yellow vest, and was performing somersaults in one of the rooms! [9] Can we really say that either the Baron or the Baroness would have been specifically *expecting* to have seen bizarre and comical apparitions such as these, though? It seems unlikely, to say the least.

A somewhat melancholy-looking individual strongly resembling alleged TV 'funnyman' Alastair McGowan is surrounded by hallucinatory household and fire-side spirits in this old aquatint, used as a frontispiece by Harry Price to his 1945 book *Poltergeist Over England*.

At a haunted farmhouse in County Cork in 1928, the farmer's children professed to be able to see crowds of fairies with "flowing beards" and wearing "high hats", as in the stereotypical image reproduced above. Less stereotypical, however, was the fact that one of these gnomes was apparently walking around on his head due to the fact that he had no feet!

A 19th-century painting by the Scottish artist John Duncan of the *Tuatha de Danaan* out riding on horseback. Now you just have to imagine them all racing around on motorbikes!

Rothesay Place in Edinburgh, and Castle Wildenstein in Germany – both the sites of alleged 20th-century gnome-sightings occurring in conjunction with poltergeist phenomena.

A solitary late-night traveller comes across a Will-o'the-Wisp. He would be wise not to follow it over any marsh-land.

Encountered outdoors, a strange light traditionally became a 'fairy'.

Seen outside of the castle here, this light floating within a grove of trees could be interpreted as being some kind of nature-spirit. If seen *inside* the castle, however, it would probably be interpreted as being a ghost. Is either perspective really entirely correct, however?

TC Kermode, who claims to have witnessed fairies dressed like tiny British Red-coats marching around within a circle of light somewhere on the Isle of Man.

TRI-STATE SPOOK LIGHT

25¢

it Actually Exists SEE for Yourself...

Authentic Guide by Bob

(ALL RIGHTS RESERVED)

A 1955 guide to US 'spooklights' ; an alternative term for 'earthlights', the phrase provides a good example of how such luminescent bodies are often personified as either ghosts or fairies. The booklet must be reliable, incidentally, as it professes to be an 'Authentic Guide by Bob'.

From this ... (above) to this (below). The temptation to personify mysterious flitting lights as being goblins – or UFOs, ghosts or demons – seems irresistible; and yet, as Patrick Harpur shows, the lights themselves are apparently real and, as he puts it, "culturally undifferentiated".

Strike a Light

The issue of UFOs in relation to this whole topic is another highly interesting one – as the basic definition of a UFO (at night, at least) is a strange light in the sky. However, strange lights are also meant to appear during poltergeist manifestations – the average witness might perhaps be expected to conclude that 'the light *is* the ghost' in such an instance – and fairies, too, were supposed to appear as bright, flitting lights. In the past, if you saw a strange light hovering in the night sky, then you would, following the cultural beliefs of your time, most probably have said that it was a fairy (or, in some societies, a witch); now, you might say that it was an alien spaceship. This, too, could be seen as being some form of metaphorical cultural *pishogue*. The lights are probably indeed there, but the explanations provided for them seem likely to be subjective.

That lights are definitely seen during poltergeist cases can be demonstrated quite easily, though. During the notorious affair of the Enfield poltergeist, for instance, mentioned earlier, one witness, a John Burcombe, saw the following odd sight on a staircase in the haunted house:

> "I saw this light ... It was the equivalent, I should say, of twelve inches vertical. It looked like a fluorescent light behind frosted glass, which burned fiercely and gradually faded away." [10]

A 1962 poltergeist case in the town of Clayton, North Carolina, which was investigated by the parapsychologist William G Roll, meanwhile, centred almost entirely around flashes of paranormal light. These illuminations had some very strange properties to them, according to one witness: "when you stand on the inside, it looks as if it's on the outside; when you go outside, it looks as if it's inside." [11] The Bell Witch, likewise, would frequently appear in the form of "lights like a candle or lamp flitting across the yard and through the field." [12] At a Scottish farmstead named Ringcroft in 1695, amidst other bizarre phenomena, actual *fireballs* were seen flying around the place [13]. The home of a Mrs D Brierley in Cheltenham, Gloucestershire, meanwhile, was haunted during WWI by typical polt phenomena such as bangings on furniture, invisible footsteps, and objects moving about. Perhaps slightly less typically, lights of two distinct different varieties were seen around the house, too; some were described as being "sort of luminous balloons floating near [the] ceiling" whilst others were "cone-shaped fountains" which leapt from around a foot above the floor right up to the ceiling, and which were "very beautiful" [14]. This list is in no way exhaustive.

In terms of the fairies, meanwhile, odd luminosities – known specifically as 'fairy-lights' – were often said to manifest around fairy-forts. Dermot MacManus, for example, spoke to a woman living near to the Irish fairy-fort of Crillaun in County Mayo, who was out late one Hallowe'en – a traditionally fairy-haunted time – and saw the fort lit up with literally hundreds of little white lights. They all flew up as one, in formation, and passed over a small lough nearby before descending down to another fort on the other side. This woman's sister also saw the fairy-lights of Crillaun; and yet when she saw them they were of many colours, red, green, blue and yellow. They were, she said, "as bright and steady as electric lights" [15]. Famously, Will-o'-the-Wisps and Jack-o'-Lanterns were also said to be fairies in luminous form. By flitting around like lamps, they would lure men to their deaths in marshes, leading many now to say that these wraiths were merely ignited marsh-gases. Sometimes, however, such lights actually appear to have had some kind of rudimentary intelligence to them. Another tale told by MacManus, for instance, is of a woman encountering a bog-light which made deliberate turns and alterations in its flight-path, apparently in order to follow her home. [16]

I saw some odd lights myself, once; they were like a swarm of little green stars, incredibly bright and glittering, which shot out of a tree when I was walking around my neighbourhood one night, only a foot or so above my head. After flying from this tree on the other side of the road, they disappeared into nothing suddenly, then reappeared on the other side of me, quite close, before blinking out as they came into contact with another tree nearby. They were, it has to be said, quite beautiful, whatever they were. If I believed, in a literal sense, in the fairy-folk, then no doubt I would have said that it was them.

Stepping Into the Spotlight
A genuinely strange subcategory of all this, meanwhile, is of sightings of mysterious lights with human-like figures inside them. These are often very fairy-like indeed. For instance, the well-known UFO researcher Jenny Randles uncovered a most bizarre tale about a retired nurse from the Wirral in Merseyside, who said that she was being bothered by strange "white footballs" of light which would hover outside her bedroom window late at night before shooting away at great speed. Often, the appearance of these lights would be accompanied by odd, poltergeist-like sounds and hums, described as being like "a thousand marbles rolling down the roof". Apparently, the woman had first heard these strange noises as a child when she was awoken in bed by them one night. Looking up, she was astonished to see a light shining on her bedroom wall. Apparently, it was "bright like the moon" and looked "like a torch beam". Perhaps it was really more of a stage-spotlight, however; as she gazed at the circle, a small being with a pointed head or cap, and looking rather like a gnome, appeared within it and smiled. Then he began to dance and spin around until the little girl let out a scream, the gnome and his limelight disappearing just before the girl's dad, alerted by his daughter's wails, arrived on the scene. So affected was she by this experience that, in later life, the girl developed a phobia of garden gnomes, believing them to be cursed somehow! [17]

Naturally, many readers may be minded to dismiss this weird vision as being merely one of those odd hallucinations which sometimes occur when a person is on the edge of sleep, and I would not disagree. However, the account is certainly interesting in that the gnome-sighting apparently occurred in conjunction with poltergeist-like phenomena – the noises – and also given the fact that, in some traditions, fairies are meant to make themselves visible in the first place by stepping out from supernatural bodies of light. Probably the most oft-cited such example was collected by WY Evans-Wentz from a Mr TC Kermode, a member of the House of Keys, the Lower House of the Manx Parliament. This informant told the industrious folklorist how, one night more than 40 years previously, during the mid-1800s, he had been travelling to a party with a friend when, near a place called Beary Farm, his companion happened to glance across a small brook and, quite casually, drew his attention to the presence of the fairies. Looking over, Kermode claimed to have seen "a circle of supernatural light", which he later came to regard as being "the 'astral light', or the light of Nature, as it is called by mystics, in which spirits become visible". Into this supernatural spotlight, Kermode and his friend supposedly saw marching "a crowd of little beings smaller than Tom Thumb and his wife", in twos and threes. They were dressed all in red like British soldiers of the time, and "moved back and forth", forming themselves into order "like troops drilling". Kermode wanted to get a closer look, but his curiously blasé friend banged on the roadside wall with his stick and shouted at the little creatures, whereupon both light and fairies vanished instantly, like ghosts at cock-crow. [18]

It seems pretty self-evident that the entities witnessed in both of these visions – or hallucinations, if you prefer – had taken on the unmistakable form of different varieties of fairy-folk. However, in some other cases, the identification of such light-dwelling figures as being fairies is a little more ambiguous. For instance, just before Christmas 1910, an unnamed Oxford student and his friend were riding their horses home from the city of Limerick in Ireland, WY Evans-Wentz tells us. When they neared the County Kerry town of Listowel, they saw a light around half a mile ahead of them, moving up and down, diminishing to a tiny spark before then building back up again to a big "yellow luminous flame". Later on in their journey, the men saw another pair of these lights around a hundred yards to the right of them. Suddenly, these also extended out into long luminous flames, six feet high by four feet wide. In the middle of each flame appeared a "radiant being", of human form. The lights then moved towards one another and joined, the two beings inside seeming as if they were walking side by side. These strange entities were, apparently, "formed of a pure dazzling radiance, white like the radiance of the sun", and much brighter than the yellow flames which surrounded them [19]. These glowing beings, it seems, were viewed as being some of the Good Folk – as would have been only natural, perhaps, in Ireland in 1910.

You Little Star

The American city of Washington in 1853, however, was not particularly well-known as being a thriving centre of the fairy-faith. Instead, Spiritualism was the new religion of choice. One spirit-circle amongst the many then in operation there gathered frequently at the home of a Mr C Laurie, in which various poltergeist-like phenomena allegedly occurred during séances. Most frequently, a ring was seen, by numerous witnesses, to float around the room and play various tricks, apparently of its own accord. These phenomena were thought to be being caused by the dead daughter of Mr Laurie, who astonished all gathered there one Sunday afternoon by manifesting herself in the form of a "bright star" upon the wall. This star's appearance was remarkable, being:

> "... so luminous as to light the otherwise darkened room to a high degree. It appeared as large as a saucer at first, but gradually contracted until it disappeared. One of the most remarkable things connected with this manifestation was the outline of a tiny human form – resembling the figure of a little girl – which was distinctly seen inside the little star. The hue of the star is described by those who saw it to have been like the most brilliant colours of the rainbow combined." [20]

The curtains were drawn back and daylight allowed in, but the star simply outshone the light of the sun; it only disappeared when Mrs Laurie approached what she saw as being her dead child with outstretched arms in an attempt to embrace her. As soon as she did so, the shining child vanished back beyond the veil.

That, then, was a poltergeist – conceived of by those present as being a spirit of the dead – appearing in the form of a human figure within a light, and not a fairy. The description of the star being somehow saucer-like is also interesting, however; it reminds one of UFOs. Are there any accounts on record of UFOs which have manifested themselves in the form of glowing lights with humanoid figures inside, too? There are many. In 1969, for example, four people were sitting in a cafe in Pontejos on the north coast of Spain, when they saw an orange rectangle, about five metres long, hovering in the night sky outside. Inside this rectangle were five men – or things that looked like men – silhouetted, and walking around. They appeared to enter into the light from either end, go to the middle of it and then vanish. Eventually, the light simply extinguished itself, leaving behind a grey object in the shape of an upturned plate, which then flew off in a blast of light.[21] Clearly, this is what most people would now term a UFO; but need it really have been an alien spaceship?

Light Fantastic

Paul Devereux, in his important book *Earthlights*, makes the proposition that some supposed 'aliens' seen in conjunction with UFOs are actually some strange extension of the UFOs (conceived of by Devereux as actually being unusual electrical or plasma-based phenomena) themselves. As proof of this, he lists a number of cases of humanoid figures forming themselves from out of bright, glowing lights. For instance, there is the odd story of a camper staying overnight near Lake Manchester in Queensland, Australia, who encountered an eight-inch electric blue sphere buzzing around him at close quarters. Astonishingly, inside this sphere was what appeared to be a "tiny, human-like entity". It was bald, sat cross-legged with its elbows upon its knees, and stared intensely at the man. Unsurprisingly, he fled!

Having been told of this experience by the unhappy camper, an unnamed psychic later went to the lake alone to see if he could encounter such a sphere for himself. He did; a small blue ball of light, with an electric quality to it, appeared. Inside it, the psychic could see "cloud-like tonings", the darker parts of which suddenly coalesced into the same tiny, cross-legged being that the earlier witness had seen. It seemed curiously disproportioned, and became clearer the more it was looked at; eventually, it just disappeared "like the bursting of a bubble." [22] Such odd spheres would appear to be the famous 'min-min lights'; flitting luminous bodies often sighted within the Outback and inside which the native aborigines believe elemental fairy-like beings live. The aborigines seemed to think that these spirits were hairy, however; which does not quite fit in with the descriptions of the non-aborigines given above. Perhaps, when it comes to what we may as well term 'fairy-lights' after all, what the luminosity eventually ends up resolving itself into is ultimately a matter of the witness' own cultural preconditioning; or *glamour* or *pishogue*, if you want to put it another way.

I think that the last word upon this whole issue must go to Patrick Harpur who, in his fêted book *Daimonic Reality*, sees such things essentially as being externalised images of the soul. He calls strange lights "the most culturally undifferentiated [type of] apparition", saying that they are:

> "... like a universal curtain which rises to initiate a drama in which the players can be a wide variety of strange beings. Some witnesses see fairies, others spaceships. Some find that the light has conferred a sudden burst of knowledge on them; others develop psychic powers. Others still return home simply to find their house infested with a poltergeist. These lights are like omens or signs which herald a bizarre experience, a different world, a new way of life." [23]

The old way of saying this might simply have been to say that strange lights signify that a person is about to enter into the realm of faery. It is just that nowadays, it seems, that realm encompasses not just the Hidden Folk, but everything from poltergeists to UFOs as being part of it as well. As we shall see in the next section, it also apparently encompasses certain elements of the discipline of cryptozoology too ...

9.

Shaggy Dog Stories: Bogey-Beasts and Phantom Animals

A nother common *glamour* which fairies apparently like to cast is to appear as animals, a trope we should be familiar with even from the world of fiction. In *A Midsummer Night's Dream*, for example, Shakespeare talks of the famous English fairy-Trickster Puck/Robin Goodfellow (even his name is changeable) being able to appear in the form not just of a dwarfish humanoid, but also as various animals and even a variety of inanimate objects and glowing lights. Or, as Robin himself puts it:

> Sometime a horse I'll be, sometime a hound,
> A hog, a headless bear, sometime a fire,
> And neigh, and bark, and grunt, and roar, and burn,
> Like horse, hound, hog, bear, fire, at every-turn. [1]

Ben Jonson, it seems, was in broad agreement with his fellow poet and playwright when he had his own literary version of Robin boast of the pranks he liked to play on unwary travellers thus:

> Sometimes I meet them like a man,
> Sometimes an ox, sometimes a hound,
> And to a horse I turn me can,
> To trip and trot them round.

It seems that strange animals – or animal-*like* beings – encountered in the lanes and by-ways of the countryside in centuries past were once thought of as being entities like Robin Goodfellow in disguise, then, as the two Renaissance playwrights clearly show. These fairy-animals – whether conceived of literally as being fairies in shape-shifted form, or else as some separate and distinct beast-like class of elf – were known generally in Britain as the 'bogey-beasts' or 'barguests', this latter term probably meaning something like 'town-ghost' [2]. They came in a variety of shapes – dogs, calves, donkeys, headless bears, even hairy ape-like beings called 'shug-monkeys' – and are thought of by most as having been purely legendary. This general opinion may actually be to some extent wrong, however, for bogey-beasts are, apparently, still being seen, albeit under different names. Their shape-shifting nature might not be so commonly reported nowadays, but it seems obvious that certain legends surrounding well-known fortean figures like Black Dogs and uncatchable Alien Big Cats (ABCs) to some extent grew from out of these older stories about bogey-beasts.

Quite a Shock

For instance, today folkloric tales about phantom black dogs with red glowing eyes are well known from across most of the British Isles, and the various local names for them, like 'Black Shuck', 'Old Shuck' and 'Shug-Dog' will no doubt be familiar to many readers. Less well-known, though, is that around 1830 an entity known as 'Old Shock' was said to have appeared in the form of either a dog *or* a calf, that in Suffolk Shuck was sometimes observed in possession of a donkey's head on a dog's body, and that another phantom dog known as 'Old Scarf' was sometimes alleged to have adopted the guise of a black goat[3]. These older, more traditional beliefs about Shuck and his kind can be summed up in the following definition of the beast given by the vicar and amateur philologist Robert Forby in his posthumously-published 1830 dialect-dictionary, *Vocabulary of East Anglia*:

> "Old Shock [is] a mischievous goblin in the shape of a great dog, or of a calf, haunting highways and footpaths in the dark." [4]

Old Shock isn't described as being the ghost of a dead dog here, or even a real but spooky animal, but is, specifically, a "goblin", that can manifest in multiple forms. Nowadays, however, the 'standard' version of the Black Dog legend appears to have pushed the old shape-shifting fairy elements of earlier stories out of the popular mind, such aspects ending up being either forgotten about or disguised. As the folklorist Jeremy Harte put it in his own discussion about Black Dogs:

> "Behind the standard phrases which describe these apparitions – 'as large as a donkey', 'as big as a calf', 'shaggy as a bear' – there are traces of earlier stories in which they had actually *been* bears, calves and donkeys." [5]

Indeed, in Harte's view, Black Dogs did not even truly exist as a separate form of apparition in genuine tradition until nineteenth-century folklorists, with their tendency towards neat classifications of such things, began to collect sightings and then write papers upon the topic.[6]

Even the original etymology of the word 'Shuck' is surprisingly ambiguous; generally, it is seen as being derived from the Old English word *scucca*, meaning 'demon/devil', although the coincidence that the common English dialect word 'shucky', meaning 'shaggy', sounds very similar to later versions of the word *scucca* also appears to have had an influence. 'Shaggy demon', then, would seem to be the best translation of the word 'Shuck' and its variants – a term which doesn't necessarily have anything specifically to do with a phantom dog at all! Indeed, one of the earliest references to Old Shuck – written '*alde schuke*' – refers not specifically to a ghostly dog, but to a poltergeist-like "invisible unwight" ('inhuman entity') who merely has the ability to *appear* in the form of a spectral animal if he so wishes. This reference can be found in a twelfth-century narration of the life of St Margaret called, simply,

Seinte Marharete [7]. The fact that, in Yorkshire, one common name for a Black Dog is merely the generic 'Barghest' is also highly suggestive.

The Cats Came Back

Another potential way of reconceptualising these old fairy-beasts as something more comprehensible to the modern mind, meanwhile, is to try and reclassify them as having been real but misidentified flesh-and-blood animals. Sometimes, this is plausible. It has often been implied that the modern form of the increasingly rare ghostly Black Dog in Britain is the Alien Big Cat, for example, and it does seem undeniable that some large non-native cat species do actually exist in the wild throughout the British Isles. Occasionally, their corpses have even been found! [8]

Sometimes, therefore, people who think that they have seen a phantom animal may well have simply misidentified a real creature of some sort in the dark or at a distance. However, whilst there may indeed be some pumas, wild-cats and even colonies of wallabies on the loose around Britain, in general this kind of theory is not tenable as being a plausible solution to the mystery of what the old fairy-beasts really were, or are. After all, whilst there are undoubtedly some real ABCs living wild in this country, there are also some accounts of mystery-animal sightings on record from these islands which sound distinctly bogey-like in their nature.

In June and July of 1981, for instance, there were a series of sightings of unusual big cats in the area around Wellington College, a private boys' school in Berkshire. First of all, a teacher said he saw a "fox-like animal" run out of some long grass at an incredible speed, estimated to be 12 yards per second. Apparently it moved in a strange "sinuous" fashion, was about the size of an Irish setter, reddish-brown in colour and had a long tail more like a cat's than a fox's (foxes being canids, not feline). The next month, two pupils saw a "jet-black" beast which they interpreted as being feline in nature, about the size of a labrador, and with a smooth glossy coat. A few days later, a local shopkeeper came forward to say that he had seen the animal, too; he said its tail was as long as its body and, most suggestively, alleged that it had "bright red eyes" which "almost seemed to flash as if ... lit by a battery". Bizarrely, though, on the same day as the boys had their sighting, a retired couple were walking in Crowthorne Woods, near the College, when they claim to have seen a lioness with a "smooth brown-gold coat" on the loose![9] Maybe several different ABCs were prowling around the countryside near Wellington College during the summer of 1981, then, and not just one – but, if so, then it seems like an almighty coincidence.

The Camera Never Lies

The similarity between bogey-beasts and the apparently shape-shifting animal(s) seen during this case are surely quite obvious; most didn't *quite* correspond to the appearance of any actual existing animals, and one even had Shuck-like glowing red eyes! Another distinctly barguest-like mystery animal was recently seen in Britain, meanwhile, when on 9th June 2007 a Devon-based falconer named Martin Whitley went out on Dartmoor with some American tourists. Whitley was demonstrating his art to these clients when one of them suddenly pointed out a strange-looking creature walking along a path about 200 yards away. According to Whitley's own words, it was "black and grey and comparable in size to a miniature pony" with "very thick shoulders, a long, thick tail with a blunt end, and small round ears." At first, he said, it moved in a way which appeared "feline", before switching to a method of locomotion more "bear-like" in its nature. Whitley's clients, being American tourists, proceeded to take out their cameras. For once some holiday snaps proved actually to be interesting, however, as when looked at separately they appeared to untutored eyes like mine to show the animal shifting its shape from frame to frame. In a fascinating discussion of these images in *Fortean Times*, the collector of ABC-lore Merrily Harpur (esteemed cartoonist sister of Patrick) compared the beast's differing appearance to that of a cat, a bear, a boar, a pony, and various breeds of dog. [10]

Examining them myself, I think it would also be possible, however, to view the creature in some frames as being seemingly headless; which is probably an optical illusion, of course, but does nonetheless echo Shakespeare's description of Puck appearing in the form of a headless bear, quoted earlier. The other animal-forms suggested for Puck by the Bard – hound, hog and horse (well, pony anyway) – were also specifically linked with the Dartmoor monster by Harpur, too. The other similarity between this animal and the bogey-beasts of old, meanwhile, is rather obvious – namely, it is all-black in colour and has what looks like extremely shaggy hair. You could, though, argue that the photos just show an ordinary animal whose apparent 'shape-shifting' is simply a trick of the eye caused by the creature moving around and thus altering the angle at which it is seen – indeed, one local woman, Lucinda Reid, did later come forward and claim that the photos actually showed unusually-framed images of her 12-stone black Newfoundland dog Troy being taken for a walk. [11]

Whatever you think of the images yourself, some modern observers have definitely tried to link the thing with the supernatural, though. According to Harpur, some locals compared the shaggy-haired beast to the so-called 'Whisht Hounds' – a pack of phantom Black Dogs who were supposed to tear around Dartmoor under the control of Satan himself in a kind of West Country version of the Wild Hunt, a legend which apparently inspired Sir Arthur Conan Doyle to create his famous *Hound of the Baskervilles*. This is in itself fascinating as it shows how old and purportedly now long-forgotten folklore about fairy-bogeys is in actual fact still alive, only under new and different names.

A New Form of Zooform?
Fairy-lore, in fact, is still very much alive in the modern world in disguised form, and I think that it would perhaps be possible to identify three main different strands of it as being present in contemporary studies into matters fortean. Firstly, there is the branch of modern fairy-lore which is most germane to this book – namely the fact that, when what we would once have called fairy-phenomena occurs within a home or other building, we would now classify the events involved under the twin headings of 'ghostlore' and 'poltergeistry'. Secondly, as observed most famously by the French writer Jacques Vallee in his seminal book *Passport to Magonia*, there are numerous old legends concerning people supposedly being taken away to fairy-land or inside fairy-hills by the Good Folk. These tales, according to Vallee's famous theory, involving as they did such now-familiar motifs as 'missing-time', bright lights and interbreeding between human and non-human fairy-races, have simply been reconceptualised and reclothed by modern ufology in the whole dubious 'alien abduction' narrative. Thirdly, though, there is the issue of fairy-animals, barguests, bogey-beasts and the like. When seen inside people's houses, strange animal-like apparitions have understandably been linked with

poltergeists and there are even a few examples of such creatures allegedly being seen in conjunction with UFOs. However, when observed outside and 'in the wild', as it were, these particular classes of fairies seem nowadays to come under the general purview of cryptozoology (or 'the study of unknown animals', as I am presuming most readers of this book will already know).

Some cryptozoologists would no doubt object to this idea – and sometimes with good reason – pointing out that what they investigate are in fact real, flesh-and-blood animals, not fairies. Often, they are correct in this assertion. The coelacanth was no supernatural bogey-beast, and nor are the thylacine or *orang-pendek*. Certain cryptozoologists have only an interest in researching demonstrably real-life, corporeal cryptids ('mystery animals') such as these, and will have no truck whatsoever with even the slightest hint of the supernatural being introduced into the subject.

An alternative and perhaps more enlightened viewpoint upon the matter, however, would have it that alongside such regular, zoological cryptids there do exist in the world other strange, animal-like beings, apparently of a supernatural nature, which are not actually animals at all. As such, I think it would be eminently possible to argue that barguests, bogey-beasts and other such fairy-animals have been reconceptualised again in recent years in cryptozoology not only as specific but limited types of animal-phantom such as Black Dogs, but also under the more generic heading of 'zooform phenomena' – a term coined by the publisher of this book, Jonathan Downes, in a 1993 essay of his for the now-defunct publication *SCAN News*. Here, Downes defined zooforms as being:

> "Apparitions which take the form of animals – usually living but which are not living things – at least in the way that we understand the term." [12]

This influential definition sounds not entirely unlike a good working description of some of the old bogey-beasts, of course ...

Animals That Aren't

Whilst interesting, all of this would be essentially irrelevant to this book, though, were it not for the fact that strange phantom animals (sometimes of a shape-shifting nature, and often not quite corresponding to usual zoomorphic norms) are alleged to have been seen during both fairy and poltergeist-hauntings, even into the present day. Indeed, sometimes old barguests were specifically spoken of as performing poltergeist or fairy-like pranks themselves. There was one notorious bogey from Northumberland known as the Hedley Kow, for example – it appeared sometimes in the form of a cow or foal and sometimes in the shape of a man or a truss of straw – which was alleged in local lore to trick servant girls outside by imitating the voices of their boyfriends before knocking over pails and pots, or else undoing their knitting and ruining their yarn and spinning-wheels inside the house [13]. Nowadays the good people of Northumberland would surely blame a poltergeist for pulling such puckish pranks, however, and not the Hedley Kow.

If one way in which bogey-beasts have been reconceptualised in modern times is through the prism of cryptozoology, another way in which they have been recast for contemporary palates is through the medium of ghost-lore, then. Take, for example, the following description of a mystery composite-beast; it was "a big animal, very heavily-muscled, with short legs" and "a bushy tail" which looked rather like "an exaggerated fox tail". Despite this fact, it had "a hyena's body", "a reddish colouring" and "short, stubby legs like a boar". It was seen hunting horses on a Utah ranch during April 1999 and, when pursued by the steeds' owner, simply "vanished into thin air". [14]

A matter for cryptozoology? You would have thought so, especially seeing as the thing is said to have physically scratched the hocks of the horses it chased. However, the above cryptid was seen during the notorious haunting at Skinwalker Ranch in Utah during the late 1990s and early 2000s, when much poltergeist (and UFO) activity was also going on around the place, as we shall see outlined briefly later. In such an outbreak of weirdness – which seems to have been a haunting of the land and sky in the area as much as it was of a mere farmhouse – the three contemporary disguised strands of fairy-lore would appear to combine to creative a narrative of what is often known nowadays as 'high-strangeness' or so-called 'window-areas' (zones in which a plethora of paranormal weirdness are alleged to occur with bewildering frequency).

The Bell Witch Bogey

Another haunting which seems to have much relevance to the more fairy-related elements of cryptozoology, meanwhile, would be the celebrated Bell Witch affair, already mentioned. Whilst it appears likely that this particular narrative has accumulated much that is purely folkloric about it, general opinion has it that there was a core of real events involved, some of which apparently involved spectral animals. Indeed, before any poltergeist activity actually broke out inside the Bell home itself, the first sign of anything untoward going on was the appearance of strange animals upon the surrounding farmland. First of all, one day in 1817, the head of the family, John Bell, was out in one of his fields when he saw a "strange animal, unlike any he had ever seen" sitting there amongst the rows of corn, "gazing steadfastly" at him. Eventually, he decided that it must have been a dog, but could not make out to what breed it belonged – which, perhaps, indicates that the beast was not really any kind of dog at all. Whatever it was, John Bell, being American, decided to shoot it first and ask questions later. Either he missed his aim or the bullet had no effect, however, as the 'dog' simply ran away, presumably unharmed – one account says specifically that it "at once disappeared", though this is probably just a figure of speech.

A few days later, meanwhile, John's son Drew saw "a very large fowl", which he thought was a wild turkey, perched on a fence outside the farmhouse. Drew ran in for his gun, but before he could kill the thing it rose up into the air and flew away, at which point he realised that it was not a turkey after all, but "some unknown bird of extraordinary size". It seems that Drew and his sister Betsy – the later focus of the Bell Witch's ire – saw other "strange creatures for which they could not account" around the place too but, frustratingly, their precise nature does not seem to have been recorded. At the time, the Bells put all this down to their being new to the area and thus unfamiliar with the local fauna, and were it not for the later poltergeist phenomena these sightings would probably all have been forgotten. It is not impossible that they were just ordinary animals which were then simply interpreted as being sinister after the ghost had appeared, after all.

However, less explicably, human apparitions were then seen around the place by Betsy Bell, too; one day, she saw a woman strolling through the orchard, who promptly disappeared into thin air as soon as Betsy spoke to her. Drew and John Bell later saw this same female wandering about near the family home as well, and it was not long afterwards that the actual poltergeist phenomena began. Significantly, some of the first things experienced inside the farmhouse were noises "as if a bird were flapping against the ceilings" and a sound like "fighting dogs chained together" with their chains trailing along the floor.[15] Interestingly, phantom Black Dogs are often supposed to have chains dragging along the ground after them in folklore too,[16] a specific association between the spook and bogey-beasts which is surely only made all the stronger by the fact that, when the Witch later developed a voice, it claimed that one of its names was 'Blackdog'.

A Man and His Dog

Perhaps it was a familiarity with such Black Dog lore which later led one of John Bell's slaves, a man named Dean, to start telling stories about his own supposed encounters with the Witch in animal form. At first, Dean seems to have alleged that, whenever he travelled to a neighbouring farm at night to see his wife Kate – this woman, rather cruelly, being owned by a *different* white farmer – the Witch was continually coming out to meet him in the form of a black hound which would follow him along to Kate's door and then disappear [17]. Telling this story to his fellow black slaves, though, Dean appears to have begun revelling in the attention it gained him, and soon he was elaborating on his theme, saying that sometimes the hell-hound had two heads, and sometimes none [18]. Before long, Dean was making up entire little folk-tales of his own about these encounters, many of which centred around a so-called 'witch-ball' that had supposedly been made by his wife Kate. This lucky charm was guaranteed to frighten off the Witch, apparently, seeing as it had been filled by Kate with various reputedly magical substances like brimstone, camphor and what is termed simply "spunk" – leading one to hope that this word had a different meaning back then than it does now.

Many a time, it appears, the Black Dog tried to get rid of this witch-ball so that it could kill poor old Dean. Once, Dean even had cause to hack into the animal's head with his trusty axe, cleaving it in two – which, he said, was what led to it having two heads the next time he set eyes on it. Another time, said Dean, the ghostly dog transformed him temporarily into a horse with a human face and rode him away down the lanes and fields all night long – a yarn which, at the very least, reveals an apparent familiarity upon Dean's behalf with old tales about both witches and fairies riding horses throughout the night and leaving them in a tired-out sweat come the morning. It also sounds not entirely unlike WY Evans-Wentz's story about the tailor being 'night-ridden' as a makeshift horse by fairies on the Isle of Man, cited earlier.

Dean's weirdest tale, however, concerned an occasion when he had trapped a possum by its tail. Seeing this, the Witch arrived on the scene, this time in the shape of a rabbit, and began talking to the possum. It seems that 'Colonel Rabbit' and 'Colonel Possum' (as Dean called them) were good friends, as the rabbit said he would set the trapped animal free. To this end, claimed Dean, Colonel Rabbit "commenced swellin', like, blowin' up like a bladder" until he was the size of a local white farmer named 'Master Frank Miles' – something else which indicates that Dean was unexpectedly familiar with Black Dog lore. After all, there are several accounts on record of phantom Black Dogs from the British Isles behaving similarly, such as a report of one seen in the Devon village of Uplyme, which supposedly "grew bigger and bigger" until he reached tree-top height before "seeming to swell into a large cloud" and floating up into the sky! [19] The bugganes, meanwhile, the bogey-beasts of the Isle of Man, were meant to frequently appear in the form of "small dogs who grow larger and larger as you watch them until they are larger than elephants" [20]. Either way, said the Walter Mitty-like slave, once he had grown to giant proportions, the ghost-rabbit was able to easily free the possum before then whacking Dean's head with a big stick, knocking him out until sunrise.[21]

Obviously these tales are, to put it politely, nonsense, and the fact that Dean appears to have told them first to his boss John Bell after turning up late and bedraggled for work, or having been found by him lying unconscious in his cabin of a morning [22], indicates that, perhaps, he simply made them up on the spot in order to account for certain unspecified night-time excursions or drinking-sessions of his which he didn't want his master to know about. Despite this, the proliferation of genuine themes and motifs from traditional British Black Dog and bogey-beast lore to be found within Dean's narratives makes them fascinating reading nonetheless.

It seems that, from whatever source, Black Dogs were actually known to black slaves in nineteenth-century America; in 1926 the American folklorist Newbell Niles Puckett published tales collected from southern blacks about Black Dogs with glowing red eyes, no heads and even one about "a little white pug dog that became bigger and bigger until it was as large as a calf", for example [23]. This last account in particular, containing as it does that telling reference to the dog becoming "as large as a calf", seems highly related to tales of old British bogey-beasts. Presumably, Dean knew all about stories such as these and merely extemporised from pre-existing narrative-templates stored inside his head whenever he wanted to impress his fellow slaves with tall tales or make up an excuse for being late for work. By doing so, however, Dean was, albeit perhaps unintentionally, linking America's most famous poltergeist back to certain obscure aspects of old European fairy-lore.

Animal Magic
However, not all of the accounts of the Bell Witch assuming animal form had their origins with Dean – although some are seemingly just as unreliable in terms of their status as evidence. One time, for example, a stray black dog turned up at the Bell house and started "cutting some antics". Seemingly, John Bell thought that it was the Witch in disguise, and went to get his gun. His wife pleaded with him not to kill it, though, and the dog lay down on the floor before rolling over and over across the room until it exited through the door. Odd canine behaviour, certainly, but it doesn't necessarily mean that the dog was a demon. [24]

Another unusual tale was related by a local girl named Fannie Sory who, together with a group of three or four pals, offered to stay up overnight with the corpse of a local eccentric named Kate Batts as a sign of respect before her funeral. This Kate Batts, the reader may recall, had been slandered by the poltergeist as supposedly being a witch, leading to most locals being reluctant to attend her wake. Fannie Sory and friends, though, regarded the idea as some kind of fun 'dare', and the tall story they put about the next day certainly made them look brave. According to the girls, Batts' house had suddenly become filled with black cats after dark, these animals spending all night jumping on the dead woman's coffin. Meanwhile, whenever

Four traditional depictions of Puck/Robin Goodfellow in either impish baby-form, or dressed as a tiny jester, as created by such influential artists as Sir Joshua Reynolds and Heny Fuseli. Visual depictions of Puck in animal-form seem much less common, however.

On the left is an image of a headless bear taken from a 1584 English witchcraft pamphlet, and on the right is the famous image of the 'Black Dog of Bungay' taken from the oft-reproduced 1577 pamphlet *A Straunge and Terrible Wunder*. Other than the fact that one has a head and tail and the other does not, however, how different are these two demons in appearance, really? Shaggy, black-haired quadrupeds – from dogs to calves to donkeys to bears and shug-monkeys – merge into one another in a confusing way in much British bogey-beast lore.

An old drawing of Northumberland's 'Hedley Kow'. As befits a bogey-beast, its precise species appears to be largely indeterminate.

One of the first signs of anything untoward occurring on the Bell family farmstead was the alleged appearance of a strange and outsized bird on the land, as (highly inaccurately) imagined here in an old US pulp-comic. "What is that weird monstrosity ... a huge bird ... a bat ... or a demon from Hades?" asks a distraught John Bell in the first frame.

Dean confronts the Bell Witch – in the form of a two-headed Black Dog – with a handy apotropaic 'witch-ball' filled up with his own wife's spunk. Enough to scare anyone off, surely.

An old illustration of John Bell's haunted farmhouse in Tennessee.

Pictures illustrating two of Dean's tall tales. In the first, Dean is transformed into a horse with a human face by the Witch and, in the second, he comes face-to-face with the Witch in the form of a giant rascally rabbit and her evil friend Colonel Possum.

Willington Mill, as viewed in the 1890s.

Epworth Parsonage, home of one of England's most famous poltergeists. Is that it running up the front path in the guise of a tiny black animal?

This road sign commemorates the Wesleys' occupancy of the parsonage, but not the poltergeist's; the Wesleys commemorated it themselves in an issue of their *Arminian Magazine* in 1784.

The strange rabbit-like creature witnessed in the kitchen at Epworth Parsonage.

England's 'Witchfinder General', Matthew Hopkins, forces two accused witches to reveal their animal-familiars, some of which – like 'Vinegar Tom', with the head of an ox and body of a greyhound – were composite or chimera-like in form. Familiarity with such ideas is what probably led Emily Wesley to conclude that the animal-spirit haunting her house was "likely to be some witch" rather than a ghost as such.

In Ireland, the wicked Earl of Rosse had his soul transformed into a black cat; in England, he could have been condemned to assume the form of a Black Dog instead.

The Irish *pooka* in the form of a big black horse with glowing eyes. Clearly it is not always viewed solely as being a 'fairy-dog', then ...

A

TRVE DISCOVRSE

of such ftraunge and woonderfull

accidents, as hapned in the houfe of M.

George Lee of North-Afton, in the coun-

tie of Oxford, being in truth and matter of

fuch efpeciall waight and confequence, as

fildome hath the like bene

heard of before.

Which begun the 19. of Nouember 1591. and continued vntill

Eafter euen laft paft 1592.

Juftified by the credit of Gentlemen of worfhip, and others

of the Countrey.

¶ Imprinted at London for Edward White, dwelling at

the little North doore of S. Paules Churh at the figne

of the Gunne.   1592.

The title page of the 1592 pamphlet telling of the alarming poltergeist phenomena and apparitions of strange dog-like creatures witnessed at the house of a Mr George Lee in North Aston. This has been said to be the earliest surviving pamphlet about an English poltergeist haunting that we have.

any of the girls went out to fetch water from the well, they claimed to have had to beat off large numbers of "black, curly-haired dogs" with a stick. Again, this simply seems like exaggeration and mischief, although no doubt there really were a few cats and dogs milling around the place, these animals being plentiful on all the local farms. [25]

Whatever you think about the Bell Witch's alleged therianthropic powers, though, there is no doubt that, upon several occasions, it boasted openly about its ability to transform itself into the shape of an animal. Frequently, it asked people whether or not they had noticed large rabbits hopping along after them whilst they were walking through the local countryside. When they agreed that they had, the Witch then informed them with glee that those rabbits were in fact her in one of her many guises. [26] One time, supposedly, the Witch metamorphosed into a rabbit and led a pack of horsemen and their hunting-dogs a merry dance, getting them to dash round and round in circles before then outrunning them at an impossible rate and vanishing into the distance, much to the spook's own amusement. [27]

This is a particularly interesting detail, as it has some very clear parallels with certain motifs to be found in tales of witchcraft; such as the confession given by the notorious seventeenth-century Scottish 'witch' Isobel Gowdie, who claimed that it was a common occurrence for her and her kind to transform themselves magically into hares and then be chased by farmers' dogs, none of whom could ever catch them [*]. [28] Once again then, in the case of the Bell Witch, we come across an example of a poltergeist narrative which, upon closer examination, proves to be made up not just of motifs from parapsychology, but also of themes derived from witchcraft, fairy-lore and even cryptozoology. Partially this is probably just because the basic core narrative of the Witch has been added to again and again in its many retellings over the past two centuries, but it also, perhaps, does much to suggest that our modern distinctions between these topics are to some degree artificial.

Trouble At t'Mill
Another very clear case of poltergeist apparitions which directly corresponded with bogey-beasts and fairy-animals, meanwhile, would be those which were seen during the infamous haunting of Willington Mill in Northumberland during the 1830s/40s. In and around this building, owned by a devout Quaker named Joseph Procter, various bizarre events occurred, some of which were classic poltergeistry – strange noises as if of a building falling down echoed throughout the air from nowhere, [29] for example, phantom footsteps were heard, and doors mysteriously unbolted themselves. [30]

However, peculiar phantom animals of a type which do not directly correspond with real physical flesh-and-blood ones were witnessed around the place, too. I was going to say that

---

* The first written account of the case, *Our Family Trouble* by Richard Williams Bell, was penned in 1846, around 25 years after the initial phenomena had ceased in 1821. Whilst Bell had been a first-hand witness to the haunting, he was only about five when it began, and ten when it ended, meaning that his memory will obviously have been suspect upon some issues. Furthermore, Bell, like later writers such as MV Ingram, a local newspaper editor who published his own investigations into the affair in 1894, will have had to rely largely when writing their books upon oral testimony from both local residents and family-members, not all of whom will have been direct witnesses, and not all of whose memories will have been entirely accurate after so many years. As such, it is obvious that at least some elements of the 'classic' narrative as told today will be to some degree inaccurate and based upon later local oral additions to the yarn.

one of these was a big white cat – but it wasn't. It was merely cat-*like*. Apparently, it was much larger than an ordinary domestic cat, and had a kind of elongated nose or snout. Also unlike most ordinary cats, it had the apparent ability to walk through garden gates, closed doors and solid walls. Most frequently, it was seen inside the Mill's furnace-room, where it was once observed "wriggling like a snake" before passing through a solid stone wall, whilst upon another occasion the fairy-cat was even seen to walk "quite calmly" into the furnace-fire and disappear! [31]

At other times, meanwhile, it appears that the creature could shape-shift. A local man named Thomas Davidson, for instance, once encountered the 'animal' outside the Mill whilst waiting there for his girlfriend. Standing around, he saw what he thought was a "whitish cat" approach and come up close. Davidson, thinking it was a real animal, tried to kick it – whereupon his foot simply passed through its body as if the thing wasn't there (a standard motif in tales of Black Dogs and other such bogeys) [32]. It walked away, and then disappeared into thin air. Then, reappearing once more, the entity hopped towards Davidson as if it were a rabbit! Again he kicked out, and again his foot went right through. Once more, the being vanished – before returning yet again, only much larger this time, supposedly being as large as a sheep and "quite luminous". Davidson didn't kick out a third time, but watched the spectre walk past him and away, whereupon it disappeared in exactly the same spot as it had done twice previously. Frightened, the young lover headed for home. [33]

At other times, meanwhile, apparitions were seen in and around the Mill in the form of "a strange-looking donkey", being "quite small with short hair of a sand colour" with a nose which "seemed to bow upwards in the middle, like a bump", as well as "an animal about two feet high" which was seen standing in the window of a particular room for 30 minutes before decreasing in size down to the point where it eventually disappeared. [34] An invisible dog was once encountered inside the Mill House too; a maid was cleaning shoes in the kitchen when she heard a bark and felt two large paws jump up onto her shoulders and press down, meaning she had to lean her hands and arms on the table in front of her to avoid being pushed over. When the Mill's owner, Mr Procter, ran in to see what all the fuss was, he could see no dog to account for the incident, however, and all the doors were shut [35]. The Willington spook was even once seen in the form of a phantom monkey, which pulled a small boy's shoe-strap before running and disappearing under a bed [36]. It also appeared in various human forms, as we shall see later.

Doing the Holden Rag
Just as odd, the ghost apparently also sometimes appeared in the form of an inanimate object – namely, a kind of white rag or cloth. One witness claimed to have seen something which looked like:

> "... a white pocket-handkerchief knotted at the four corners, which kept dancing up and down, sometimes rising as high as the first floor window." [37]

Another time, a woman was tidying one of the bedrooms in the Mill House when she saw what she took to be "a white towel" lying on the floor. When she went to pick it up, though, this 'towel' rose into the air, flew behind the dressing-table and then landed back down on the floor again before escaping under the door. At this point, the sound of a "heavy step" was heard walking down the stairs by several people, and the flying towel could be seen no more.[38]

This all seems extremely bizarre. And yet, as we have seen, it was absolutely standard belief amongst country-folk in the past that bogey-beasts and fairy-animals, being consummate shape-shifters, had multiple forms in which they could potentially manifest – including not just beasts like cats, dogs, calves, donkeys and rabbits, but also inanimate objects such as pieces of cloth or towels. For example, a bogey called the Holden Rag, which was alleged to have haunted the lonely lanes and by-ways of rural Yorkshire during the 1800s, was meant to appear to unfortunate travellers sometimes in the form of a big black dog, and sometimes in the form of a rag of white linen caught on a thorn-bush[39]. Another Yorkshire tale, meanwhile, from the town of Norton, concerns two men who were allegedly astonished one day to see a "beautiful white heifer" standing near some water suddenly transform itself into a roll of Irish linen[40]. In a place called Petty Lane near the village of Glowrowram in County Durham, likewise, another bogey would supposedly appear initially in the form of a woman, but, when approached, fall to the ground and spread itself out in the form either of a great sheet of linen or a large pack of wool. Allegedly, so the legend goes, this shape-shifting barguest only disappeared for good when the road was dug up and a skeleton of some unnamed woman, presumably a murder victim, was found buried beneath it [41].

Phantoms at the Parsonage
Despite these clear similarities, though, it does not appear, from contemporary records, that any connections were made between the Willington Mill haunting and the then still-current belief in bogey-beasts by the people who were directly involved in it. This seems initially surprising, because the north-east of England was one of the main 'hot-spots' for belief in such creatures in Britain, with several of the most famous barguests, like the notorious Hedley Kow, hailing from the area. A connection *was* made, however, by the Mill's owner, Joseph Procter, between the events he had experienced and another well-known haunting, that which took place at Epworth Rectory in Lincolnshire between December 1716 and January 1717. This was an extremely well-known tale, as it occurred in the home of the Reverend Samuel Wesley, father of John Wesley, the founder of Methodism.

We know that Joseph Procter was aware of the basic history of this haunting, as there exists some correspondence between him and a local doctor named Edward Drury in which passing reference is made to the affair at Epworth with no accompanying explanation of what exactly it involved, making it obvious that both reader and writer assumed one another to have been familiar with it. In any case, the details of John Wesley's life were at the time very well-known to other educated Non-Conformists, such as the Quaker Procter, and it is a simple fact that the nick-name of 'Old Jeffrey' was used of the ghosts at both Epworth and Willington Mill, which surely cannot have been mere coincidence. [42]

The most interesting similarity for our present purposes, however, is that at Epworth, too, strange animal-like apparitions were seen, just like at Willington. Most famously, Samuel Wesley's wife saw "something ... like a badger, only without any head" scuttling from under a bed in the family nursery one day, running beneath the petticoats of one of her daughters, and then disappearing. Intriguingly, Mrs Wesley had only looked beneath the bed in the first place because a number of apparently intelligent raps, so characteristic of poltergeists, were heard to be emanating from its head and feet. The implication, perhaps, is that the 'badger' made them!

This animal was later seen sitting in front of the fire in the dining-room by a household servant, Robert Brown, who seems to have disturbed its slumbers. As soon as he entered into the room, the thing got up, ran past him and out into the hallway, where it vanished beneath the stairs. Another time, meanwhile, Brown was sitting alone by the fire in the kitchen when he saw something white that looked "like a rabbit, but less", with ears that lay flat upon its back and "little feet" which "stood right up" shoot out from what is termed the "copper hole" or "oven stop" in the hearth (a typical fairy-haunt). It turned around five times very swiftly, and Brown tried to catch it with a pair of tongs but it, too, eluded his grasp. Just like at Willington Mill, however, the ghost was also observed to manifest in human shape; one night, it is said, a spectre "something like a man in a loose night gown trailing after him" chased one of Wesley's daughters down the stairs.[43]

Badger-Witch

The interpretations of all this weirdness upon the Wesleys' behalf, however, fitted in with both their own highly religious preconceptions and concerns, and the time in which they lived. John Wesley, for instance, seemed to blame the affair upon the wrath of God, who was angry with his father Samuel for some silly indiscretion, and ever since the family's original letters relating to the case appeared in the *Arminian Magazine* (a long-running monthly Methodist publication) in 1784, the Wesley haunting has been used by religious Non-Conformists in the English-speaking world as a key example of the reality of the spiritual world and the existence of otherworldly powers [44].

A different view held by one of the main witnesses at the time, meanwhile, had it that witchcraft was to blame. According to Emily Wesley, one of the many daughters of the household, the white rabbit/headless badger seemed "likely to be some witch", presumably in shape-shifted animal form, which she pledged to shoot if she ever got the chance. Furthermore, Emily said, there had been a recent case of witchcraft in the vicinity and, for several weeks prior to the poltergeist's initial appearance, her father had been preaching from his pulpit about the dangers of having traffic with that once-common class of benign white witches and English countryside herbalists known as 'cunning folk' [45]. Perhaps taking their cue from Emily's musings, both Harry Price and Sacheverell Sitwell, authors of two of the twentieth century's most influential books upon polts, have linked the animal apparitions of Willington and Epworth to the so-called 'familiars' well-known to us from Renaissance English witchcraft trials – those funny little demons in the form of small animals which were alleged to have been gifted to witches by Satan to act as their servants [46].

Nobody, however – as far as I know – has tried to link either haunting to the idea of bogey-beasts, either now or at the time they occurred. Returning spirits, God's wrath and witchcraft have all been preferred as providing potential explanations, at least by those who have written about the cases. Presumably, this is because the primary witnesses to both hauntings – and, indeed, people like Price and Sitwell, who have covered them since – were literate and educated persons. To people like the fairly well-to-do Procters and Wesleys, even the slightest talk of fairies or their animal analogues would no doubt have seemed, by definition, absurd. Given their unswerving religious background, however, notions of unquiet spirits and witchcraft perhaps would not have done.

Maybe the whispers of the less well-educated local people would have linked the incidents back to the barguests of old, however; we cannot really know, oral testimony and lore being naturally more perishable than their written counterparts. Certainly, though, belief in bogey-beasts amongst ordinary rural folk did outlast both of the hauntings at Willington and Epworth, so it seems curious that the apparently obvious connection between them was not made at the time. I can only presume that the connection *was* in fact made, but only amongst people from lower social classes, and never in writing, only in gossip – though I fully admit, of course, that this is mere presumption!

A Cat Shows Its Claws

Another intriguing poltergeist infestation which would seem to have been amenable towards being assimilated into local fairy-traditions but surprisingly wasn't involved the so-called 'Black Cat of Killakee', a notorious feline phantom which supposedly haunted Killakee House in County Dublin, Ireland, throughout the 1960s and 1970s. When a Mrs Margaret O'Brien bought the derelict house – actually a former hunting-lodge – in 1968, intending to use it not only as a home but also as a centre for the exhibition of Irish art, she was warned by locals that the property had been haunted by a huge black cat, as big as an Airedale dog, for over 50 years; well beyond the lifespan of any ordinary cat, it need hardly be said. Soon, Mrs O'Brien herself was seeing glimpses of a large black animal lurking around the grounds, but this did not shake her too much. After all, it need not necessarily have been a *phantom* cat she was seeing.

Rather more undeniably abnormal, however, was the incident which befell the Dublin artist Tom McAssey, who was helping to redecorate the front hall of Killakee House with two other men one night in March 1968. He told his terrifying tale to an Irish radio reporter:

> "I had just locked the heavy front door, pushing a 6-inch bolt into its socket. Suddenly, one of the two men with me said that the door had opened again. We turned, startled. The lock was good and the bolt was strong, and both fastened on the inside. We peered into the shadowed hallway ... and, sure enough, the door stood wide open, letting in a cold breeze. Outside in the darkness, I could just discern a black-draped figure, but could not see its face. I thought someone was playing a trick and said "Come in. I see you." A low, guttural voice answered: "You can't see me. Leave this door open." The men standing behind me both heard the voice, but thought it spoke in a foreign language. They ran. A long, drawn-out snore came from the shadow, and in panic I slammed the heavy door and ran, too. Halfway across the gallery, I turned and looked back. The door was open and a monstrous black cat crouched in the hall, its red-flecked, amber eyes fixed on me." [47]

Soon, the cat (which McAssey later painted) turned poltergeist; paintings were torn into long, thin strips, pottery smashed and heavy furniture hurled about, turned upside down and pushed into corners. One medieval oak chair was methodically dismantled into tiny pieces, with the brass tacks from its tapestry lined up on the floor in orderly little rows. After dark, doorbells rang even though they had all been removed and, weirdest of all, dozens of hats, from top-hats to caps with woollen pom-poms, appeared around the building, hanging from picture-hooks and furniture. Mrs O'Brien's plans to create a new centre for Irish art were, like the artworks themselves, in ruins.

Reasons for the manifestation of the entity were soon sought – and quickly found. Behind Killakee

House stood Montpelier Hill, atop of which were the charred remains of another hunting-lodge which, from about 1737, had been used to house the Irish chapter of the Hellfire Club, a society dedicated to the performance of morally transgressive acts. The first Earl of Rosse, Richard Parsons, had converted the lodge for this express purpose, and, what is more, he seemed to have an abiding prejudice against black cats. On one occasion, or so it is said, he had drenched one in spirits, set it on fire, and then taken great delight in watching it running down the hill spitting and squealing, terrifying locals who swore blind it was the Devil. Another time, after Satan had failed to appear at a Black Mass he was staging, Parsons supposedly placed a black cat on a throne in his stead in an act of mock-worship [48]. It does not take a great leap of logic to associate these unlikely incidents with the ghostly black cat which began haunting the area in the twentieth century, of course – even though there must be a suspicion that these tales were perhaps invented by locals in order to account for the cat's appearance *after* it had first been seen, rather than the other way around.

Pooka People
That, at least, is the standard story, implausible though it may seem. However, another surprising aspect about the alleged haunting at Killakee House is that it does not seem to have been linked more by witnesses and commentators with the *pooka*, a well-known type of fairy-animal from Irish lore. This *pooka* is generally said to be a fairy-dog, but sometimes appears to be a kind of indefinable mixture of both cat and dog in certain witness accounts. Dermot MacManus tells us that this should be no surprise, as the *pooka* is essentially a shape-shifter, able to appear as a shaggy pony, calf, ass, bull or goat, but always with black hair and "blazing fiery eyes" of sinister aspect [49]. In other words, then, it is yet another bogey-beast! By comparing an account of the *pooka* as seen by a friend of MacManus with a contemporary eye-witness account of the Black Cat of Killakee, it will become obvious that we are apparently looking at different encounters with the same basic type of 'animal'.

MacManus' friend, a certain Mr Martin, then a student at Dublin's Trinity College, met the *pooka* whilst back home in County Derry for the holidays. He was out fishing by a country river, when all of a sudden he saw a "huge black animal" appear, padding through the water. Significantly, it looked entirely like neither cat nor dog – he could not decide whether it was canine or a panther – and had "fearsome, blazing red eyes ... like live coals". Sensibly, he jumped into a tree and waited until it had safely passed by [50]. The account from Killakee, meanwhile, comes from Val McGann, a former Irish pole-vault champion who lived in a caravan within the House's grounds. He said that he had seen the Black Cat several times, and, just like Mr Martin, commented upon both its "terrible eyes" and the fact that it was built not like an ordinary cat, but was, rather, "the size of a biggish dog". He had often tried to track and shoot it, but always it managed to elude his aim [51]. A further possible connection with fairy-animals, meanwhile, can be found in the legends about the soul of the evil Earl of Rosse returning to the area in feline form. After all, such legends are known from England, too – except there the wicked aristocrat is cursed by God to return in the form of a stereotypical Black Dog rather than a black cat. [52]

The 'cat' at Killakee, then, sounds in many ways very much like a *pooka* or barguest; and yet, by the 1960s and 1970s, belief in such beings was obviously dying out, even in the countryside of Ireland. As MacManus had distastefully predicted years beforehand, belief in things like poltergeists had replaced it. Even though the animal was black, had blazing eyes, and could apparently shape-shift into human form and talk (if we believe Tom McAssey, in any case), local legend-mongers apparently preferred to link it back to things like ancient curses and the activities of the Hell-Fire Club, rather than the old fairy-faith. Such, it seems, were the signs of the times ...

Phantom Pets

Maybe it is because fairy-animals and bogey-beasts were mostly just glimpsed outside, in fields or fairy-glens, rather than inside haunted houses, that associations between them and poltergeist phenomena grew fairly weak amongst the general populace. However, phantom animals *are* still seen inside polt-haunted houses, even today. An excellent modern example reputedly occurred in 1994 in a home in the Norwegian town of Kongsvinger. Initially, footsteps and voices were heard around the residence in question, and doors would open by themselves. Then, a black cat suddenly appeared inside the house one day; it walked through a door (whether open or closed the original report does not say) and then disappeared. Weirdly, it stopped coming back when the house's owners bought their own pet feline. Instead, the poltergeist now preferred to show itself in the fairy-like form of a little woman wearing an apron, who once allegedly appeared turning a roasting-spit in the kitchen. Another time, chairs began screeching about in the presence of the man of the house before the fairy-woman then appeared, started spinning around, uttered some words in a "croaking voice" and then suddenly flew up out of the house through the roof! [53]

Another curious tale of a fairy-animal was told to WY Evans-Wentz by one of his many informants from the Isle of Man, who expounded to the wandering folklorist about a little white dog which would supposedly appear in his grandmother's house when she and her daughters were spinning, acting as a warning that the rest of the Good Folk were approaching. Being thus informed, the human family would drop their work, leave out fresh water and light the *sidhe* a fire, before hurrying up to bed. Once there, they could hear the fairies banging around like polts downstairs, but never once did they actually see them – only their pet dog and herald. [54]

Phantom cats and dogs also pop up during some full-blown poltergeist cases in which the Good Folk themselves are not even mentioned, however. For example, during a 1676 poltergeist haunting at the Blackfriars home of a man named Edward Pitts in Puddle Dock, London, a ghostly cat, "about the size of a mastiff", and with no visible legs, supposedly appeared [55]. The comparison of the cat's size to that of a dog's seems a curious echo of legends about bogey-beasts. Another poltergeist in animal-form, which caused crowds to gather outside a haunted house in Baldock in Hertfordshire during January 1878, was also described using terms typical of barguests. This phantom animal, which caused beds to lift up and windows and doors to open and close by themselves was, apparently, small and white with "eyes like saucers" – just like Shuck and his kin were frequently (and probably metaphorically) said to have in old descriptions of them [56]. At the haunted house of a man named George Lee in the Oxfordshire village of North Aston in 1591/92, meanwhile, amongst more typical phenomena, a series of "grotesque dogs" and other animals were observed. One time a "black object like a dog" appeared in the courtyard, and another time "a creature like a great brindled [streaked] dog without legs" was found in a tub used to sift meal in [57]. The repeated use of the phrase "*like* a dog" here is surely significant. Just as interesting was the 1722 haunting in Sandfeldt, Germany, where as we saw earlier a race of "little crooked people" were supposedly busy teleporting innocent kids underground and offering them money to stay.

Similarly fairy-like, however, was the vision seen by the children on 26th February when they supposedly witnessed "a cavalcade of strange rough things almost like calves, but smaller" flying out of a shed, and being flogged forward by a big man with a whip. [58]

Acting Catty

An account of a Frenchman named Ferdinand Estève, recorded in 1899, mentions another phantom cat being sighted in conjunction with such things, but the implication here is that the spectre was no fairy, but a dead soul returning to earth in animal form. Visiting a female relative, Estève was put up for the night in the room in which this woman's husband had previously died. He was awoken from his slumbers, however, by the sound of dishes and plates flying about and smashing in the kitchen downstairs. Then, after silence had returned, he heard something rushing up towards his room from the foot of the stairs.

As it entered, he saw some small animal, which he took to be a cat, jump onto his bed and then hurl itself out of the window. Getting up to check, however, he found that the window was closed shut; which, it will be recalled, is just how the *cait sidhe* had exited from the farmer's house during the 1928 County Cork case, mentioned earlier. Furthermore, when he went downstairs into the kitchen, Estève found that the crockery had not even been touched, in spite of the infernal racket he had just heard. Three days later, Estève's mother slept in the same room and experienced exactly the same phenomena. The French scientist Camille Flammarion, discussing this case in his unimaginatively-titled 1924 book *Haunted Houses*, blamed "subjective impressions ... produced by external causes" (i.e. objective but misleading visions being made by the dead man's spirit), for the bizarre occurrences. [59]

In order to get a more traditional perspective upon this particular haunting, however, perhaps Estève's account, coming as it does from France, could usefully be compared with a description of beings called *follets* – what some French people used to call fairies, remember – taken from the Renaissance demonologist Pierre Le Loyer's 1605 book *Discours, et Histoires des Spectres*:

> "There are plenty of houses haunted by these spirits and goblins, which *ceaselessly disturb the sleep* of those who dwell in them; for now they will *stir and overturn the utensils, vessels, tables, boards, dishes, bowls,* and now they will draw the water from a well, or make the pulley squeak, the slates and tiles fall from the roof, throw stones, *enter chambers, imitate now a cat,* now a mouse, now other animals, lift up persons lying asleep in their beds, pull the curtains or coverlets, and perpetrate a thousand tricks. These follets do not bring any other nuisance than disturbing or ... hindering their sleep; for *the household vessels, all of which they seem to have smashed and broken, are found the next morning to be intact."* [60]

Clearly Estève's cat must have been a *follet*, then. My basic point is simply that, in the past, these poltergeist-related phantoms could legitimately have been viewed as being fairy-animals who had, for whatever reason, come in from their usual haunts in lonely lanes and deserted fields and taken up residence within people's houses instead. Now, however, we tend to think of such apparitions in terms of other things. The specific terminology used inevitably shifts over time. The phenomena themselves, though, are still in many ways basically the same as they ever were – elusive, mysterious and endlessly fascinating.

10.

The Same Old Haunts: Fairies and Poltergeists Around the Home

Where, ultimately, did the belief in alternately helpful/malicious domestic or tutelary fairies like brownies and boggarts actually come from? It could be proposed that such beliefs were based at least partially upon the actual observation of genuine supernatural events in the past, but a more widely accepted suggestion would be that they have their origins in the Classical world, namely in the old Roman concept of household spirits known as *lares* and *penates*.

The exact nature, origin and function of the *lares* is slightly uncertain, but the easiest thing to say is that they were guardian deities of some kind – though not necessarily always of the house and home. They could also extend their blessing and protection across fields, roads, boundaries, or even entire towns or cities; as such, there were supposed to be several different sub-species, the most relevant for us here being the *lares familiares* and *lares domestici*, the household and family versions of the spirits. When the *lares* were protecting a home, however, they seem also to have merged somehow with the *penates*, a closely-related class of minor deity whose name means 'gods of the storehouse', or *penum*, the innermost part of a Roman house where supplies of food, wine, oil and other such valuable substances were kept. The ultimate origin of such beings is contested, but it appears possible they were originally conceived of as being the souls of a family's ancestors.

It was said that looking after your *lar* would bring good fortune but that neglecting it was unwise, a parallel notion to the later European idea that a helpful brownie would turn into a malevolent boggart when riled. According to some ancient commentators, such negligence could lead to a *lar* becoming a *larva* or *lemur*, malicious and formless spirits which would bother people in their beds at night, and otherwise cause a nuisance of themselves. Other commentators, however, suggested that a person who neglected the state of their own soul in life would be punished for their sins by being turned into a *larva* after death; whereas, if they cultivated and honoured it properly, they would become a helpful and benign *lar*. This idea would thus seem to imply that all *lares*, *larvae* and *lemures* were in fact variant forms of *manes* – the generic Roman term for the spirits of the dead. The later Christian interpretation, of course, was that all such ghosts were simply evil pagan demons. As with the fairy-folk, then, the conception of what precisely the *lares* were and how they came into existence in the first place are deeply confused. [1]

There are even those who have claimed that malign *lemures* and *larvae* were nothing more than what the Romans called poltergeists, despite there being no detailed accounts of specific poltergeist phenomena occurring in relation to any of these entities to be found in what survives of Classical Roman literature. The association of *lares* with tutelary fairies is, however, a little more substantial; the fact that they were meant to live inside hearths and fireplaces, for example, is most suggestive, seeing as this is precisely where boggarts and brownies were most often said to reside, too. According to the fairy-folklorist Katharine Briggs, the *lares* were sometimes thought of as being the spirits of ancient hearth-sacrifices, accounting for their choice of abode [2]. In the view of the French demonologist Pierre Le Loyer, writing in 1586, however, the reason for their occupancy of fireplaces was probably that in early Rome the dead bodies of family members used to be buried beneath the hearths of the very same houses in which their descendents continued to live [3]. This is essentially guesswork, though. We might as well just say that they were thought to be the 'spirits of the flame' who kept the household fires going – after all, statues of a specific sub-class of *lar*, the *lares praestites*, were deliberately housed by the Roman State near to the Temple of Vesta, in which a sacred flame was kept burning at all times in order to preserve the safety of the city [4].

A Family Affair
Furthermore, the ancient *lares* seemed to combine in the one same figure what Katharine Briggs herself deemed to be the two main types of post-Classical tutelary fairy; namely, the household drudge, who would do work around the home, protect it and bring it luck just so long as he was looked after, and the ancestral spirit, who was attached to a particular family no matter what, often bewailing their future tragedies like the Irish *bean sidhe*, or 'fairy-woman'. [5] The household drudge was free to go should he ever so desire, and was not necessarily specifically related in some way to the particular family he happened to be aiding at any one time, whereas with the ancestral spirit the matter was quite different.

The link between poltergeists and such ancestral spirits is an underexplored one, but it does exist. After all, tales of essentially one-off poltergeist-like events functioning as family death-omens are legion; the French meteorologist and psychic researcher Camille Flammarion collected hundreds. In his 1924 book *Haunted Houses*, for instance, Flammarion reproduces a letter sent to him by a certain Mlle Meyer, who told of how her grandparents' coffee service had spontaneously shattered itself at the very same hour that their son had died in Africa. Then, years afterwards, the coffee service which they had bought as a replacement repeated the feat, suddenly leaping from its shelf and breaking into a "heap of fragments" on the same morning that their son-in-law died [6]. Traditionally, rapping and drumming noises were also said to foretell of deaths within various English aristocratic families – deaths amongst the Wood family of the village of Brize Norton in Oxfordshire were reputedly preceded by knockings on tables, doors and shelves, for example, whilst a family called the Burdets had advance notice of a forthcoming departure by virtue of loud drumming which would begin issuing from their manor house's chimneys for several weeks beforehand. [7]

An extraordinary tale told to the sixteenth-century astrologer, mathematician and physician Gerolamo Cardano by his father Fazio is also worth citing here. Fazio, it seems, had once taught Latin to the three sons of a man named Johannes Resta and, one of these lads being sick, Fazio had been invited to stay with him in his new capacity as a medical student. Whilst there, probably sometime during the 1480s, Fazio was repeatedly disturbed by knocking from within the walls of his room. Asking one of the sick youth's brothers about this, he was told not to mind it; it was simply the household *follet*, a type of being which he specifically described as a "familiar spirit". It was harmless, he said, but was acting up at present – he did not know why. Later that night, Fazio thought he had worked out the answer. Waking up to find a disembodied and invisible ice-cold hand crawling over his face and sticking two fingers into his mouth, he threw it off, presuming that the sick boy had died and that he was being visited by his ghost. Going up to the boy's bedroom, the sound of the phantom hand could be heard knocking on the walls of the turret before him. Entering his patient's room, however, Fazio found him to be still alive – but, when he entered, a loud noise "as if the house was falling" was heard by several people. The boy died the next evening [8]. If the idea of the poltergeist did indeed grow, in a roundabout way, from the idea of the household fairy-familiar or ancestral spirit, as several persons before me have speculated, then perhaps tales and traditions such as these are the last dying embers of such a connection?

Eating You Out of Hearth and Home

It is not upon the poltergeist's occasional function as family death-messenger that I wish to focus here however, but, rather, upon the surprising fact that they are sometimes associated very strongly with ovens, hearths and chimneys, just like the Roman *lares* were (and, indeed, as the death-knockings of the Burdets were). Of course, I don't wish to overstate my case here – most polts have nothing whatsoever to do with fireplaces or ovens, after all – but there is a definite sporadic connection. Certainly, there is a persistent connection between these areas in a home and the fairy-folk. In centuries past, the fire and/or oven were the very centre of a person's home; much more so than in these days of central-heating and microwaves, they were essential to life. As such, if there were any household spirits that you wanted to propitiate, it was definitely the hearthside ones.

It appears that one of the most common locations in which people imagined a 'fairy-house' could be found within their home was beneath the fireplace, with the hearthstone being the trapdoor leading down into it. Katharine Briggs, for example, tells of a house in Airlie in Scotland where there was a crack in the hearthstone. It was said locally to have been haunted by fairies because several cakes which had been left baking by the fire had mysteriously disappeared. Eventually, the house was demolished, and a solution to the 'mystery' found; the cakes had simply been falling down the crack in the hearthstone, several mouldy ones being found beneath it whilst the work was being done. In Briggs' opinion, though, the truth was likely to have been somewhat different; probably people had been purposely slipping the cakey treats down the crack as secret offerings for the household brownies.[9]

The pot-hook which usually hung over open fireplaces before the dawn of twentieth-century domestic comforts was also often said to be a favoured spot of the fairy-folk. For instance in Scottish folklore there was a specific type of fairy known as Wag-at-the-Wa', who just loved to sit on the pot-hook whenever it was empty. If you were foolish enough to idly swing or spin this item around, then you were asking to be paid a visit from the creature, who had many of the classic attributes of a brownie; he disliked lazy servants, for example, could be heard laughing from thin air, and was of grotesque appearance. He wasn't hairy like most brownies, though. Wag-at-the-Wa' was an ugly old man with blue breeches, grey cape, a nightcap and red coat, and a bandage tied around his face due to persistent toothache. Further south in Herefordshire, however, it was common-or-garden brownies who were meant to sit on the pot-hook all day, not Wag-at-the-Wa'. Here, the crook in the hook, useful for hanging kettles on, was termed the 'brownie-sway'. If there was no crook, then this was considered bad form, an upside-down horseshoe being put on the hook instead so that brownie still had his seat. This was a wise precaution to take because, if brownie took offence at your neglect of him, he could easily make your life unpleasant. [10]

Figures in the Fire
This intimate association between fairies and fireplaces must have lasted well into the modern era, as there are some surprisingly recent accounts of people claiming to have witnessed such entities sitting in their hearths. For example, a letter printed in the now-defunct magazine *John O'London's Weekly* in 1936 from a Marjorie T Johnson of Nottingham, described an experience she claimed to have had in her childhood. Lying in bed one morning she "suddenly ... felt compelled" to sit up and look at the empty fire-grate. There, "on a filmy cobweb on the bars", sat perched a "strange little creature" with a "broad grin on its face" which she could only call an "elf" or "nature-sprite". It had "very large" ears, was 4-6 inches in height, and its body was of a "glimmering green" hue. She stared at it, and it stared back, with a "blank expression which showed very little intelligence". Eventually, Marjorie tried to approach it, whereupon the dim-witted elf disappeared. Getting back into bed and turning to face the fire again, however, Marjorie found that the fairy had returned. This game of hide-and-seek continued until eventually she brushed away the cobweb and the sprite vanished from her fireplace for good. [11]

Dermot MacManus has another such story, which supposedly occurred to a female friend of his one day when she was five and living in a house in the south-east London suburb of Wandsworth. Dancing in a room there one day, she was surprised to see a "little figure" dressed all in green except for his red "jelly-bag" cap, sitting cross-legged on the coals in the unlit fireplace. He filled the hearth and was bigger than the little girl herself. She thought that it was a big doll that had been left there for her as a present – until it moved. The pixie began smiling and nodding his head repeatedly, before evaporating completely as the child tried to pick him up in her arms. [12]

Both of these tales, of course, involving as they did lone children, could be quite easy to dismiss. However, a bizarre account of a fairy being sighted in an oven by an adult was reported on in the Romanian Press in 1883. This woman, named only as 'Mrs AG', lived in Szemerja, in Transylvania, and returned home one evening in March that year to find the moon shining on her oven through the window. This light allegedly allowed her to see that a little man was sitting next to it. He was about the size of a man's arm and dressed in red with a black cap on his head. Significantly, the fairy was also rather furry – his face and hands were covered with hair, making him sound even more like an oven-dwelling brownie. The housewife stood there staring before eventually the thing got up, walked a few steps and then vanished. She wasted no time in fumigating the oven and scrubbing the room with garlic – not just useful against Transylvanian vampires, evidently – but to no avail. The next night, the goblin returned. Mrs AG said she threw a can at him, whereupon the intruder jumped on her, knocked her to the ground and scratched her forehead. She fainted in fear and was bedridden for three days until, finally, she scraped up some dust from the place where the brownie had been sitting and swallowed three mouthfuls as well as having the oven fumigated three more times. Supposedly, the little man was also seen by three other people, and he is said to have left some footprints, "like those of a goose", behind after him. Rather implausibly, the Romanian Press blamed an escaped monkey for causing the panic.[13]

Fairies, then, were once very definitely associated with hearths, ovens and their attendant chimneys. But what has this to do with poltergeists, exactly? After all, these last few first-hand sightings – or hallucinations, if you prefer – aside, it seems obvious that talk of Wag-at-the-Wa' and brownie-sways are just folklore. Maybe so, but as always, there are some puzzling cases on record in which both folklore and apparent real-life events seem to have begun to merge into one ...

Oven-Ready Brownies
It appears that a Welsh farm known as the Trwyn in the Monmouthshire parish of Mynyddislwyn was reputedly bothered, around 1700 or so, by an invisible spirit of some kind (Job John Harry, then the farm's owner, did not know quite what to call it) which acted very much like a poltergeist, playing all of the usual tricks like knocking on the door and throwing stones. It also took to speaking to people from out of the oven by the hearthside – although what about is sadly not recorded. It is no wonder, then, that the spook came to be known as a *bwca* by local people in the years after the haunting had ceased. After all, it had apparently lived in the hearth, and this was just what *bwcas* – which were simply what the Welsh called brownies – were supposed to do in legend. According to the researches of the former US Consul to Wales Wirt Sikes, in his classic 1880 book *British Goblins*, for example, it was highly recommended for any right-minded Welsh servant-maid to make a good fire in the hearth overnight and leave out an offering of fresh cream for the household *bwca* on the hob where he lived before going to bed. Then, in the morning, she would find that the butter had all been churned, saving her a long and tedious job [14]. It is obvious that a *bwca* is simply a brownie, then; and yet the poltergeist at the Trwyn does seem to have been a matter of direct experience rather than a mere folk-invention.

By the end of the nineteenth century, however, memories of the original, possibly genuine, incidents had accumulated their own folkloric additions, and it was being said that the *bwca* had once been a helpful little beast around the household before Blodwen, a mischievous servant girl of half-fairy blood, had soaked its nightly offering of bread in a bowl of piss (then commonly used as a household dyeing agent) as a joke. Then the fairy had turned bad, beating up Blodwen and spending its days bothering the cattle and its nights throwing things around the house. Supposedly, it appeared at one point in the form of a white, disembodied hand with a ring on one finger. A neighbouring farmer, Thomas Evans, is said to have threatened to shoot the *bwca*, but was showered with stones which flew at him from all directions, even when he was surrounded by a circle of people trying to protect him, which does have a certain ring of truth to it.

An account of the *bwca* playing Will-o'the-Wisp and leading poor Job John Harry to the edge of a precipice, in which place he stayed precariously balanced all night until daybreak, however, sounds most unlikely [15], as do later additions to the tale in which the *bwca* moved farms and became embroiled in a version of the Rumpelstiltskin legend, in which a cunning servant lass gained power over it by guessing its name ('Gwarwyn-a-Throt', since you ask). Eventually, Gwarwyn fled to another farm where he made friends with a servant who went off to fight Richard III – quite an achievement, seeing as the original haunting is meant to have occurred several hundred years after Richard's death – and ended up being banished to the Red Sea by a local wise man, like many a fictional ghost of the past [16]. Thus, folklore and real-life incidents can happily coexist in such narratives, it seems – but, whatever the truth of certain elements of the tale, the original *bwca* really did seem to speak to people from out of an oven. Or was that simply a later invention, too? If a stone-throwing polt was thought to in fact be a *bwca*, then tales about it talking from an oven would hardly be impossible for some gossipy local to invent, after all. Have any poltergeists *really* spoken to people from out of ovens or hearths, then, or is the idea all just a myth?

Spanish Practices
Surprisingly, talking ovens do have one very notable parallel within poltergeist lore rather than remaining exclusively the property of heavily embellished fairy-stories. The case of the 'Saragossa Spook' (or '*La Duende de Zaragoza*' – 'the Zaragoza Fairy' – as it was called in Spanish) was once well-known, but seems to have been rather neglected in recent years, possibly because it all sounds so silly. Either way, it caused a media frenzy back in November 1934, when the occurrences first began and were reported on in *The Times* under the curious headline 'A Polite Spanish Ghost'. It seemed that the spirit was manifesting itself in a flat in the Aragonese city of Zaragoza, lived in by the Palazon family and their 16-year-old servant-girl, Maria Pascuela. The polt here had only the one trick up its sleeve, or so it seemed; it liked to talk to people down the chimney-flue of what the original news-reports called an "economical cooker" in the kitchen. This voice was intelligent, could answer questions, addressed persons by name and demonstrated a certain dry sense of humour. When an architect and workmen were called in to investigate, they searched the apartment-building from roof to cellar, but could find no practical jokers. Finally, the architect ordered his men to measure the flue, presumably thinking that some recording-device was hidden away in there. "You need not trouble, the diameter is just 6 inches", the ghost informed them politely from within the empty chimney-pipe. They measured it anyway ... and found that the *duende* was exactly right.

The trouble began one morning when Maria the maid was lighting the fire in the kitchen, intending to cook breakfast. As she did so, the voice began coming out of the cooker-chimney, greeting her "effusively". She was startled and made a great fuss, as is perhaps only to be expected, and her mistress came in to see what the matter was, only to be greeted by the sound of the voice addressing her as well. From then on, the oven just wouldn't shut up. Some days, it talked "almost incessantly". The police were called out, but could do nothing. How do you arrest a ghost – or indeed a cooker? Eventually, the voice seems simply to have gone away; 20 people were present during its final appearance, including policemen, doctors and a local magistrate. They all heard the spook speak in broad daylight. Their ultimate explanation for the affair was that young Maria was something called "an unconscious ventriloquist" and that the voice was not an actual ghost, but merely "a psychic phenomenon produced only in certain circumstances." [17]That description isn't really very clear, but it seems that the observers felt that the maid was creating a voice from inside her head and then externalising it inside the oven-flue somehow, using some kind of alleged (and ill-defined) psychic or ventriloquistic powers.

I don't think that the Spanish officials had the slightest idea of what the Saragossa Spook really was; but they had to say that it was something, and so plucked an appropriate-sounding explanation from the mental landscape which then prevailed in the society around them. Job John Harry didn't know what to call the invisible thing which was speaking from his oven in eighteenth-century Wales, either – but other people did. It was a spirit, and it lived in a hearth, so it must have been one of those fairies known as a *bwca*. What the witnesses chose to call the ghosts in their ovens was largely a matter of what they personally felt culturally-sanctioned to. The idea of ghosts entering stoves and then haunting them is, after all, one of surprising antiquity – in ancient Greece, for example, a grotesque prophylactic mask or moulding of a Gorgon's monstrous face was placed upon the door of many ovens and kilns in order to frighten off any evil spirits or bogeys who might otherwise have taken up their abode within and interfered with the baking process [18]. Given this ancient provenance of the trope, it is no surprise that interpretations of haunted stoves and hearths have shifted many times over the years.

Hell's Kitchens
For Martin Luther, for example, paranormal phenomena occurring in or near ovens and chimneys were down to neither fairies nor spooks but, rather, the Devil himself. Twice in his life, Luther tells us, he experienced polt-like phenomena in relation to ovens – once, when "a loud noise" erupted from behind a stove in front of which he was praying and, a second time, when an invisible force began throwing hazelnuts at him from behind a different stove. Both times, he blamed Satan [19]. (It may be worth noting in relation to these facts, incidentally, that in German speech of the time, the area behind an oven was known as the 'Helle' – meaning, literally, 'Hell' – although presumably this was due to the heat of the place rather than because they were all haunted by diabolic spirits!) In the town of Oberdorf in the Alsace region of what is now France sometime during the 1700s, however, mysterious knocking and hammering sounds heard coming from within a chimney were blamed by worried locals not upon the Prince of Darkness, but upon the unquiet soul of a murder victim – a murder victim, apparently, who could not rest until the entire house had later been consumed by fire. [20]

More commonly, though, chimney and stove-dwelling spooks were thought of as being brownies or other varieties of fairy-folk, as already stated. Perhaps in light of this fact, we should reconsider what precisely the main sin of John M'Laughlin, the Northern Irish farmer mentioned right of the start of this book, was – was it really cutting down the fairy-thorn which drew down the *sidhe*'s wrath, or was it, rather, the double-offence of him then using this item to sweep out his chimney with, thereby upsetting the home of an understandably disgruntled boggart, too?

The ambiguity of these old superstitions can be well observed in a case cited by Claude Lecouteux. According to him, there was once a house in the town of Ampfersbach, in what is now French Alsace, which was supposedly haunted by the Devil (no date is given for this tale, regrettably). Satan manifested himself there, it would appear, largely by producing poltergeist-type noises; unseen chains would rattle, heavy but invisible objects would pound against the door, and the pots and pans in the kitchen would clang and jangle against one another throughout the night. These otherworldly noises returned every evening until, surprisingly, the householder carried out a rather bizarre form of exorcism – he had a bread-oven installed! [21] Clearly this particular spook was not Satan at all then, but a homeless household familiar in need of appropriate shelter. I suppose, these days, you could have just bought him a microwave. [22]

Coming Down the Chimney Tonight
An unexpected link between witchcraft and polt-infested chimneys, meanwhile, can be found in an amazing 1612 haunting from the Bourgogne region of France generally now known as the case of the 'Devil of Mascon'. Here, in the house of a Huguenot Minister named François Perrault [*], all kinds of poltergeist-related wonders occurred – the explanation for all this, supposedly, being that the clergyman had been cursed by a witch. Perrault, it transpires, only got his new house at the expense of its previous female occupant, who had been dispossessed of the property by court order. Seeing as Perrault had benefited from this decision, the woman blamed him for her misfortune and, one day during the haunting, she was discovered by Perrault hiding inside his chimney-breast, making ritual curses and invoking Satan. Naturally, Perrault reported this to the law, and the woman was ordered to appear before local magistrates and bound over to end her persecutions upon December 22nd – the very day that the poltergeist activity in Mascon in fact ceased [23]. Significantly, when the poltergeist did finally depart, it was obliged to provide Perrault with a leaving present; it hung two little bells upon a nail in the chimney-breast, and then was heard from no more. [24]

This is all very interesting for a number of reasons. For one thing, it is well-known that the hearth was once thought to be one of the main centres of domestic magic. This makes sense because, just like a door or window, it represented a potential symbolic opening into the home through which malign and evil influences or spiritual entities could potentially pass. As such, many magical items like 'witch-bottles' (bottles filled with pins, rags, bones, hair, feathers, urine and other such supposedly magical substances), mummified cats, and empty pots intended to catch spirits are often found buried beneath hearthstones or stuffed up chimneys when old houses are demolished. These items are said to have what is termed an 'apotropaic' function; that is to say, they were meant to ward off evil [25]. If some cursed item was buried beneath the hearth instead, however, or evil spells muttered within a chimney-breast, then it would be reasonable to assume that this would have had an opposite effect. As well as being used to toast crumpets and boil kettles, then, household fireplaces were also once thought of as

---

* Some sources say 'Perreaud' and call the place Mâcon – the place's modern name – not Mascon.

A lar holding up a cornucopia ('horn of plenty'), a traditional symbol of success in the harvest. This particular idol comes from 1st-century Roman-occupied Spain, showing how belief in the beings was exported out across the Empire. Do brownies and other such tutelary fairies have their ultimate origins in such ancient household and hearthside gods?

Another lar, this time with *two* cornucopias; evidently the family which he looked after the fortunes of must have been doing rather well for themselves. On the right, meanwhile, the Roman goddess Vesta does her best to keep the home fires burning.

Gerolamo Cardano, the archetypical 'Renaissance Man', whose father Fazio had a genuinely strange encounter with the disembodied hand of a *follet* acting as a family death-omen.

Wag at the Wa' throws a pot from off its hook. Evidently, his adopted family must have been neglecting either him or their household duties.

In *The Fairies Are Out*, by the Victorian illustrator James Nasmyth, hundreds of tiny beings gather around their natural home – the fireplace.

According to the former US Ambassador to Wales Wirt Sikes, in his 1880 book
British Goblins, this is what a *bwca* looks like. He claims that a "Welsh peasant"
drew the above cartoon with a lump of coal (what else?) when asked to describe
one of the beasts.

The story of the Saragossa Spook seems to have been the basis for a local theatre company's play, sadly never translated into English.

Some puzzled Spanish policemen inspect the famous 'talking oven' of Saragossa whilst Maria Pascuela herself tries to get it to engage in yet another fireside chat with her.

Goya's typically grotesque depiction of some Spanish *duendes*. You wouldn't want
to find *them* living inside your oven!

Scottish 'Green Lady' *glaistigs* are not the only kind of '*fée verte*' in existence …

being potentially dangerous spiritual battlefields.

There seems to be some evidence, for example, of an old tradition that chimneys could be appropriate places for priests and cunning men to 'lay' troublesome ghosts inside ('laying' being a kind of temporary exorcism, popular in many old tales, wherein a spirit is 'conjured' to live within some inaccessible location, like a deep well, for a certain period of time, often a hundred years). Bagley House near the town of Bridport in Dorset, for instance, was supposed to have been haunted during the 1880s by a male phantom wearing old-fashioned clothing, who would cause various auditory phenomena, such as footsteps, rappings and rustlings to echo around. Often, doors could be heard opening and closing and crockery being tossed about, only for closer inspection to reveal that none of these events had actually occurred at all. As is the way with these things, an explanatory narrative was invented for the polt, and it was said that it was the ghost of a former owner of the house named Squire Light, who had drowned on a hunting trip many years before. Having caused much bother to the house's inhabitants at the time, it was said, a group of clergymen had supposedly pooled their powers to lay the unquiet Squire inside one of the house's chimneys for a set number of years – a term of imprisonment which had sadly expired by the 1880s.[26]

Woolly Reasoning

Perhaps the oddest account of a poltergeist coming and going down a chimney, meanwhile, involved the Bell Witch. The final initial act of this remarkable entity is supposed to have come one evening whilst the Bell family were relaxing in front of the fire after a meal. Suddenly, according to the testimony of one of the Bell sons, John Jr, "a ball, something like a cannonball", rolled down the chimney and out into the room, before then "bursting like a smoke-ball". Once it had exploded, the Witch spoke to announce its temporary departure. "I am going and will be gone for seven years," it announced. "Good-bye to all." [27] What precisely happened after those seven years had passed is disputed, but the most famous version of the Witch's later return also involved the family's chimney. According to the testimony of Joel Bell, the family's youngest son, one autumn afternoon in 1828 he and his mother were sat around discussing family matters, when all of a sudden:

> "... a dense sulphur smoke filled the hallway from floor to ceiling, and as soon as the smoke cleared away, a black ball as large as a water bucket, seemingly composed of black wool, rolled softly across the hall floor ... to a wide open fireplace and went up the chimney." [28]

The Witch, they both instantly knew, had at last returned, just as it had promised.

Nandor Fodor, the well-known Freudian parapsychologist, saw these chimney-related acts as being fraught with unlikely sexual symbolism, or "guilt-release", as he put it [29]. Perhaps he would have done better to have tried pointing out the fairy-motifs implicit within these tales, however. There are not only the obvious parallels to do with haunted chimneys and absences of precisely seven years here, but also curious echoes of various British bogey-beasts in the Witch's alleged transformation into inanimate objects like a ball of black wool. Quite apart from the several instances of barguests morphing into rolls of linen and suchlike which we examined earlier, for example, there is a nineteenth-century account on record from Leeds of a female traveller seeing a Black Dog "rolling along on the ground before her, like a woolpack". Here, whilst the phrasing is ambiguous, it does seem more than possible that the woman involved is meant to have specifically seen it transforming itself into a bale of wool, as opposed to simply behaving like one by rolling around on the floor [30]. There is even one version of the tale of the Trwyn *bwca*, meanwhile, which alleges that it travelled to Trwyn Farm in the first place in the specific form of a possessed ball of wool which rolled across the Welsh valleys until the goblin finally reached its new home. [31]

Perhaps the most notable instance of a barguest manifesting as a ball of wool, though, is meant to have occurred to the respected nineteenth-century Dorset dialect-poet and friend of Thomas Hardy, William Barnes. He used to enjoy telling people the story of how, when he was riding by a reputedly haunted house on a lane between the village of Bagber and the small market-town of Sturminster Newton one day, he saw the place's ghost appear to him in a very strange form. It looked, he said, like a "fleece of wool" which rolled along until it got under the legs of his horse, which supposedly then went lame [32]. Did the Bell family know about tales like these before they told their own tales of the Witch to future generations? Did their possible knowledge of such folklore influence the way they then perceived any real poltergeist phenomena, or did they simply use it in order to embroider their narrative? Or, on the other hand, was the spook ideoplastic, and so able to accommodate its appearance to the family's pre-existing mental expectations of how such things should appear? Or, rather more simply, was the 'Witch' really just a fairy? I am afraid you will have to draw your own conclusions upon the matter.

Cursed Coal
In his book *Wild Talents*, meanwhile, Charles Fort records yet another example of a haunted hearth, that which was reported from within the household of a Mr J. S Frost of the North London district of Hornsey in 1921. Around 1st January, it seems, this Mr Frost brought home some coal. Soon, it was exploding inside his fireplace and even in its storage-buckets, without the stuff being lit. Suspicious, Mr Frost called out the police – and a constable not only witnessed coal mysteriously detonating but also hopping out of fire-grates and sauntering along floors. An Inspector then made his way to Hornsey and picked up a piece of coal to examine it more closely. As he did so, however, it split itself into three separate pieces within his hands before simply vanishing into nothing. Soon, things got worse. Various fireside objects, such as buckets and irons, began to dance around, and objects repeatedly fell to the floor without breaking. Burning coals now not only jumped from grates, but passed through solid walls into other rooms and showered to the ground from thin air. Interestingly, a pot hanging over the fire took to swinging about of its own accord – perhaps it was a 'brownie-sway'? There were many witnesses to all this, and eventually a public meeting was held about the matter. One of Mr Frost's children, Gordon, even ended up being hospitalised with nerves and another child, Muriel, actually died during the haunting – supposedly from fright. [33]

Another weird event involving a hearth is said to have occurred during the unjustly obscure haunting of the home of a Swiss lawyer and journalist named Melchior Joller in 1860-62. Here, Joller's maid lit a fire in the kitchen-range one evening. However, the dark chimney then suddenly became filled with light and she was nonplussed to see a "sugar-loaf-shaped object with innumerable little blue flames" floating down it. This then disintegrated, producing an appreciable amount of water as it did so, drenching the newly-lit fire. One piece of the 'sugar-loaf' fell down into an adjoining unlit hearth, where one of Joller's children was playing with the kettle. Both the kettle and the maid's jacket then somehow became covered with the same little blue flames which had previously been seen on the floating object, leading the maid and her young charge to flee from the house in tears, the pair of them later being found cowering in the outhouse like little girls. [34]

With an account like this, though, we have a problem; the rest of the Joller case did not centre around fireplaces, chimneys or ovens at all. So should we consider this particular aspect of the haunting as being possibly fairy-related or not? There are dozens of examples on record in which polts have reputedly done things like throw stones down chimneys, but this would not necessarily be to say that they were all brownies. After all, if there is a fireplace, oven or chimney inside a haunted house – as there usually is – then why should a ghost not haunt this as well as a bedroom or a cupboard? The accusation could be made that I am looking for patterns where none actually exist.

Don't You Open That Trapdoor
In fact, however, the connection between modern poltergeists and old domestic fairy-dwellings is more substantial than just this. Brownies were, in the past, alleged to have lived not just inside ovens, chimneys and hearths but also in what might be termed the 'liminal' parts of a home; namely, those parts of it which were not exactly at the heart of the house, or used for living in. These neglected corners of a dwelling – attics, cellars, garrets or junk-rooms – were often alleged to be inhabited by *kobolds*, sprites and brownies, perhaps simply because they were inherently dark and spooky [35]. (It may not be insignificant, incidentally, that an eighteenth-century German word for store-rooms and junk-rooms is *polterkammer*, meaning 'noise/commotion-room'!) [36]

An absolutely model example of a ghost acting up only in and around these 'classic' haunted zones is said to have occurred within a farmhouse in France's Ille et Vilaine region, named Barre de Cicé. Here, the owners were awoken one night at some unspecified time in the past by the "terrifying noise" of "a gigantic log" falling down into the main fireplace. Going to check, however, they found nothing there. Then, the haunting spread to both attic and cellar. Invisible footsteps could be heard after dark, climbing up and down the ladder to the attic above, and the door to the cellar below was continually found standing open, in spite of it having been barred. Eventually, a priest had to come and say a mass for the dead in the attic, thereby dispelling the spirit for good. [37]

In this instance, clearly, the poltergeist was conceived of as being an unquiet soul rather than a fairy – but, if so, then why did he/it only seem to operate in and around the typical places that a household fairy-familiar was meant to haunt? Nowadays, the average poltergeist probably haunts bedrooms and living rooms as much as he does cellars, junk-rooms and attics, but this old pattern is by no means extinct. Tabloid tales of allegedly haunted pubs, for instance, always seem to feature the idea of there being 'something sinister in the cellar', for example, even if we may be justified in suspecting that most of these stories have been concocted for publicity purposes.

A Smashing Time
One plausible example of a haunted pub cellar, however, came from a 1900 haunting in a wine shop/inn in the Italian city of Turin. This was investigated by none other than the famous Professor Cesare Lombroso, whose controversial 1876 book *Criminal Man* has often led to him being described as the 'founder of criminology'. Here, much to the distress of the establishment's owner, a Signor Fumero, the wine-bottles in his cellar had taken to jumping off their shelves and breaking for no apparent reason, as well as rolling themselves into a big heap behind the cellar-door, making it hard to open. Lombroso bravely descended downstairs to inspect the uncanny events for himself; by candlelight, he observed three empty bottles, which had been standing upright on the floor, suddenly "spin along as if twirled by a finger" and break nearby, as well as seeing several descend from their shelves "without any violent motion, but rather as if they had been lifted down by someone" before bursting. At other times, meanwhile, the bottles would simply shatter of their own accord, without even being dropped. It was no wonder, then, that the cellar floor was, Lombroso said, "drenched with wine" before he even went in. [38]

It may not be irrelevant to mention in relation to this haunting that, according to popular Irish lore, the clurichaun – a kind of house-dwelling cousin of the leprechaun – was often said to live down in people's cellars where he would make his presence known by laughing and making the bottles move around noisily [39]. Some traditions regarded this fairy as being the 'night-form' of the leprechaun, and implied that if he was treated well he would protect your wine-cellar but if ignored or mistreated would do his best to ruin it [40]. One old tale from Ireland tells of an offended clurichaun who was so displeased with a cold meal which had been left out for him in the cellar one day that he dragged the family cook out of bed and down the stairs, leaving her battered and bruised [41]. Perhaps one of these beings had temporarily decamped from the Emerald Isle to Turin for its summer holidays that year, then? Other types of cellar-haunting fairies/spirits from England, meanwhile, would include the 'Thrummy-Cap' of the North Country, and the prosaically-named 'Cellar Ghost', who was meant to guard wine-supplies from thieving servants [42]. Perhaps in such figures we can even detect faint echoes of the old Roman *penates*? Or alternatively, it could just be that cellars, as inherently 'spooky' locations – filled with damp, darkness, dust, rats and spiders – make good locations for people to imagine that they have encountered ghosts in.

There is one extremely unusual case of a fairy within a cellar, though, which seems very much like it involved some kind of makeshift shrine to a tutelary spirit. The tale comes from a place called Manor Farm in the Lincolnshire village of East Halton where, around the turn of the twentieth century, the folklorist Mabel Peacock found a strange legend attached to an old iron pot which was kept in the cellar. Supposedly, this item contained a store of children's thumb-bones and, if you were stupid enough to stir these remains around, then you would make the farmhouse's resident fairy 'walk'. When the then-current owner of the farm, a 'Mr S', was being shown around the place prior to buying it, it is said that his female guide stopped warily before descending into the cellar, saying that it was haunted by a hobthrust, a type of brownie or boggart. When asked by Mr S what one of these beings was, the woman replied that it was a "kind of devil", and told of how it had bothered the old owners of the house, who had stayed there for more than a century, and who had ultimately had it sealed in the iron pot, a traditional Lincolnshire means of trapping ghosts.

Mr S, intrigued, demanded to see the vessel. The woman acquiesced, and led him downstairs, locking the cellar door behind them so the hobthrust could not escape. There was indeed an iron pot down there; Mr S was not allowed to touch it, but he could see that it was half-full of sand. The woman alleged that it had lain there undisturbed for 200 years now and that, so long as the pot was not touched, all would be well on Manor Farm but that, if it were felt or removed, the spirit (described as being "a little fellow with a big head") would be freed and misfortune inevitably follow [43]. Seeing as alternative traditions about this particular brownie said that he did work around the place unseen overnight, however, it could well be said that the old occupants of Manor Farm quite literally kept their 'luck' down in the cellar.

Yet More Trouble At t'Mill
Another obviously related trope to be found in a number of poltergeist narratives, meanwhile, involves the idea of a dead body being buried in a cellar. One key such example was uncovered by the writers and researchers Mike Hallowell and Darren Ritson during their investigation into the haunting of Willington Mill – home, as we saw earlier, of various apparent bogey-beasts. During their researches, Hallowell and Ritson unearthed an interesting tale, far too convoluted to describe here (read their book!), which led them to conclude that a murder had taken place on the premises and a body been buried in a cellar there, thus partially explaining the haunting. [44]

Surprisingly, this idea can actually be linked back to the notion of bogey-beasts infesting the place. After all, it is a confusing fact that, in much old folklore, fairy-bogies could sometimes appear in human as well as animal shape, something which could lead to them merging with murder-victims and the restless dead in the popular mind. For instance when, at the Lincolnshire village of Kirton, a bogey was seen first in the form of a dog-like creature, then a fox-like animal with a bushy tail, and then finally a White Lady with blood dripping down her dress, it would be no surprise if locals had come up with fictional tales of murder and buried corpses in order to account for the strange apparition [45]. It was likewise with another White Lady who, in the 1800s, was supposedly seen by a stream named 'White Lass Beck' near the small market-town of Thirsk in Yorkshire, sometimes in the form of a fair maiden but also in the guise of a white dog or an "ugly animal" which made a "tremendous clitter-my-clatter". How to account for all this weirdness? Simple. Locals invented the legend that this barguest (for that is what they called it) was the spirit of a female murder victim whose bones, as if to prove the fact, were allegedly then dug up from a nearby gravel pit. [46]

However, it must be said that it is perhaps debatable as to whether the Black Dogs, White Ladies and other bogeys which were said to appear at murder-scenes and suicide-spots were always thought of as being literally the wandering souls of those persons who had supposedly died there; rather, they could almost be considered as being spectral symbols of there now being something 'wrong' about the location more than anything else. As Jeremy Harte put it, such apparitions may "bear witness to a bad death" rather than being the dead returning in animal form.[47]

Maidens Fair

It seems that, with their hypothetical tale of murder taking place at Willington Mill, Hallowell and Ritson have inadvertently tapped into this old tradition. They do, after all, catalogue several sightings of phantom ladies who were allegedly witnessed there along with all the phantom animals, including some of an unidentified Grey Lady with empty eye-sockets [48]. Even more suggestive is another account from Willington of a ghostly woman dressed in "greyish garments" with bowed head and one hand pressed upon her chest "as if in pain" with the other extended towards the ground with her index finger pointing downwards – perhaps towards the location of her secret grave [49]...

However, given that the Willington Grey Lady was sighted in conjunction with various other fairy-animal apparitions and that, as we have just seen with the examples of Thirsk and Kirton, there is a pre-existing pattern of White Ladies and Grey Ladies being merely variant forms of bogey-beasts, perhaps we should be careful about taking this particular phantasm's appearance literally and saying that she was a returning spectral murder victim. Many commentators have often seen the figure of the White/Grey Lady less as being the spirit of any one particular person, and more as some kind of impersonal and archetypal figure, perhaps linked back to old traditions of fairy-ladies or even fairy-queens. However, as time went on and the fairy-faith began to die out, it has been suggested, such beliefs became 'degraded' and the *fays* turned into mere phantoms with invented and predictably tragic back-stories then being created for them in order to account for any further sightings. [50]

There is even one specific fairy-figure from Scottish lore which seems – in some traditions – to represent a halfway point in this process, namely the *glaistig*. Like many fairy sub-breeds, *glaistigs* were thought of in different ways by different people, and the image of them as hostile, water-dwelling half-woman-half-goat creatures is irrelevant here [51]. However, a competing idea of them as being helpful brownie-like tutelary spirits with a penchant for performing invisible housework is germane to us now, as according to this tradition *glaistigs* were in fact the ghosts of actual human females who had, since death, inexplicably taken on fairy nature – as can be seen, perhaps, in the fact they are now often said to appear in the form of so-called 'Green Ladies', the alleged colour of their dresses being most appropriate. It is easy to come across stories of such *glaistigs* playing typical polt pranks like pulling away bedclothes, making objects vanish and float, bothering cattle and throwing clods of earth at people [52]. A *glaistig* haunting the home of a certain Mac'ic Alasdair in Strathglas was especially polt-like. She would pull Alasdair's bedsheets from him and giggle, steal milk and cheese from his dairy, and cause his jacket to appear and disappear repeatedly. So famous did this polt become locally that groups of people used to go out to the haunted house to listen to the strange noises the ghost made and see pots leave their 'brownie-sway' over the fire and drop down to the floor inexplicably in front of their own eyes. [53]

However, tales told of one specific *glaistig* known as the 'Maiden of Inverawe' (or 'Green

Jean'), said to haunt Inverawe House in West Scotland, are even more interesting, as not only did this fairy-polt move furniture and knock over water-stoups during the night, she also had a stereotypically lurid origin-story attached to her. This 'Maiden', it was said, was none other than a sinful former mistress of the house who had been condemned to be buried alive (I'm guessing in the cellar – though the corpse of one Scottish Green Lady is supposed to have been stuffed, equally suggestively, up a chimney [54]) after having an affair with some illicit lover [55]. When she was first encountered, however, it seems reasonable to speculate that the Maiden will have had no such tall tale attached to her at all. The fact that she was meant to be particularly well-disposed towards the Campbell family, who first owned Inverawe, and that she was said occasionally to have performed helpful actions like laying out towels and soap, would seem to imply that she was originally thought of as being a female ancestral spirit rather than the victim of a murder [56]. Indeed, in some traditions the *glaistig* would let out a wail to warn of a forthcoming death in the family to which she was attached, making it obvious she was really just a Scottish version of the Irish *bean sidhe* [57].

Something Under the Floorboards
Also like the banshee, these White/Grey/Green Ladies are said to attach themselves to particular families, following them around from place to place, and not being confined to just the one location. Such, it seems, was the case with the White Lady which was said to have shadowed the Prussian royal family during centuries gone by. Supposedly, she was the soul of one of the Countesses of Orlamunde, and her appearance was an infallible omen of forthcoming death in the family, as indicated by her wearing a widow's band and veil. However, her presumable origin as some kind of fairy-like ancestral spirit seems to have been signified in one particular tale told about her, which is alleged to have been true, though it seems unlikely. One day, it seems, two teenage sisters of a companion to a lady of the Prussian Court were sitting around in some apartments associated with one of the royal residences when they were disturbed by the sound of a harp being played. Significantly, the source of this music was a stove in the corner of the room. One of the sisters, "half in fear and half in fun", took a stick and struck the stove, to see what would happen. The music instantly ceased, but the stick, the girl said, was snatched from her hand by an unseen force.

This girl then fled the room, but, upon her return, found her sister lying on the floor unconscious. It transpired that she had fainted after hearing more music coming from the stove after which the White Lady had emerged from it and approached her. It being thought that the Lady's appearance betokened the presence of treasure under the stove [*], the floorboards were dug up; but gold there was none. All that lay beneath was a kind of secret cellar, empty except for "a very unwholesome vapour" and a quantity of quicklime, a substance once used for the quick disposal of corpses. The Prussian King, upon being informed, is said to have expressed no surprise. The hidden cellar must have been the final resting place of the Countess of Orlamunde, he explained, who had been buried alive there by her lover after she had poisoned her own children for reasons both elaborate and unlikely. She was, he said, seen by children once every seven years, with her appearance always preceded by harp music, she having been a very skilled player whilst alive [58].

---

* In the Roman playwright Plautus' comedy *Aulularia*, a *lar* reveals secret treasure hidden beneath a hearth.

The fairy elements here should seem obvious to readers by now; the heavenly music, the seven years motif, the association with stoves, all are much more fairy-like than ghostly. The idea of the woman being buried alive in the cellar is also a clear parallel with the tale of the Glaistig of Inverawe. It would appear that in the past, when there was an unquiet cellar, a fairy was generally held culpable, not a revenant. However, as time has moved on, explanations have moved on with them, and ghosts are now blamed, including that particular variety now known as the White or Grey Lady. To modern ghost-believing minds since at least the late 1700s, it has seemed obvious that the 'explanation' for a cellar being haunted is that there is a dead body lying undiscovered down there. To our earlier ancestors, however, this 'fact' may not have been anything like so evident.

Popular contemporary variants of the 'buried body' idea, meanwhile, now include the notion that a cellar has unfortunately been built over a cemetery – or, since the release of the Hollywood film *Poltergeist*, on top of an old Indian burial-ground. In 1875, for instance, a certain Mr Penhey, the owner of an oil-paint shop in Kingston, Surrey, made the seemingly sensible decision to extend his cellar to increase storage space for his stock. Sadly, it transpired that the cellar was built right next to the old parish churchyard, and workmen dug up several skulls and old bones during the extension work. This, it is alleged, was the trigger for poltergeist phenomena then breaking out around the building – including, on one occasion, large chunks of plaster falling down from the ceiling for no apparent reason [59]. Presumably, the excavations had simply caused some subsidence, though. Either way, we shall have cause to return to the idea of poltergeists being released by building-work soon.

Attic Attack
It seems that ghosts still inhabit all of the traditional fairy-haunts around the home, then – including attics. It would be tedious to list case after case in which ghostly footsteps have been heard coming from above bedrooms; it is one of the standard stereotypes of poltergeistry. Catherine Crowe gives a good one, though, about an English family renting an old house in the French city of Lille during 1786, which had been empty for some time on account of it being haunted by what the locals termed a *revenant*. Sure enough, the English travellers were repeatedly awakened during the night by a "heavy step" emanating from the unoccupied garret above. There was a yarn abroad locally that this wandering ghost was the unquiet soul of a young man who had been kept locked inside a cage up there, treated cruelly, and then killed. The English occupants scoffed at this romance but, upon climbing into the attic, they claimed to have actually found an old iron cage there, as well as a rusty chain with a collar on the end attached to one of the walls [60]. Even if, like me, you find this story too melodramatic to be true, it does nonetheless clearly show how a movement away from fairy-stories and towards tales of ghosts and murder was taking place across Europe's haunted attics as well as down within its unquiet cellars as the eighteenth century turned into the nineteenth.

The other liminal part of a house which was meant to be haunted by fairies, meanwhile, was the junk-room or store-room. Harry Price gives a good example of such a haunting, from an old disused mill which stood on the banks of the River Eden in Westmorland, Cumbria. This was bought in 1887 by a Mr Fowler and his family, who wasted little time in trying to make the place fit for human habitation. The first thing Fowler did was take the mill-wheel out and extend the kitchen, the remainder of the old wheel-room being partitioned off and used as a junk-room. Soon afterwards, however, it seemed as if this room had acquired a ghost; loud blows and voices were heard coming from within, and one of its windows was smashed by a flying pebble. One time, a flaming piece of paper was found in a corner of the junk-room, its origins a complete mystery. Alarmed, Mr Fowler sealed the place off, barring its door. This did not stop the poltergeist, however; it now came through the partition-wall to cause havoc in the newly-extended kitchen. Not long after, the packing cases which had been left inside the junk-room by the family were heard being dragged around all over the place. Not wanting to unfasten the barred door and investigate, the Fowlers went outside and peered through the junk-room window from a safe distance. From here, they could see boxes, crates and even an old pram floating past, as if being carried by some invisible person. The next morning, fearing that they might release the spook into the rest of the house if they undid the door, a ladder was placed next to the window so they could examine the room more closely. Looking in, it was found that all of the boxes had been piled into a big mound against the sealed-off door [61].

Conversion Disorders
Interestingly, once again it appears that the initial 'trigger' for this haunting was some kind of building-work taking place. We have already seen this supposedly being the case with a cellar being extended, and there was a recent case from Fife in 2000 when the act of converting an attic into a childhood bedroom supposedly caused poltergeist phenomena to occur [62]. Oddly, this is a recognised pattern. A 2007 survey carried out by the SPR, for example, found that a surprising 9% of hauntings in their sample were associated in some way with building or renovation-work going on. [63]

But why would such an association exist? Nobody knows, but one folkloric parallel could be with the old idea of people's houses becoming haunted by the *sidhe* if they should ever be foolish enough to extend them into the way of a fairy-path. Dermot MacManus, for instance, tells the curious tale of a man named Michael O'Hagan, who in 1935 was incautious enough to have built an extension to his home which, sadly for him, jutted onto an invisible path between the two nearest fairy-forts. As a result of this idiocy, so it is said, several of his children sickened and died, his second-to-last child only being saved from doom by virtue of O'Hagan demolishing his extension with a pickaxe overnight [64]. Are tales like this the true ancestors of modern-day stories about poltergeist infestations being caused by building-work? We may be tempted to speculate so.

If fairy-ghosts are often meant to be tutelary spirits, however, then another possibility opens up. Are such entities simply expressing their disapproval of the 'desecration' of their ancestral homes when playing poltergeist during building-work? You could, perhaps, argue this quite plausibly if looking at some such narratives purely from a folkloric perspective, and saying that they are mere fictions containing a hidden social message. However there is, yet again, the problem that some such tales purport to be true. The last reported sightings of the Maiden of Inverawe were in 2001, for instance, when she was reportedly seen wandering Inverawe House during repair work which was being done on its roof. One guest at Inverawe during this period claims to have been kept awake for an entire night by the sound of banging doors and phantom footsteps around the place. Another account from 1912 seems just as suggestive; as the castle was changing ownership, the sellers had stripped all the furniture from one particular room as a preparation for moving. The night before they left, however, they heard loud female screams coming from within that very room. Their explanation was that the house's resident *glaistig* was shocked upon entering it that evening to find it bare, and unwanted change going on around her home. By haunting a household during building-work, perhaps such spirits are merely showing their concern for it?[65]

Where exactly this whole connection comes from is one of the biggest problems we face in our analysis, though. Do modern polts sometimes seemingly live inside hearths, ovens, attics and cellars because they really are, literally, the fairies of old? Or are such accounts merely unconscious echoes of old fairy-lore which have found their way, unexpectedly, into that type of modern folk-tale we now call the 'ghost story'? Or, alternatively, is it the case that poltergeists are real but inherently ideoplastic in their nature, and so pick up on their victims' childhood knowledge of old fairy stories whenever they choose to manifest themselves? I suspect that there will be a few readers of this book who will end up subscribing to each of these different theories – or even come up with their own. I suppose that's just how living folklore works.

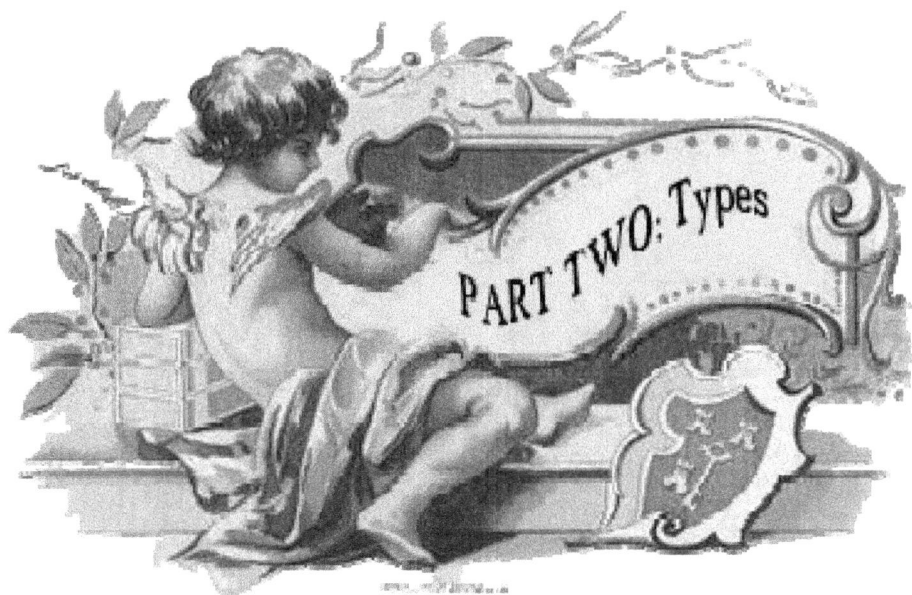

PART TWO: Types

1.

The Poltergeist as Brownie

There are many different types of fairy mentioned in the annals of folklore but the three specific subcategories which are most relevant to poltergeistry are brownies, boggarts and *stallspuks*. Collectively, these are known in England as the 'hobmen', 'hobhursts', 'hobthrusts' or 'hobs' * – and, basically, they were generally-invisible fairies conceived of as living and working inside houses, farms and stables. Of these, brownies are the most well-known, being generally depicted as performing unseen labour upon a farm or within a household overnight in return for little more than some simple offerings of food. For example, during the nineteenth century a man named Daniel Burton owned a farm in Levenshulme, on the road between Manchester and Stockport, where he was supposed to have had a friendly brownie named Puck. According to one account:

> "... during the night everything was cleaned up, and all was in apple-pie order when ... [the servants] came into the kitchen at daybreak; the milk churned, the cows foddered, the necessary utensils filled with water from the well, the horses ready harnessed for their day's work at the plough, and even a week's threshing done and the barn left as tidy as though it had just been emptied and swept." [1]

Whether things like this really happened or not, it seems that some people in the past genuinely believed that they did. The most likely actual explanation for such tales springing up, however, is that jealous farmers used them to try and explain their rivals' success in agriculture. Daniel Burton's farm, after all, was apparently "a model one in its way" with "the old man raising finer crops than any other farmer in the district", according to James Bowker, who first recorded the story in his 1878 book *Goblin Tales of Lancashire*. Maybe this was just luck – Burton's farm may have had better soil than others – or perhaps he was more industrious and had better staff. It seems that other local land-owners could not take this fact, though, and, in Bowker's words:

---

* The term 'hob' is probably a corruption of 'Rob', short for 'Robin', rather than a reference to an oven's hob.

> "... finding a reproach to their own idleness not only in the old man's success but also in the careful, industrious habits of his everyday life, [they] were not slow to insinuate that there was something more than farming at the bottom of it." [2]

This theory of Bowker's seems likely to have been the true explanation for the narrative. After all, one other idea locally was not that Burton had a brownie or 'household luck' ("his 'luck' became proverbial", Bowker says) living upon his farm but, rather, that he had sold his soul to Satan to guarantee a good income from his fields; nowadays French farmers seem to have pulled off a similar deal with the even more sulphurous agency of the European Union. [3]

Poetic Licence

Such notions of helpful household familiars were once very well-known, the belief being alluded to in much pre-modern English literature such as Milton's poem *L'Allegro*, wherein a country-lad:

> Tells how the drudging goblin sweat
> To earn his cream-bowl duly set,
> When in one night, ere glimpse of morn,
> His shadowy flail hath threshed the corn
> That ten day-labourers could not end,
> Then lays him down the lubber fiend,
> And stretched out all the chimney's length,
> Basks at the fire his hairy strength;
> And crop-full out of door he flings,
> Ere the first cock his matin rings.

Here, the 'lubber fiend' (or 'beneficent goblin') has been left out offerings of food in order to induce him to perform his household duties. The great fairy-scholar Katharine Briggs tells us that an alternative name for Milton's helpful goblin was 'Lob-Lie-by-the-Fire', and that he was a hairy spirit with a long tail, who would work through the early hours of the night upon his adopted farm before lying down and resting in front of the hearth with his bowl of cream [4]. Once he is 'crop-full' of this particular food, Milton tells us, Lob then 'flings' or rushes out of the door before cock-crow sounds his doom amidst the morning light. Had these offerings not been left, however, Lob would either not have done the work, or started to bother everyone with poltergeist pranks in the guise of a boggart.

The standard folkloric interpretation of such legends, of course, is that they were used to both encourage and strike fear into a farm or household's workers; as one informant put it in 1734, the domestic fairies would "do good to the industrious people, but they pinch the sluts" [5]. Misbehaving or lazy servants, then – to be 'sluttish' used to mean to be untidy and slatternly – would be punished, whereas good workers might get some fairy-money as a reward for their virtue. Telling your staff such tales, it is said, would be a good way to keep them in line; such a pleasant fiction was a much more romantic solution than employee-employer contracts, at any rate. Some people might wish we could still have them. As Bishop Corbet put it in his (premature) seventeenth-century lament for the passing of the fairy-faith, *A Proper New Ballad, Entitled the Fairies' Farewell*:

> Farewell, rewards and fairies,
> Good housewives now may say,
> For now foul sluts in dairies
> Do fare as well as they;
> And though they sweep their hearths no less
> Than maids were wont to do,
> Yet who of late for cleanliness
> Finds sixpence in her shoe?

Who indeed? Next to no one these days, sadly.

Robin's Jest

However, whilst this is obviously a highly sensible interpretation of the brownie-myth, there is one small problem with it; namely that, once more, there are some cases on record in which obviously fictional old tales of fairy-hauntings appear to merge away in a peculiar fashion into perhaps more credible tales of modern poltergeist-infestations. A helpful fairy known as 'Robin Round-Cap', for instance, was meant to have haunted the Yorkshire manor-house of Spaldington Hall, apparently down into the 1700s. This particular brownie was the standard friendly little chap, happy to lend a hand with farm-work on the estate. However, like many a brownie, he also had a polt-like side to him; so the stories went, Robin enjoyed playing childish pranks like knocking over milk-pails, putting out fires and mixing wheat with chaff. Eventually, three clergymen were said to have magically sealed Robin in a nearby well, where he was doomed to remain trapped for a set number of years.

As time progressed and belief in fairies began to fade, though, locals did not just stop believing in the spook at the Hall. Instead, they simply 'rationalised' Robin into being a ghost. Robin Round-Cap, it was now said, was merely the spirit of a jester of that same name who had resided in the Hall during the reign of James I, and had enjoyed playing the same tricks as his shade now did [*]. His pranks becoming annoying to the Hall's Jacobean residents, they had kicked him down the stairs to his death one day, so this invented narrative goes, leading him to haunt the place thereafter.

This might just seem like replacing one fiction with another. However, it is a curious fact that, around 1800, the Hall was demolished and some of its stones re-used to build a new farmhouse nearby – a farmhouse which, according to the 1989 book *Yorkshire Holy Wells and Sacred Springs*, was still being haunted by a mischievous poltergeist even at the end of the twentieth century. This was put down by locals to Robin now being "out of the well", his term of imprisonment having come to an end [6]. In this changing story, we can see in microcosm the historical development of explanations for such phenomena progressing down from fairy to ordinary ghost to poltergeist.

---

[*] This kind of spurious 'rationalisation' of poltergeist pranks has other direct parallels – for instance, modern polt phenomena allegedly occurring in Muncaster Castle in Cumbria are nowadays often blamed upon the returning ghost of the castle's alleged former jester, Tom Skelton (ghost-jesters being now considered more 'plausible' than puckish fairies, evidently). Needless to say, there appears to be no real basis for identifying the spook as being Tom beyond our old friend wishful thinking; indeed, the 'coincidence' that his surname is Skelton, the name also sometimes given to the Cauld Lad o'Hilton (see below) further speaks of a kind of folkloric contamination taking place between some of these tales.

A Lad Called the 'Cauld Lad'

Surely the most notable example of this kind of process in action involved the celebrated 'Cauld Lad o' Hilton', a sprite who was once meant to haunt a fifteenth-century manor house known as Hylton Castle, in Sunderland. Here, according to the original version of the tale, the Cauld Lad was a kind of invisible household brownie who would take impish delight in rearranging things in the kitchen. If the servants tidied up properly before they went to bed at night, then the Cauld Lad would spend the whole evening throwing everything around, breaking plates and causing a mess. If the servants themselves left the place in a mess overnight, though, then the rather dim brownie would spend his time tidying everything up and putting things back in their proper order instead, still thinking he was causing mischief. Eventually, however, the goblin was banished by virtue of being given a new set of clothes, a standard motif in such narratives; "Here's a cloak, and here's a hood/The Cauld Lad o' Hilton will do no more good", he is said to have rhymed before vanishing forever.

However, as time passed, and tales of brownies began to be deemed silly by most, the Cauld Lad became a ghost. Some said that he was the spirit of an abused child who had been kept locked inside a cold cupboard, thereby accounting for his name. Yet others said that he was the ghost of a servant-boy who had been drowned in a pond by one of the Castle's former owners. The antiquarian writer Robert Surtees, who visited Hylton in the early 1800s, thought that this latter story may have been based upon fact. He unearthed records of an old coroner's inquest which stated that in 1609 a certain Roger Skelton had been accidentally killed with a scythe by Robert Hilton, a member of the family who owned the castle. Hilton was pardoned and the offence deemed manslaughter not murder, but Surtees thought the event could have been the ultimate basis for the story of the Cauld Lad being dumped in the pond. More likely in my view, however, is that the tale about the drowned boy was merely a nineteenth-century invention added to an older story about a brownie-like being in order to try and make the narrative make greater sense to more modern ears. [7]

Witch-Switch

Another way in which to adulterate these stories was to bring in witchcraft in order to account for brownie-poltergeist phenomena occurring around a home. This seems to have been the case with a tale from Upleatham in Yorkshire where a family by the name of Oughtred were reputed to have been aided on their farm by a friendly brownie from nearby Hob Hill. Like the Cauld Lad o' Hilton, however, he ultimately took offence at being offered some clothing and fled. Or, at least, this was one version of the story. Another had it that, just after the brownie left, a local witch named Peggy Flaunders came and cursed the Oughtreds' farmhouse. Then, late one night, a loud knocking was heard at the door and, when it was opened, a "thing like a blazing pig" was stood there. The maid who saw it fled without shutting the door, allowing the evil spirit to gain entrance to the building. As per usual, the spook in this instance smashed up crockery, broke machinery and tormented cattle. It was only eventually exorcised by virtue of the Oughtreds engaging in an act of counter-witchcraft by stuffing a black cockerel full of pins and roasting it alive over a fire to exorcise the polt.

This element of witchcraft in the tale, however, seems likely to have been a Victorian invention, the 1800s being a century when magic was more likely to be believed in by most rural folk than fairies were. In the original older narrative, it is probable that the brownie, offended by having been offered some clothes, was the one who had actually acted like a poltergeist, not Peggy Flaunders' pet imp. We can tell this because of the fact that, at one point, so the yarn goes, the Oughtreds had packed up all their belongings to move out of their haunted house when a neighbour popped in and asked if they really meant leaving. "Aye, we're going to move in the morning," said the demon, popping its head out of the packed furniture, leading to the exasperated farmers deciding to stay put in any case [8]. This, as we shall see in the next chapter, is an absolutely standard motif of many fairy-stories, but with a boggart standing in for the imp. The demon-poltergeist in this instance was, we can be certain, originally a thoroughly annoyed brownie.

Friendly Ghosts
Did the legend of the brownie have any actual real-life basis to it, though? Perhaps. It is a surprising fact that there are several tales on record of modern poltergeists helping out around the home, even if the spooks' more destructive aspects now tend to predominate. It seems that, for instance, a 1960s Yorkshire ghost known as the 'Black Monk of Pontefract' once helpfully laid out the table ready for tea before its adopted family came home – even if, in general, its activities were rather less benign [9]. Janet Bord, meanwhile, tells us that a certain Welsh postmistress of slatternly habits was, for years, very grateful for the services of an invisible helper she called 'Billy' at her village post-office. Leaving everything out in a muddle overnight, she was overjoyed to find that Billy would invariably have straightened everything up by the next morning, a service for which she habitually thanked him out loud. This tidy brownie appears to have been somehow attached to the postmistress rather than the post-office building itself, however. In the woman's own words:

> "When I retired, Billy went. No need for his services, see." [10]

In his book *On the Trail of the Poltergeist*, likewise, the parapsychologist Nandor Fodor tells of a home haunted by some unseen being which particularly enjoyed cleaning the windows and mirrors. They never needed polishing, and the family concerned didn't understand why. As a test, they deliberately smeared over the panes before going to bed one night. In the morning, however, they were all spotless – and yet nobody human had got up after dark to clean them. [11]

Occasionally, such phenomena are rationalised by modern witnesses as being down to the spirits of dead household staff. A ghostly serving-maid, for example, was said to inhabit the vicarage of St Mark's Church in Cambridge, at least according to a TV show broadcast in 1997. Canon Bill Loveless, who used to live there, heard loud crashes at night, and his wife had once awoken to see a young girl standing by her bed. The house's next occupant, Canon Philip Spence, found lace doilies rearranged tidily under glass covers, and discovered a disused serving-hatch forced open, leading him to draw his conclusion about a spectral house-maid residing there [12]. We can also read of a phantom char-lady who supposedly haunted the council-flat of the Usher family of Bow Road, East London, in 1975. Apparently, the ghost was that of a bad-tempered looking woman in a white dress and blue slippers, who liked to make the beds, clean the bathroom and tidy cupboards. As proof of their experiences, the Ushers said that their lavatory door opened by itself every day at 12.50pm. Clearly, this was a spirit of regular habits. [13]

Faithful Servants
A further classic instance of this kind of rationalisation taking place was recorded by

Catherine Crowe, who had the story first-hand off somebody she calls, rather vaguely, "the daughter of the celebrated Mrs S". This woman and her husband were travelling through Wales at some point during the 1800s, it seems, when they stopped at a lodging-house in Oswestry. Here, they found two causes for complaint; firstly, the rooms were all filthy and clearly hadn't been dusted for years. Secondly, however, they were kept from sleep by the loud and annoying noise of the servants sweeping, polishing and moving furniture about all night. Had the staff been shamed into action by the couple's arrival? Apparently not; the next morning, they found the house as untidy as ever. Complaining, the visitors were given short shrift. It was not the servants making fake cleaning noises during the night, the staff said, it was a ghost. Furthermore, they had no energy left to actually clean the place up during the day, as their elderly mistress was so scared by the noises that they were obliged to stay up with her all night, then sleep through the daylight hours instead. It seems that the rumour locally was that this old woman had murdered one of her maids some years beforehand and that the girl was now returning from the grave to take revenge [14]. From this yarn we can probably conclude less about the lady's supposedly murderous proclivities, however, and rather more about the fact that belief in fairies must by this point in time have been very much on the wane in Oswestry.

Crowe gives us another such example, that of a house in the German village of Quarrey, in which a housekeeper in the employ of a Catholic priest had died. The man soon hired a new servant, but he need not have bothered – all the fires were lit, the rooms swept and tidied and, in fact, "all the needful services performed by unseen hands" without the new maid having to lift a finger. Eventually, the new servant quit, finding her services unnecessary. Apparently, word got around about the haunting, so much so that King Frederick the Great of Prussia sent some soldiers to examine the place. As they approached the house, their progress is said to have been attended by marching music coming from thin air, and when they went into the parlour and saw furniture being moved around with their own eyes, the captain in charge was supposedly slapped in the face by the spook. Frederick was so disturbed upon hearing all this that he ordered the priest's house be torn down and paid for him to have another built some distance away [15]. That, at least, is the story as Crowe tells it, though it sounds somewhat embroidered to me.

The most recent example of a brownie-haunting that I could find was also blamed upon a spirit of the dead, although not a maid in this case. In 2008, and again in 2011, it was reported in the Scottish Press that an establishment called 'Laura's Cafe' in the village of Cardross was haunted by a ghost that sometimes played brownie. Upon one occasion, for instance, Laura McKirdy, the cafe's proprietor, knocked some lollipops from their jar just before locking-up time and didn't bother to tidy them away properly. The next morning, however, she found that all the lollipops had been picked up and placed back inside their correct jar by the helpful ghost. At other times, however, the spook preferred to act like a boggart; it knocked pictures off walls, made crumbs appear on freshly-cleaned tables and left displays of Kit-Kats "in disarray". Nobody thought to claim that a fairy was responsible, though. Instead, local Spiritualists laughably preferred to blame the ghost of "an old lady who loved to touch sweets". [16]

The Sleep of Reason Brings ... Chips!
Sometimes, meanwhile, those of us who read the weirder recesses of the Press come across accounts of alleged burglars whose idea of a successful raid is to break into someone's house and tidy up after them. At this point we may start to wonder ... who says it had to be burglars? In 1992, for example, a couple from Hove, Sussex, returned home to find that their living room and kitchen had been cleaned and their dishes all washed up, dried, and put away in their cupboards. Most curiously of all, during the day an insurance man had called at the house and been told by an elderly lady who had answered the door that she was the new cleaner. But who was she really, and how on earth had she got inside? [17] In 1999, likewise, it was reported that German police were searching for a gang whose *modus operandi* was to break into houses, spend hours mopping, polishing and dusting, and then disappear taking nothing but some food from the fridge [18]. Real-life brownies, performing their services and then taking their traditionally-allotted tribute, it seems to me!

Another recent news story which seems relevant to brownie-lore concerned a 50-year-old woman named Claire Bartlett from Newport in South Wales, who, it was reported in 2013, was suffering from a bizarre somnambulistic disorder which led her to clean up during her sleep. According to Press reports, this behaviour could occur as often as three times a week. The housewife would simply wake up in the morning to find her dishes done and her windows polished, with no memory of having performed these chores whatsoever. She wasn't looking to be cured, though – in fact, she had taken to leaving her dirty plates out unwashed overnight deliberately, hoping that her subconscious would make her get up and clean them, leaving her next day free! [19] Other people, meanwhile, have reported cooking in their sleep, such as Rab Wood, a chef from Glenrothes in Scotland, who gets up as often as five nights a week and cooks dishes such as chips, spaghetti bolognese and omelettes – but never eats any of them. Instead, he simply awakes in the morning to find that his cooking has already been done for him. [20] It seems likely that such strange somnambulistic or amnesiac disorders could account for certain tales of brownies from the past – but not, surely, all of them.

The story of Mr Wood cooking in his sleep, however, does have its parallels with the occasional tale told about benign household familiars concerning themselves with culinary matters. One such example is cited by Katharine Briggs and was meant to have happened around 1960 or so, her source being a vicar's wife and thus, you would have hoped, a trustworthy source. According to this lady, her husband had 'exchanged pulpits' with the curate of a little church in Devon for their holidays one year. The vicarage attached to this church was "very old indeed, long and low and thatched ... always very dark", and seemed to be inhabited by brownies. One day, the vicar's wife forgot to light the fire so that some stew could cook. Returning home, she and her husband were resigned to a cold meal, but were surprised to find the fire mysteriously lit and the stew piping-hot. Another time the same happened in reverse. The woman forgot to take the evening meal off the fire, meaning it should have been burnt to a crisp. However, returning home she was surprised to find that it had been removed from the stove before this could happen. Furthermore, she told Briggs that she had been advised to shout up the chimney for help if she was ever having trouble lighting the fire. Was somebody just playing tricks upon the vicar's wife here? Maybe the brownies themselves were; whilst this may all sound like benign helpfulness, it could also be considered as being rather a rebuke to the woman's domestic skills. After all, as Briggs herself rather tartly put it, "this lady seems to have been a rather casual housewife". [21]

Matters of Conscience

As we said briefly earlier, whilst many brownies simply offered good examples of industry to be followed, some also provided a threat by playing poltergeist tricks upon those workers, housewives and servants who just couldn't be bothered to do their jobs properly – so maybe the vicar's wife was lucky to get away without being pinched black-and-blue. Sometimes, this relationship between domestic misdeed and subsequent household haunting seems so clear that a reader may almost be tempted to speak of the 'fairy' involved actually being some kind of externalisation of a person's guilty conscience. This, for example, is the account of one Irish informant about what happened one night after she had not cleaned her kitchen properly:

> "I was never to leave anything on the table but a cup of water and the kettle left on the hook; the house had to be left spotless. One night I was just too tired after a day's work and I didn't wash up after the supper. I said I would just leave it in the basin until morning and I thought every cup that was in the basin was going to be broken with the racket that went on in the house that night. I've never left the house dirty at night since." [22]

Here, I suppose the obvious thing to guess is that the woman felt guilty about transgressing her social role and that, as such, experienced some kind of auditory hallucination which she then put down to the fairies (or the dead – she wasn't entirely sure which) punishing her for her slatternly misdeed. However, an alternative interpretation would be to say that the poltergeists producing the noise did have a kind of objective reality and were, perhaps, actually some kind of RSPK-style projection of the lazy woman's guilt out onto the physical world around her.

Embarrassed by an Elf

Surprisingly, poltergeists do actually appear occasionally to have enjoyed causing embarrassment by the public revelation of people's moral misdeeds – whether these should relate to trivial offences like unwashed dishes or crimes which are rather more serious in nature. In this way they can almost be seen to be fulfilling some kind of regulatory role. Misbehave in private, some poltergeists seem to threaten their victims, and they will reveal the fact to the whole world, like some kind of weird, externalised conscience. This seems analogous to the threats and humiliations imposed upon slack workers in brownie-lore – something to which we shall return after a slight digression.

During one of the very first poltergeist cases we have on record, for example, from near the German town of Bingen in the year 858, the ghost in question denounced people's sins and revealed embarrassing evidence of sexual misconduct. This spook's activities were first chronicled in the *Annales Fuldenses*, a medieval chronicle written by a monk named Rudolf from the Benedictine monastery of Fulda, and have been oft-cited since. In a house belonging to a poor farmer, said Rudolf, a "malignant spirit gave a clear sign of its wickedness" by throwing stones and banging against the walls "as though it were using a hammer." Then, it developed a voice, and delighted in "fomenting quarrels" between the locals with the things it revealed. Eventually, the polt focused its ire upon one particular farmer, who it claimed was a great sinner. Loudly and dramatically, it listed his alleged moral transgressions, which in some accounts included the sin of sleeping with his foreman's daughter. Worse, the spirit implied that it was only persecuting the other locals because of this particular individual's vile misdeeds, and started to set fire to any house that the man went inside, including his own. The man and his family ended up having to sleep outside in the fields, but this did no good either – the demon simply set all of his crops aflame instead.

Angered by the hellish vengeance that seemed to be being brought down upon the whole community by this man, it seems that the other families of Bingen were ready to kill him. However, he underwent the ancient legal ordeal of trial by iron (holding a red-hot iron bar to see if he was guilty) and so 'proved' his innocence. Thus, the Bishop of Mainz was petitioned to send out some exorcists, though they fared little better. The "ancient Enemy", as Rudolf called it, just started hurling stones again, this time with such ferocity that blood was spilled. Then, the invisible entity said that the exorcism was of no use because one of the priests performing it was his "very own slave", and let him hide beneath his cap. According to the disembodied voice, this exorcist had slept with – or perhaps raped, the original account is ambiguous – a local girl at the demon's suggestion, and so was a dreadful sinner himself. As such, the ritual had no effect and the entity stayed around for three years, during which time it allegedly burned down almost every home in the vicinity. [23]

We can see here, quite clearly, how the precise nature of the embarrassing revelations made by the ghost must have led to the reinforcement of certain social mores, namely those which say that adultery and rape are immoral acts. The farmer and the priest were publicly caught out in their alleged misdeeds; so presumably would as a result have thought twice about doing the same thing again (if they were even guilty in the first place). We can see hints of this idea in the way that Rudolf wrote the whole thing up, being quite willing to co-opt the affair for his own moralistic purposes. Indeed, the learned monk even went so far as to quote Matthew 10:26 in his account of the haunting, to the effect that "Nothing is hidden which will not be revealed", as if to hammer home the Christian warning against sin which he saw contained in it all. Given this, we may well suspect that the tale has been somewhat exaggerated to act as Church propaganda, but if so, then there are still several other tales on record which sound suspiciously similar ...

Ghostly Guilt
For example, we could look at the behaviour of the infamous Pembrokeshire spirit of 1184, one of the very first known British poltergeists, whose deeds were originally recorded by the medieval clergyman and chronicler Giraldus Cambrensis ('Gerald of Wales'). Here, in the house of a man called Stephen Wiriet, as well as throwing lumps of dirt – or possibly excrement – about, the spirit:

> "... used to talk with men, and when people bandied words with it, as many did in mockery, it taxed them with all the things they had ever done in their lives which they were least willing should be known or spoken about." [24]

Curiously, both this entity – and another Pembrokeshire spirit mentioned by Giraldus, which is said to have repeatedly ripped up cloth in the house of a man named William Not – proved immune to attempts at exorcism, even when copious amounts of holy water were splashed around. This fact puzzled the chronicler at the time – but, suggestively, it may have led some contemporary observers to think these Welsh spooks to be fairies, rather than demons or ghosts as such. After all, according to the opinion of the time evil spirits were compelled unfailingly to flee in the face of holy rites; it was only entities of more ambiguous nature, like fairies and elementals, who could hope to resist the power of the crucifix [25]. Around 1190, meanwhile, at Dagworth in Suffolk, that fairy-like spook identifying itself as 'Malekin', whom we encountered earlier, is also said to have revealed "the secret doings of other people" in both English and Latin [26]. It is especially interesting that three such early cases should all feature this particular yet actually fairly rare poltergeist motif; perhaps people in those more Christian days were just more attuned to the idea of their sins being found out and then punished by a superior (or infernal) and invisible agency?

Getting Inside Your Head

More modern instances of the trope do exist, though. A very famous 1930s poltergeist known as Gef the Mongoose, for instance – he supposedly appeared in the form of such a creature, albeit one with human hands and the ability to talk – seems to have particularly annoyed John Cowley, a motor mechanic at the local Isle of Man bus company, by spying on him and his colleagues going about their private business before then revealing their every embarrassing personal foible to the world. Amazingly, so annoyed was Cowley by this behaviour that he actually set up a trap to electrocute Gef on the undercarriage of his bus! In Cowley's own words:

> "This animal, or whatever it is, knows a darn sight too much. He seems to hear what we talk in the bus-shed, behind closed doors, in the early morning hours, when no one is about. I can imagine a rat hiding under the floor of the waiting room, but I can't see how a rat could tell Mr Irving [in whose house Gef 'lived'] whose coming we used to dread. He made us uncomfortable by telling us every ridiculous thing that we have been doing, as for instance, heating plugs over the stove in the office, etc. He never came to see me, and I have never been to [Irving's haunted farm-house] Doarlish Cashen. He said Gef told him. It is damn strange." [27]

Stalin must have dearly wished he had a whole army of creatures like Gef at his disposal; no good police state should ever be without one.

Surely the most notable sin-revealing entity, however, was the Bell Witch, who made embarrassing revelations quite frequently. One such instance came when the Witch was listening to a discussion in the Bell household about covetousness and sin. One guest made the observation that he did not feel that it could ever be a sin for a man to steal food when he was starving. Instantly, the Witch butted in, asking the man sarcastically "if he ate that sheepskin". At this point, the unfortunate fellow shut his mouth and left. The Witch had revived an old scandal, long-forgotten, in which the man had been accused of pinching a sheepskin, seemingly finding it amusing after all these years to reveal that the man was indeed guilty of the crime. [28]

A watercolour illustration by William Blake to John Milton's great poem *L'Allegro*. That giant spirit with the threshing equipment and empty bowl is Blake's slightly eccentric interpretation of Lob-Lie-by-the-Fire, the familiar spirit or brownie who helps out around the farm.

LOB LIE-BY-THE-FIRE

OR THE LUCK OF LINGBOROUGH

BY JULIANA HORATIA EWING

WITH ILLUSTRATIONS BY RANDOLPH CALDECOTT

LONDON
SOCIETY FOR PROMOTING CHRISTIAN KNOWLEDGE,
NORTHUMBERLAND AVENUE, CHARING CROSS. W.C;
43, QUEEN VICTORIA STREET, E.C.;
26, ST. GEORGE'S PLACE, HYDE PARK CORNER, S.W.
BRIGHTON; 135, NORTH STREET.
NEW YORK: E. & J. B. YOUNG & CO

The brownie Lob-Lie-by-the-Fire, being such a hard-working spirit, provided a good figure through whom to spread a 'morally educative' message to children – as this book published in 1883 by the Society for Promoting Christian Knowledge shows.

Bishop Richard Corbet, who in a 17th-century poem lamented that fairies no longer leave any sixpences inside the shoes of cleanly servant-maids.

The Jacobean jester Tom Skelton, whose soul allegedly haunts Muncaster Castle in Cumbria in the form of a poltergeist. But was the spirit originally a brownie?

The Cauld Lad o'Hilton, as depicted in Joseph Jacob's 1890 book *English Fairy Tales*.

EASTMAN KODAK CO.'S BROWNIE CAMERAS $1.00

Make pictures 2¼ x 2¼ inches. Load in Daylight with our six exposure film cartridge and are so simple they can be easily

Operated by any School Boy or Girl.

Fitted with fine Meniscus lenses and our improved rotary shutters for snap shots or time exposures. Strongly made, covered with imitation leather, have nickeled fittings and produce the best results. Forty-four page booklet giving full directions for operating the camera, together with chapters on "Snap-Shots," "Time Exposures," "Flash Lights," "Developing" and "Printing," free with every instrument.

Brownie Camera for 2¼ x 2¼ pictures,				•	•	•	•	$1.00
Transparent-Film Cartridge, 6 exposures, 2¼ x 2¼,		•	•	•	•	•	•	.15
Paper-Film Cartridge, 6 exposures, 2¼ x 2¼,		•	•	•	•	•	•	.10
Brownie Developing and Printing Outfit,	•	•	•	•	•	•	•	.75

The Brownie Camera Club.

Reward ofttimes is slow
to fall
To those who earned it best
of all.

One of our main sources for the modern stereotypical visual appearance of brownies was the Canadian cartoonist Palmer Cox (1840-1924), whose popular 'Brownies' characters appeared in their own comic-strips and books, and were even used to advertise the early 'Box-Brownie' portable cameras. Kodak deliberately named their device after Cox's characters in order to piggy-back on their immense popularity.

A brownie hard at work. There are certainly worse varities of poltergeist to be haunted by ...

Palmer Cox's brownies lend a hand around the farm.

A brownie makes the crockery clatter. Were such events – whether thought of as being auditory hallucinations or not – the sign of an untidy housewife's guilty conscience?

The Bell Witch, it appeared, had the power to spy upon not only the actions, but also the inner thoughts of the local community. Once, it repeated a couple's entire private conversation in public, advising everyone present "not to talk too much" as it did so, then adding that nobody had better think any bad thoughts about its favourite member of the Bell family, Lucy, because it could read their minds [29]. At other times, the spook took delight in publicly shaming persons who fell asleep in church and threatening those who did not attend services regularly [30]. Fear of embarrassing revelations being made soon grew strong. Before long, people's behaviour was being forcibly regulated by the entity, known by many as 'Kate'. Apparently:

> "Citizens of the community soon learned to respect Kate's presence and councils, as they feared and abominated the Witch's scorpion tongue. Everybody got good; the wicked left off swearing, lying and whiskey-drinking ... The avaricious were careful not to covet or lay hands on that which belonged to their neighbours, lest Kate might tell on them. No man allowed his right hand to do anything that the left might be ashamed of."

It all sounds rather totalitarian – and yet, the level of criminality in the neighbourhood is said to have dropped as a result of the Witch's activities:

> "No citizen thought of locking his smoke-house or crib door, or of staying up through the night to guard his hen-roost or watermelon patch." [31]

Crime and Punishment

This particular aspect of the Witch's tale seems exaggerated, but there are a few slightly less extreme cases on record of people supposedly being turned away from the path of crime by polts. For example, a haunted house in Westmorland, Cumbria, known locally as the 'boggart-house', was visited sometime in the 1840s by an engine-driver and his fireman. On the way there, they passed a farm and stole some eggs. As soon as they entered the boggart-house, however, the fireman's cap was snatched from his head and slapped into his face, and an egg hurled at him. According to the recorder of this story, the Scottish dialect-poet Robert Leighton:

> "... the egg incident seemed to give his mind a serious turn. Certain it is, that he was afterwards afraid to tamper with hen's nests that did not belong to him, lest other eyes than his own be upon him." [32]

Even more dramatic was the tale of a stolen saddle which, during a haunting at the home of the Gast family in the Somerset village of Little Burton in 1677, began acting very strangely indeed. It would leap from its hook and "hop about the house from one place to another", even jumping on the table. Taking this to be a warning to return the saddle to the relative from whom they had borrowed it with no intention of giving it back, two women from the household, on their way to do so, were attacked by flying sticks and stones, and even had the shawls on their shoulders knitted together, one with the other. Still the trouble did not cease, however – that night, the very same saddle was hurled onto a bed from nowhere. The object was then chopped into pieces and scattered on a public highway, after which it bothered the Gasts no more – but a coat that had also been stolen flew into the fire, where, amazingly, it did not burn! Bizarrely, it took three people to remove the item from the flames, as it suddenly became inexplicably heavy. A stolen hat was then knocked from Mr Gast's head whilst he was having dinner [33]. I'm sure that at this point the householders got the message – you should always return that which does not belong to you.

From Ireland, meanwhile, there comes a curious tale from Upper Ballygowan in Northern Ireland where, in 1866, two families who had repaired their houses with materials taken from an abandoned (because allegedly fairy-haunted) home had been subsequently plagued by showers of stones and turf. The folklorist Richard P Jenkins speculates intriguingly about this case that:

> "... a degree of communally recognised ill-behaviour may have been involved. The deserted house was abandoned because the previous owner had been forced to leave by the fairies ... Thus those who used its fabric as building material were, in effect, profiting from someone else's misfortune." [34]

I take it that, here, Jenkins is talking about the story as being a piece of *untrue* local folklore, the families' immoral behaviour being "communally recognised" by virtue of an invented tall tale. But could such stories ever actually have been real? The psychologist Julian Jaynes, in his master-work *The Origin of Consciousness in the Breakdown of the Bicameral Mind*, inadvertently provides some possible evidence that they could. Jaynes' controversial book posits the view that, up until relatively recently in man's history, he did not have any kind of meaningful 'inner-life' or consciousness. Instead, he was the subject of various auditory and visual hallucinations which he personified as being 'gods' – though Jaynes asserts that they were in fact merely products of the brain – who guided him through life, telling him how to behave. In essence, he implied, 'bicameral' people (those guided by the 'gods' and not themselves) had no internal sense of right and wrong. They relied instead upon voices – apparently coming from outside the head, though in reality from within – to warn them what was a sin. It was only once the state of bicamerality began to die out that people could feel the emotion we now call guilt. "No one before 1000BC ever felt guilt", [35] he says, and then gives various pieces of evidence for such a claim, drawn from ancient Greek drama.

But he could also, perhaps, have looked for such evidence in fairy-lore. A story collected by WY Evans-Wentz from the Isle of Barra in the Outer Hebrides, for example, tells of a man being sent to get some medicine for a dying woman. On his way, this man selfishly stops for a rest next to a fairy-hill and falls asleep in the warm sunshine before being awoken by a voice singing the words:

> "Ho, ho, ho, hi, ho, ho. Ill it becomes a messenger on an important message to sleep on the ground in the open air." [36]

Was this really a fairy talking, or a late example of Jaynes' 'bicamerality' in action?

God Forgive Me!
Perhaps those poltergeists which enjoy embarrassing people through indelicate public revelations – and thence regulating their future behaviour somewhat – are some kind of

strange, externalised remnant of this now almost-vanished quality of bicamerality? Maybe some people are born more naturally 'bicameral' than others, and then inadvertently project their interior 'god voice' out into the world in the guise of the RSPK-derived 'noisy ghost'? I make no claims, only suggestions; this is all incredibly speculative. After all, the stories given above could simply be untrue, the morals they contain being taught through fiction masquerading as fact. But consider the life of the ever-curious Curé d'Ars, Jean Baptiste Vianney, whom we met earlier. He was persecuted by his *grappin* – the name he gave to the invisible demon which haunted him – for about 30 years; one of the longest hauntings on record. He must have hated this constant satanic persecution, we might suppose.

We would suppose wrong. He absolutely *loved* it! But why? Because this strange man was constantly beset by hysterical fears about his degree of moral worth, despite the fact that he barely ate or slept for most of his adult life due to performing acts of charity for his parishioners and the thousands of pilgrims who made their way to his village to meet him. When he was ill in bed one time, for instance, he cried to God that he did not wish to die, being "not yet ready to appear before Thy dreadful judgement seat." This wholly unreasonable opinion was backed up for the Curé by a troop of hallucinatory demons which then appeared to him, constantly repeating "We have him; we have him!" in a terrible voice [37]. Eventually, he recovered.

Hell, then, was an irrational yet ever-constant fear for the Curé; and *grappin* kept on inadvertently exhorting him to avoid it by providing him with both public insults and opportunities to demonstrate whole new heights of asceticism. Thus, he actually felt that the poltergeist was of some moral use to him. The following disembodied cajolement, for example, was heard not just by Vianney in his head, but also by an independent witness:

> "Vianney, Vianney, what are you doing there? Get along, get along!" [38]

Not a moment's self-indulgent rest for the Curé in this life, then; *grappin* as represented here sounds not unlike having the ghost of Calvin forever at your ear, reminding you mercilessly that each poor sinner will have to account for every last second of their miserable little lives before the all-seeing and merciless Court of God come Judgement Day. On one occasion, meanwhile, *grappin* is meant to have burnt the Curé's bed to ashes. Vianney's reaction to this event was particularly unhinged. Was he not upset about it all, he was asked? Not at all! His opinion upon the matter in fact ran thus:

> "For a long time past have I been asking this grace of the good God, and He has heard me at last. Today I think I am really the poorest man in the parish. They all have their beds – and now, thank God, I have none." [39]

We might of course question whether or not the strange Monsieur Vianney burnt his bed himself, consciously or otherwise, in order to procure this fortuitous outcome for his soul – but, apparently, the conflagration displayed certain ostensibly unnatural characteristics to it. The flames, it seemed, stopped burning just as they reached a relic of St Philomena, "as if by a line drawn with geometrical precision", burning all on one side of the holy item and nothing on the other [40]. Supernatural or not, though, the blaze certainly gave the Curé yet another chance to engage in an act of public mortification. In the final six months of his life, however, *grappin* finally abandoned Vianney altogether, "as if," speculates his biographer Alfred Monnin, "the enemy had withdrawn his forces in despair." [41] One would certainly like to think so; if the Curé d'Ars couldn't get into Heaven after the life he had led, then I don't think the rest of us can have much hope.

Cleanliness Is Next to Godliness

Another type of socially-unacceptable behaviour besides lack of godliness, acts of theft or taking advantage of another person's misfortune, however, would be having a dirty, unkempt house, and here at last we return specifically to the subject of brownies. The alleged tactics used by such beings to discourage slatternliness through causing open embarrassment were various. The 1960s Pontefract poltergeist, for example, not only provided a good domestic example by laying the table but also, less praiseworthily, liked to make a mess with food. One morning at four o'clock, for example, Mrs Pritchard, the woman of the haunted house, found that several door handles had been smeared with jam and wrapped in lavatory paper, a mixture of marmalade and mustard having also been poured down the stairs. Joe, her husband, told her to come back to bed and leave it. But, being a typical Yorkshire housewife, Mrs Pritchard got up straight away, filled a bucket with hot water and scrubbed up immediately. As Colin Wilson, who investigated the case, commented:

> "It is an interesting thought that if Jean Pritchard had been an indifferent housewife who could ignore untidiness, 'Fred' [the ghost] might have given up a great deal sooner." [42]

Very true; but if somebody had called at the house early that morning and seen the state of it, I'm sure that poor Mrs Pritchard, being commendably house-proud, would have been most embarrassed – mortified, even. Here, then, it is almost as if the poltergeist is taunting its victim, and goading her into performing what she viewed as being her accepted social role – that of the clean, industrious Yorkshirewoman. By occasionally turning boggart in this way, the brownies of folklore actually acted to insist upon cleanliness, forcing the household staff to do what Mrs Pritchard found she too had to do; namely, to get down on their knees and scrub. For example, the obscure British fairy known as 'Brownie-Clod' – a household familiar who, if he found a home's level of cleanliness not to his liking, threw clods of earth at the lazy servant-women – only made further work for his victims even as he went about punishing them. [43]

However, brownie could be even more oppressive than this, in his way. The historian Robert Chambers, in his 1826 book *The Popular Rhymes of Scotland*, stated of such fairies that:

> "The least delinquency committed either in barn, or cow-house, or larder, he was sure to report to his master, whose interests he seemed to consider paramount to every other thing in this world, and from whom no bribe could induce him to conceal the offences which fell under his notice. The men, therefore, and not less the maids, of the establishment usually regarded him with a mixture of fear, hatred and respect." [44]

If the brownie-familiar reminds us of the Bell Witch's reign of moral terror here, then the farm-workers he kept an eye over also remind me of people who were still living in what anthropologists once called a 'shame society'. The idea went that there were two types of society operating to regulate people's behaviour in existence – 'shame societies' and 'guilt societies'. The latter were seen as being morally higher, as in a guilt society you regulated your own behaviour yourself because you had an innate sense of right and wrong and did not wish to transgress it, whereas people living in shame societies only did not wish to perform transgressive acts in public. It is almost as though the spy-master brownie in Chambers' description is a kind of 'person-substitute' for people still living in such shame-regulated societies, people who know that doing a half-hearted job when unsupervised is wrong, but who still feel the need of an external presence in order to force them to work hard. For some potential sinners God probably performs the same function, with his famed 'all-seeing eye'. Maybe, then, when people stuck at this lower level of moral development perform a lazy or wicked act they can subconsciously externalise their guilt, and we are left either with embarrassing public revelations being made, or with annoying boggart-like polt phenomena as we saw with the clattering dishes which had been left out uncleaned by the Irishwoman earlier on.

Clean Up Your Own Mess

An alternative perspective upon the matter, of course, would be that all such tales are mere fictions and that, whilst brownie may once have played a useful role in regulating people's behaviour, he was in fact no more real than is the bogeyman with whom parents still threaten their misbehaving children. The historian Keith Thomas, in his monumental 1971 book *Religion and the Decline of Magic*, sums up this sort of position thus:

> "Modern social anthropologists, studying the survival of fairy-beliefs among the Irish peasantry, have been able to show that such notions can ... help to enforce a certain code of conduct ... It would be an exaggeration to say that ... serving-maids only did their work conscientiously because they were afraid of being tormented by the fairies, but the direction in which fairy-beliefs influenced those who held them is obvious enough ... They even upheld the virtues of neighbourliness by lending out household utensils and insisting upon their prompt return; those who delayed bringing back the spits and pieces of pewter they had borrowed were never helped by the fairies again." [45]

Perhaps such tardy persons were also bothered with poltergeist phenomena, as with the haunted saddle at Little Burton? Society being what it once was, moralising fairy-stories of this kind were particularly aimed at women. According to the writer Jeremy Harte, for instance, tales told to young girls about fairies leaving behind coins and silver for diligent housemaids:

> "... acted as sweeteners for the feminine role that lay ahead of them. After all, cleaning and sweeping is hard work ... and if you are going to spend the rest of your life doing it, you might as well have a story or two to give it some magical allure. Getting that bucket of fresh, bright water is a chore, but

maybe, just maybe, there will be a piece of bright silver shining at the bottom of it." [46]

This is all very sensible, but we should be careful of simply dismissing *every* such tale in these terms. Here, for example, is an account sent in to *Fortean Times* in 2006 by a woman named Jennifer McGhee, of Greenock in Scotland. It transpires that, whilst tidying her bathroom one day, Jennifer was kneeling on the toilet seat in order to dust the shelves above. When she had finished, she was surprised to find a crisp £20 note on the toilet, where there had been no note before, lying "perfectly flat as if it had just come out of a cash machine." She texted her boyfriend, and he suggested that Jennifer say thank you for this, so she did – and at that very moment there came a knock on her bedroom door, even though she had thought she was alone in the flat [47]. Admittedly, this is pure anecdote – but can we really just ignore it?

Mother's Little Helper
One of the most commonly-known facts of poltergeistry is that such phenomena tend to focus with disarming regularity upon teenage girls – exactly the type of person who would in the past have been highly likely to be employed in domestic service. Certainly, this was the case with the Devil of Mascon. Here, it was noticed that a Bressan servant-girl in the haunted household of the Huguenot Minister, François Perrault, was on particularly close terms with the ghost; within a different cultural context, it may have been said that she had 'a bit of fairy' in her blood. They liked mocking and making jokes about one another, it seems; the spirit called her "my Bressan girl", and jokingly imitated her local patois. Interestingly, he also used to help her around the house, like many a brownie. Upon one occasion, she chafed him for never making her labours lighter by bringing her any firewood. Immediately, he threw a faggot down the stairs so that she wouldn't have to fetch it herself, by way of amends. Furthermore, when the maid temporarily left Perrault's service, the Devil bothered her replacement at night by beating and pouring water on her until she fled – something which furthers, perhaps, the suspicion that the poltergeist here might well have been an inadvertent RSPK-emanation of the Bressan girl's own personality [48]. If this were indeed the case, then it is hardly any surprise that it should have proved so handy with the housework.

We can easily find other such examples of poltergeists proving helpful upon request. At Poona for instance, the spirit would sometimes fetch things when asked to; you only had to say "shoe-polish, please" for this item to float over and land next to your foot [49]. Matthew Manning, meanwhile, an English faith-healer and one-time poltergeist medium, could also supposedly benefit in this way from his spook. In January 1972, for example, he was unable to find a copy of the Ringo Starr record he wanted in any shops. However, returning home, he was delighted to find a brand-new copy of it sitting there on his desk! Another time, he wished to make a bonfire, but was short of material to burn. He went and asked his mother if she had anything appropriate, but she did not. Going back out, however, Matthew found to his amazement that a large stack of wood and logs had appeared in the garden from nowhere. He received many other such useful apports, too; a bag of sugar, some gloves, stamps, other records and, predictably, bank-notes. One time, feeling hungry on a train, he wished he had brought something to eat with him. Unzipping his bag, he found an apple pie and a bottle of beer, just waiting there for him. [50]

We can also sometimes read of brownies taking their servant-girls' side and turning against any persons who may have mistreated them. A *lutin* which caused certain "noises and extraordinary disorders" at the house of a wealthy merchant in the Italian city of Bologna in 1579, for example, attached itself to one of the serving-maids, following her wherever she went. Once, when her mistress had become annoyed with her, the *lutin* exacted revenge upon the girl's behalf, slapping and pinching her employer, tearing her head-dress and even throwing cold water over her as she lay in bed, as with the replacement maidservant at Mascon. Bizarrely, the *lutin* in question was finally exorcised by the master and mistress of the house force-feeding the maid excessive amounts of food, something which supposedly angered the spook so much that it left the house forever! [51]

A Woman's Work Is Never Done
However, if sometimes such spirits aided housemaids then, at other times, they simply made them even more work to do, just like Brownie-Clod. For example, showing a visitor up to a bedroom one day, François Perrault found that the bed, blankets, sheets and bolster had all been thrown across the floor by the Devil of Mascon. The maid was called and ordered to re-make the bed, which she did in Perrault's presence, but, when he later re-entered the bedroom, the whole bed was "undone and tumbled down on the floor, as it was before." [52] There is also the tale of the polt (called a *kobold* by its victim) which followed a young Austrian servant-girl named Hannie during the 1920s. Her master, a Commander Kogelnick, in his account of the spirit's activities, speaks of such irritating things as an ink-stand materialising one day and then shattering, staining everything black. Hannie, of course, had to clean the ink-stains up, together with Kogelnick's wife. As they were doing so, pieces of coal were thrown at them. Then, a flower-pot sailed across the room, sprinkling soil across the newly-mopped floor as if to spite them [53]. When we read about poltergeist cases, of course, we do not tend to stop and think about the fact that someone has to get down on their hands and knees and sweep up all those broken plates after them, but someone does; and, in the past, it was highly likely that that person would have been a servant-girl.

If these ghosts really are nothing more than emissions of RSPK-forces upon such girls' behalf, as many modern critics would claim, then it is easy enough to see why they would make helpful brownies appear. But why on earth would they also cause these fairies to dirty up the place, smash crockery and generally act like bothersome boggarts? The sceptical historian Owen Davies asked himself the same question, and produced an interesting answer:

> "One recognises the insecurities and frustrations that must have been a common experience for young servants ... They were removed from their families and familiar environments at a formative age, and had to live with strangers and negotiate the inequalities and sexual politics between masters and servants ... [such a servant] found expression for her emotional state through a form of displacement activity that enabled the release of pent-up frustration through vandalism, whilst at the same time attracting the attention she obviously craved ... poltergeist activity can be read as a way in which adolescents can and did transform the supernatural into domestic power, radically altering the dynamics of household relationships." [54]

Whether the young servant-girls at the centre of many old poltergeist hauntings did this deliberately through hoaxing, or inadvertently, through the emission of psychic powers, is a decision which can only be left to the individual reader. Maybe, by creating more work for themselves by smashing crockery, messing up beds and dirtying floors, these women were simply expressing, by proxy, their frustration and boredom with their work. By doing such things, whether supernaturally or otherwise, they were actually inverting their intended domestic roles and dirtying the place rather than keeping it clean. Frequently, if the ghost was indeed deemed to be attached to them somehow by their employers, such girls would then be sacked, thereby freeing them (temporarily) from the prisons of their drudgery. If they were not dismissed, however, then at least they were making their workplaces a bit more interesting! Such narratives could actually have been some kind of folk-expression of a deep, underlying social truth, then; that the life of a female servant around the house or farm was one of unremitting and ill-rewarded drudgery.

2.

The Poltergeist as Boggart

We can see that just as common as tales of fairies' rewards and help, then, are cases of household familiars exacting revenge against those who slight them or to whom they simply take a dislike. Whenever this happens, we might usefully say that brownies become boggarts – or malicious poltergeists, if you prefer to view it that way. If you were stupid enough to turn a brownie into a boggart, then he would mess the place up, make objects disappear, pull your bedsheets off at night, make animals go lame and tug on a person's ears. Hanging a horseshoe on the door of your house was meant to keep a boggart out, but if he did get inside you generally just had to put up with him; once attached to you and your family, he would follow you around to the ends of the earth. [1]

Most purported boggart-narratives are just folklore, of course; but many are also surprisingly modern, feature named witnesses or participants, and are supposed literally to be true. Perhaps my favourite such contemporary tale is that of a certain Jenny and Peter Bolton, who were allegedly told by the former occupants of their new house that there were brownies living at the bottom of the building's garden, who would happily perform simple household tasks for them. Amazingly, this appeared to be true; when the couple were at work, the washing-machine would be turned on and the wet clothes placed in the tumble-drier, and the garden shed would be tidied. Mrs Bolton went to see a doctor, presuming that she had been doing these things herself and then suffering from amnesia, but he could find nothing wrong. However, one day, perhaps placed under stress by the continuing weirdness, Jenny is said to have lost her temper with her invisible helpers and, thereafter, the brownies turned bad. Plugs were put in sinks and taps turned on, furniture knocked over, soap-powder poured onto vegetables and jam smeared into their carpet. Eventually, so the story goes, things became so bad that the couple had no choice but to move out. [2]

The psychic-healer Matthew Manning, whom we met in the previous chapter, must also have occasionally annoyed his childhood poltergeist however, as it didn't just limit its activities to providing useful services like bringing him free Ringo Starr records. Sometimes it used to mess his house up something awful. One Easter Monday, for example, Matthew says that he and his parents arose to find that nearly every room in the house "looked as though a bomb had hit it". Chairs and tables were turned over and piled on top of one another, ornaments thrown across the floor and pictures dismounted. Wearily, the family began to tidy everything up, starting in the sitting-room before then moving on to the dining-room. In here, they found some object which really should have been in the sitting-room. Upon taking it back, however, Manning and his family found that the sitting-room was once more in a state of "total disarray", only a few minutes after they had tidied it. Once more, they set right the sitting-room – only to find that, whilst they had been doing so, the dining-room had again been disarranged! [3]

The folklorist RL Tongue, meanwhile – not necessarily the most reliable of sources, admittedly [4] – supposedly spoke in 1964 with an unnamed woman living next to an establishment called The Holman Clavel Inn near Somerset's Blackdown Hills, which was meant to be haunted by a mischievous fireside hob called 'Chimbley Charlie' who could sometimes be the very opposite of helpful. One time, this woman said, when the inn's maids had been asked to prepare a dinner for a certain local farmer, Charlie acted just like a boggart. Supposedly, the servants carefully laid out all the silver and the linen, and spruced the place up beautifully. Whilst talking, however, one maid said of the farmer in question that "Oh! Charlie don't like 'ee [him]!" After this observation had been made, the staff knew what was coming, but all they could do was shut the kitchen-door and hope for the best. According to Tongue's informant, this is what happened next:

> "... before the guests arrived [the maids] went in again, to make sure that everything was all right. The doors had been kept closed, but ... the table was quite bare. All the tankards were hanging up again on their hooks; the silver had been put neatly in its place. Charlie certainly didn't like him." [5]

The fairy-expert Katharine Briggs gives another interesting example of a brownie that could turn boggart. The tale concerns Lemmington Hall outside Newcastle, which was occupied in the early twentieth century by two old women by the name of Hoyle and what they called a 'Silkie' – a type of entity defined by Briggs as being White or Grey Ladies clad in silk, "something between ghosts and brownies", who were said to haunt certain houses in the North of England [6]. The place being rather too large for these two old women, they were grateful indeed for the spirit's services, cleaning, as it did, the hearth and laying logs in the fire-place, as well as leaving out nice fresh flowers on the stairs. However, by WWII, both Hoyles were dead and a new occupant had moved into the Hall. Unfortunately, says Briggs, "he was not the kind of person to get on with fairies", and the banging noises and poltergeist pranks which soon broke out there became so bad that he was ultimately forced to leave. [7]

Have You Seen My Keys?
Another example of a mortally-offended domestic fairy comes from Herefordshire, a county where, it was said, the household brownies and boggarts (just like Wag-at-the-Wa') used to sit on the 'sway' – the iron bar above the hearth where pots and kettles hung. Accordingly, whenever the hobgoblin was deemed to have been offended, small offerings of food were left out by the fireplace as a means of appeasement. According to the Herefordshire folklorist EM Leather, writing in 1912:

> "Brownie sometimes took offence at what he considered slights to himself, and his favourite and chief form of revenge was to hide the household keys; there was only one way in which they could be brought back. The members of the household sat in a circle round the hearth, after placing a little cake upon the hob, as a peace-offering. The party sat in absolute silence with closed eyes, when the keys would be flung violently at the wall at the back of the sitters." [8]

This was recorded as having been done at the Portway Inn in the Herefordshire village of Staunton-on-Wye, in the 1840s or so. Many modern-day people, too, have also had recourse to the invocation of invisible powers when searching for lost items such as keys, however; it is just that, nowadays, they do not tend to term these unseen gods boggarts or brownies. For example, an Andrew Shilcock once wrote in to *Fortean Times* to tell them how, whilst staying in the Surrey town of Haslemere in the summer of 2004, his wife lost their hotel door-key. Turning the room upside down they could not find it anywhere, so Mr Shilcock resorted to extreme measures; he stood by the door and asked out loud for it back. A few minutes later, he heard his wife yelp – a cupboard by the door had moved itself out from the wall and the missing key lay in the depression in the carpet where the wardrobe had stood previously. Mr Shilcock said 'thank-you' out loud and then went to bed [9]. At a haunted garden centre in the London suburb of Bromley in 1973, meanwhile, the ghost used to enjoy stealing the car-keys from one employee's pocket. An investigator who was present during such an episode calmly asked for their return – whereupon, it is said, they suddenly appeared sitting on the floor where they had not been before. [10]

Here's another case which sounds exactly like what took place at Herefordshire's Portway Inn all those years ago. It happened to a certain Graham Oxley and his wife in 1989, when they were refurbishing an old house in Dumfries, Scotland. Having put a bunch of heavy old keys on the floor and left the room momentarily, Graham was surprised to return and find they were no longer there. A lengthy search ensued, but to no avail. Later, however, when he and his wife sat down on the only two chairs in the house in one of the bare and as-yet unfinished rooms, the keys were thrown across the floorboards at them from "out of nowhere ... skidding to a halt" a few feet away [11]. Patrick Harpur, we will recall, christened these phenomena with the appropriate name of pixilation. An alternative option, though, would be to say that such vanished items have been 'boggled' – a word ultimately derived from the terms 'bogey' and 'boggart'. Perhaps it is not too hard to see why ...

A Moving Story

Modern tales like these are generally cited with no real context to them; they are simply presented in books and magazines as being odd, isolated events which have happened to people. Essentially, they are anecdotes. With older boggart-narratives, however, there often seems to have been some kind of subsequent accretion of obviously untrue folkloric elements around what may originally have been genuine, actual occurrences. One particularly striking case of such a process seemingly taking place surrounds the activities of a Yorkshire boggart originally described during the 1750s. An early account of the fairy is described by one commentator as being "pure poltergeist", and goes like this:

> "The children's bread and butter would be snatched away, or their porringers of

bread and milk would be dashed down by an invisible hand ... One day the farmer's youngest boy was playing with the shoe-horn, and as children will do he stuck the horn into a knot-hole ... The horn darted out with velocity and struck the poor child over the head. Time at length familiarized the preternatural occurrence, and that which at first was regarded with terror, became a kind of amusement ... Often was the horn slipped slyly into the hole, which never failed to be darted forth at the head of one or other; but most commonly he or she who placed it there was the mark at which their invisible foe placed the offending horn." [12]

The yarn being told about the Gilbertsons – the family at the epicentre of these apparently real-life poltergeist disturbances – by the 1800s, however, was much different. In fact, it was merely a locally-specific version of one of the most widely-spread of all British folk-narratives, being lent some superficial credence by the addition of genuine, named personages to its telling. It is, in fact, the tale of the 'flitting boggart', and tells of how a family (in this case the Gilbertsons), affected by any number of irritating phenomena being inflicted upon them at the hands of an evil fairy, pack up all their belongings on a cart and try to move on to pastures new. Stopped by a neighbour who expresses his sorrow at their departure, the head of the family replies with words to the effect that "It's only because of the boggart we're flitting!" whereupon he is answered by a deep voice from inside the milk-churn saying something like "Ay, it's only because of me we're flitting!" At this point the patriarch, reasoning he may as well stay in a house he knows and be plagued by the bogey as move to an unfamiliar one and be bothered by him, turns straight back around and unpacks again.[13] This tale-type was once so well-known that Tennyson even wrote a verse-version of it, namely his 1824 poem *Walking to the Mail*.

Could it possibly have had any truth to it, however? It could be said that the story-type of the 'boggart-flit', as it is known to folklorists, almost sounds like a riff on the modern idea that a poltergeist is associated with a focus-person rather than with a specific place, so moving house would actually do polt victims no real good. However, the motif is explained much more plausibly by the writer Jeremy Harte by virtue of the fact that such tales probably in fact summed up a kind of no-nonsense attitude once held amongst old Yorkshire farmers that you were better off trying to make the best of things on your own farm rather than swanning off in search of pastures new. As Harte says, "at the end of the day your luck [in both senses of the word] will travel with you." [14]

A good explanation, of course. But then, perhaps, ostension * comes in, and we get apparently real-life accounts of ghosts which torment fleeing residents with the prospect of moving house along with them. The Willington Mill polt, for instance, put the fear of god into Joseph Procter and his wife, the mill's owners, upon the night of their eventual removal from the haunted building in 1847. Edmund Procter, one of their sons, described his parents' final hours in the structure in the *Journal* of the SPR in 1892:

"My parents have both repeatedly told me that during the last night they slept in the old house ... there were continuous noises during the night, boxes being

---

* A term used to denote the apparent real-life acting out of fictional folklore motifs, intentional or otherwise.

apparently dragged with heavy thuds down the now carpetless stairs, non-human footsteps stumped on the floors, doors were, or seemed to be, clashed, and impossible furniture corded at random and dragged hither and hither by inscrutable agency; in short, a pantomimic or spiritualistic repetition of all the noises incident to a household flitting. A miserable night my father and mother had of it ... not so much from terror at the unearthly noises, for to these they were habituated, as dread lest this wretched fanfaronade might portend the contemporary flight of the unwelcome visitors to the new abode." [15]

Thankfully for the Procters, however, it did not; their new home was, by comparison, almost blissfully quiet.

The Unfortunate Travellers
Or, at least, this is how the standard version has it. In fact, recent researches into the case by Michael J Hallowell and Darren W Ritson uncovered testimony suggesting that, actually, the boggart *did* flit along with the Procters after all! According to them, there is an account that one of the Procters' maids from Willington Mill moved to their new home in the Tyneside town of North Shields a short while after her employers themselves. Naturally, prior to leaving, she put her meagre possessions into a "securely corded and locked" box and sent it on ahead of her. When the woman herself arrived at the North Shields residence, though, she was reputedly shocked to find that all of her belongings had been scattered about her new room – despite the box itself still being locked and sealed exactly as she had left it. Talking to the cook, another long-term family employee, the maid was told that the spook had played the same trick upon everyone else in the house, and that it was now common gossip about the Procters that "the ghost had followed them" [16]. They may as well have just stayed put with the devil they knew, then, as was the moral of the old folk-tales.

There are a few other accounts on record of poltergeists apparently making a noise as if of persons packing, or else of previously-dormant polts starting up again on the day their original victims were supposed to move out, which purport to be genuine, too [17]. There is even one very elaborate description of what might be termed 'phantom removal-men' being at work inside a polt-haunted house known as 'Beth-Oni' in the Oxfordshire village of Tackley, from 1908. Here, one night, according to a diary-entry of the house's then-resident, a Miss Ada Sharpe:

"From 9.50pm till 12.15am I heard sounds as if heavy furniture was being removed from every room in the house, without five minutes' cessation. I distinctly heard footsteps in the big attic as well as on the tiles in the hall. I heard a heavy van draw up outside the front windows and men talking and loading. They seemed to come in at my side window ... to fetch a chest of drawers which I was watching and which they seemed [audibly, but not visually] to take quite easily through the window, which, by the way, looks out on the glass top of the greenhouse. When they had finished loading, the van moved off and all was silent." [18]

With narratives such as this, we are left in a quandary; after all, the tale of the 'boggart-flit' is just folklore. The Willington Mill haunting, however, seems to have been real. Was the flitting element of it merely invented, then? Or could it, perhaps, be the case that poltergeists simply adapt themselves to the prevailing notions of the society around them about how precisely they should manifest? Maybe the Procters were already familiar with the tale of the 'boggart-flit' (well-known in the North-East at the time); and, perhaps, that is why the spook chose to manifest in a way which fitted in with that particular tale-type? I have no definite answers for you here, I'm afraid.

Big Hairy Men

From looking at these tales, the boggart, it would appear, is half-benign, half-malicious, half-real, half-folkloric, half-fairy and half-poltergeist. Descriptions of him also make him sound half-human, half-animal; he is most often presented as being a big, hairy, naked man living inside a chimney[19]. Another description depicts him as being "dark and hairy with long yellow teeth," [20] and he is sometimes said to wear tattered garments like the legendary *woodwose*, or 'wild man of the woods'. Another description has him being "a squat hairy man, strong as a six-year-old horse, and with arms almost as long as tacklepoles" [21]. He seems, in short, to sound a little like a Bigfoot – a type of creature, together with its cousins the yowie, sasquatch and yeti, that are often abbreviated down to BHMs, or Big Hairy Men. Is *that* what a boggart really is, then, rather than a fairy or a poltergeist?

At first glance this seems rather counterintuitive but, according to Patrick Harpur, a Bigfoot is simply yet another type of what he calls a "big fairy". As evidence for this assertion, Harpur gives the case of the Bigfoot that bothered Randy and Lou Rogers of the Indiana town of Roachdale in 1972. This beast, like many such beings, seemed to be as spectral in nature as it was physical. Its appearance was heralded by a luminous object hovering over a nearby cornfield and exploding, after which noises began to be heard in the Rogers' yard at night. Soon, the Bigfoot announced its presence more confidently with loud, polt-style knockings on the walls of their trailer for several nights in a row. Curiously, Lou Rogers said that he could sense the beast approaching somehow, a strange atmosphere in the air getting stronger and stronger until the rapping would begin. Then, the Rogers began to see the Bigfoot – heavily built, six-foot tall, covered in black hair and smelling of "dead animals or garbage" – and noticed that it was playing games with them. For instance, when Randy was washing dishes, she would see it bobbing up and down outside the window, as if playing hide-and-seek. Being kind souls, the Rogers left it out some food, treating it almost like a pet. Clearly, however, this 'pet' was no ordinary animal, as on occasion it appeared semi-transparent and left no footprints, even in thick mud. Another time, it was shot at by some local farmers, something which had absolutely no effect. Phantom or not, though, it still took the food which the Rogers left out for it – much like a boggart would once have been expected to do with its own food-offerings. [22]

A different Bigfoot visited the Lee family who lived near the town of Nowata in Oklahoma two years later, in 1974. Eventually, the Lees rather lost their fear of this beast, and began to play a game with it. Every morning, the Bigfoot left an old feed pail in front of their barn and every day they took it away and hid it – much to the man-beast's delight as, each night, he went around looking for it. He never failed to find it, and each morning the pail was found left outside the Lees' home once more. Significantly, we are told that the only time the Lees heard the being make a noise was when it seemed to laugh [23]. A further account of a BHM playing deliberate games with its human 'friends' comes from the case of Sue and Jerry O'Connor, an Australian couple who claimed to be in psychic communication with a yowie (the Australian version of a Bigfoot). Apparently, Jerry began to interact with the creature by leaving intricate patterns of sticks on the ground near his property. After a few days, he would return to find these structures had been "thoughtfully rearranged", and felt that the yowie had enjoyed this simple game [24]. According to Lisa Shiel, author of a book called *Backyard Bigfoot*, BHMs on her property communicate with her in a similar fashion, by leaving "carefully arranged" piles of twigs lying around on the floor. She also often awakes of a morning, she claims, to find her horses with "intricate braids" tied in their hair – a sure sign, she believes, of a visit from Bigfoot, but also, from another perspective, a classic sign of a *stallspuk,* as we shall see soon.[25]

Specific links between BHMs and modern-day poltergeist hauntings are not exactly unknown either, though. According to the respected Australian cryptozoologist Tony Healy, for example, yowies frequently turn up in the close vicinity of poltergeist infestations, citing the disturbing example of one supposedly encountered in 1946 near the small town of Wilcannia in New South Wales. The story goes that, in this year, a man named George Nott and his family moved into an old homestead in the area. As soon as they had done so, the Notts realised that something was horribly wrong. Large, five-toed tracks began appearing on the farm, and horses started panicking over nothing. Soon, typical polt phenomena were occurring; objects flew around the house, doors opened by themselves, banging came from inside the ceiling and stones cascaded onto the roof like pouring rain. Worse, what was termed a "bloody big gorilla", about six-foot tall and covered in "brownish fur", allegedly then invaded the house. Supposedly, it grabbed Mr Nott by the neck, an event which led to the family abandoning their new home for good. [26]

Feeding and Heeding
However, in accounts such as this one, we can see a real difference from the benign stories of the Lee and Rogers families. When comparing such narratives, we are back, it seems, with the whole 'boggart-brownie' dichotomy, discussed earlier. Some fairy-like BHMs are friendly, and so thus could be said to resemble brownies. Others, meanwhile, appear hostile, and so seem more like boggarts. Maybe this is all just down to their mood at any one particular time?

After all, some such creatures have apparently shown two distinct different sides to their personalities. For example, if the Lee family's pet Bigfoot enjoyed a laugh after playing 'hunt-the-pail' with its human friends, then it also reputedly showed a propensity for taking a joke rather too far. It appears that the Lees eventually tired of their bucket-game and stopped playing it, whereupon the Bigfoot began making a nuisance of itself in the barn, smashing a window and stealing a neighbour's chicken. Eventually, Deputies were called in to shoot it. The next day, Mrs Lee heard a loud thump on the wall whilst in the shower, and that was that – no more Bigfoot. Like many offended domestic hobs, the BHM had simply upped sticks and returned to fairyland [27]. Patrick Harpur says that this is "a sad tale, and a cautionary one", opining in his excellent analysis of the matter that the Lees' BHM only became a nuisance when ignored because poltergeists and fairies:

> "... do not literally need feeding; they need *heeding*. We must give them their

due, leaving a portion of the harvest for them or something off the table. Otherwise they might take something for themselves. The Lees got off lightly with only the loss of a neighbour's chicken. To be visited by fairies ... is good luck, if we treat them right." [28]

Maybe Harpur is right. During the 1972 wave of BHM sightings in Roachdale, for example, the Rogers family – who, we will recall, kindly left out food for the entity – were essentially left alone by the thing. Other than banging on their trailer, it did them no harm. Other Roachdale residents were not so sensible, however; local farmers found that food which had been left out in buckets for their pigs – and not for the Bigfoot at all! – had been stolen by the beast anyway. Presumably, they will have taken steps to prevent these annoying thefts; and maybe this was why the creature was later held responsible for the disappearance of around 200 chickens from the area's smallholdings. Apparently, the BHM didn't actually eat them, it just killed them and scattered their remains around all over the place. One pair of farmers, named Carter and Junior Burdine, even caught it red-handed inside their chicken-house. Junior said it had no neck, was covered in long brownish hair, looked "like an orang-utan or a gorilla" and was groaning. They shot it, but to no avail; it seemed immune to bullets[29]. Perhaps they would have done better to have just left out a bowl of milk for it overnight ...

Hairy Horrors

Are there any actual poltergeists (rather than just poltergeist-like BHMs) which have been hairy and looked like boggarts, though? Apparently, there are not too many. However, we could always look at the testimony of a man named Patrick McGowen, who, upon being offered the chance to shake the hand of the Bell Witch, "felt something in his hand which felt like a hairy substance." But then again, a Calvin Johnson, who also shook the Witch's hand, described "that which he felt, like unto a woman's hand." [30] Meanwhile, returning to his poltergeist-haunted Edinburgh flat late one night in 1979 and reaching out to switch on the light, an ex-soldier (and, later, dinosaur-hunter!) called Bill Gibbons said that he felt "a cold furry thing" that grasped his wrist. Running upstairs screaming and peering over the banister into the "inky blackness", Gibbons then saw "two slitted yellow eyes" staring up at him [31]. That certainly sounds not unlike a domestic Bigfoot, in a way.

Accounts of actual hairy humanoid-like figures being directly witnessed during poltergeist cases are, however, exceedingly rare *. A case from Coventry in 2011 featured the detail that a seven-foot tall figure, described as being "like an animal" (presumably meaning that it was hairy) had been sighted at a window [32], and Harry Price gives a brief mention of a polt-haunted boy who claimed to have seen "a great tall thing covered with fur, with a long tail" [33], but such alleged glimpses of boggart-like entities are not common. I did find one Scottish poltergeist haunting from 1995 in which the ghostly figure of an orang-utan with a human face was allegedly seen [34], and an American case from the 1950s in which another orang-utan-like spirit dressed in a one-piece suit supposedly attacked people [35], but both accounts seem dubious in the extreme. Undoubtedly the most notorious hairy humanoid seen during a poltergeist haunting, however, was encountered during what came to be known as 'the case of the Hexham Heads'.

---

* Although see my book *Terror of the Tokoloshe* (CFZ Press, 2013) for numerous modern accounts of African poltergeist-hauntings being blamed upon hairy little fairies.

The famous German *kobold* Hinzelmann (we'll meet him properly later) takes part in a German version of the 'boggart-flit' story. No matter how fast the house-holder's horses go, Hinzelmann will keep up with them until they reach the very ends of the earth.

'Beth-Oni' in Oxfordshire. On the left is the greenhouse over which the 'phantom removal-men' made such a racket shifting around invisible furniture.

A bold knight takes on the might of a fierce *woodwose* within the depths of the forest.

A statue of a yowie, to be found in Queensland. Why are such beings often associated with poltergeists?

Patrick Harpur feels that we have to interact with hairy fairies, as depicted in this old woodcut, if they are not to turn into malicious boggarts on us.

The much-reproduced image on the left is often labelled as being a *wulver*, but its obvious similarity to other European images of 'mere' werewolves, as seen on the right, would seem to indicate that it probably isn't.

A marvellous illustration of the headless Longridge Boggart, taken from James Bowker's 1878 book *Goblin Tales of Lancashire*. Not all boggarts were BHMs, then!

Cist in Hob Hurst's House.

HOB HURST'S HOUSE.

View of Hob Hurst's House.

It is clear that boggarts (or 'hobhursts') were thought to live in the wild as well as indoors, simply from the name of landscape features such as 'Hob Hurst's House', a bronze-age barrow in Derbyshire.

An early 20th-Century photograph showing the entrance to 'Boggart Hole Clough', now a large urban park in Manchester, but whose name strongly implies that it was once thought to be the haunt of terrifying spirits of the wilderness – like the rest of Manchester undoubtedly is.

A Wolf in Sheep's Clothing

This oft-told story begins in 1971 in the Northumberland town of Hexham, where an 11-year-old boy, Colin Robson, and his brother were weeding the garden of their council-house. A dull chore was soon enlivened, however, when Colin's trowel turned two strange objects up from the soil – a pair of small, roughly-carved stone heads. Taken into the house, these objects seemed to be the catalyst for poltergeist phenomena breaking out. Before long, both heads were turning around spontaneously during the night, allegedly so that they could face back in the direction of the garden. At the very spot where the heads had been unearthed, meanwhile, a strange light could supposedly be seen glowing spookily, whilst the noise of a baby crying could also be heard. Furthermore, objects in the house were breaking for no discernible reason, doors unlocking themselves, taps turning on and off and things jumping off walls. Glass would also leap from photo frames and smash, a mirror was found lying in pieces inside a frying-pan, and a dye-bottle was seen to suddenly explode one day.

Most striking of all, however, the heads became associated with the apparition of what appeared to be some sort of werewolf (or weresheep)-like creature! This first appeared to the Robsons' next-door neighbour Mrs Ellen Dodd, who had gone into her ten-year-old son Brian's bedroom to comfort him one night during a bout of toothache. She described the event thus:

> "Brian kept telling me he felt something touching him. I told him not to be so silly. Then I saw this shape. It came towards me and I definitely felt it touch me on the legs. Then, on all fours, it moved out of the room."

The creature, which Mrs Dodd described as being "half-human half-sheep" (accounts differ as to which half was which!), then padded down the stairs and away. When she followed it, she found that the front door – previously locked – was hanging wide open. As a result of her terror, Mrs Dodd was actually later rehoused by the council. This was not simply some idle fiction being perpetrated by a woman who fancied a new house, however; the 'werewolf' allegedly later reappeared several times to the family of the noted Celtic scholar Dr Anne Ross, who took the heads home from the Robsons to examine. Dr Ross explains how she awoke one night and saw the beast:

> "It was about six feet ... high, slightly stooping, and it was black against the white door. It was half-animal and half-man. The upper part, I would have said, was wolf and the lower part was human. It was covered with a kind of black, very dark fur. It went out and I just saw it clearly and then it disappeared and something made me run after it ... I felt compelled to run after it. I got out of bed and I ran and I ran, and I could hear it going down the stairs. Then it disappeared toward the back of the house. When I got to the bottom of the stairs, I was terrified."

This strange apparition continued to be seen for as long as the heads remained in the house – the entity was even said to be quite noisy. The most disturbing sighting occurred to Dr Ross' 15-year-old daughter Berenice who, returning to what she thought was an empty house one day, saw what she described as being "a black thing ... as near a werewolf as anything" coming down the stairs. It jumped over the banister and landed "with a kind of plop" on the floor before padding away with "heavy animal feet" towards the back of the house, where it disappeared. Understandably, Dr Ross disposed of the heads and the phenomena all stopped – but the speculation did not [36]. It was declared by Dr Don Robins, an inorganic chemist, that the heads could have been acting as some kind of psychic storehouse for an obscure entity named the *wulver*, a half-man, half-wolf creature from the folklore of the Shetland Islands – a novel variation upon the old 'fairy-cursed stone' motif, maybe? After all, this *wulver* is sometimes classified as being yet another breed of fairy. Might we, however, also say that the Hexham wolf-man was a boggart? After all, it was a big, hairy man-beast which caused poltergeist phenomena to occur – some of which even centred around a chimney!

Apparently, during the original haunting of their home, the Dodd children said that they could often hear "a pitter-patter akin to a cat or dog walking on a laminated floor" coming from the direction of the chimney, in which a noise like "birds nesting" could also be heard – together with the sound of soot falling down into the grate. Whenever the grate was actually checked, however, it was found to be completely empty [37]. All of this sounds fairly suggestive – but perhaps we should not be too hasty in drawing our conclusions here. After all, I've yet to come across any account of a boggart which had a wolf's or a sheep's head perched up there on its shoulders!

Of Boggarts and Barguests
However, in thus far describing boggarts purely as being (sometimes-invisible) big hairy men, I have in fact been oversimplifying somewhat. There are, in truth, a number of different physical varieties of boggart we can read about in folklore. There is a celebrated fictional boggart which was meant to have haunted the country lanes around the small town of Longridge in Lancashire, for example, in the form of a hooded woman carrying a basket in her hand. Upon closer inspection, however, unwary travellers would find that the woman's hood was empty, and that her severed head was in fact contained within the basket; once seen, the head would chase a person home, with its teeth snapping away at their heels [38]. On the other hand, in Lincolnshire a boggart known as the Lackey Causey Calf was supposed to appear from a tunnel near a stream, often in the form of a headless cow, and try to drown people in the water; because of this fact, local legend said that such boggarts were very likely the ghosts of suicides, taking on animal form as cattle, dogs or rabbits [39]. The Yorkshire 'Boggart of Longar Hede' was said to be a shaggy-haired calf-sized being with eyes "like saucers" trailing a long chain behind it, meanwhile, whilst a Lancashire bogey known as the 'Boggart of Hackensall Hall' was supposed to appear in the shape of a huge horse. [40]

Evidently, then, when a boggart was seen outdoors, it seems to have merged with the bogey-beasts or barguests; those odd, shape-shifting fairy-entities we discussed at length earlier. Indeed, the 'separation' of boggarts from barguests and bogey-beasts is clearly an artificial trick of the language; it is obvious that, when people once referred to an outdoors bogey as being a 'barguest' rather than a 'boggart', this was an issue of differing dialect rather than of competing demonology. However, it is equally clear that at least some persons in the past thought both domestic poltergeist phenomena, and sightings of weird beast-like zooforms outdoors, to be essentially two different sides of the same supernatural coin. Boggarts, it seems, could be both domestic and wild. There is one particularly boggart-like form of outdoor bogey that we have not so far examined in this book, however – namely, the fearsome 'shug-monkey'.

The shug-monkey has returned to the public eye somewhat in recent years, due largely to the researches of the cryptozoologist Nick Redfern, whose interesting 2007 book *Man-Monkey* is subtitled 'In Search of the British Bigfoot'. That subtitle says a lot about what the book is about – namely, a series of unexpected recent encounters with what would seem to be hairy yowie-like monsters in various spots around the British Isles. However, are these sightings really evidence of the existence of some hitherto-undiscovered species of large anthropoid ape lying hidden from the eyes of man in the wilder and more remote parts of our nation? Presumably not, as Redfern himself explains at length. The idea that genuine big apes could be hiding somewhere within perhaps the most well-mapped area on earth is simply absurd. As the two main stalwarts of the CFZ, Jonathan Downes and Richard Freeman, put it in their own 1998 discussion of BHM sightings in Britain:

> "As two of this country's few working cryptozoologists, we are quite prepared to accept the possibility that various species of undiscovered primate ... await discovery in various far-flung parts of the world ... [However] to ask us to believe that a hitherto-undiscovered species of primate is lurking anywhere in Europe, let alone in the wilds of ... [Britain] is asking us to suspend disbelief to an unacceptable degree. We must look for alternative rationalisations of these phenomena." [41]

Indeed we must – and one such alternative rationalisation of them is to say that these things are just the modern-day reconceptualisations of boggarts and barguests.

Are You a Man or a Monkey?
In fact, this does seem to be a plausible idea, if you look at some modern BHM-sightings from the UK and compare them back with descriptions of shug-monkeys from past centuries. For instance, the case that set Redfern off writing his book is most suggestive. This narrative – now often given the title of 'The Man-Monkey of Ranton' – was first set down in writing by Charlotte S Burne in her 1883 book *Shropshire Folk-Lore*. Here, she talks of "a very weird encounter with an animal ghost" which supposedly took place on 21st January 1879, when a labourer was transporting a cart from Ranton in Staffordshire to another village, named Woodcock, along a road following the path of the Shropshire Union Canal. On his way, just before reaching a particular bridge, this man was reportedly shocked to encounter "a strange black [ape-like] creature with great white eyes" which jumped from the roadside bushes and onto the back of his horse. Naturally, the man struck out at the spectral animal with his whip, but it just passed through it impossibly. Terrified, the man allegedly dropped his weapon and watched as his panicking horse ran onwards with the thing clutching to its back before, eventually, the monster disappeared, though he knew not how. A mile further on, at the nearest village, Woodseaves, the man told his tale before retreating to bed for several days. His whip, so the yarn goes, was later found abandoned at the scene of the attack. [42]

In their comprehensive book *The Lore of the Land*, a superlative compendium of England's most famous myths, legends and folk-tales, the authors Jacqueline Simpson and Jennifer Westwood specifically call the Ranton Man-Monkey a bogey-beast, and compare it directly with a shug-monkey which was alleged to be seen haunting the road between the Cambridgeshire villages of West Wratting and Balsham during the first half of the twentieth century [43]. This beast was described by a certain Constable A Taylor, who had heard tales about the shug-monkey as a child, as being:

> "... a cross between a big rough-coated dog and a monkey, with big shining eyes. Sometimes it would shuffle along on its hind legs and at other times it would whizz past on all fours." [44]

Whilst this animal was not actually seen by Taylor, and it seems likely the shug-monkey's presence was just invented by wary parents who wished their children to avoid the road after dark, the description still sounds similar to what was supposedly seen by the carter near Woodseaves in 1879; namely, it resembled a monkey and had "big shining eyes". The description of it being halfway between a dog and an ape is also significant, as we shall now see; it appears that Black Shuck and the shug-monkey, as their similar names imply, were very close cousins indeed.

Simon Says
During his researches, Redfern uncovered a bizarre account from a man named Simon of a BHM he claimed to have seen one day in 1982 in the woods alongside the Shropshire Union Canal, only about three quarters of a mile away from where the monkey-man of 1879 was allegedly witnessed. Simon alleges that he heard a loud noise like a screaming fox coming from the trees on the other side of the canal from him. Looking across, he was shocked to see "this bloody great thing like a gorilla" stand up and then run into the woods. Curiously, Simon noticed that it had "a very long muzzle" and "long flattened ears like a dog" on the side of its head. He thought it looked "just like a werewolf", showing, perhaps, how old lore about bogey-beasts and shug-monkeys has now been almost completely obliterated by images from modern horror films in the popular mind. [45]

A further connection between the Ranton Man-Monkey and dog-like bogey-beasts, meanwhile, was uncovered by Redfern in the form of testimony from a man named Nigel Lea, who claims to have been driving through Cannock Chase (a large forest through which the Shropshire Union Canal runs) one night in 1972 when a "strange ball of glowing blue light" slammed into the road ahead of his vehicle, releasing a "torrent of bright, fiery sparks". Obviously, Lea stopped his car and got out to investigate. He saw no light, however; only "the biggest bloody dog" he had ever seen in his life, muscular and black in form, with pointed ears and a "wild, staring look" in its yellow-tinged eyes. Eventually, the dog walked into the trees by the roadside and Lea drove off. Lea felt that the sighting presaged a close friend's death in an industrial accident two weeks later – an idea which does fit in with traditional lore about Black Dogs sometimes being considered death-omens. [46]

It appears, then, that within the same smallish area encounters have been had with a kind of monkey-spirit, a large BHM with dog-like muzzle and ears, and a phantom Black Dog which allegedly functioned as a supernatural death-warning. Talk about living folklore! Remarkably, it does seem that tales of shape-shifting bogey-beasts are still alive in the heart of England, even today – it is just that the language we use to talk about them has now changed. No longer do they fall under the traditional purview of 'fairy-lore', but under the new heading of 'cryptozoology'.

The real clincher in terms of demonstrating that the Ranton Man-Monkey was probably originally thought of as being some kind of boggart or barguest, though, comes in the form of a curious coda to Charlotte S Burne's original telling of the tale in her book of 1883. Here she related how, some days after the ghost-sighting, a policeman called at the home of the carter's master. Word about his experience having spread, the local bobby had got the wrong end of the stick and concluded that the man had been attacked by a thief. When the carter's employer put the constable straight about the matter, however, he is alleged to have replied in a surprisingly calm fashion, thus:

> "Oh, was that all, sir? Oh, I know what that was. That was the Man-Monkey, sir, as does come again at that bridge ever since the man was drowned in the cut." [47]

The policeman's words provide particularly compelling evidence that the ghost-monkey's appearance was being explained locally at the time in terms of the general framework of a then-prevailing belief in bogey-beasts. After all, local legends of many barguests were often 'explained' by puzzled residents as them being the spirits of the unquiet dead in animal-like form, as we demonstrated earlier, lurid tales of murder or suicide then being attached to the spots where these beasts reputedly appeared, presumably falsely [48]. It seems likely that a similar kind of legend-generating process took place in the Ranton case too, whether a man really did drown in the canal or not (and we have no evidence either way, really). Ghosts usually need a 'reason' for appearing – and it appears that the man supposedly drowning in the cut was the Man-Monkey's.

If You Go Down to the Woods Today ...

Whilst this is all undoubtedly very interesting, it must be asked whether it really has anything much to do with poltergeists, though. I would say, in light of cases like the Hexham Heads, and of contemporary American and Australian encounters with BHMs which acted more like polts than they did real, flesh-and-blood animals, that it probably does. The distinction between boggarts and shug-monkeys in the wild and the more classical, house-dwelling boggart-poltergeists was once somewhat more blurred than it is now. After all, the words 'boggart' and 'bogey' both derive from the Middle English *bugge*, which is in turn derived from the Welsh *bwg*, which seems in itself to have been a variant form of *bwca*, one of those hairy creatures we saw talking from an oven at Trwyn Farm earlier on, showing how both wild and domestic spirits were linked in the very derivation of their names. Furthermore, seeing as boggarts were also meant to be a type of hob, it is interesting that the words 'hobhurst' and 'hobthrust' derive according to some authorities from the phrase 'hob o't'hurst', or 'hobgoblin of the woods' – the very place, of course, where modern BHMs are now meant to roam. Some modern scholars, however, like the Anglo-Saxon specialist Bruce Dickins, prefer to derive the word from the Old English *thyrs*, later *thurse*, meaning 'a giant of the wilderness' (Grendel in *Beowulf* was a *thyrs* [49]) – a pretty good description of a BHM, I would have thought! [50]

In the folklorist Jeremy Harte's own discussion of this issue, he notes how it must be significant that, whilst there are innumerable names for domestic fairies in English, the vast majority of them can also be used to refer to what he calls "frightening spirits of the wild". His theory is that the use of the same word to describe lane-haunting boggarts and chimney-dwelling boggarts was simply a way for old tale-tellers to "hint at a savagery which has been only temporarily domesticated" in these spirits when they happen to have appeared indoors, living inside people's ovens and fireplaces. [51] Maybe so. After all, even the friendliest household brownie can suddenly and maliciously turn boggart if it wants to, as we have repeatedly seen.

All this seems to indicate one thing about the 'true' nature of boggarts above all else, though; that they had no one stable form, just as they had no one stable name. They could appear or be conceived of as things as varied as invisible hearthside spooks, big hairy men living up chimneys, shape-shifting Black Dogs, shug-monkeys, odd lights glimpsed flitting down country lanes or White Ladies seen standing near rivers, beckoning people on to drown themselves. Given this infinite variety in appearance and behaviour, then, it seems clear that, the closer you look at the word 'boggart' – just like the words 'fairy' and 'poltergeist' – the less it actually appears to really mean.

LAIR OF THE CELEBRATED ANTIGONISH GHOST AND THE WRAITH HUNTERS

DeWALKER FRANKLIN PRINCE the GHOST HUNTER

THE ANTIGONISH GHOST HOUSE and BARN

DETECTIVE CARROLL WHO SAYS the GHOST SLAPPED HIM

MARY ELLEN MacDONALD DECLARES SHE HAS BEEN REPEATEDLY SLAPPED by the ANTIGONISH GHOST

At Antigonish, Canada, in 1922, a poltergeist was on the loose which knotted cows' tails, frightened horses and ruined crops; the textbook behaviour of a typical *stallspuk*.

3.

The Poltergeist as Stallspuk

The other main fairy-identity that the poltergeist has sometimes adopted is that of the *stallspuk*, a rather obscure entity from medieval European folklore. This creature, probably first referred to in print in the French bishop William of Auvergne's 1225 work *De Universo* [1] (but likely to be of much older origin) is perhaps best defined as being a kind of 'barn-fairy' whose particular area of invisible expertise was to frighten horses and cattle in their stalls, saddling or unsaddling them, setting them free from their tethers and knotting or braiding their manes and tails in the night. Sometimes, they would even assault or wound livestock or ride horses around after dark, causing them to break into sweats and fevers which rendered them unusable come the morning. The *stallspuk* also liked to interfere with farm-produce, making milk go sour, mixing wheat with chaff and stealing butter. Poltergeists are also supposed to have pulled exactly these kinds of tricks too, however, during a surprisingly large number of cases.

The Amherst poltergeist, for instance – that unruly Canadian spirit we encountered earlier on tormenting a young girl named Esther Cox with pins – repeatedly milked a certain red cow on the Cox farmstead, even though it had been locked inside its stable with a watch placed over it [2]. The Devil of Mascon, meanwhile – already seen by us playing both brownie and boggart – occasionally manifested as a *stallspuk* too, apparently. According to François Perrault's account:

> "Sometimes he would be the groom of my stables, rubbing my horse and plaiting the hair of his tail and mane, but he was an unruly groom, for once I found that he had saddled my horse with the crupper before and the pommel behind [i.e. put the saddle on back-to-front]." [3]

The tale of the so-called 'Maid of Orlach' – well-known in Germany, if not elsewhere – also featured similar tropes. Here, events surrounded a young peasant girl called Rosina Magdalena Gronbach, of the town of Orlach in Württemburg, around whom, beginning in 1831, inexplicable fires broke out, and from whose mouth strange entities supposedly spoke, leading many to conclude that she had been possessed. However, the haunting in this case began initially in a cow-shed where Rosina worked, and where cattle were found to have been moved around and had their tails knotted mysteriously during the night [4]. Such things still reputedly occur. In 1951, for example, a priest from the small German village of Neusatz investigated a poltergeist in a farmhouse occupied by a mother and her mentally disabled 30-year-old son. Clothes and linen were cut up and torn, the living room curtains took to disappearing ... and, in the stable, the tails of the cows kept on getting braided [5].

Even the famous Harry Price, during his first-ever ghost-hunt as a child, had cause to investigate a *stallspuk* – although he at no point dignified it with such a name. To him, it was a plain old poltergeist. When a schoolboy, it seems, Price and his family often spent their holidays in a tiny English hamlet which he chose to disguise under the name of 'Parton Magna'. Here there was an old manor house, whose barns and woodsheds were apparently haunted by a typical *stallspuk*. Animals were untethered at night, pans of milk overturned themselves in the dairy and securely-fastened stable doors opened of their own accord after dark. The worst-affected area was the woodshed, where pebbles were thrown and piles of logs scattered around. This *stallspuk* had no desire to allow itself to be observed at work, however. When a farm-hand hid behind a stack of logs to keep watch for the ghost overnight, nothing happened inside the shed. Instead, as if to spite him, pebbles were flung down onto the roof *outside*. When a watch was kept both inside *and* outside, meanwhile, nothing was seen at all – although, bizarrely, the sound of pebbles hitting and then rolling down the corrugated iron roof was still clearly audible. Suddenly, however, the *stallspuk* left the barns and woodsheds and took up residence inside the manor house itself, raking embers out from the hearths and disturbing utensils in the kitchen like a boggart, as well as creating loud thumps, as if from heavy boots, which trod the upstairs gallery and paced the stairs during the night. Being given permission to investigate one evening, Price says that he heard these noises himself, and even made an unsuccessful attempt to photograph the ghost. Supposedly, the sound of his flash going off startled the spirit so much that it actually fell down the stairs! [6]

The Antigonish Antagonist

Nobody, however, nowadays talks much about *stallspuks*. Even Harry Price didn't, as we have just seen. Most readers, before picking up this book, probably wouldn't even have heard the word. Even when we hear of a modern case which clearly seems to involve one, we prefer to simply label it as being a poltergeist manifestation. For example, the Antigonish poltergeist of 1922, from Nova Scotia in Canada, did all the usual things a *stallspuk* does, and several that generic poltergeists are generally held to do, too. According to a contemporary newspaper report:

> "It braids the tails of cows, chases horses into a lather of sweat, in the dead of night starts mysterious fires, bewitches cattle, consumes unconscionable quantities of stored victuals and keeps up such a rattling and rapping about the house that rest or sleep within its walls even for the canny MacDonalds [the affected family] became a physical and mental impossibility."

There was no mention of a *stallspuk* in the original Press reports of this case, though. This was the twentieth century, well into the era of established psychical research and its associated jargon, and in the opinion of a contemporary "scientific ghost hunter" from the Boston SPR called Dr Walter Franklin Prince, who found himself plastered all over the Canadian newspapers, the haunting was not really down to any kind of actual 'ghost' at all. He held that the MacDonalds' 15-year-old adopted daughter Mary Ellen was responsible – although she was not, however, deemed by Dr Prince to be "morally culpable" for it all. In his view Mary Ellen had bothered the cattle and set fires whilst in "an altered state of consciousness" and thus did not realise what she was doing. However, Prince did add as a caveat that there was a certain possibility that her altered state of consciousness was "brought about by a discarnate intelligence" – or, in other words, that she was possessed by an evil spirit. The author and prominent Spiritualist Sir Arthur Conan Doyle looked into the case too, as he seems to have insisted upon doing back then, pronouncing that:

> "Mary Ellen was not the ghost, but the medium of the ghost which probably was that ... of some naughty boy whom not even death could cure of his mischievousness." [7]

No actual *evidence* is presented for this viewpoint by him, of course – it's just that, this pronouncement being made in the 1920s, it could hardly have been plausibly maintained by him that *stallspuks* were responsible for it all (even if Conan Doyle did, notoriously, actually believe in fairies himself). As ever, we view these things in the light of our own times.

Witches' Kitchen

At a remote Breton farm in 1913, for instance, the prevailing social prism through which to view such events was still, apparently, that of witchcraft. A certain Jean Mettois and his friend, who went out to the place to investigate, were greeted by the woman of the house with the query "Are you good sorcerers?" They replied by saying that they *might* just have enough magical powers to dispel any evil forces bothering her, hoping to hear her spin them a good yarn – which she did. When asked what exactly was going on, she replied thus:

> "Ah, Monsieur, our horses and beasts die, our oats melt away, our corn is eaten. If you slept on the farm for a single night, you might die of fright. Every night there is an uproar which does not give us a minute's sleep. Look, there [the woman pointed to the chimney] stones fall one by one with a terrible clatter. It sounds as if thunder broke in the chimney. About midnight we seem to see white forms trailing burdens on the ground, the locked doors open of themselves, the horses get loose and run wildly about the yard, the cows low with fright. It is enough to drive one mad."

She herself was not mad, however; Mettois stayed the night and experienced some of the phenomena for himself. In the middle of his sleep he was awoken by:

> "... furious blows, as if somebody armed with a battering-ram were trying to force the door ... [or] as if somebody were trying to break the chimney." [8]

Accordingly, Mettois got a ladder, climbed onto the roof and looked down into the flue. It was empty – and yet still the blows continued to shake the fireplace below.

The French scholar Claude Lecouteux, however, cites another account from his homeland in which a woman blamed her dead husband for causing an outbreak of *stallspukery*, not witchcraft. After this man had died, his widow heard tapping sounds around her farmhouse, and saw furniture moving. Initially, she did not associate this with her dead spouse. However, one night she was awoken by the sound of rattling chains coming from the stables. Going inside, she found that all the oxen were running free, their chains having been inexplicably removed. At this point, the solution to the mystery struck her – her husband's unquiet soul needed to have another Mass said to enable it to find rest. She therefore arranged for one, and that was the end of it all [9]. Elsewhere in France, though, the Devil could be blamed for haunting barns, the French folklorist JB Bardin informing his readers that, according to village elders in the Isère region, Satan frequently "moves into the farms, tangling the manes of the horses and making unusual noises in the stables and haylofts". [10]

Frightening the Horses

Probably the most common habit of the *stallspuk* was its frequent botheration of horses and cattle, panicking them and making them sweat, something which, again, has found itself allegedly occurring during a surprisingly large number of poltergeist cases from the past. The well-known haunting at Calvados Castle in Normandy, France, during 1875-6, for instance, featured the interesting detail that the horses in the castle stables frequently seemed spooked, being sometimes "found in the morning drenched in sweat as if they had been ridden a long time" with straw having been tossed about all over the place inside their stalls. [11]

Another example of horses supposedly being interfered with reportedly took place during the famous seventeenth-century haunting at Tedworth where, as we saw earlier, the ghostly 'Drummer' also liked to pretend to be a fairy by producing the sound of chinking coins. According to Joseph Glanvil, who investigated the disturbances in John Mompesson's house, one day:

> "... my Man coming up to me in the Morning, told me that one of my Horses ... was all in a sweat, and lookt as if he had been rid all Night. My friend and I went down, and found him so. I enquired how he had been used, and was assured that he had been well fed, and ordered as he used to be, and my Servant was one that was wont to be very careful about my Horses. The Horse I had had a good time, and I never knew but that he was very sound. But after I had rid him a Mile or two, very gently over a plain Down from Mr Mompesson's house, he fell lame, and having made a hard shift to bring me home, dyed in two or three days, no one being able to imagine what he ailed. This I confess might be accident or some unusual distemper, but all things being put together, it seems very probable that it was somewhat else." [12]

Such cases don't necessarily sound overly-convincing, of course, and the suspicion naturally arises that the idea of horses having been 'night-ridden' could just have been an old folk-explanation used to account for fevered or knackered nags. This is a reasonable assumption; it used to be standard practice for farmers to lock their animals in stalls and byres which were too low and small, giving them insufficient air to breathe. The result was that the beasts would stamp and fret overnight, leading to them being found exhausted and covered all over in sweat come the morning. The fact that one way of exorcising such stalls was to open the windows to 'let out the Devil' is very telling – the real exorcising force at work here being, of course, simply fresh air [13]. However, another occasion at Tedworth, when John Mompesson entered his stables and found his favourite horse lying on the ground "having one of his hinder Leggs in his Mouth, and so fastened there, that it was difficult for several Men to get it out with a Leaver" is far more difficult to explain in such terms [14].

Taken for a Ride

However, the Bell Witch, at least, was reputedly directly witnessed in the act of frightening horses – although, again, how much of this is mere folklore is anybody's guess. Supposedly, the Witch delighted in scaring the steed of a Mr Jerry Stark, a frequent visitor to the Bell household, always at the same point near a large tree on a lane outside the farmstead. Here, a "rustling sound" would be heard in the leaves before "something apparently the size of a rabbit" (the Witch in animal form, presumably) would jump out, causing Stark's horse to bolt.[15]

The Witch is also famously meant to have had the ability to stop horses in their tracks; allegedly, the spook once caused the wagon of the future US President General Andrew Jackson to come to a complete halt by bewitching his horses so that they could not move [16], a story which has sadly since been found to be untrue. As usual, this particular aspect of the Witch's behaviour has its parallels in British fairy-lore – namely, in stories told about a White Lady-like bogey named 'Silky' who reputedly inhabited the countryside around the Northumberland village of Black Heddon and took pleasure in interfering with passing steeds. She is supposed to have found it amusing to stop them dead in their tracks in such a way that it was impossible to get them moving again without their owners going off and getting some branches of rowan or ash, traditional dispellers of witchcraft and evil. [17]

There is also what sounds like a classic example of a horse being night-ridden by the Bell Witch on record – albeit with the highly unusual caveat that its owner happened to be mounted upon it at the same time too! This man was a local resident named Billy Wall who, having heard about the wonder of the talking spirit, decided to go over to the Bell farmstead and hear it for himself. Nearing the place, a disembodied voice asked Billy if he was on his way to see the Witch. He replied in the affirmative, after which the voice said that it was going there too, and would hitch a ride behind Billy on his "fat horse". Billy agreed and at that moment:

> "… he felt his horse squat, as if some heavy weight had fallen upon him and then [the horse] commenced wriggling, prancing and kicking up. He threw one hand behind to feel what it was and then the other hand, but found nothing and yet, he said, 'the damn thing kept up a continual palavering at my back, asking me all sorts of hell-fired questions, while my horse continued in a canter, squealing and kicking up, and every damn hair on my head stood straight up, reaching for the treetops. It wasn't any fun for me but the damn thing kept on laughing and talking about my fine race-horse, and how pleasant it was to ride behind on his broad fat back, telling me what a fine suit of hair I had, and how beautifully it stood up, making me look like a statesman.'" [18]

One imagines that, after such an ordeal, the poor old nag would have been left fit only for the knackers' yard.

Are there any accounts of spirits being directly witnessed bothering horses actually *within* their stables, however? There is one, as it happens, and the observer was none other than the father of our old friend Dermot MacManus. Supposedly, he used to like to tell MacManus Jr the tale of how, when a boy of 14, he was playing hide-and-seek with his brother one day. Searching through an attic-top granary, and hearing sounds of horses in apparent distress coming from the stable below, he thought that he had discovered his sibling's hiding place. He hadn't. Opening the attic trap-door and looking down, he saw two horses in "a mad panic of terror, trembling and snorting with fear". Then, the boy claims to have seen something horrible. Crouching on the stable floor in a "compact ball" was "a figure of evil" with "baleful eyes, blazing red like glowing coals of fire". Its hands were particularly horrible; they were "a dirty greyish-brown" with fingers which were all bone and sinew, ending in "curved, pointed claws." He slammed the trap-door shut and fled.[19] Whether you find this tale plausible or not, it is at least interesting that MacManus Sr apparently conceived of the visible form of a *stallspuk* as being remarkably similar to that of a malevolent brownie or boggart.

Locking the Stable Door After the Horse Has Bolted
Another thing which *stallspuks* were supposed to do in the stables after dark was to let the animals loose, or move them around from place to place. During a haunting at the German town of Töttelstedt during 1581, for instance, in which a farmer's family were bothered by such demonic delights as sharp objects flying after them in their house, the poltergeist also played tricks upon the cattle, repeatedly cutting their tethering-ropes during the night [20]. Obviously, however, ropes can snap by themselves without any ghosts or fairies being responsible for it, and sometimes the idea of the *stallspuk* was merely a convenient supernatural fiction to account for such misfortunes. A breed of Norfolk fairies known as the 'Hyter Sprites', for example, were once blamed by locals for entirely ordinary occurrences such as donkeys working themselves free from their stakes and then tangling their ropes up in hurdles overnight [21]. However, some *stallspuks* have purportedly managed to liberate livestock in a rather more remarkable fashion than this ...

For example, one May morning in 1906, a Mr JC Playfair of the Kent village of Lamberhurst went into the stables of his poltergeist-haunted mill and found that all of his horses had been turned back-to-front in their tight and confined stalls, a feat which should have been physically impossible. Worse, one of them was missing. He did not have to look too far to find it, however – it was discovered standing in the hay-room nearby. This hay-room had only a very narrow doorway, however, through which a man could barely enter, never mind a horse. Eventually, a wall had to be demolished in order to free the animal. Apparently, it had been teleported there! [22]

Sheep are also bothered in such ways by *stallspuks*, it seems. During the incredible haunting at a Scottish farmstead called Ringcroft, located near to the coastal village of Rerrick in Dumfries and Galloway in 1695, for example, the poltergeist involved took great pleasure in tying sheep together in their byres with lengths of rope which, supposedly, the entity made itself by twisting together pieces of straw from the stables [23]. The very earliest phenomena to have occurred at Ringcroft were acts of *stallspukery*, it would appear; the first inkling that Andrew Mackie, the farm's owner, had that it was haunted came one morning in February when he awoke to find that all his cattle had escaped from their sheds, their tethering-ropes having been broken after dark. The next night, the same thing was found to have occurred, with one very odd addition; one of Mackie's cows had been fastened to a high beam with a rope pulled so tight that the poor animal's hoofs barely even touched the ground, leaving it trapped in a very awkward and uncomfortable position.[24]

Perhaps the weirdest example of livestock being interfered with by spirits after dark, however, supposedly occurred during September 1909 at a haunted farm near the town of Issime in Italy. Here, not only were cows found detached from their usual fastenings one morning and chained awkwardly up to one another instead, but also – if you can believe this – two goats were reportedly discovered having been dressed up "comically" in men's clothing overnight! More standard polt phenomena were witnessed in the haunted stable, too; stones fell from thin air and flew around in bizarre zig-zag patterns, hitting both men and cattle, to the extent that it became impossible to milk the cows without being injured. One witness described these animals as being in a state of "terror" and "pulling against their chains as if trying to escape" whenever the ghost appeared on the scene. [25]

At other times, meanwhile, horses are supposed to have been helpfully saddled by spooks; Catherine Crowe, for instance, tells a story of a German couple who awoke one morning after a night spent being disturbed by various ghostly noises, apparitions and lights, only to find that their horse had been released from its stable beneath their bedroom, with its halter on and the stable door still closed behind it [26]. According to the writer Sacheverell Sitwell, likewise, he knew of a place called Toadpool Farm not far from his ancestral home in Derbyshire, where a poltergeist would rap and throw pebbles. Even odder, however, were the occasions when the cart-horses were allegedly found having been ready-saddled and harnessed in their stables of a morning. To add atmosphere, we may point out that, according to Sitwell, Toadpool Farm was surrounded by mushroom rings – around which were meant to dance the fairy-folk in popular lore [27]. In such unlikely tales, *stallspuks* could perhaps be said to merge back into useful brownies.

One particularly clear example of a helpful *stallspuk* shading away into other varieties of benign fairy-being can be seen in tales told about a so-called 'screaming skull' which was, for hundreds of years, kept on an isolated hill-farm in Derbyshire called Tunstead Farm. As usual with these macabre objects from English tradition, it is said that if 'Dickie', as the skull was known, was moved from his rightful place upon the farm, then various misfortunes – including outbreaks of poltergeist phenomena – would occur. However, if left alone, then Dickie would fulfil the functions of both brownie and friendly *stallspuk* – he would saddle the horses, open gates for horse-drawn carriages and carts to pass through as they approached, watch over calving cows, wake the servants of a morning so they would not oversleep, and open doors for people. Strangely, Dickie also had the multiple forms of a barguest available to him, too; he would reputedly appear around Tunstead Farm in the guise of both a White Lady dressed in silk and a Black Dog, which used to follow people along a particular lane and then vanish inside a nearby hill (a particularly fairy-like touch) [28]. Clearly, the figure of the *stallspuk* – like all such domestic fairies – can never be looked at purely in isolation.

Space Cowboys
For example, the motif of 'teleporting livestock' is nowadays no longer associated purely with *stallspuks*, but rather more often with UFOs. In 1967 for instance, it was reported that an entire herd of cows had supposedly been teleported from the middle of their field only to reappear there again, just as mysteriously, the next day. Seeing as this field lay in the quiet village of Chitterne, near the Wiltshire town of Warminster – the major supposed 'UFO hotspot' in England at the time – aliens were inevitably blamed, not elves. [29]

The infamously strange occurrences at Skinwalker Ranch in Utah during the 1990s, meanwhile, must surely rank as being one of the most bizarre series of events ever to have (allegedly!) happened. Whatever it was that reputedly bothered the Gorman family, a group of hardy and experienced cattle-breeders, over a number of years there could hardly just be called a mere poltergeist. As well as all the usual polt tricks, the tale also involved UFOs, cattle mutilations, giant bullet-proof wolves, semi-sentient flying orbs filled with luminous liquids, sightings of tunnels in the sky, ancient Indian curses and, as we saw earlier, the appearance of zoomorphically-impossible animals. There was also, it seems, a *stallspuk* present upon the ranch.

Faced during 1994-95 with the mutilation and killing of animals on their property by unusual means, Tom Gorman and his wife Ellen had become extra-vigilant about the safety of their livestock. It is understandable why they should have felt this way; the animals seemed to be inexplicably vanishing – once, a cow's footprints simply disappeared into thin air in the middle of a deep snowfield [30] – or were found dead in the most gruesome circumstances imaginable. In April 1995, Tom's son Tad noticed a heifer had fallen into a shallow canal and was struggling to climb back up the slippery embankment. Returning 20 minutes later to rescue the animal, which had been in no danger due to the shallowness of the water, Tad found the heifer lying motionless, her entire rear-end having been carved out. The cut, apparently, was "flawless", looking as if a six-inch "perfectly circular" saw had been shoved into the cow's anus and then used to suck out its entire guts without any blood being spilled [31].

The weirdest act of *stallspukery*, though, was yet to come. Setting out one day upon a routine mission to count their cattle, the Gormans passed by the bull-enclosure, in which lived their four Black Angus cattle; each one worth more than $100,000 and the main basis for their economic well-being. As they passed by, therefore, an obvious thought crossed their minds; that they would be ruined if those four particular beasts were ever found slaughtered. It is easy to imagine their feelings then, when, on their way back, the Gormans found these very same bulls to now be missing. After some frantic searching, however, the ranchers found the animals not lying dead in a field, but trapped inside a small trailer nearby, the only entrance to which was a small tightly-locked door through which they could not possibly have passed. All were apparently subject to some kind of suspended animation. Banging on the trailer, Tom awoke the bulls from their bizarre fugue and, in panic at the situation in which they now found themselves, they charged through the trailer's metal walls and back outside. [32]

A case of teleporting livestock which beats even that story in scale, however, supposedly occurred at a place called Ripperstone Farm in South Wales in 1977. Here, UFOs, *stallspuks* and poltergeists seemed to co-exist, just like at Skinwalker Ranch. Late one night in

The only known image of William of Auvergne, author of *De Universo* (*The Universe of Creatures*), apparently the first book in which the word '*stallspuk*' is used.

A goblin ensures that this particular horse will be 'night-ridden' to within an inch of its life, in this marvellous illustration to James Bowker's 1878 book *Goblin Tales of Lancashire*.

Geschichte

des

Mädchens von Orlach.

Dargestellt

von

Dr. Justinus Kerner.

Stuttgart,

Druck von J. Wachendorf.

1834.

The frontispiece to an 1834 edition of Justinius Kerner's book *The Story of the Maid of Orlach*, in which the supernatural knotting of cows' tails is noted.

A rider hits out at some invisible force which is spooking his horse; well, either that or he's hitting out at his horse itself ...

General Andrew Jackson's horses are halted in their tracks by the Bell Witch (top) and a French *lutin* bewitches a plough-boy and his cattle (below). Do both illustrations merely depict different culturally-appropriate variations upon the same myth, though? After all, animals really do act strangely sometimes, and ideas like these can be used to 'explain' the fact.

An extremely unflattering photograph of General Andrew Jackson. Recent research appears to cast great doubt upon the story of him meeting the Bell Witch; disappointingly, there is no reliable record of him being in the area of John Bell's farmstead during the time of the haunting at all. Yet another dubious addition to the Witch's tale, then ...

What goes on inside the stables after dark.

A 15th-century illustration of a cow being sucked up into the clouds by the power of the sun's rays. Teleporting cows are still being reported even nowadays, however ...

WEEKLY WORLD NEWS®

THE WORLD'S ONLY RELIABLE NEWSPAPER

ARE UFOs ABDUCTING COWS?

BEFORE

AFTER

DOZENS MISSING!
– SHOCKING EYEWITNESS REPORTS

Undeniable proof for sceptics that aliens really do want to kill our cattle.

September, the head of the household, Bill Coombs, was checking on his cattle when his telephone rang. It was another local farmer, wanting to know why he had allowed his herd to escape onto his land and start trashing the place. Bill said that he hadn't; he had just been in the cowsheds looking at them. The other farmer said that this was nonsense; Bill's cows had been trampling all over his property for an hour now, and he had been trying to phone Bill all that time with no answer. Bill knew that this could not have been true. Upon returning to the sheds, however, he was in for a shock – every last one of his stalls was now empty. Going to the other farm, he found that the cows on the rampage were indeed his own; and yet how could they have been there on the other man's land for an hour when he had been with them himself throughout that time? This incident presents a real mystery, if true [33]. (Which it may not be; some sightings of silver-suited 'aliens' around Ripperstone Farm were proven hoaxes, and the whole Welsh 'UFO-flap' of the time seems to have been somewhat exaggerated.[34])

More tales of extraterrestrial *stallspukery* exist from Ripperstone, though. One time, two cows were reputedly found locked together in the same stall, despite the fact that they had been placed in separate ones when put away that night. Several times the entire herd were supposedly transported from their gated paddock and into the field next door [35]. It is said that five animals just disappeared forever, with no trace of them ever being found [36]. In particular, though, the cows kept on teleporting down the road to the nearest farm. Bill Coombs would have to trudge down there in the middle of the night, make up some embarrassingly feeble excuse for their escape, and take them all back home. Then, as soon as he went indoors, he would receive another irate phone call; his cows were rampaging on his neighbour's property yet again. Bill claimed that this once happened to him three times in the same night! [37] He blamed aliens; readers of this book might know better.

Ripping Yarns
Something else which would once have been blamed upon *stallspuks* but which is now generally linked with UFOs is the unpleasant phenomenon of nocturnal assaults upon farm-animals. Often, people account for these crimes – dubbed 'cattle-mutilation' and 'horse-ripping' – by pointing the finger at criminals or sadists, but the main way in which the issue has reached public consciousness is through its association with UFOs. Numerous implausible conspiracy-theories exist about ETs being in league with the CIA and getting permission to cut up cattle in order to perform hideous biological experiments upon them – something which, if true, does rather beg the question of why the CIA don't just *buy* the aliens some cows and let them dissect them in secret!

Cattle-mutilations have actually been known of since Classical times, however, when aliens and the CIA were less frequently blamed. The ancient Romans knew of the phenomenon, and appear to have guessed that demons did it. The modern wave of mutilations, though, began around 1973 in the American Midwest, when mysterious black helicopters – often reputedly soundless and unmarked – were reported as hovering over herds of cattle and acting suspiciously. By 1974, actual UFOs and their occupants were being witnessed in cattle-mutilation areas. Equally often, however, their presence was simply inferred. What was not in any dispute, though, were the weird and disturbing deaths that cattle suffered during the night; their ears, lips, eyes, tails and udders were removed, their corpses exsanguinated, and their internal organs extracted in a clean-cut manner ostensibly inconsistent with the idea of natural predation. Just as odd, there were said to be a total lack of footprints or blood to be found at the scenes of the animals' deaths, and incisions made upon some of them appeared to have been performed with laser-like implements, due to their impossibly straight nature. Furthermore, it has been noted that these animals seemingly failed to put up any kind of struggle, leading some to speculate that the cows had been drugged or otherwise disabled – just like, perhaps, Tom Gorman's bulls in their trailer [38]. This, at least, is the popular legend of the so-called 'mutes' – though much plausible criticism of the whole idea does exist. [39]

Cows and bulls were not the only animals found dead and mutilated in this way, of course – horses, too, have been killed, the most famous being a Colorado mare named 'Snippy', which in 1967 was found with the flesh eerily stripped from its head and neck (although it actually later turned out to have been shot and garrotted, an unpleasant though in fact quite explicable death). Despite this connection, horse-ripping itself is generally viewed as being a slightly different phenomenon from that of cattle-mutilation, centring as it does largely upon the nocturnal violation and torture of unattended horses in their stables. They are stabbed, have their genitals maimed, their tails cut off or snipped, and are raped with blunt or sharp instruments, such as broomsticks with barbed wire curled around them. Once again, these animals do not seem to have put up much of a struggle, leading some to speculate that they may have been drugged by sexual perverts. [40]

Poultry, too, have sometimes been found killed in unusual ways. In his book *Lo!*, for instance, Charles Fort famously detailed the activities of a particularly nasty chicken-killing polt at a place called Binbrook Farm near Grimsby. Between 1904 and 1905, the farmhouse in question had been the scene of spontaneous movements of objects and various inexplicable fires had been reported there (including one which broke out upon an apparently entranced maidservant's back without her even noticing!), creating quite a mystery. Just as strange was the peculiar predator that had been at work on the farm's chickens. A journalist from the *Louth and North Lincolnshire News* went out to investigate and interviewed the farm's owner, a Mr White, reporting back that:

> "Out of 250 fowls, Mr White says he has only 24 left. They have all been killed in the same weird way. The skin around the neck from the head to the breast has been pulled off, and the windpipe drawn from its place and snapped. The fowl-house has been watched night and day, and whenever examined four or five birds would be found dead." [41]

No animal, then, was seen either entering or exiting the chicken-house. Furthermore, no known animals are recognised to kill their prey in this way, and no poultry were actually found *eaten* in any case – just dead (rather like with the Bigfoot killings on Carter and Junior Burdine's farm in 1972, mentioned earlier). No aliens were held responsible for the Binbrook carnage, though; in 1904/05 it just would not have occurred to anyone sensible to do so. *

---

* See also my book *Paranormal Merseyside* (Amberley, 2013) for a polt killing 50 pigs in 1950s Runcorn.

We Have the Technology

My point here isn't necessarily that animal-mutilations are all genuine paranormal phenomena – readers will no doubt hold differing viewpoints upon the matter – merely that they are compatible with a number of different supernatural traditions, both ancient and modern. Probably the thing which makes people nowadays think more of aliens or the CIA killing cattle rather than poltergeists or *stallspuks*, for instance, is the strange, apparently high-tech nature of many of the assaults. Cored-out rectums and laser-like incisions certainly *sound* more like the result of advanced top-secret alien technology than the invisible handiwork of ghosts and fairies. However, things were once rather different; in the past, the *sidhe* were said to have had access to a type of technologically-advanced weaponry of their own, namely the 'elf-shot' which the fairy-host would fly around shooting horses and cows with. The Scottish fairy-folklorist Robert Kirk described this elf-shot as being:

> "... like to yellow soft flint shaped like a barbed arrowhead, but flung as a dart with great force. These arms (cut by art and tools it seems beyond human) have somewhat of the nature of a thunderbolt, subtly and mortally wounding the vital parts without breaking the skin, of which wounds, some have I observed in beasts and felt them with my hands ... With their weapons they ... pierce cows, or other animals ... whose purest substance [i.e. their souls] ... these subterraneans take to live on ... leaving the terrestrial [i.e. the actual meat] behind." [42]

There's a key phrase about elf-shot in there – that these amazing arrows were "cut by art and tools it seems beyond human". This was actually because the old prehistoric flint arrow-heads found in fields and then mistakenly called elf-shot had been knapped and pressure-flaked [43] (techniques unknown to Kirk), but some preferred other explanations for their seemingly advanced nature. The celebrated Scottish witch Isobel Gowdie, for instance, in her famous confession of 1662, claimed to have entered into the 'Court of Fairy'; "a fair big room, as bright as day" hidden magically within the Dounie Hills. Here, she said, was where the fairies made their missiles:

> "The elves and the Arch-fiend laboured jointly at this task, the former forming and sharpening the dart from the rough flint, and the latter perfecting and finishing ... it." [44]

What is this, if not an old-fashioned version of the more modern notion of advanced 'alien technology' being blamed for the nocturnal wounding of cattle? It is just that the one takes fairy-lore, and the other science-fiction, as its basic source of imagery. Satan's magic fairy-forge inside the Scottish hills is really just a different way of presenting an alien weapons factory located near Alpha Centauri – and both are but fictions used to 'explain' the same phenomenon. In this way, the incomprehensible is rendered temporarily comprehensible, and unusual events brought back into line with a person's own pre-existing mental worldview.

Tied Up in Knots

Not everything that *stallspuks* and their modern equivalents are meant to have done to cattle is necessarily as unpleasant as all this, however. Sometimes, for instance, such fairies were said to be quite content to simply tie braids and knots in horses' manes and cows' tails. Like many other elements of fairy-behaviour, this trait must once have been well-known amongst the general populace, as it is mentioned as a matter of common knowledge in much pre-modern literature. Shakespeare makes reference to it in *Romeo and Juliet*, speaking of the 'fairy queen' Mab, who:

> ... plaits the manes of horses in the night
> And bakes the elf-locks in foul sluttish hairs,
> Which once untangled, much misfortune bodes. [45]

The French *lutins* were also associated with this kind of thing; there was actually a specific French word, *lutines*, which could be used to describe what a fairy had done to a horse when its mane or tail was tangled. This tradition followed French settlers to Canada, where in 1980 the folklorist Gary R Butler set out to interview residents about traditional *lutin*-beliefs in the Newfoundland region. He found people who believed in their activities even then, coming across a man named Emile Benoit who actually claimed to have had a real, live *lutin* in his barn, which braided the mane of his horse so elaborately that it took him ages to comb it straight again. Oddly, Benoit thought for some reason that these *lutins* came from outer space, so was bemused as to why they needed to braid horses' hair and then ride them during the night, as legend said they did. [46]

The supernatural plaiting of manes is no longer now just an Old World tradition, then; a breed of South American elves known as the *duende*, for example, are also said to ride horses during the night but, being so small, are obliged to make stirrups for themselves from the animals' manes, which they knot in such a way that they are able to rest their feet upon them [47]. However, such notions came originally to South America from Spain with the *conquistadors* – horses, of course, being unknown in the New World until they were shipped over during the Spanish conquest. The fact that the word *duende* comes ultimately from the Spanish word *dueño*, meaning 'owner' (as in the 'real owner' of a house) indicates that this particular type of Latino fairy had its origins in some kind of Iberian belief in brownie-like house-sprites and hearthside gods. The French folklorist Paul Sébillot, writing in 1905, said that an exactly parallel idea, right down to the detail about the braids being used for stirrups, was current in nineteenth-century France, meanwhile, so it seems certain that the ultimate origin of this South American belief was indeed European. [48]

This is not all simply a thing of the past, though; there was also an outbreak of horses' manes being plaited in the West Country in 2009. Devon and Cornwall Police suggested these braids were surreptitious 'tags' left behind on animals by horse-thieves, so that they would know which horses to target at a later date. This theory was rather undermined, however, by the fact that no such thefts were actually reported from the area during this period. Dorset Police, meanwhile, preferred to pass it all off as being the result of some kind of pagan ritual; apparently, there is a type of spell known to contemporary Wiccans as 'knot magick', which the police thought might have been relevant. However, if pagans were indeed responsible, then they seem to have been able to bypass security measures – and, indeed, catch the horses – with bemusing, fairy-like ease. Perhaps realising that both official explanations were unlikely, some commentators tried to pass it all off as being down to the horses' hair getting tangled up in brambles and barbed-wire. This also was not tenable, however, as the interlacings on the beasts were actual elaborate plaits, weaved into clear patterns, and not simply random tangles. Some people at the time did mention the idea of fairies in relation to all this – but not, specifically, *stallspuks*, which have now evidently long been forgotten about. [49]

Playing With Food

Seeing as *stallspuks* were supposed to live on farms, it should not be too much of a surprise to learn that they were also said to enjoy playing tricks with the farm-produce, such as stealing, spilling or ruining milk, butter and crops. Again, an obvious sociological explanation is likely to occur to readers here; aren't such tales merely old attempts by people to explain away the unfortunate loss of foodstuffs which have been stolen or ruined by natural means? In general, I would not disagree. However, once again, there is the awkward fact of apparent first-hand testimony to account for. The Bell Witch, for instance, is said to have once stolen enough calcium-rich milk to give it strong bones for life. Apparently, a neighbour of the Bells, a Mrs Betsy Sugg, called at the haunted household one day to pay a visit to Mrs Bell. Whilst talking:

> "... Mrs Bell spoke of her new dairy-house and invited Mrs Sugg out to show her how nicely it was arranged. She had just finished straining and setting the milk for cream, locked the door and put the key in her pocket. The milk was set in pewter basins ... with wooden covers. Mrs Bell took the key from her pocket, unlocked and opened the door, and to her surprise and chagrin there was not a drop of milk there, and the basins were turned bottom up and the covers placed over them." [50]

It was an old tradition that fairies loved dairy-products, and that any spilled milk should be left as their share [51], so possibly the Bell Witch's milk-theft was only to be expected, all things considered. One legendary Scottish *glaistig*, meanwhile, from a farm in Glen Duror of Appin in Argyll, used to happily look after the farmstead's cows in return merely for a small offering of milk being poured over a certain stone for it. Some new tenants refused to perform this simple service, however, so it is said that the *glaistig* turned *stallspuk*, not only moving cattle around in their sheds overnight, but also stealing the milk from their udders. [52]

Maybe if, as Patrick Harpur suggested earlier, such farmers had taken the time to feed and heed the *stallspuks* living on their farms, then these fairies would have happily taken their tributes and left them well alone. Many have preferred simply to ignore or abjure them, however, which could perhaps be one reason why there are so many cases on record of ghosts apparently taking great delight in ruining food on farmsteads.

In 1669, for instance, a farm in the Hertfordshire village of Burton was bothered by a spook (called a 'hag' at the time) which loved to ruin the food and crops. During the night, cabbages were pulled up from their rows and arranged in the pattern of crosses and fleurs de lys, piles of grain and pulses were burned or adulterated, loaves, cheese and meat were hidden in silly locations and, supposedly, the flesh upon a roast pig inexplicably disappeared, leaving only bare bones behind [53]. A farmhouse near Daventry in 1658, likewise, was reportedly plagued by a typical *stallspuk* which liked to move, break and spill milk-vessels, as well as mixing sand with beer and salt with bread, crumbling cheese into atoms and showering wheat down over people, ruining it [54]. Perhaps less typical, though, is a tale which Harry Price recorded of a polt which disturbed an incubator used for hatching chickens; apparently, it extinguished the heat-lamp then hard-boiled all of the eggs! [55]

Are *stallspuks* really a specific sub-species of fairy-polt, then? Personally, I think not. The fact that so many spooks from years gone by apparently used to enjoy spilling milk, bothering cows and saddling horses is surely simply down to the fact that society was much more rural in the past. Now that Western society has become infinitely more urbanised, there are far fewer barns or cowsheds available to be invaded by poltergeists and fairies – and so they have to make do with haunting attics, bedrooms and kitchens instead. In this instance, I do not think it is the behaviour of the spirits themselves that has changed over time but, rather, the nature of the society which surrounds them.

4

Foreign Fairies

The word 'poltergeist' is still essentially unknown to ordinary people in some parts of the world – and would have been entirely so until part-way through the twentieth century. And yet, if such things are real, then poltergeist phenomena must still have occurred, whether in Russia or Arabia, Japan or Sumatra. So what did the inhabitants of such places put these disturbances down to? Generally, they had their own specific domestic fairies to blame, many of which were supposed at certain times to be invisible. This cannot hope to be anything like an exhaustive discussion – space would not allow it – but we shall examine a few of the key sometimes-invisible goblins of other cultures briefly here. They, too, seem to exist in a state part-fairy, part-poltergeist.

Foxy Ladies

This, for example, is a description of the so-called 'fox spirits' and 'fox-elves' which play a prominent role in both Chinese and Japanese folklore:

> "Like ghosts, foxes sometimes haunt a room of a house. Sometimes they let the family use the room during the day, but insist upon having food and wine laid out for them so they can have a private feast at night. Sometimes they throw things around and break everything they can lay their paws on unless they're given the room for the entire day ... They are almost always invisible, usually but not always solitary ... and always in need of a good, strong exorcism." [1]

In Japan, these fox-spirits are called the *kitsune*, and they are Trickster-like figures who enjoy playing pranks. One of their favourite japes is cutting off people's hair – a trait attributed to them in both China and Japan. Strange as it may seem, there have been numerous hair-clipping panics across Asia which have been blamed upon the actions of fox-spirits, the earliest known occurring in China in AD 477. Chester Holcombe, a missionary and US diplomat stationed in Peking, even declared in the 1870s that such occurrences took place almost every year in some part of China [2]. As well as the *kitsune*, however, the Japanese also had another spirit-entity who was sometimes blamed for acts of paranormal hair-clipping, the so-called *kurokamikiri*, or 'black hair-cutting monster' [3], which was said to bite off people's locks and eat them. This chubby black-skinned being was vaguely humanoid, and was said to enjoy creeping up behind its victims and biting off their hair whilst going 'mogaaaa!' There are several named persons on record as supposedly being victims of this entity, one of Japan's many *yokai*, or 'legendary monsters'. Just as notorious was its close cousin the *kami-kiri*, a being with a bird-like beak and face, the body of a wizened old man and sharp crab-like pincers for hands. Naturally, it would use these appendages to snip people's hair with, supposedly as a punishment for vanity, and was particularly fond of attacking servant-girls in the bathroom. Tales of *kami-kiri* attacks even made it into Japanese newspapers during the Meiji Era (1868-1912), so must have been taken seriously by some, although it is hard to say in such cases where reality ends and myth begins. [4]

One particular Japanese folk-tale about the matter of supernatural hair-cutting was collected by the English diplomat and writer AB Mitford in his 1871 book *Tales of Old Japan*. This story details how a boastful carpenter, Tokutarō, sits drinking with his friends one night when the conversation turns to the *kitsune*. Tokutarō drunkenly bets that he can travel across the notoriously fox-haunted Maki Moor alone, and return unscathed. Whilst walking across the moor, however, he notices a fox dash into a bamboo grove, from which then emerges the daughter of the village headman. Requested to accompany her back home, Tokutarō agrees but suspects she is a fox in shape-shifted form. Once at the headman's house, Tokutarō informs the girl's parents that the girl is probably not their daughter at all. Offering to help, Tokutarō grabs the girl, ties her up and roasts her alive, hoping to make her reveal her true form. However, the girl dies and still she is not revealed as a fox. Obviously, Tokutarō has made a horrible mistake! Tied up himself and told to await execution, Tokutarō is saved only by the timely arrival of a Shinto priest, who offers to save his life on the condition that he too becomes a monk. Tokutarō agrees, the family of the dead girl also consenting, but only on the proviso that the murderer has his head shaved and thus be ordained immediately, before their very eyes. What happens next is best recounted in the words of the original fairy-tale:

> "... the reverend man stood up behind him, razor in hand, and, intoning a hymn, gave two or three strokes of the razor, which he then handed to his acolyte, who made a clean shave of Tokutarō's hair. When the latter had finished his obeisance to the priest, and the ceremony was over, there was a loud burst of laughter; and at the same moment the day broke, and Tokutarō found himself alone in the middle of a large moor. At first he thought it was all a dream ... He then passed his hand over his head, and found that he was shaved quite bald." [5]

At the end of his retelling of this old story, AB Mitford adds that "There are a great many tales told of men being shaved by the foxes." Why is this, though? Could these yarns to some extent possibly be based upon the observation of actual paranormal hair-cutting incidents which were then simply put down to the fox-elves? Well, Western poltergeists are sometimes spoken of as engaging in such activities themselves. In his book *Wild Talents*, Charles Fort gives a few such instances, being the first to juxtapose them with the larger outbreaks of mass hair-clipping then taking place in China [6]. One such case occurred in the town of Clarendon in Quebec in 1889, upon the farm of a certain George Dagg, where a rather incredible polt developed a voice which liked to both sing hymns and swear. The actual hair-clipping here took place upon the heads of Dagg's little boy and of Dinah McLean, an 11-year-old orphan-girl whom the family had adopted. According to Fort:

> "One afternoon little Dinah felt her hair, which hung in a long braid down her back, suddenly pulled, and on crying out, the family found her braid almost cut off, simply hanging by a few hairs. It had to be cut off entirely, and looked as if a person had grabbed the braid and sawed it with a knife. On the same day the little boy began crying, and said somebody pulled his hair all over. Immediately it was seen by his mother that his hair had also been cut off in chunks ... all over his head." [7]

Another strange example, taken by Fort from a weekly Chicago-based Spiritualist newspaper, the *Religio-Philosophical Journal*, is also instructive. It concerns a certain Mr Lynch, of Wisconsin, who had moved from Indiana with his children after his first wife had died, and then apparently wasted little time in acquiring a new one:

> "Lynch went to town one day, and returned with a dress for his [new] wife. Soon afterward, the dress was found in the barn, slashed to shreds ... Lynch bought another dress. This was found, in the barn, cut down to fit one of the children. Eggs rose from tables, tea cups leaped, and a pan of soft soap wandered from room to room ... One day one of the children, named Rena, was standing close to [the new] Mrs Lynch. Her hair was sheared off, close to her scalp, and vanished." [8]

There are other such cases to be found. The seventeenth-century astrologer and occultist John Heydon, in his 1662 book *The Harmony of the World*, told how one of his mother's maids was at the centre of a love-triangle, one of her suitors, a John Stringer, ending up being murdered by a jealous rival. Lying in bed one night, behind three locked doors, this maid claimed to have been assaulted by Stringer's furious ghost; she said she was pulled out of bed and had the entire right side of her hair "clean shaved or cut away" by the vengeful spirit [9]. More recently, the prominent American Episcopalian Bishop James Pike told of the odd poltergeist disturbances he experienced after his son's suicide in 1966. Significantly, one such phenomenon was the inexplicable cutting of the hair of Pike's female assistant; she awoke one day to find the bangs singed from off her head in a completely straight line, something which occurred again the next morning. The actual hair that had been burned away could not be found. The clear implication was made that the Bishop's dead son had done this – apparently, whilst alive, he had never liked the woman's hairstyle! [10] We would blame ghosts, then; and the Chinese and Japanese would no doubt blame their fox-elves.

Dastardly Djinn

The famous Islamic spirits known as the *djinn* (singular *djinni*) are not usually classified as being fairies, but if you look at the stories which are told about them throughout the Arab world, they do sound an awful lot like them in many ways. For Muslims, the Koran itself gives sanction to a belief in such entities. Apparently created by Allah as one of three classes of being from 'smokeless fire' – the other two classes being humans made from clay, and angels from light – the *djinn* are shape-shifting spirits, sometimes corporeal and sometimes not, sometimes appearing in beast-form as cats and dogs, sometimes manifesting as humanoids, sometimes as composite creatures ... rather like the old British bogey-beasts, in fact!

Other similarities between the fairies and the *djinn* are that these strange Arabian spirits were supposed to steal people's food, and to live in some kind of 'otherworld' broadly analogous to the Western concept of fairyland. Here, many lived supernatural versions of 'ordinary' lives, working and playing, just as the fairies were meant to. They sometimes left this realm to interact with human beings, however – by having sex with them, for instance. There is, just as with the European fairies, also some confusion about where the *djinn* first came from; some say that they were originally ancient pagan gods who became degraded to the level of earth-spirits after the spread of monotheism, others that they were once the personification of otherworldly forces associated with remote, sacred or unhallowed locations. Furthermore, they were sometimes said to travel in the wind like the Irish *sidhe*; the sight of a dust-storm or whirlwind in the desert could be explained as a *djinn* passing. When such a 'dust-devil' was seen, the Arabs would shout "Iron! Iron!" as the *djinn* were reputedly just as terrified of this substance as the European fairies were [11]. Like brownies, the *djinn* were also supposed to take up their abode in people's ovens and to enjoy playing with children. Interestingly, some scholars have tried to link the ancient *djinn* of the Syrian oasis-city of Palmyra – where they were known as *gny* or *ginnaya* – with the Roman *genius* or *lar*; in nineteenth-century Britain, the term *genii* was used by scholars to describe not just Roman household deities but also the Arabic *djinn*, as if there were no difference at all between the two. [12]

If the *djinn* sound much like fairies, though, then they also sound not entirely unlike poltergeists. For one thing, they are said to haunt houses. The famous nineteenth-century Orientalist Edward Lane, for example, provided some notes on the *djinn* in his translation of the *Thousand and One Nights*, saying that:

> "... malicious or disturbed Jinnees are asserted often to station themselves on the roofs, or at the windows, of houses, and to throw down bricks and stones on persons passing by." [13]

Likewise, according to the Persian theologian and philosopher Avicenna, writing in the eleventh century, when annoyed *djinn* will "pelt the folk in the house with missiles and utensils." [14] A sub-species of *djinn*, meanwhile, the *iblises*, were meant to live inside walls; where, presumably, they would make the same rapping and scratching noises as polts do [15]. Furthermore, just like poltergeists, the *djinn* were usually supposed to be invisible – the term '*djinn*' actually means something like 'hidden from sight' [16]. Unlike polts, however, one folk-explanation of this invisibility was that it let them spy on humans getting undressed without their victims realising it! [17]

There are even some modern instances of *djinn*-hauntings which are impressive in their resemblance to poltergeist phenomena. For example, in 2009 a family in Saudi Arabia took a *djinni* before a court of Sharia Law, accusing it of engaging in polt-like tricks such as throwing stones at them, stealing their mobile phones and leaving them threatening voicemails [18]. Apparent 'possession' by *djinn* is also not unknown, just like in the occasional poltergeist case; in 2010, it was reported that a 29-year-old man, identified only as 'Turki', had been kept shackled up in a room by his family due to his supposedly being possessed by one. When clerics came around to cast the spirit out of him, they were terrified to hear a female voice telling them that she was a royal *djinni*, and that nobody could possibly exorcise her from Turki's body without him dying in the process. Apparently, Turki now survives on social security benefits! [19]

There is even a curious tale of a *djinni* which haunted the Portuguese town of 'Ulya (now Loulé) during that period when southern Iberia was controlled by the Arabs, which involves the spirit acting as a kind of 'externalised conscience', much as we saw various poltergeists doing earlier. The story concerns a Sufi master – a type of Islamic mystic – named Abu Ja'far al-'Uryani, who had been expelled from 'Ulya by the citizens, who thought he was some kind of sorcerer. Seemingly, he was; decamping to Seville, he is supposed to have conjured up a *djinni* called Khalaf and ordered it to go and haunt the home of a certain prominent citizen of 'Ulya who had led the calls for al-'Uryani to be kicked out. The *djinni* spoke from thin air in this man's house, and gave orders that the townspeople should gather there. They did, and the *djinni* promptly revealed that another man had fallen in love with the prominent citizen's wife, and was having an affair with her. This proved to be true and, having demonstrated his powers, the *djinni* began systematically exposing the hidden crimes and vices of the townspeople to all and sundry, driving them to such despair that, after six months of torment, they sent word to Seville to ask al-'Uryani to return and free them from the pest. [20]

Another tale of a polt-like *djinni* can be found in a fifteenth-century tract written by a Dominican Friar named Felix Fabri, concerning a pilgrimage he made to the Holy Land during 1483/84. Whilst in the Middle East he visited Egypt, and learned of a haunted house close to the Nile. The house currently lay empty and, should anyone be foolish enough to try and stay there, they would soon find their belongings being thrown out of the windows, and be subjected to attacks of what we would now call 'sleep paralysis' at night. Despite this, the house's owner was not losing any money because of the spirit; once per month, in one of the rooms, he would find a sum equivalent to his usual charge of rent, wrapped up neatly in a piece of cloth. Presumably, the ghost was paying it! [21] (Fabri doesn't specifically mention the word '*djinni*' in relation to this tale, incidentally, but it is clear that it was meant to be one.)

The fact that the *djinn* are supposed to be made from 'smokeless fire' is also interesting as, frequently, both polts and *djinn* are alleged to start mysterious fires – some of which are meant to have been curiously smokeless themselves. For six months in 2010, for instance, a series of ghostly fires broke out around the house of a 73-year-old widow, Zainab Sulaiman, in the village of Kota Bharu in Malaysia. In addition to typical polt-pranks like objects appearing and then disappearing (a pair of trousers eventually turning up inside the family fridge), food being ruined by huge quantities of salt and clothes being cut to shreds, odd blazes began to occur in the household. There were large numbers of these – 78 in one day – and they occurred everywhere from on clothes, rugs and lino to inside mattresses. All were easily extinguished, and the house did not burn down; but, significantly, neither did the fires produce any actual smoke, as photographs taken at the time seem to prove [22].

A similar case occurred during 2012/13, meanwhile, this time in Turkey, when the family of a street-vendor named Zeki Toprak began being bothered by a spook which set fire to walls, ceilings and a variety of household objects at their home in the town of Siirt. Upon one occasion, the three-year-old son of the household was found asleep with his blanket ablaze on top of him. When a cup of water was thrown over the fire, however, it was instantly extinguished and the toddler was found to have no injuries whatsoever; even his clothes were left unsinged. Clearly, these fires were utterly abnormal in their nature – as was the conflagration which broke out inside the family's ice-cool refrigerator one day when, in a curious parallel with the haunting of Mrs Sulaiman's house in 2010, clothes were placed inside the appliance by the spook and then set ablaze. Other typical polt-like tricks occurred to the Sulaimans, too – plates vanished from a breakfast table and were found arranged neatly out in the garden, keys turned in their locks when the family were not at home, leaving them locked out, and salt mixed itself into a sugar bowl whilst a water-bottle mysteriously filled up with vinegar, ready for some unwary person to drink [23].

Modern Westerners, of course, would surely blame poltergeists for such childish and antisocial actions; but, as the Australian researcher Paul Cropper discovered when he investigated both hauntings on the spot, many imams, local residents and even the families directly involved preferred to say that it was all down to the actions of some troublesome *djinn*. Given the nature of their cultural background, who could blame them?

Household Help
We have already examined the brownie in this book at length, but I think that, without going over too much old ground, it might be worthwhile stopping for a moment to look at a few other breeds of (sometimes) helpful fairies from across Europe; for many cultures seemed to be aware of the same basic phenomenon, or at least had their own national and ethnic myths about it. The widespread nature of these tales, the varying names of their elfin protagonists notwithstanding, seems likely to me to speak volumes for their being at least partially based upon actual reality. [24]

The first of our foreign brownies to be examined here is the Russian *domovoi*, a small, hairy little man who acts as a kind of household guardian; the term literally means 'he of the house'. Like many fairies he is a shape-shifter, sometimes being seen in his hairy form, but at other times as a little old man with a beard, as a cat or dog, or as the double of the master of the household. Usually however, he was invisible. Traditionally, each home was meant to have its own guardian *domovoi*, who would help out around the house and farm by performing chores and field-work. In return for guaranteeing a household's prosperity, he would be left offerings of milk and biscuits in the kitchen overnight. A further similarity with hobs and *bwcas*, meanwhile, is that they were meant to live in or beneath stoves and ovens (or, alternatively, at the threshold of the house, under the doorstep). If you wanted to attract one to live with you, then the best thing to do would be to place some bread in front of the oven to tempt one inside.

However, as you will no doubt have guessed, a *domovoi* who was displeased with his 'owners' (due to their neglect of either it or the household chores) could turn poltergeist and play all the usual nasty tricks; it would smash crockery, bang on pots and walls, moan and groan, leave muddy footprints and move and rattle small objects. He could also act like a *stallspuk*, and torment horses in their stables overnight (rather like the *domovoi's* Slavic cousin, the *dvorovoi*, or 'spirit of the courtyard', which delighted in harming livestock, especially if it had white fur). No doubt because of these characteristics, an alternative and pejorative Russian word, *barabashka*, can be used to describe a *domovoi*. It means, literally, 'rattler', and is used to describe the *domovoi* purely in terms of its poltergeistic aspect, rather than in its more helpful, brownie-like form. However, even when he was being helpful, the *domovoi* could act like a poltergeist. For example, if he wished to warn a woman of the house that she was getting herself involved with an unsuitable man, he would pull and tug her hair, just like many modern-day spooks have done. If he laughed invisibly, meanwhile, it was a portent of good times to come, but if he wept and groaned, it boded ill – a family death was on its way. If he made unseen music appear, however, perhaps by strumming a comb, then it indicated a wedding was in the air.[25]

The Slavic *kikimora*, meanwhile, another type of Eastern European house-spirit, performed many of the same actions a *domovoi* would. Unlike the *domovoi*, however, the *kikimora* was conceived of as being female (some traditions say she is the wife of the *domovoi*), the entity being stereotypically described as either an average-looking woman with her hair down, or a small hump-backed lady dressed in dirty clothes. Again, like the *domovoi* or hob, she used to live in stoves or ovens; or else haunted the cellar. As usual, in a well-kept household, the *kikimora* was said to do the housework and look after the chickens; in a poorly-kept home, however, she would break crockery and keep the family up at night by making strange noises and whistling. There were meant to be two types of *kikimora* which could live inside a person's home; forest ones, and swamp ones. You could tell if you had a swamp one if wet footprints turned up around the place. Clearly, they were thought of as being malevolent as well as helpful, as it was a habit of builders and repair-men who didn't like the householders for whom they were working to make a doll in the fashion of a *kikimora* and hide it somewhere in the house in order to magically introduce one of these beasts into the dwelling. [26]

The Scandinavian *tomte* (in Sweden), *tonttu* (in Finland) or *nisse* (in Norway and Denmark) – all three words refer to the same basic thing – is another household fairy of note. This *tomte* was generally envisaged as being a small old man, often with a beard, dressed as a farmer, who would protect and look after the household at night. Again, he was a shape-shifter, being able also to appear as a giant, or with one single, large, cyclopean eye, or as the more usual hair-covered creature with pointed ears and glowing eyes – although, naturally, he was meant to be invisible most of the time. Originally, he was supposed to be the soul of the initial founder of a farm, therefore having links to the ancient practice of ancestor-worship, as with the Roman *lares*. If you wanted the *tomte* to look after your farm though, then, unsurprisingly, you had to leave him out offerings of porridge and butter, particularly at Christmas (something which has actually seen him merge with Father Christmas in the area in more modern times). Failure to do so meant that *stallspuk*-like phenomena would occur; cattle could be killed or harmed, cows' tails tied together and objects be broken or overturned. If he caught someone on the farm engaging in bad behaviour, meanwhile, like swearing, mistreating the animals or pissing in the barn, he would waste no time in boxing them around the ears or administering a good thrashing with unseen hands. In Sweden, whilst belief in the *tomte* has since been largely replaced by belief in poltergeists, as in other Western countries, the term still lives on as an expression for someone who performs an anonymous favour for you unseen, or is used to refer to the human caretaker of a property, under the variant form *hustomte*. [27]

Kobold Chaos
From those lands we now call Germany and Austria, meanwhile, we can read of beings called *kobolds* [28]. Like the English word 'fairy', the German word *kobold* seems to have been an umbrella term used to refer to non-human spiritual entities as a whole. For example, miners frequently blamed rapping and hammering sounds heard underground upon a race of subterranean gnomes they called *kobolds*. Some thought these noises were warnings that the

mine was about to collapse; others that the direction the knocks were coming from indicated where the most valuable ores were to be found. Seeing as these spirits mainly manifested by making rapping sounds, however, they also sound a bit like poltergeists. Either way, these mine-*kobolds* were certainly a matter of widespread belief; the poisonous element cobalt was actually named after them.

Another unusual class of *kobold* was the *klabautermann*, who was meant to haunt wooden ships which had inadvertently been made from the tree that he had previously inhabited. Some sailors said that these beings brought a craft luck; but others described them as playing polt-like pranks such as tangling the ship's ropes and laughing at the sailors. Most often, he just made knocking sounds, as if with a hammer, upon the planks and masts – his name is actually derived from the German verb '*klabastern*', meaning 'to rumble' or 'make a noise' [29]. (In 1791, incidentally, it is said that a Scottish carpenter named John Spence was constructing a boat for a client on the Isle of Orkney when mysterious knocking sounds, as if from an invisible hammer, were heard coming from the craft. When he had finished his work, the rappings followed Spence home – evidently he had accidentally cut down a *kobold*-haunted tree to make his boat, too! [30])

Yet a further sub-class of these beings, meanwhile, was the *bieresal*, or 'beer spirit', who would haunt the beer-cellars of inns and perform the work of invisible bar-staff by washing glasses, cleaning tables and looking after the barrels. Clearly, he was the German equivalent of the Irish clurichaun, and, I would guess, the distant ancestor of all those contemporary pub-ghosts who are said still to pour pints or spoil beer, depending how the fancy takes them.

In general, however, the *kobolds* seem to have been thought of, once more, as being domestic fairies, sometimes helpful, sometimes not. Records show that, in the 13th century, German homes often had a carved wooden effigy of a *kobold* in their main room, to bring luck. It has been speculated that such practices reflect a continuation of ancient pagan beliefs in Germany after Christianisation, the word *kobold* often being said to derive from the Old German *kofewalt*, or 'room spirit'. Others claim that it derives from the phrase *kuba-walda*, meaning 'the one who rules the house', which sounds plausible – a house's *kobold* was often referred to colloquially as 'the steward' or 'manager'. Another idea, meanwhile, has it that the word actually comes from the word *kobalos*, a breed of tricksterish little sprites spoken of by the ancient Greeks, and about whom little is known.

Either way, the word's basic meaning as referring to a household god is quite clear; something made all the more obvious by the fact that *kobolds* were also frequently said to reside in hearths and ovens like *lares* and brownies. Some sources even tell us that *kobolds* manifested frequently as masses of flames and fire, entering and exiting a house through its chimney. Not unexpectedly, the *kobold* was meant to be a shape-shifter too, able to appear as animals, human beings and even inanimate objects, such as candles. One alleged first-hand description of some *kobolds*, recorded in 1820, described them as being small dancing lights, "round, and about the size of a cheese plate", surrounded by "the dim outline of a small human figure, black and grotesque ... like a little image carved out of black shining wood". The witness, a Madam Kalodzy, claimed that these lights were actually the creatures' hearts. Most frequently they are conceived of as being small dwarf-like humanoids, however – when they are seen. It

Japanese folklore is full of all kinds of different goblins and fairies which we don't have here in the West; they call them *yokai*, and some of them occasionally act like poltergeists.

A Japanese *kitsune* (fox-spirit) creeps up on someone in disguise; maybe he wants to snip their hair off?

The 17th-century English occultist John Heydon, whose mother's maid allegedly had her hair shaved off her head by a vengeful ghost.

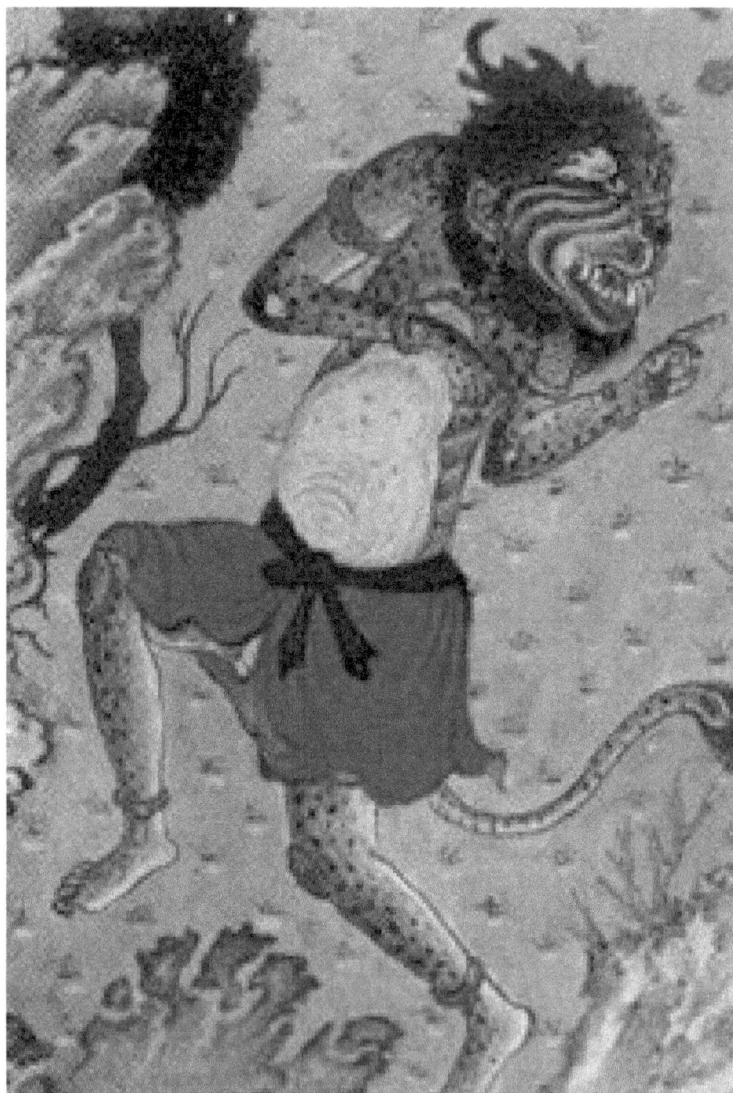

A very animal-like depiction of a dancing *djinni* from an old Islamic text. He looks like one of the *ThunderCats*!

The hairy Russian *domovoi*, depicted crawling around near its traditional home of the household oven.

The Slavic *kikimora*, one of the most obscure of all European house-sprites.

A Scandinavian *tomte* sweeps out his master's stables.

A cute little *nisse*. If you look carefully, you'll notice he has cat's whiskers.

To judge by this old engraving, one variant of the Hinzelmann legend had it that he was actually the spirit of a murdered child, like the Cauld Lad o'Hilton.

should go without saying by now that *kobolds*, too, are generally invisible in their nature.

As per usual, *kobolds* were supposed to perform domestic chores for those they favoured, or to play poltergeist tricks upon those who neglected or angered them. Some traditions held that the classic sign that a *kobold* has come to stay would be waking up in the morning to find that woodchips have been strewn everywhere and cow-dung and dirt dropped into the milk-cans. The fact that these fairies were hard workers can be proven, however, by the existence of a nineteenth-century German idiom; when you encountered an efficient or hard-working woman, you would say that she "had the *kobold*" about her.

Other similarities with poltergeists are that *kobolds* would reputedly beat and strangle people with invisible hands, and make noises at night to keep householders awake. They were also supposed to punish vices and reveal people's secret moral transgressions. That they have continued to be associated with poltergeists in Germany even into modern times can be seen in the fact that a 1909 German dictionary specifically defined a polt as being a "*kobold* [or] household spirit" [31]. The main participants in some of the most-anthologised ghost-stories from Germany have specifically called their spooks *kobolds*, too. For instance, the haunting of the home of a German Lutheran Minister named Jeremias Heinisch in Gröben during 1718 pops up in many a polt book. Here, the main phenomenon to be encountered were our old friends flying stones, which rained down on a cowshed, flew through windows and sailed around corners, leading to Heinisch blaming "eines insgemein sogennantenten Kobolds" – 'so-called *kobolds*' – for the disturbances in the title of a pamphlet he later published about the affair. [32]

How real were *kobolds*, though? Presumably most tales told about them were just legend, but there could still have been a certain core of truth to some stories – especially a few of those told about the most famous *kobold* of all, Hinzelmann of Hudemühlen. This yarn, taken as a whole, is a celebrated German folk-tale. However, for a folk-tale, it has some odd elements to it. For one thing, it has specific dates and locations attached, this particular *kobold* first making his presence known in 1584 by knocking on the walls of Hudemühlen Castle in the region of Lüneberg, near what is now Hanover. This in itself is odd for a fairy-tale – does anybody know what exact year Cinderella went to the ball, for instance, or in which specific castle the handsome prince lived? Either way, the Hudemühlen sprite certainly seems to have had many obvious poltergeist-like qualities to him. For instance, he developed a disembodied voice, and began to speak familiarly to both the servants and their master. He even sang and laughed, telling people who wanted to know it his entire biography. His name was Hinzelmann, he said, he had a wife named Hille Bingels, and he hailed from the Bohemian mountains [*]. His usual companions were living in the Bohemian Forest, but had recently fallen out with him, obliging him to take temporary refuge inside the castle with the "good people" who lived there until such time as his old friends should desire reconciliation.

This kind of bizarre and childish pseudo-account of Hinzelmann's life has parallels in other

---

[*] Interestingly, the very name 'Hinzelmann' would have had obvious fairy-connotations for a German. Derived from a diminutive form of 'Heinrich', the term 'Hinzelmännchen' was famously used to describe a race of brownie-like dwarves from Cologne, well-known figures in German legend. A spirit announcing his name was Hinzelmann, therefore, would be the rough equivalent of an English ghost saying his name was Robin.

cases, too. 'Malekin' had a back-story equally as improbable, as did Reyneke the ghost-hand, both of whom we encountered earlier – and, indeed, as have some modern polts such as Gef the Mongoose, who claimed somewhat implausibly to have been born in Delhi, India, on Monday 7th June 1852 [33]. (A further curious similarity with Gef, meanwhile, is that Hinzelmann was said sometimes to appear in the shape of a large black marten – an animal not entirely dissimilar to a mongoose in basic form.)

Soon, Hinzelmann was acting like a typical brownie, performing any number of tasks around the castle, such as scrubbing the pans and dishes, finding lost items, cleaning tubs and brushing down the horses in the stable. He also acted as an invisible supervisor of the servants, encouraging the good ones and whacking the lazy ones with a stick. As a reward, the cook left him out a dish of sweet milk for breakfast each morning. He was even given his own room, with a bed. He was never seen sitting upon this, but a little impression, about the size of a cat, could often be observed in the mattress. Sometimes, he was said to eat at his master's table, the food vanishing from his plate only to later be found hidden in various places around the room. Generally, then, Hinzelmann was a benign presence, his pranks being far more mischievous than they were malicious.

Was Hinzelmann indeed a kind of poltergeist, then? Not according to him. When he was asked if he might be a *kobold* or 'knocking spirit' (*polter geyst*, in the German of the time), he haughtily denied it, saying:

> "What have these to do with me? They are the Devil's spectres, and I do not belong to them!"

(Gef the Mongoose also virulently denied that he was a polt in this way, too.) Devil's spectres or not, however, Hinzelmann certainly acted like a typical poltergeist when an exorcist came to try and dispel him; he is supposed to have snatched the Bible from his hands and torn it to shreds before squeezing and scratching the poor man until he fled in terror. Plenty of invisible ghosts are meant to have acted like that; though, admittedly, rather fewer have explained, like Hinzelmann, that he only did so because:

> "I am a Christian like any other man, and I hope to be saved."

If Hinzelmann wasn't really a poltergeist, though, then he could certainly perform a good impression of one. For one thing, he locked doors and hid their keys, upon one occasion leaving a maid who had slighted him to spend the whole night in the cellar, the keys then being found lying in plain sight in front of the cellar-door the next morning. Also like a typical polt, Hinzelmann seems to have attached himself to young girls; he took such a shine to two in particular that they ended up remaining unmarried. If any rivals for their affections stayed the night, he bothered them with loud bangs on their walls and threw things at them, until eventually they gave up and went away. At other times, he would make golden writing appear upon walls before the girls' suitors, warning them off, and would sometimes be seen – in the form of a small depression in their bedclothes – sleeping at their feet to keep watch over them in the night. When a secretary was making love to a chamber-maid in secret one evening, meanwhile, he jealously intervened by pulling them apart, throwing the secretary out of the door, and beating him with a stick. These actions of *coitus interruptus*, too, have their close parallels within several other poltergeist cases. Also worth noting is that Hinzelmann, like many fairy-polts, was fond of children; sometimes infants at play in the castle were supposedly joined by another child, of "beautiful countenance", with curled yellow hair and dressed in a coat of red silk – Hinzelmann in disguise. [34]

Hinzelmann stayed at Castle Hudemühlen for four years, announcing his departure in 1588, leaving us with a legend as picturesque as it seems initially unlikely. There is much more to the tale than I have described here, and numerous fictional fables – including a version of the 'boggart-flit' narrative, no less – have certainly attached themselves to the overall story of Hinzelmann. And yet, taken element by element, rather than as a whole, there are few parts of the yarn which do not have their parallels in genuine poltergeist cases. Either Hinzelmann really was an actual spook, then, or the people who invented these stories certainly knew what a real-life poltergeist did and looked like.

Invisible Indians

Similar accounts really can be found from all over the world. Certain American Indian tribes, for example, believed in an entity called the *hobomokko*, a kind of invisible sprite which could manifest by moving furniture and producing rappings in tents and wigwams. [35] The Cherokee Indians of North Carolina, meanwhile, called the fairies the *Yunw Tsunsdi*, and conceived of them as being a race of elf-like Indians who left tiny footprints behind them in the snow. To track these prints, however, would be dangerous as the little people would begin hurling stones at you, like a poltergeist. Another description of the activities of these Cherokee fairies, provided by a high-school counsellor called Lois Calonehuskie in 1987, sounds equally polt-like:

> "Sometimes at night people will wake up and hear footsteps and voices in their houses. When they get up to see who is there, they find nothing. But in the morning, when they go to the kitchen and they find some food missing, they know the Little People have been there." [36]

The Yakima Indians, likewise, believed in a mysterious fairy-race called the *Wahteetas*, who sounded a little like brownies in some ways; the ancient examples of 'picture-writing' found on rocks around the rivers of Washington and Oregon were supposed to be cleaned up by them overnight. According to legend, if you dirtied these pictures with mud, they would be found "all bright and fresh as ever" the next morning. The Coeur d'Alene Indians also believed in invisible dwarfs who would cause people to fall into a swoon as they approached them. When they awoke, they might find themselves hanging upside-down from a tree or with some of their clothing missing. These dwarfs can supposedly still be heard, hitting trees with sticks – or making rapping-noises, to you and me – and making wails and groans during the night. [37]

I again say here that this list is in no way exhaustive, however; lack of space and my equal lack of competency in foreign languages mean it can be no other way. The brief taster of foreign fairy-types provided in this chapter, though, is surely sufficient enough to show two things; that fairy-like beings have been believed in in most cultures around the world and that, when described, they often sound very much like what we modern Westerners would now term poltergeists. Given the consistency of their supposed behaviour in the tales which are told about them, it seems to me that we are then left with two main options about how to interpret this fact – either they all had some kind of mysterious common source of folkloric origin, or else these tales are based at least partially upon the global observation of actual supernatural phenomena. Only the individual reader can decide which notion they find to be the more plausible or intellectually appealing to them. Either way, it does seem obvious from looking at the evidence I have presented that the modern figure of the poltergeist in Europe, at least, grew from out of the ancient idea of the guardian or tutelary spirit of a family or household. Perhaps it is not just Santa Claus (who partially originated in the figure of the Scandinavian *tomte*, remember) for whom we should occasionally be leaving out offerings of food and drink of a cold winter's night, then ...

Conclusion:

A Ghost By Any Other Name ...

I think it is fair to say that this book has shown that fairies and poltergeists have much in common. Can we say that they are *exactly* the same thing, however? It is undoubtedly possible to make such a claim, and there are those who would look at certain contemporary hauntings, even today, and see not spooks at work but some obscure and specific sub-species of fairy instead. For example, there is a recent poltergeist case from the Essex town of Frinton-on-Sea which was looked into by the well-known paranormal investigator Michael J Hallowell, whom we met earlier. However, as he probed the case further, he and his fellow researcher John Triplow were, in Hallowell's words:

> "... slowly drawn to the conclusion that the bizarre phenomena were being carried out not by a poltergeist at all, but by a powerful elemental creature of ancient provenance – the brag."

This brag, of course, is a little-known variety of barguest from the folklore of Durham and Northumberland in the North-East of England, where it generally adopts the form of a shaggy horse or donkey (brags, like most bogey-beasts, being able to shape-shift). Whilst in this form, it is said to try and tempt people to sit on its back before throwing them off into a pool of water and then running away laughing – just like in certain legends told about Scottish kelpies, or 'water-horses', another form of legendary shape-shifting fairy-beast.

These descriptions don't really make the brag sound much like a poltergeist, however ... but whatever it was that was infesting the home of Nial Coghlan and his partner Caroline in Frinton-on-Sea in 2010 certainly did sound like a polt, and a particularly unpleasant one at that. For one thing, it lit fires, sometimes by performing such anti-social actions as putting a tea-towel inside a toaster and then plugging it in. For another thing, it made phantom footsteps and odd noises, and moved and hurled objects around as well as hiding keys. Furthermore, its activities were not limited to the house itself, the thing once causing a scene in a pub by making strange sounds and pushing a table about violently. It was even able to create mysterious flows of liquid; one time a small cloud supposedly formed itself out of nothing about 15 inches below the ceiling, from which actual rain then began to pour – but rain made from piss! All of these phenomena (even the appearance of urine) have their parallels within several other poltergeist cases.

Given this fact, what evidence, then, is there that it was actually a brag and not a 'mere' poltergeist haunting the Coghlans? Well, for one thing, it left behind animal-like footprints after itself; once the entity had rained wee down all over the stairs, it climbed up them, leaving imprints of its feet in the wet carpet. In the words of Nial Coghlan, some of these prints looked like they had been made "by a wolf or something" and had claws sticking out of them. A police officer who arrived on the scene, meanwhile, said that some were "hoof-shaped" – as you may expect a bogey-beast's footprints to be. Furthermore, according to Hallowell, he has found certain historical (surely folkloric?) sources which purport to demonstrate that, as he puts it, the brag has "an almost unrivalled propensity for violence", these entities, he says, having supposedly severely injured and even killed people in the past. The Frinton spirit was also incredibly aggressive, Hallowell tells us; one time, as the Coghlans were driving back from the pub, it began beating the head of Nial's brother Mark with invisible hands and tried to strangle another man in the car with his hooded top. As the car was brought screeching to a halt, the brag laughed at the trouble it had caused; it made, quite audibly, the sound "Ho ho ho!" which, according to Hallowell, is "a verbal signature which brags have used for centuries." [1]

Nothing to Brag About

So, then; the spook was actually a brag. Or was it? Actually, the evidence is more ambiguous than that. Let's look at what the entity actually did. For one thing, it lit fires; but, as we've just seen, *djinn* (who could also manifest as beast-like creatures) can do that too, being the acknowledged masters of 'smokeless fire', so the spirit was hardly unique in that respect. In actual fact, there are dozens of poltergeist pyromaniacs on record; were these all brags, too? The Frinton brag also made liquid appear from nowhere; but so have many other ghosts. For example, in 1919 at Swanton Novers rectory in Norfolk, literally gallons of paraffin, petrol, methylated spirits, water and sandalwood oil famously poured from walls and ceilings with no apparent source detectable for where it was all coming from – events which are, nowadays, generally blamed upon a poltergeist. [2]

If you want a case of urine manifesting during a haunting, meanwhile, then you need look no further than the unquiet home of the Boulter family in Leicester where, in 1991, puddles of slimy liquid began appearing all over the place; pools of it simply materialised inside electrical appliances, over clothes and furniture, even inside closed handbags. So much ended up in the fish-bowl that it killed the family's pet goldfish! After being analysed at Leicester University, the goo was found to be animal urine – and, in fact, the apparition of a goat was actually seen around the Boulter household. If it had left behind footprints, presumably they would have been hoofed [3] ... Mysterious clouds have also, very occasionally, been witnessed inside haunted houses, too – during an 1860s Swiss case, for example, a servant girl claimed to have witnessed "a transparent, grey little cloud" which floated through a kitchen-window and then hammered itself against a door. [4]

The physical attacks made by the Frinton brag, meanwhile, have any number of parallels; we

Strange barguest-like beings have always been claimed to attack people within their homes. But should we necessarily always take such tales literally?

Bogey-beasts which lurked near ponds and rivers – like the kelpie and certain bar-guests – could sometimes adopt the form of White Ladies and try to entice people on to drown themselves in the water, as with these nubile fairy-maidens depicted in *Hylas and the Nymphs* (1896) by John William Waterhouse. You really could imagine such beings in whatever form you liked.

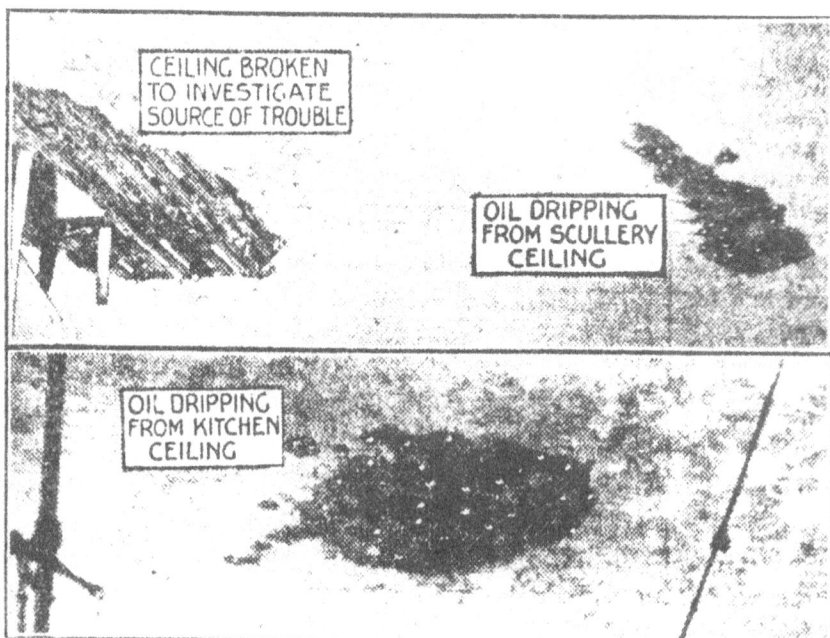

A contemporary newspaper illustration of the mysterious flows of liquid observed at Swanton Novers Rectory in Norfolk during 1919.

Melchior Joller and his family, in whose home a poltergeist manifested in the form of a flying cloud.

A Japanese *kappa*, or 'water-goblin'. These, too, have been said to leave wet footprints around people's homes.

have already had a chapter about supernatural assaults, so need give no further examples here. The brag's supernatural movement of objects, likewise, is the very stereotype of poltergeistry. The appearance of animal footprints, too, is not unknown; Gef the Mongoose left several such tracks behind after him, for example, which were analysed by the British Museum. They said that they had been made by a dog, a raccoon and some other creature [5]. The fact that the brag's tracks resembled wolf-prints may also remind us of the creature seen during the Hexham Heads haunting – except for the fact that *that* particular bogey-beast, of course, was identified not as a brag, but as a *wulver*. We might also recall that one of the signs of having a swamp-*kikimora* inside your house was to find wet footprints there. There is even a case on record from June 1991, in which the appearance of a trail of dozens of small, four-toed wet footprints inside a house in the Japanese town of Saito was blamed upon neither a brag nor a *kikimora*, but a *kappa* – a kind of Japanese water-goblin. [6]

Nothing to Laugh About
Even the entity's triumphant cry of "Ho ho ho!" is not unique, historically-speaking, to the brag specifically. The Russian *domovoi*, for instance, was meant to say "Hee Hee Hee" or "Ho Ho Ho" when happy or excited [7], and Shakespeare's Puck does likewise. This extract from the 1628 poem *The Mad Merry Pranks of Robin Goodfellow*, probably by Ben Jonson, backs Shakespeare up, describing Robin, as it does, as a typical laughing, brownie-like poltergeist:

> When house or hearth doth sluttish lie,
> I pinch the maidens black and blue;
> The bed-clothes from the bed pull I,
> And lay them naked all to view.
> 'Twixt sleep and wake,
> I do them take,
> And on the key-cold floor them throw.
> If out they cry
> Then forth I fly,
> And loudly laugh out, ho, ho, ho!

In Northamptonshire, meanwhile, there was an old adage, 'to laugh like Old Bogey', whilst the Germans spoke of someone 'laughing like a *kobold*', indicating that all such fairies enjoyed a good giggle, and not just brags [8]. Indeed, according to Sir Walter Scott, in his 1802 book *Border Minstrelsy*, there was no such specific bogey as a 'brag' in existence anyway; in his view, the very word was just a dialect-term used in the villages of the North-East instead of the word 'barguest'. [9]

A brief examination of a few of the most well-known brags from the rural North-East should make it quite evident that they are merely barguests or bogeys by a different name. One of the most famous, for example, was the Hylton Lane Brag, which reputedly haunted a path leading between Sunderland and the Durham village of Hylton during the 1800s in the form of a dog, calf, horse or White Lady, following keelmen along the road [10]. Even more infamous was the Pelton Brag, which roamed the village of that name. This beast, as per usual, could appear in many forms; a calf with a bushy tail and a white handkerchief tied around its neck, various species of horse, an invisible phantom coach, or even a big white sheet like a fake ghost from

Scooby-Doo [11]. Clearly, these brags are just generic barguests, rather than any kind of specific sub-species of the breed.

Back Where We Started

Therefore, the identification of the Frinton-on-Sea ghost as being a brag tells us nothing much at all. Hallowell isn't wrong as such in his claim (I'm not trying to criticise him – his idea is a novel and interesting one and in many ways anticipates my own); it's just that the term itself is essentially meaningless, or at least deeply ambiguous. But then, as we have seen throughout, so are the terms 'poltergeist' and 'fairy'. Do all these names merely mean the same thing, then? Not exactly, perhaps. You wouldn't call a poltergeist a brownie if it never cleaned up for you, I suppose; but if it cleaned up sometimes and threw around soil at others, would you be justified in calling it a boggart? Maybe. I'm not sure there is a right or a wrong answer here. Instead, it seems to me that brownies, brags, boggarts and poltergeists are all just competing versions of one another, or else varying aspects of one ultimately mysterious root 'thing' which remains at present unknowable to us. When we talk about encountering one of them, what we really mean is that we have witnessed some kind of inexplicable or apparently supernatural activity; and this, of course, was the original English meaning of the word 'fairy' back when it was still being used as an adjective, as we saw in the introduction. One man's brag is just another man's poltergeist in the end then, I suppose.

What do I myself think these things are, though? The more I research them, the less sure I become, frankly. There's *something* there at the heart of all this, for sure – the basic phenomena have been testified to right throughout history – but what this something is, exactly, will bear many competing masks being hung upon it. Personally, I think that these things are over and above all else puckish shape-shifters; though whether that quality is one which is inherent within poltergeist and fairy phenomena themselves or a product of the mental landscape and cultural preconditioning of the persons who observe them, I leave it for you to decide. Both poltergeists and fairies can be whatever you want them to be; and that, I think, is the best piece of evidence that they might just be basically the same thing that you could ever hope to come across.

BIBLIOGRAPHY OF PRINTED WORKS CITED

NOTE: the publication dates listed in brackets are those of the specific editions which I used personally. Many may not represent the works' original publication dates or publishers.

- Appleyard, Brian (2006) *'Aliens: Why They Are Here'* Scribner: UK

- Aubrey, John (2006) *'Miscellanies Upon Various Subjects'* BiblioBazaar: USA

- Bord, Janet & Bord, Colin (1985) *'Alien Animals'* Panther Books/Granada: UK

- Bord, Janet (1997) *'Fairies: Real Encounters with Little People'* Michael O'Mara: UK

- Bowker, James (2011) *'Goblin Tales of Lancashire'* General Books: USA

- Briggs, Katharine (2002) *'The Fairies in Tradition and Literature'* Routledge Classics: UK

- Brookesmith, Peter (Ed.) (1995a) *'Marvels & Mysteries: Ghosts'* Parallel: UK

- Brookesmith, Peter (Ed.) (1995b) *'Marvels & Mysteries: Strange Talents'* Parallel: UK

- Budden, Albert (1995) *'UFOs: Psychic Close Encounters'* Blandford: UK

- Burton, Robert (2001) *'The Anatomy of Melancholy'* New York Review of Books: USA

- MacGregor, Alasdair Alpin (1937) *'The Peat-Fire Flame: Folk-Tales and Traditions of the Highlands and Islands'* The Moray Press: UK

- Carrington, Hereward & Fodor, Nandor (1951) *'Haunted People: The Story of the Poltergeist Down the Centuries'* EP Dutton & Co: USA

- Cassirer, Manfred (1993) *'The Persecution of Mr Tony Elms: The Bromley Poltergeist'* Privately Printed: UK

- Clanny, William Reid (1841) *'A Faithful Record of the Miraculous Case of Mary Jobson'* MA Richardson/JR Smith: UK

- Clark, Jerome & Coleman, Loren (2006) *'The Unidentified'* [2006a] & *'Creatures of the Outer Edge'* [2006b] AnomalIst Books: USA

- Clarke, David & Roberts, Andy (2007) *'Flying Saucerers: A Social History of Ufology'* Heart of Albion Press: UK

- Crowe, Catherine (2000) *'The Night Side of Nature'* Wordsworth: UK

- Davies, Owen (2007) *'The Haunted: A Social History of Ghosts'* Palgrave Macmillan: UK

- Devereux, Paul (1982) *'Earthlights: Towards an Understanding of the UFO Enigma'* Book Club Associates: UK

- Devereux, Paul (2007) *'Spirit Roads: An Exploration of Otherworldly Routes'* Collins & Brown: UK

- Eliade, Mircea (2004) *'Shamanism: Archaic Techniques of Ecstasy'* Princeton University Press: USA

- Evans, EP (2009) *'The Criminal Prosecution and Capital Punishment of Animals'* The Lawbook Exchange: USA

- Evans, Hilary & Bartholomew, Robert (2009) *'Outbreak! The Encyclopaedia of Extraordinary Social Behaviour'* Anomalist Books: USA

- Evans, Hilary & Stacy, Dennis (Eds.) (1997) *'UFO 1947-1997: Fifty Years of Flying Saucers'* John Brown: UK

- Evans-Wentz, WY (2008) *'The Fairy-Faith in Celtic Countries'* BiblioBazaar: USA

- Flammarion, Camille (1924) *'Haunted Houses'* T Fisher Unwin: UK

- Fodor, Nandor (1959) *'On the Trail of the Poltergeist'* Arco: UK

- Fort, Charles (1997) *'Lo!'* John Brown: UK

- Fort, Charles (1998) *'Wild Talents'* John Brown: UK

- Foster, RF (2005) *'WB Yeats A Life, Vol II: The Arch-Poet'* Oxford University Press: UK

- Freeman, Richard (2010) *'The Great Yokai Encyclopaedia: The A-Z of Japanese Monsters'* CFZ Press: UK

- Gauld, Alan & Cornell, AD (1979) *'Poltergeists'* Routledge & Kegan Paul: UK

- Gooch, Stan (2007) *'The Origins of Psychic Phenomena'* [originally published as *Creatures from Inner Space*] Inner Traditions: USA

- Goss, Michael (1979) *'Poltergeists: An Annotated Bibliography of Works in English, circa 1880-1975'* Scarecrow Press: USA

- Graves, Robert (1999) *'The White Goddess: A Historical Grammar of Poetic Myth'* Faber & Faber: UK

- Hallowell, Michael J (2007) *'Invizikids: The Curious Enigma of 'Imaginary' Childhood Friends'* Heart of Albion Press: UK

- Hallowell, Michael J & Ritson, Darren W (2011) *'The Haunting of Willington Mill'* The History Press: UK

- Hardinge, Emma (1870) *'Modern American Spiritualism'* The New York Printing Company: USA

- Harold, Clive (1979) *'The Uninvited'* Star Books: UK

- Harpur, Patrick (2003) *'Daimonic Reality: A Field Guide to the Otherworld'* Pine Winds Press: USA

- Harte, Jeremy (2004) *'Explore Fairy Traditions'* Heart of Albion Press: UK

- Henderson, Jan-Andrew (2008) *'The Ghost that Haunted Itself'* Mainstream: UK

- Holder, Geoff (2013) *'Poltergeist Over Scotland'* The History Press: UK

- Hough, Peter & Randles, Jenny (1999) *'Mysteries of the Mersey Valley'* BCC: UK

- Hubbell, Walter (1916) *'The Great Amherst Mystery'* Brentanos: USA

- Innes, John (Ed.) (1999) *'The Fortean Times Book of UnConventional Wisdom'* John Brown: UK

- Jaffé, Aniela (1963) *'Apparitions and Precognition'* University Books: USA

- Jaynes, Julian (2000) *'The Origin of Consciousness in the Breakdown of the Bicameral Mind'* Mariner: USA

- Joynes, Andrew (2001) *'Medieval Ghost Stories'* Boydell & Brewer: UK

- Kelleher, Colm A & Knapp, George (2005) *'Hunt for the Skinwalker: Science Confronts the Unexplained at a Remote Ranch in Utah'* Paraview Pocket Books: USA

- Kirk, Robert (2007) *'The Secret Commonwealth of Elves, Fauns and Fairies ...'* New York Review of Books: USA

- Lang, Andrew (2006) *'Cock Lane and Common Sense'* BiblioBazaar: USA

- Lecouteux, Claude (2012) *'The Secret History of Poltergeists and Haunted Houses: From Pagan Folklore to Modern Manifestations'* Inner Traditions: USA

- Lebling, Robert (2010) *'Legends of the Fire Spirits: Jinn and Genie from Arabia to Zanzibar'* IB Tauris: USA

- Lewis, CS (1994) *'The Discarded Image: An Introduction to Medieval and Renaissance Literature'* Cambridge University Press: UK

- MacKaye, Charles (1995) *'Extraordinary Popular Delusions and the Madness of Crowds'* Wordsworth: UK

- MacManus, Dermot (1979) *'The Middle Kingdom'* Colin Smythe: UK

- Manning, Matthew (1987) *'The Link'* Colin Smythe: UK

- McGovern, Una (Ed.) (2007) *'Chambers Dictionary of the Unexplained'* Chambers: UK

- Mitford, AB (2000) *'Tales of Old Japan'* Wordsworth: UK

- Monnin, Alfred (1862) *'Life of the Curé d'Ars'* Burns & Lambert: UK

- Moore, Steve (Ed.) (1995) *'Fortean Studies 2'* John Brown: UK

- Moore, Steve (Ed.) (1996) *'Fortean Studies 3'* John Brown: UK

- Moore, Steve (Ed.) (1998) *'Fortean Studies 5'* John Brown: UK

- Moretti, Nick (Ed.) (2006) *'The Bell Witch Anthology'* no publisher listed: USA [includes *'Our Family Trouble'* by Richard Williams Bell, *'The Bell Witch, A Mysterious Spirit'* by Charles Bailey Bell, *'An Authenticated History of the Famous Bell Witch'* by MV Ingram, and *'The Bell Witch of Middle Tennessee'* by Harriet Parks Miller]

- Narváez, Peter (Ed.) (1997) *'The Good People: New Fairylore Essays'* University of

Kentucky Press: USA

- Owen, ARG (1964) *'Can We Explain the Poltergeist?'* Helix Press/Garrett Publications: USA

- Pilkington, Mark & McNally, Joe (Eds.) (1998) *'Fortean Times Weird World 1999'* John Brown: UK

- Playfair, Guy Lyon (1975) *'The Flying Cow: Research into Paranormal Phenomena in the World's Most Psychic Country'* Souvenir Press: UK

- Playfair, Guy Lyon (1976) *'The Indefinite Boundary: An Investigation into the Relationship Between Matter and Spirit'* Souvenir Press: UK

- Playfair, Guy Lyon (2007) *'This House Is Haunted: The Investigation into the Enfield Poltergeist'* Sutton: UK

- Price, Harry (1945) *'Poltergeist Over England'* Country Life: UK

- Redfern, Nick (2007) *'Man-Monkey: The Search for the British Bigfoot'* CFZ Press: UK

- Rickard, Bob & Michell, John (2000) *'Unexplained Phenomena: A Rough Guide Special'* Rough Guides: UK

- Roll, William G (2004) *'The Poltergeist'* Paraview Special Editions: USA

- Scott, Sir Walter (2001) *'Letters on Demonology and Witchcraft'* Wordsworth: UK

- Sitwell, Sacheverell (1959) *'Poltergeists: An Introduction and Examination Followed by Chosen Instances'* University Books: USA

- Steiger, Brad (2008) *'Otherworldly Affaires: Haunted Lovers, Phantom Spouses and Sexual Molesters from the Shadow World'* Anomalist Books: USA

- Thomas, Keith (1991) *'Religion and the Decline of Magic'* Penguin: UK

- Thurston, Father Herbert, SJ (1954) *'Ghosts and Poltergeists'* Henry Regnery: USA

- Trubshaw, Bob (Ed.) (2005) *'Explore Phantom Black Dogs'* Heart of Albion Press: UK

- Tucker, SD (2013) *'Terror of the Tokoloshe: The Untold True Story of Southern Africa's Hairy Invisible Ghost-Rapist'* CFZ Press: UK

- Tucker, SD (2013) *'Paranormal Merseyside'* Amberley: UK

- Vallee, Jacques (1975) *'Passport to Magonia: From Folklore to Flying Saucers'* Tandem: UK

- Westwood, Jennifer & Simpson, Jacqueline (2005) *'The Lore of the Land: A Guide to England's Legends, from Spring-Heeled Jack to the Witches of Warboys'* Penguin: UK

- Wilson, Colin (2000) *'Poltergeist! A Study in Destructive Haunting'* Caxton Editions: UK

- Wilson, Colin (2003) *'The Occult'* Watkins: UK

- Wilson, Colin & Evans, Dr Christopher (1991) *'The Giant Book of the Unknown'* Magpie: UK

- Yeats, WB (1993) *'Writings on Irish Folklore, Legend and Myth'* Penguin Classics: UK

REFERENCES

NOTE: It will be noticed that, when it comes to old and rare texts from the European past, I have largely quoted from translations provided within more recent twentieth/twenty-first century books. This proved unavoidable. However I have, where possible, made use of multiple modern versions to try and spot any inconsistencies.

INTRODUCTION

1. Report in the 'Coleraine Chronicle' (Northern Ireland) for 26th January 1907 cited in Bord, 1997:15-16 & Fort, 1997:35; Fort spells the man's name 'McLaughlin'
2. Bord, 1997:16
3. Playfair, 1975:251
4. 'Alligator' is derived from the seventeenth-century Spanish phrase 'el lagarto', meaning 'the lizard'
5. Lecouteux, 2012:15; not everything in this chapter is actually specifically about poltergeists, though …
6. Lecouteux, 2012:15-16
7. This isn't the famous literary critic William Hazlitt, but his rather more obscure son. His translation can be found at http://www.ccel.org/ccel/luther/tabletalk.txt – Christian Classics Ethereal Library
8. Davies, 2007:31 & Crowe, 2000:292
9. Goss, 1979:ix
10. Price, 1945:277
11. Lang, 2006:57
12. Ludwig (Lewes) Lavater, 'Of Ghostes and Spirites Walking by Nyght …' cited in Davies, 2007:2
13. Lang, 2006:32
14. Lang, 2006:214
15. Lang, 2006:32
16. Wilson, 2000:285

17. Owen, 1964:157
18. Noel Williams, 'The Semantics of the Word Fairy: Making Meaning out of Thin Air' in Narváez, 1997:457-478
19. Williams in Narváez, 1997:459
20. Williams in Narváez, 1997:462
21. Williams in Narváez, 1997:463
22. Williams in Narváez, 1997:463-464
23. Williams in Narváez, 1997:468
24. Williams in Narváez, 1997:469
25. Harte, 2004:3
26. Harte, 2004:4-5
27. Bord, 1997:2
28. See Harte, 2004:65-67 for an excellent discussion of the probable socioeconomic origins of this motif
29. 'The Irish Fairies' in Yeats, 1993:9
30. MacManus, 1979:139
31. Foster, 2005:467-468
32. MacManus, 1979:14-15
33. 'Irish Fairies' in Yeats, 1993:63-64
34. 'An Irish Storyteller' in Yeats, 1993:79
35. Sir William Barrett, 'Poltergeists in Ireland and Elsewhere' in Sitwell, 1959:343

PART ONE

1. HIGH SPIRITS

1.   Alan Bruford, 'Trolls, Hillfolk, Finns and Picts: The Identity of the Good Neighbours in Orkney and Shetland' in Narváez, 1997:135 & Holder, 2013:95-96
2.   Kirk, 2007:19
3.   Kirk, 2007:44
4.   Antonio de Torquemada, 'The Flower Garden', differing translations cited in Lecouteux, 2012:123-124 & Owen, 1964:48-49
5.   Johannes Praetorius, 'Anthropodermus Plutonicus', cited in Lecouteux, 2012:19
6.   Pierre Viret, 'Le Monde a l'Empire et la Monde Demoniacle fait par Dialogues', cited in Lecouteux, 2012:120
7.   Lecouteux, 2012:56-58
8.   Montague Summers, 'Demonality or Incubi and Succubi' cited in Gooch, 2007:25-26
9.   Vallee, 1975:58
10. Gerolamo Cardano, 'De Rerum Varietate' cited in Burton, 2001: 1.2.1.2, p.193
11. Lecouteux, 2012:120-121 & 215-216
12. MacManus, 1979:96
13. Letter from J Keen in Fortean Times 137, p.52-53
14. Briggs, 2002:286

15. Hardinge, 1870:157-164
16. Linda-May Ballard, 'Fairies and the Supernatural on Reachrai' in Narváez, 1997:53
17. Gauld & Cornell, 1979:120
18. Henderson, 2008:163
19. Barthélemy Jacquinot, 'Adresse Chrétienne Pour Vivre Selon Dieu dans le Monde ...' cited in Lecouteux, 2012:128-130
20. MacManus, 1979:90-94
21. http://www.nytimes.com/2005/07/13/international/europe/13elves.html?_r=0 – New York Times.com
22. Brookesmith, 1995b:94
23. http://www.spr.ac.uk/expcms/index.php?section=74 – SPR website
24. http://www.spr.ac.uk/expcms/index.php?section=74 – SPR website
25. AJ Bell, 'Procession of the Gracious: Fallout of the Damned' in Fortean Times 20, p.14-17
26. Crowe, 2000:310
27. Patrick Harpur, 'The Problem of Pixilation' in Fortean Times 209, p.54-55

2. THE LEY OF THE LAND

1. Briggs, 2002:163-164
2. Devereux, 2007:50
3. Devereux, 2007:149
4. Devereux, 2007:159
5. Devereux, 2007:158
6. MacManus, 1979:102-103
7. Devereux, 2007:158
8. This survey has been criticised, however; for more details, see http://en.wikipedia.org/wiki/Hulduf%C3%B3lk – Wikipedia
9. Fortean Times 74, p.16
10. Ingolfsson lays out his full sceptical views upon the matter of elves interfering with construction projects at http://old.qi.com/talk/viewtopic.php?t=10615&start=15&sid=58a34d913d5c8a38d837a430e496a749 – QI Talk Forum
11. Claire Smith, 'The Land of the Hidden People' in Fortean Times 201, p.42-27 & http://old.qi.com/talk/viewtopic.php?t=10615&start=15&sid=58a34d913d5c8a38d837a430e496a749 – QI Talk Forum & http://www.ismennt.is/vefir/ari/alfar/alandslag/aelvesmod.htm – Elves in Modern Iceland
12. http://www.magazine.bilfinger.com/en/Magazine/Archive/Edition-1-07/Interview – Bilfinger Berger.com
13. http://www.icelandreview.com/icelandreview/daily_news/Angry_Elves_Said_to_Have_Wreaked_Havoc_in_West_Fjords_0_379383.news.aspx – Iceland Review Online & http://www.icenews.is/2011/07/02/icelandic-town-hopes-angry-elves-have-been-soothed-by-songs/ – IceNews
14. http://old.qi.com/talk/viewtopic.php?t=10615&start=15&sid=58a34d913d5c8a38d837a430e496a749 – QI Talk Forum

15.   http://www.icelandreview.com/icelandreview/daily_news/?
       cat_id=29314&ew_0_a_id=390052 – Iceland Review Online
16.   Westwood & Simpson, 2005:396
17.   Wilson, 2000:188-189 & Price, 1945:301-302
18.   'The Witch of Scrapfaggot Green' by Robert Halliday in Fortean Times 303, p.30-35
19.   Price, 1945:302
20.   Westwood & Simpson, 2005:422-423
21.   Wilson, 2000:189-191, citing 'Leicester Mercury' for Aug 26th 1980
22.   Wilson, 2000:190
23.   Bord, 1997:5
24.   Bord, 1997:44
25.   Devereux, 2007:103
26.   Devereux, 2007:151-153
27.   'Columkille and Rosses' in Yeats, 1993:49
28.   'The Tribes of Danu' in Yeats, 1993:143
29.   Germaine Laisnel de la Salle, 'Croyances et Légendes du Coeur de la France Vol. 1'
       cited in Lecouteux, 2012:81-82
30.   Lecouteux, 2012:81-82
31.   Parks Miller in Moretti, 2006:257-258
32.   Ingram in Moretti, 2006:138
33.   Briggs, 2002:45
34.   Sam Hanna Bell, 'Erin's Orange Lily', cited in Bord, 1997:46
35.   Letter from 'Faustus' in Hardinge, 1870:448
36.   Letter from 'Faustus' in Hardinge, 1870:451
37.   Letter from 'Faustus' in Hardinge, 1870:452

3.   ASK AND YE SHALL RECEIVE

1.   Letter from John Mompesson cited in Gauld & Cornell, 1979:49-50
2.   Gwyndaf, Robin, 'Fairylore: Memorates and Legends from Welsh Oral Tradition' in
       Narváez, 1997:177
3.   Monnin, 1862:251-255
4.   Fodor, 1959:51
5.   Letter from Jack Romano in Fortean Times 280, p.75
6.   Lewis, 1994:130-131
7.   'The ghost in my garage' – 'The Daily Mail' (London), 6th April 2010, p.31
8.   Maxwell-Stuart, 2011:222
9.   Account of Miss H Kohn cited in Thurston, 1954:151
10.   Fort, 1997:36
11.   Fortean Times 55, p.24
12.   Gwyndaf in Narváez, 1997:185
13.   Bord, 1997:11
14.   Letter from Mike Bending in Fortean Times 191, p.76
15.   Harpur, 2003:137

16. Lady Augusta Gregory, 'Visions and Beliefs in the West of Ireland', cited in Harpur, 2003:137; the full text is available online at http://www.sacred-texts.com/neu/celt/vbwi/vbwi07.htm – SacredTexts
17. Williams in Narváez, 1997:465
18. Kirk, 2007:19-20
19. Both quotes contained in a letter from Everard Feilding cited in Carrington & Fodor, 1951:93; for the full case see pp92-96 in this book
20. Carrington & Fodor, 1951:94-96
21. Fortean Times 36, p.26
22. 'Gazette des Tribunaux' (Paris), Feb 2nd 1849, cited in Flammarion, 1924:72
23. Fort, 1997:36
24. Aikki Perttola-Flink, 'On the Fringe of Human Knowledge', cited in Fortean Times 45, p.48-49

4.   PINS AND NEEDLES

1. Hubbell, 1916:122
2. Owen, 1964:221
3. Carrington & Fodor, 1951:78
4. Holder, 2013:52-54
5. Playfair, 1976:242-246
6. Henry Durbin, 'A Narrative of some extraordinary things ...' cited in Thurston, 1954:23-24
7. Durbin in Thurston, 1954:23
8. Barbara Rieti, 'The Blast in Newfoundland Fairy Tradition' in Narváez, 1997:289
9. Rieti in Narváez, 1997:285
10. Rieti in Narváez, 1997:288
11. Rieti in Narváez, 1997:286
12. Rieti in Narváez, 1997:291
13. Rieti in Narváez, 1997:286
14. Rieti in Narváez, 1997:286
15. Rieti in Narváez, 1997:288
16. Thurston, 1954:25-26
17. Vallee, 1975:95
18. Holder, 2013:40-45
19. Ingram in Moretti, 2006:206
20. Holder, 2013:45
21. Interview with Lucinda Rawls cited in Ingram in Moretti, 2006:206-207
22. Parks Miller in Moretti, 2006:252-253
23. Interview with Lucinda Rawls cited in Ingram in Moretti, 2006:208
24. Aubrey, 2006:93
25. Testimony of Schuppart cited in Owen, 1964:260
26. Gauld & Cornell, 1979:133
27. Durbin cited in Gauld & Cornell, 1979:123
28. Aubrey, 2006:137

29. 'Irish Witch Doctors' in Yeats, 1993:271
30. Durbin cited in Thurston, 1954:22
31. Durbin cited in Thurston, 1954:25
32. 'The Broken Gates of Death' in Yeats, 1993:179
33. 'The Broken Gates of Death' in Yeats, 1993:172

5. WALKING THROUGH THE AIR

1. Joseph Glanvil, 'Saducismus Triumphatus' cited in Owen, 1964:225-226
2. Owen, 1964:226-227
3. Statement of T Leece cited in Evans-Wentz, 2008:154
4. Statement from Marian Maclean cited in Evans-Wentz, 2008:138-139
5. Account from E Hamer, 'Parochial Account of Llanidloes' cited in Bord, 1997:14
6. Letter from Rev Andrew Paschal cited in Aubrey, 2006:112-113
7. Scott, 2001:79
8. Owen, 1964:218
9. Gauld & Cornell, 1979:115
10. Statement of a Mrs Ketkar cited in Gauld & Cornell, 1979:114
11. Letter from JD Jenkins cited in Owen, 1964:230
12. Playfair, 2007:151-152
13. Playfair, 2007:153
14. Fortean Times 23, p.6-7
15. Letter from 'W' to the 'Boston Post' cited in Hardinge, 1870:268
16. Account of Rev Haraldur Nielsson cited in Thurston, 1954:8-9
17. Lang, 2006:78-79
18. Fortean Times 22, p.13-14
19. Evans & Bartholomew, 2009:329
20. Owen, 1964:228-229
21. Eliade, 2004:428-430
22. Eliade, 2004:140
23. Eliade, 2004:126
24. Raymond E Fowler, 'The Allagash Abductions' in Evans & Stacy 1997:135
25. Extract from Joseph Glanvil, 'Saducismus Triumphatus' cited in Owen, 1964:222
26. 'Witches and Wizards in Irish Folk-Lore' in Yeats, 1993:370
27. 'A Note on The Hosting of the Sidhe' in Yeats, 1993:208
28. 'The Broken Gates of Death' in Yeats, 1993:185
29. 'The Irish Fairies' in Yeats, 1993:9
30. 'Scots and Irish Fairies' in Yeats, 1993:26
31. Fort, 1997:148-149
32. http://www.answers.com/topic/pansini-brothers – answers.com
33. Fort, 1997:21
34. Fort, 1997:31

6.   THE STOLEN CHILD

1.   Ralph de Coggeshall, 'Chronicon', cited in Thurston, 1954:190
2.   Westwood & Simpson, 2005:667-668
3.   Thurston, 1954:191
4.   Maxwell-Stuart, 2011:27
5.   George Waldron, 'A Description of the Isle of Man', cited in Harte, 2004:108
6.   See 'The Invisible Made Visible: The Fairy Changeling as a Folk Articulation of Failure to Thrive in Infants and Children' in Narváez, 1997:251-279
7.   Susan Schoon Eberly, 'Fairies and the Folklore of Disability: Changelings, Hybrids and the Solitary Fairy' in Narváez, 1997:232
8.   Harte, 2004:109
9.   Wirt Sikes, 'British Goblins' cited in Rickard & Michell, 2000:134
10.   JO Halliwell, 'Illustrations of the Fairy Mythology' cited in Rickard & Michell, 2000:134
11.   Evans-Wentz, 2008:153
12.   Playfair, 1975:257
13.   Letter from Chris Pollard in Fortean Times 266, p.71
14.   Cited in Clark & Coleman, 2006a:65
15.   Homem Christo, extract from 'Le Parc du Mystère' cited in Flammarion, 1924:166
16.   Playfair, 1975:275
17.   Extract from Alcuin, 'Vita Willibrordi' cited in Thurston, 1954:188
18.   Maxwell-Stuart, 2011:17
19.   Father Ludovico Sinistrari, 'De Daemonialitate' cited in Vallee, 1975:120-123
20.   Letter from Darcy Frederiksen in Fortean Times 133, p.53
21.   Hallowell, 2007:8
22.   Hallowell, 2007:46
23.   Fortean Times 43, p.14-15
24.   Hallowell, 2007:42
25.   Hallowell, 2007:43
26.   Hallowell, 2007:44
27.   Hallowell, 2007:52
28.   Hallowell, 2007:2
29.   Hallowell, 2007:91
30.   Hallowell, 2007:79-80
31.   Hallowell, 2007:117
32.   http://en.wikipedia.org/wiki/Duende_(mythology) – Wikipedia

7.   FROM OUT OF THIN AIR

1.   Evans-Wentz, 2008:61-62
2.   MacManus, 1979:96-98
3.   Account of Thomas Wood cited in Bord, 1997:13
4.   Elias Owen, 'Welsh Folk-Lore' cited in Rickard & Michell, 2000:130 & Bord, 1997:81-82

5.   Jaynes, 2000:377-378
6.   Crowe, 2000:318-319 & Clanny, 1841:15, 28, 42, 45 & 55
7.   Letter from LM Austin cited in Hardinge, 1870:398
8.   Extract from EW Capron, name of work not given, cited in Hardinge, 1870:57
9.   Evans & Bartholomew, 2009:719
10. Gwyndaf in Narváez, 1997:174
11. Westwood & Simpson, 2005:209
12. Bell, R in Moretti, 2006:45
13. Parks Miller in Moretti, 2006:242-243
14. Gauld & Cornell, 1979: 226
15. Gervaise of Tilbury, 'Otia Imperialia', cited in Lecouteux, 2012:55
16. Henry of Hereford, 'Memorable Histories', cited in Lecouteux, 2012:166 & Joynes, 2001:116-117
17. These competing accounts can be found detailed in Maxwell-Stuart, 2011:22-23 & Lecouteux, 2012:51-53
18. Martin del Rio, 'Disquisitionum Magicarum' cited in Lecouteux, 2012:125-126

8.   SEEING THINGS

1.   Bord, 1997:107-108
2.   Bord, 1997:108
3.   John Keel, 'Anomaly', cited in Budden, 1995:169-170
4.   Article by William Martin from 'Folk-Lore' cited in Bord, 1997:32-33
5.   Thurston, 1954:181-186
6.   Thurston, 1954:181
7.   Holder, 2013:131-133; this case exists in two wildly different versions, one of which doesn't mention Mrs van Hoorne seeing a fairy at all, but, rather, the apparition of the dead sailor himself. The fairy-tale version appears (according to the careful researches of the writer Geoff Holder) only to have surfaced during 2001, in a popular book about alleged Scottish hauntings.
8.   http://www.mysteriousbritain.co.uk/hauntings/castle-wildenstein.html – Mysterious Britain and Ireland.com
9.   Bord, 1997:65-66
10. Playfair, 2007:49
11. Roll, 2004:81
12. Bell, R in Moretti, 2006:24
13. Crowe, 2000:305
14. Price, 1945:349-350
15. MacManus, 1979:111-112
16. MacManus, 1979:115
17. Hough & Randles, 1999:110-111
18. Testimony of TC Kermode cited in Evans-Wentz, 2008:165-166
19. Evans-Wentz, 2008:109-110
20. Letter from 'E' cited in Hardinge, 1870:113-114

21.   Harpur, 2003:9
22.   Devereux, 1982:45-46
23.   Harpur, 2003:10

9.   SHAGGY DOG STORIES

1.   'A Midsummer Night's Dream', III.i., lines 103-106
2.   However, the etymology is disputed. Sir Walter Scott thought it to be derived from the German '*bahrgeist*', meaning 'spirit of the bier'; see Devereux, 2007:49-50
3.   Westwood & Simpson, 2005:500
4.   Robert Forby, 'Vocabulary of East Anglia' cited in Jennifer Westwood, 'Friend or Foe? Norfolk Traditions of Shuck' in Trubshaw, 2005:61
5.   Jeremy Harte, 'Black Dog Studies' in Trubshaw, 2005:7
6.   Jeremy Harte, 'Black Dog Studies' in Trubshaw, 2005:5
7.   Westwood & Simpson, 2005:501 & Jennifer Westwood, 'Friend or Foe? Norfolk Traditions of Shuck' in Trubshaw, 2005:62-63
8.   Probably the best single introduction to the topic of big cat carcasses being found in Britain remains Dr Karl PN Shuker, 'British Mystery Cats – The Bodies of Evidence' in Moore, 1995:143-152
9.   Harpur, 2003:72-73
10.   'Alien Big Cat Diary' by Merrily Harpur in Fortean Times 226, p.26-27
11.   http://news.bbc.co.uk/1/hi/england/devon/6929397.stm – BBC News
12.   Downes, Jonathan & Freeman, Richard, 'Shug-Monkeys and Werewolves' in Moore, 1998:178
13.   Westwood & Simpson, 2005:559
14.   Kelleher & Knapp, 2005:189-192
15.   Bell, CB in Moretti, 2006: 70 & Ingram in Moretti, 2006:138
16.   Jeremy Harte, 'The Black Dog in England: A Bibliography' in Trubshaw, 2005:108
17.   Bell, CB in Moretti, 2006:70
18.   Bell, R in Moretti, 2006:35
19.   Bord & Bord, 1985:86
20.   Sophia Morrison, 'Manx Fairy Tales' cited in Briggs, 2002:130
21.   See Ingram in Moretti, 2006:189-196 for Dean's tales in full
22.   Bell, CB in Moretti, 2006:79
23.   NN Puckett, 'Folk Beliefs of the Southern Negro' cited in Bord & Bord, 1985:86
24.   Ingram in Moretti, 2006:212
25.   Ingram in Moretti, 2006:208
26.   Bell, R in Moretti, 2006:42 & Ingram in Moretti, 2006:217
27.   Bell, CB in Moretti, 2006:89
28.   Scott, 2001:171
29.   Hallowell & Ritson, 2011:210
30.   Hallowell & Ritson, 2011:119
31.   Hallowell & Ritson, 2011:139 & 142

32.   Jeremy Harte found 18 English examples of stories in which a blow went through a Black Dog; see Jeremy Harte, 'The Black Dog in England: A Bibliography' in Trubshaw, 2007:108
33.   Hallowell & Ritson, 2011:141-142
34.   Hallowell & Ritson, 2011:142-143
35.   Hallowell & Ritson, 2011;143
36.   Hallowell & Ritson, 2011:96-97
37.   Hallowell & Ritson, 2011:143
38.   Hallowell & Ritson, 2011:174
39.   Jeremy Harte, 'Black Dog Studies' in Trubshaw, 2005:7
40.   Westwood & Simpson, 2005:561
41.   Westwood & Simpson, 2005:233
42.   Sitwell, 1959:98 & 105-106
43.   Letters from various members of the Wesley household cited in Price, 1945:89, 91, 95, 98 & 103
44.   Price, 1945:82
45.   Letter of Emily Wesley cited in Price, 1945:91
46.   Price, 1945:4-5 & Sitwell, 1959:100-104
47.   Cited in Brookesmith, 1995a:96
48.   Brookesmith, 1995a:94-97 & Wilson & Evans, 1991:385-387 & http://en.wikipedia.org/wiki/Montpelier_Hill – Wikipedia
49.   MacManus, 1979:64-65
50.   MacManus, 1979:67-69
51.   Testimony of Val McGann cited in Brookesmith, 1995a:96
52.   Jeremy Harte, 'Black Dog Studies' in Trubshaw, 2005:10
53.   Undated report in the 'Glåmdalen' newspaper of Norway cited in Lecouteux, 2012:174-175
54.   Evans-Wentz, 2008:155
55.   Maxwell-Stuart, 2011:145
56.   Davies, 2007:35
57.   Gauld & Cornell, 1979:37 & http://www.bl.uk/eblj/1977articles/pdf/article20.pdf – British Library Catalogue
58.   Gauld & Cornell, 1979:113
59.   Letter from Ferdinand Estève cited in Flammarion, 1924:244-245
60.   Pierre Le Loyer, 'Discours et histoires des spectres' cited in Bord, 1997:16-17 [the italics are mine]

10. THE SAME OLD HAUNTS

1.   All of this information is widely available; I used Wikipedia.
2.   Briggs, 2002:47
3.   Briggs, 2002:12
4.   http://en.wikipedia.org/wiki/Lares – Wikipedia
5.   Briggs, 2002:30
6.   Letter from Mlle Meyer cited in Flammarion, 1924:137

7. Rickard & Michell, 2000:210
8. Gerolamo Cardano, 'De Rerum Varietate' cited in Maxwell-Stuart, 2011:69-70
9. Briggs, 2002:118
10. Briggs, 2002:43; in some parts of Scotland, though, a 'Wag-at-the-Wa' was a colloquial term for a wall-hanging clock with a pendulum dangling down from it.
11. Letter from Marjorie T Johnson cited in Bord, 1997:49
12. MacManus, 1979:48-50
13. 'Nemere' (Romanian newspaper), 16th March 1883, cited in Bord, 1997:66
14. Wirt Sikes, 'British Goblins' cited in Briggs, 2002:37
15. Wirt Sikes, indeed, has the 'goblin-precipice' story down as being a generic one told about all *bwcas*, not just the Trwyn sprite.
16. Details about the Trwyn bwca compiled from Harte, 2004:67-69 & Briggs, 2002:36-37 & the account of W Jenkyn Thomas from 'The Welsh Fairy Book' (available online at http://tinyurl.com/69seezm – Sacred Texts) Details differ greatly in every one of them!
17. Carrington & Fodor, 1951:104-112
18. Graves, 1999:225
19. Martin Luther, 'Table Talk' cited in Lecouteux, 2012:17
20. Lecouteux, 2012:68
21. Lecouteux, 2012:96
22. In fact, there are now several (dubious) tales of allegedly poltergeist-haunted microwaves in circulation on the Internet; e.g. see http://www.yawp.com/3rd-i/vol4/vol4No9/microwave.html – YAWP.com
23. Maxwell-Stuart, 2011:115-116
24. Maxwell-Stuart, 2011:111
25. Maxwell-Stuart, 2011:115
26. Westwood & Simpson, 2005:209
27. Bell, CB in Moretti, 2006:108
28. Testimony of Joel Bell cited in Parks Miller in Moretti, 2006:283
29. Carrington & Fodor, 1951:166
30. Jeremy Harte, 'Black Dog Studies' in Trubshaw, 2005:7
31. W Jenkyn Thomas, 'The Welsh Fairy Book' (available online at http://tinyurl.com/69seezm – Sacred Texts)
32. Westwood & Simpson, 2005:205-207
33. Fort, 1998:96
34. Gauld & Cornell, 1979:8-9
35. Lecouteux, 2012:23
36. Lecouteux, 2012:18
37. Claude Seignolles, 'Les Evangiles du Diables' cited in Lecouteux, 2012:64
38. Cesare Lombroso, 'Ricerche sui Fenomeni Ipnotici e Spiritici' cited in Lecouteux, 2012:194-196 & Wilson, 2000:14-17
39. Lecouteux, 2012:122
40. http://en.wikipedia.org/wiki/Clurichaun – Wikipedia
41. http://zeluna.net/fairy-list-Clurichaun.html – FairyTales.net
42. Briggs, 2002:280 & 45
43. Westwood & Simpson, 2005:445

44. Hallowell & Ritson, 2011:183
45. Jeremy Harte, 'Black Dog Studies' in Trubshaw, 2005:7
46. Westwood & Simpson, 2005:840
47. Jeremy Harte, 'Black Dog Studies' in Trubshaw, 2005:10
48. Hallowell & Ritson, 2011:133 & 149
49. Hallowell & Ritson, 2011:86
50. Davies, 2007:22-23; for an excellent discussion of the White Lady as an archetype, see Jaffé, 1963:85-103
51. Briggs, 2002:274
52. Holder, 2013:64-65 & MacGregor, 1937:61-62 & 65
53. MacGregor, 1937:65-66
54. http://en.wikipedia.org/wiki/Glaistig – Wikipedia
55. Holder, 2013:64
56. http://www.smokedsalmon.co.uk/inverawe-ghost-stories+pu+ghost+1 – Inverawe Scottish Smoke House & http://www.fife.50megs.com/inverawe-house.htm – TourScotland
57. MacGregor, 1937:59-60
58. Crowe, 2000:226-228
59. Davies, 2007:50
60. Crowe, 2000:236
61. Price, 1945:204-212
62. Holder, 2013:197
63. 'Renovation Hauntings' by Peter A McCue in Fortean Times 268, p.30-35
64. MacManus, 1979:103-105
65. http://www.smokedsalmon.co.uk/inverawe-ghost-stories+pu+ghost+1 – Inverawe Scottish Smoke House

PART TWO

1. AS BROWNIE

1. Bowker, 2011:13
2. Bowker, 2011:13-15
3. Bowker, 2011:13-15
4. Briggs, 2002:276
5. Harte, 2004:39
6. Westwood & Simpson, 2005:840
7. Westwood & Simpson, 2005:238-239 & Sitwell, 1959:152-153; there are an infinitude of slightly differing versions of the whole legend available, none of which can ever really be considered to be 100% 'definitive'.
8. Westwood & Simpson, 2005:827
9. Wilson, 2000:349
10. Bord, 1997:136-137

11. Fodor, 1959:29
12. Pilkington & McNally, 1998:57
13. Fortean Times 21, p.4
14. Crowe, 2000:222-223
15. Crowe, 2000:264
16. Holder, 2013:210-211
17. Fortean Times 65, p.8
18. Fortean Times 126, p.13
19. http://www.mid-day.com/news/2013/may/230513-woman-does-housework-in-her-sleep-hatke-news.htm – mid-day.com
20. http://www.dailymail.co.uk/health/article-2336618/Yes-CAN-drive-100mph-sleep--cook-spag-bol-scale-130ft-crane-sex.html – MailOnline
21. Briggs, 2002:164-165
22. Patricia Lysaght, 'Fairylore from the Midlands of Ireland' in Narváez, 1997:32
23. Rudolf, 'Annales Fuldenses' cited in Maxwell-Stuart, 2011:17-19 & Jacobus de Voragine, 'The Golden Legend' cited in Wilson, 2000:96-97
24. Giraldus Cambrensis, 'Itinerarium Kambriae' cited in Thurston, 1954:7
25. Lecouteux, 2012:60
26. Ralph of Coggeshall, 'Chronicon' cited in Thurston, 1954:190
27. Carrington & Fodor, 1951:201
28. Bell, R in Moretti, 2006:29-30
29. Bell, CB in Moretti, 2006:93
30. Bell, CB in Moretti, 2006:91-92
31. Ingram in Moretti, 2006:141
32. Letter from Robert Leighton cited in Thurston, 1954:113-114
33. Report of James Sherring cited in Price, 1945:68-69
34. Richard P Jenkins, 'Witches and Fairies: Supernatural Aggression and Deviance Among the Irish Peasantry' in Narváez, 1997:317
35. Jaynes, 2000:464
36. Evans-Wentz, 2008:143
37. Monnin, 1862:179
38. Monnin, 1862:119-120
39. Monnin, 1862:118
40. Monnin, 1862:117-118
41. Monnin, 1862:116
42. Wilson, 2000:156-157
43. Harte, 2004:72
44. Robert Chambers, 'The Popular Rhymes of Scotland' cited in Harte, 2004:63
45. Thomas, 1991:730-731
46. Harte, 2004:74-75
47. Letter from Jennifer McGhee in Fortean Times 206, p.75
48. Perrault cited in Thurston, 1954:45
49. Owen, 1964:119
50. Manning, 1987:97-98

51. Gooch, 2007:27 & Lecouteux, 2013:125, both citing Girolamo Menghi, 'Compendia dell Arte Essorcistica seu Possibilità delle Mirabili'
52. Perrault in Thurston, 1954:44
53. Thurston, 1954:36
54. Davies, 2007:176-177

2.   AS BOGGART

1.   http://en.wikipedia.org/wiki/Boggart – Wikipedia
2.   Colin Parsons, 'Encounters with the Unknown' cited in Bord, 1997:17; 'Jenny' and 'Peter' are actually pseudonyms, so I have no idea as to how reliable this story actually is …
3.   Manning, 1987:36
4.   Harte, 2004:19-20
5.   Briggs, 2002:44
6.   Briggs, 2002:279
7.   Briggs, 2002:33
8.   EM Leather, 'The Folk-Lore of Herefordshire' cited in Briggs, 2002:43-44
9.   Letter from Andrew Shilcock in Fortean Times 200, p.77
10. Cassirer, 1993:12
11. Letter from Graham Oxley in Fortean Times 133, p.51
12. Account of 'P' cited in Harte, 2004:70; a slightly different version is available at http://www.sacred-texts.com/neu/eng/efft/efft39.htm - Sacred Texts
13. Harte, 2004:70
14. Harte, 2004:71
15. Diary of Edmund Procter cited in Price, 1945:188
16. Hallowell & Ritson, 2011:126-127
17. See Price, 1945:338 & 342 for two such examples
18. Diary entry of Ada Sharpe cited in Gauld & Cornell, 1979:186
19. Harte, 2004:67
20. McGovern, 2007:79
21. http://en.wikipedia.org/wiki/Boggart – Wikipedia
22. Harpur, 2003:79 & Bord & Bord, 1985:155-156 & Clark & Coleman, 2006a:14-16
23. Harpur, 2003:80
24. www.herper.com/miscpdfMMPapersAust.pdf – Herper.com
25. Fortean Times 235, p.18
26. 'Fetch the Holy Water, Maude – it's a Yowie!' by Tony Healy in Innes, 1999:65
27. Harpur, 2003:80
28. Harpur, 2003:80
29. Bord & Bord, 1985:155-156 & Clark & Coleman, 2006a:17-18
30. Ingram in Moretti, 2006:201
31. Fortean Times 55, p.58
32. 'Mum, there's a poltergeist in my bedroom!' in the 'Daily Mail' (London) 2nd April 2011, p.26-27

33. Price, 1945:353
34. Holder, 2013:184
35. Steiger, 2008:138-143
36. This whole story is compiled from Brookesmith, 1995a:70-73 & Fortean Times 15, p.4-5; the poltergeist phenomena referenced are taken from both these sources and also from Screeton, 2012:18,21,24,25 & 32
37. Screeton, 2012:32
38. Westwood & Simpson, 2005:403
39. Westwood & Simpson, 2005:442
40. http://en.wikipedia.org/wiki/Boggart – Wikipedia
41. 'Shug Monkeys and Werewolves' by Jonathan Downes & Richard Freeman in Moore, 1995:185
42. Charlotte S Burne, 'Shropshire Folk-Lore' cited in Redfern, 2007:10-13
43. Westwood & Simpson, 2005:675
44. Testimony of A Taylor cited in Westwood & Simpson, 2005:70
45. Redfern, 2007:57-59
46. Redfern, 2007: 131-132
47. Charlotte S Burne, 'Shropshire Folk-Lore' cited in Redfern, 2007:13
48. Westwood & Simpson, 2005:442
49. Harte, 2004:24
50. Westwood & Simpson, 2005:165 & 828
51. Harte, 2004:67

3.   AS STALLSPUK

1.   Gauld & Cornell, 1979:29
2.   Hubbell, 1916:141
3.   Perrault cited in Thurston, 1954:44
4.   Fortean Times 293, p.32 & 37
5.   Roll, 2004:97
6.   Price, 1945:213-219
7.   'The Antigonish Poltergeist' by Theo Paijmans in Fortean Times 256, p.34-36; Conan Doyle's pronouncement is actually a paraphrasing of his ideas made by the contemporary Press
8.   Letter from Jean Mettois cited in Flammarion, 1924:223-225
9.   Jean-Pierre Piniès, 'Croyances Populaires des Pays d'Oc' cited in Lecouteux, 2012:63
10. JB Bardin, 'Le Pays de Septème' cited in Lecouteux, 2012:96-97
11. Letter from a 'Monsieur Morice' cited in Lecouteux, 2012:131
12. Glanvil in Price, 1945:54
13. Evans, 2009:8-9
14. Glanvil in Price, 1945:55
15. Ingram in Moretti, 2006:236
16. Ingram in Moretti, 2006:196-201
17. Westwood & Simpson, 2005:549-550
18. Ingram in Moretti, 2006:238

19. MacManus, 1979:136
20. Gauld & Cornell, 1979:29
21. Westwood & Simpson, 2005:502
22. Report in the 'Daily Mail' (London) for 28th May 1906, cited in Price, 1945:30
23. Holder, 2013:35
24. Price, 1945:76
25. Account of a local priest named Grat Vesan cited in Lecouteux, 2012:142-143
26. Crowe, 2000:286
27. Sitwell, 1959:65-66
28. Roberts, Andy & Clarke, David, 'Heads and Tales: The Screaming Skull Legends of Britain' in Moore, 1996:134-139
29. Appleyard, 2006:144
30. Kelleher & Knapp, 2005:67
31. Kelleher & Knapp, 2005:69
32. Kelleher & Knapp, 2005:118-119
33. Harold, 1979:90-92
34. Clarke & Roberts, 2007:201
35. Harold, 1979:97-99
36. Harold, 1979:119
37. Harold, 1979:140-144
38. Rickard & Michell, 2000:146-150
39. For a particularly devastating dismissal of the whole phenomenon, see Fortean Times 302, p. 46-49
40. Rickard & Michell, 2000:147
41. Extract cited in Fort, 1997: 119-121
42. Kirk, 2007:16-17
43. Harte, 2004:148
44. Scott, 2001:100 (These are Walter Scott's words, not Gowdie's)
45. I.iv. lines 87-89
46. Gary R Butler, 'The Lutin Tradition in French-Newfoundland Culture' in Narváez, 1997:12-14
47. Patrick Harpur, 'Straight from the horse's mane' in Fortean Times 259, p.52-53
48. Butler in Narváez, 1997:9
49. Patrick Harpur, 'Straight from the horse's mane' in Fortean Times 259, p.52-53
50. Ingram in Moretti, 2006:236
51. McGovern, 2007:217
52. MacGregor, 1937:65
53. Maxwell-Stuart, 2011:144
54. Price, 1945:66
55. Letter from an Ethel Wilkinson cited in Price, 1945:344

4. FOREIGN FAIRIES

1. http://academia.issendai.com/fox-abodes.shtml – Issendai.com
2. See Steve Moore, 'Hair Today ..' in Fortean Times 177, p.42-46 for an excellent introduction to such panics
3. Freeman, 2010:203-204
4. Freeman, 2010:149-150
5. Mitford, 2000:223-227
6. Fort, 1998:30-31
7. Fort, 1998:28
8. Fort, 1998:29
9. Davies, 2007:48
10. Wilson, 2003:631
11. Lebling, 2010:110
12. Lebling, 2010:13
13. Lane cited in Lebling, 2010:253
14. Avicenna cited in Gooch, 2007:25
15. Lebling, 2010:8
16. http://en.wikipedia.org/wiki/Jinn – Wikipedia
17. Lebling, 2010:112
18. Fortean Times 254, p.8
19. Fortean Times 268, p.8
20. Lebling, 2010:50-51
21. Maxwell-Stuart, 2011:68
22. Paul Cropper, 'Pyro-Poltergeists' in Fortean Times 281, p.40-44
23. Paul Cropper, 'Angel and the Fire Demon' in Fortean Times 302, p.42-45
24. I must be honest and admit at the outset that this entire section is based upon information found upon Wikipedia about these entities, meaningful detail about them in the English language being hard to come by.
25. http://en.wikipedia.org/wiki/Domovoi – Wikipedia
26. http://en.wikipedia.org/wiki/Kikimora – Wikipedia
27. http://en.wikipedia.org/wiki/Tomte – Wikipedia
28. Unless stated otherwise, all info here is taken from http://en.wikipedia.org/wiki/Kobold – Wikipedia
29. http://en.wikipedia.org/wiki/Klabautermann – Wikipedia
30. Holder, 2013:58
31. Lecouteux, 2012:25
32. Maxwell-Stuart, 2011:166 & Thurston, 1954:36-37
33. Hallowell, 2007:60
34. See http://www.sacred-texts.com/neu/celt/tfm087.htm for a useful complete summary of Hinzelmann
35. Price, 1945:369
36. Cited in Bord, 1997:63
37. Clarke & Coleman, 2006a:63-65

CONCLUSION

1. Mike Hallowell, 'The Ruler of the Roost Part Two' in Paranormal Magazine issue 62, p.52-56
2. Fort, 1997:36-40
3. Fortean Times 65, p.13
4. Gauld & Cornell, 1979:11
5. Hallowell, 2007:63
6. Freeman, 2010:163
7. http://en.wikipedia.org/wiki/Domovoi – Wikipedia
8. http://en.wikipedia.org/wiki/Kobold – Wikipedia
9. Westwood & Simpson, 2005:560
10. Westwood & Simpson, 2005:236
11. Westwood & Simpson, 2005:241-242

Terror of the

TOKOLOSHE

The Untold True Story of Southern Africa's Hairy Invisible Ghost-Rapist

S.D.TUCKER

From the same author...

- **Paperback:** 228 pages
- **Publisher:** cfz (14 Jun. 2013)
- **Language:** English
- **ISBN-10:** 1909488100
- **ISBN-13:** 978-1909488106

Who, these days, still believes in goblins? Well surprisingly, millions of people do, right the way across the countries of southern Africa, where such creatures are known as tokoloshes. Little known in the West, these entities - hairy little men with gigantic magical penises and the ability to turn themselves invisible through the aid of an enchanted pebble - are a matter of everyday belief in nations such as South Africa, Zimbabwe, Namibia and Lesotho.

In this, the first ever full-length book to be published upon the topic in the West, the consequences of this bizarre belief are explored in immense detail. It is not just that poltergeist-hauntings and UFO-sightings are blamed upon the activities of this nefarious little imp; so are everyday misfortunes such as a person's lack of success in love or business. Rather more outlandishly, tokoloshes are also held responsible for supposedly raping innocent women in their beds at night and then impregnating them with goblin-children; court cases have arisen in which people have been accused of murdering such unfortunate infants whilst under the genuine impression that they were evil tokoloshe-babies. But this is not all - tokoloshes have also been linked with witchcraft, zombies, paranormal stone-showers, murder, ancient Trickster-gods, sightings of unknown animals and outbreaks of mass hysteria. In no other book can you read about topics as diverse and strange as haunted toilets, killer one-eyed Cyclops-men made from porridge, severed penises being used as magical batteries and a deformed baby goat born with the head of Homer Simpson. All this, and the full uncensored tale of the man who claimed to have been molested in the night by a big gay hippo-monster ... Lavishly illustrated and all fully-referenced, this book is not only filled with dozens of unusual, amusing and hitherto-unexamined real-life stories, it also tries to place prevailing contemporary southern African belief in the tokoloshe into some kind of plausible social context. The tokoloshe may not be a genuinely real creature, but it certainly occupies a position of social reality in the minds of those who believe in it - with truly wide-ranging and often unexpected consequences.

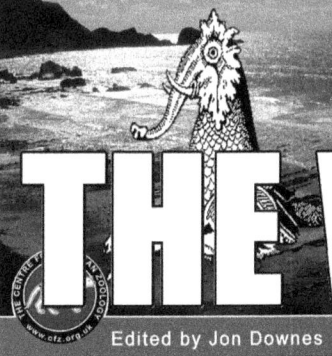

THE WORLD'S WEIRDEST PUBLISHING COMPANY

HOW TO START A PUBLISHING EMPIRE

Unlike most mainstream publishers, we have a non-commercial remit, and our mission statement claims that "we publish books because they deserve to be published, not because we think that we can make money out of them". Our motto is the Latin Tag *Pro bona causa facimus* (we do it for good reason), a slogan taken from a children's book *The Case of the Silver Egg* by the late Desmond Skirrow.

WIKIPEDIA: "The first book published was in 1988. *Take this Brother may it Serve you Well* was a guide to Beatles bootlegs by Jonathan Downes. It sold quite well, but was hampered by very poor production values, being photocopied, and held together by a plastic clip binder. In 1988 A5 clip binders were hard to get hold of, so the publishers took A4 binders and cut them in half with a hacksaw. It now reaches surprisingly high prices second hand.

The production quality improved slightly over the years, and after 1999 all the books produced were ringbound with laminated colour covers. In 2004, however, they signed an agreement with Lightning Source, and all books are now produced perfect bound, with full colour covers."

Until 2010 all our books, the majority of which are/were on the subject of mystery animals and allied disciplines, were published by `CFZ Press`, the publishing arm of the Centre for Fortean Zoology (CFZ), and we urged our readers and followers to draw a discreet veil over the books that we published that were completely off topic to the CFZ.

However, in 2010 we decided that enough was enough and launched a second imprint, `Fortean Words` which aims to cover a wide range of non animal-related esoteric subjects. Other imprints will be launched as and when we feel like it, however the basic ethos of the company remains the same: Our job is to publish books and magazines that we feel are worth publishing, whether or not they are going to sell. Money is, after all - as my dear old Mama once told me - a rather vulgar subject, and she would be rolling in her grave if she thought that her eldest son was somehow in `trade`.

Luckily, so far our tastes have turned out not to be that rarified after all, and we have sold far more books than anyone ever thought that we would, so there is a moral in there somewhere…

Jon Downes,
Woolsery, North Devon
July 2010

CFZ PRESS

CFZ Press is our flagship imprint, featuring a wide range of intelligently written and lavishly illustrated books on cryptozoology and the quirkier aspects of Natural History.

CFZ Classics is a new venture for us. There are many seminal works that are either unavailable today, or not available with the production values which we would like to see. So, following the old adage that if you want to get something done do it yourself, this is exactly what we have done.

Desiderius Erasmus Roterodamus (b. October 18th 1466, d. July 2nd 1536) said: "When I have a little money, I buy books; and if I have any left, I buy food and clothes," and we are much the same. Only, we are in the lucky position of being able to share our books with the wider world. CFZ Classics is a conduit through which we cannot just re-issue titles which we feel still have much to offer the cryptozoological and Fortean research communities of the 21st Century, but we are adding footnotes, supplementary essays, and other material where we deem it appropriate.

http://www.cfzpublishing.co.uk/

Fortean Words is a new venture for us. The F in CFZ stands for "Fortean", after the pioneering researcher into anomalous phenomena, Charles Fort. Our Fortean Words imprint covers a whole spectrum of arcane subjects from UFOs and the paranormal to folklore and urban legends. Our authors include such Fortean luminaries as Nick Redfern, Andy Roberts, and Paul Screeton. . New authors tackling new subjects will always be encouraged, and we hope that our books will continue to be as ground-breaking and popular as ever.

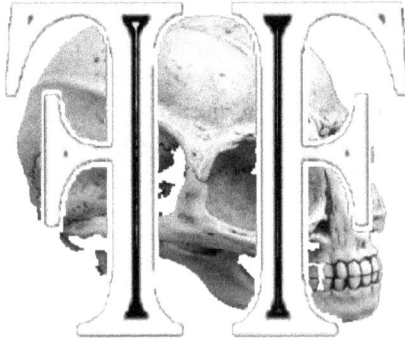

Just before Christmas 2011, we launched our third imprint, this time dedicated to - let's see if you guessed it from the title - fictional books with a Fortean or cryptozoological theme. We have published a few fictional books in the past, but now think that because of our rising reputation as publishers of quality Forteana, that a dedicated fiction imprint was the order of the day.

http://www.cfzpublishing.co.uk/

www.ingramcontent.com/pod-product-compliance
Lightning Source LLC
Chambersburg PA
CBHW070017100426
42740CB00013B/2531